THE UBER FIGHTS
The Inside Story of the Regulators vs Rogue Apps

By Connor J. McGee

Army of Pencils Publishing, LLC

ISBN 978-0-692-094173-7 (Paperback)
ISBN 978-0-692-094173-4 (e-book)

Cover by Ebook Launch (https://ebooklaunch.com)
Copyediting by Nell McPherson

First edition, 2017.

Visit https://www.ConnorMcGeeAuthor.com.

For my niece.

Table of Contents

Introduction

When I started this project in the fall of 2015, I was a few years out of government performance auditing, a fascinating job for a policy wonk like me. I had earned a Master's Degree in Public Administration from Cornell University. And in my first real job, every few months I'd learn about a new area of state and local governments while investigating their inner workings. I had access to confidential files and restricted areas, and I was taught how to organize data and write lengthy reports on what our teams had uncovered. It was both eye-opening and a great high.

But in the wake of the Great Recession, the work soured. Fearful of their perceived usefulness during a budget downturn, audit agencies started demanding reports completed faster and faster. Thoughtful investigations took time, but that no longer mattered. At each layer, pressure from the top compounded increasingly to the next rung below. Directors pressured deputies, who pressured managers, who pressured auditors. Adding further strain, overtime was generally prohibited. Performance auditing was already stressful, but the recession dialed it up to eleven, and at times, I had panic attacks.

It didn't just occur in my workplace. Morale sank across the industry. At conferences, I noticed a wide variety of auditors inquiring about job openings at agencies other than where they were working at that moment. The industry had turned into a bizarre game of musical chairs, and no one else seemed to notice the vicious cycle.

In 2012, after 3.5 years, I left and vowed never to return.

Having moved back to my home town of Austin, Texas, I found work as an analyst for a Norwegian oil company, but I couldn't get my head out of research or public policy. I missed the paper chase too much. There were things I still wanted to learn.

Between 2014 through 2015, I started to independently investigate and write articles about local subjects that fascinated me. I wrote about why the 2013 Austin City Limits Music Festival's ticket prices had crashed. I wrote about a children's indoor play center my friends and I loved when we were kids but had shut down in the '90s.

On a whim, one day I started looking at jobs online and noticed that Uber was looking for public policy analysts. At the time, I knew very little about the company, except that my friends liked their service and they seemed popular. I assumed Uber wanted help with their regulatory fights, and I thought it might be interesting to work there. So, I did what I do for any job application: I researched the kinds of challenges they encountered. Specifically, I looked at their regulatory battles.

With a few Google searches, I also learned that employees who worked for Uber's corporate offices often put in 60-80 hours per week. And that was well beyond my stamina. I wasn't in my 20s anymore, and I chose not to apply.

But the fights were interesting. Uber had a unique talent for cajoling its users into contacting elected officials on their behalf. The tactic seemed like the future of disruptive companies. Within a month, it occurred to me I could write a book about these battles as a how-to guide. "Are you a disruptive startup that wants to overcome regulatory obstacles? Here's how Uber did it."

I started tracking the history and evolution of the fights. I imagined Uber improved their tactics after each one, and I wanted to see how they pulled them off over time. But then the more I looked, the more I noticed one critical detail:

The regulatory fights weren't independent of one another. They were connected as part of an ongoing campaign by the taxi *regulators* themselves.

My fascination took a turn. Why were a group of state and local government employees, who were scattered across the US, embarking on this campaign? I dug more deeply, and my goal in this book shifted. I wanted to know why and how it all happened.

This project is the culmination of 1.5 years of research, dozens of public information requests, and nearly thirty hours of firsthand interviews. The objective of this book was not to review the regulatory fights of *every* American city or state – that would be an encyclopedia, not a narrative nonfiction story. Instead, I chose what I felt were the more critical battles.

The ones that not only accomplished certain "firsts" but where one could examine the evolution of tactics on both sides.

In my research, I've noticed that many writers have painted Uber's stories by rooting for one side or the other. A common theme is to point to either the regulators or Uber and shame one of them for their intransigent behavior. I didn't come into the narrative rooting for either side. Like an auditor, I wanted an honest evaluation. Mostly, I wanted to understand what I couldn't see in the news stories. Why did each side maneuver as they did? What motivated their goals? What context lied beneath the surface?

What the hell actually happened?

This is my report.

CHAPTER ONE

Tug of War

At three in the morning in New York City, January 1925, a young couple exited Club Epinard, a Greenwich speakeasy named after a popular French-owned racehorse of the Prohibition era.[1] He was a twenty-year-old student from an upper-class family preparing to enter Yale. She was a young and impressionable art gallery employee living in Brooklyn. It had already been an eventful night, the embodiment of youthful exuberance in the Roaring Twenties: dinner, theater, and dancing.[2]

They hailed a random cab and made their way to her home in Brooklyn, just across the bridge. En route, the jubilant mood began to fade. The ride took much longer than it should have. It was dark, and the driver was unfamiliar with the area.[3] He was so lost he pulled over on Wyckoff Avenue and asked a fellow cab driver for directions.[4]

Finally, after roughly two hours, they pulled over across the street from her home. The young man's date headed up the stairs while he argued about the fare with the driver. He took off his raccoon coat and handed the cabbie a five-dollar bill, asking for a dollar in change. But the driver immediately protested. Although they had agreed not to use the taximeter, he felt that seven dollars was more reasonable than four.[5]

"I lost time. I didn't know where it was," the driver explained.[6]

"Well, I didn't expect to drive all over Brooklyn," replied the young man.[7]

The difference might have seemed small, but in 1925, an extra three dollars was enough to buy a pound each of bacon, coffee, steak, butter, and cheese and still have enough left over for a half gallon of milk and ten pounds of potatoes.[8] It was a lot.

Their argument continued. Tired, the driver gave in and handed over the dollar in change. Once more the young man chided him, adding that he intended to give the dollar as a tip but changed his mind. Figuring he'd had the last word, he walked toward the stairs.[9]

The driver pulled a U-turn in the middle of the street. Facing the couple, he yelled and screamed through the passenger window, reportedly threatening to come find the young man in Greenwich Village where he had picked them up. The boy took two steps toward the driver, who then pointed a revolver from his cab and shot him in the abdomen and chest, felling him to the ground. The driver sped off, returning his car to a garage in Manhattan.[10]

The shots and the young woman's screams drew a police officer from the nearby Ralph Avenue subway station. The young man survived the immediate shots but remained in critical condition as he was carried away to St. Mary's Hospital. But more notably, city officials quickly learned that this was not just any young man. He was Dennis Kenny, son of William F. Kenny, owner of the popular Tammany Hall hangout the Tiger Room and a close lifelong friend of then–New York Governor Al Smith.[11] Politically speaking, the young man was a royal prince.

Tammany Hall, which had existed in practice since the 1850s, was one of the most influential political machines in American history. In concept, a "machine" was a highly organized political party where candidates doled out money in exchange for the promise of votes. District leaders in the machine were well connected within their neighborhoods and intimately knew who and how to press for constituents' support. If turnout successfully produced a victory for the candidate, he was expected to perform several favors at the request of the machine's boss, including appointments to well-paying government jobs.[12]

Governor Smith and William Kenny were both beneficiaries of the machine. The two had known one another since childhood when their fathers were stationed in the same firehouse on the Lower East Side. Over time, William earned wealth through contracting and real estate, making a number of sizable deals in the New York City area. The year before young Dennis was shot, Governor Smith received the Democratic nomination for US president, and although he lost, his friend William donated $25,000 to clear the debts of the Democratic National Committee.[13] On that cold morning that Dennis was rushed to the hospital, William Kenny was on vacation in Florida with the Tammany boss of Kings County (Brooklyn).[14]

Almost immediately, a heated search began for Dennis's assailant. Before returning home, his date searched through mug shots for the driver, described as a tall man of Italian descent with a long, thin face. The police questioned fellow taxi drivers in the Greenwich area. Although many cab drivers were territorial and had preferred "spots" to wait for fares, the shooter had apparently switched up his routine. The police broadened their search, and a dozen police detectives reportedly combed the streets questioning taxi drivers.[15]

A week later, they heard gossip of a new driver waiting at the taxi stand of the Municipal Building who used to hack on the east side of town. Detectives asked the taxi drivers to point him out, and he was a solid match for the description.[16] They arrested a dimwitted twenty-four-year-old John Leventine. At first, he denied the accusations but was told during interrogation that Kenny was dying and they were about to arrest the young woman he'd been with. According to one newspaper, Leventine replied, "Huh, I don't want to see any dame in a jam on my account. I'll come through."[17] He then gave a confession, and the police found his revolver.[18]

The police and newspapers quickly pointed out that Leventine, originally from Hartford, Connecticut, had a long track record of arrests.[19]

After hearing of the shooting charge, his distraught mother said she had placed him in a New York asylum until age sixteen.[20] Not long after getting out, he was arrested multiple times for charges such as auto theft, burglary, and federal grand larceny.[21]

Leventine had also never obtained a chauffeur's license, a requirement for all NYC taxi drivers. Because of his criminal history, he was afraid he wouldn't qualify. The investigation revealed John Leventine had a brother, Joseph, who was also a taxi driver. Joseph's chauffeur license had been issued to him as "J. Leventine," and it was believed John borrowed the license, representing it as his own, to rent a cab from the garage.[22]

The shoddy oversight was not surprising. A legislative committee's investigation years earlier had found that the Department of Licenses was prone to graft and mismanagement. Twenty-two convicted felons were active cab drivers, and hundreds more had arrest records. Some drivers testified that inspectors were only willing to approve of a cab in exchange for a bribe of one dollar. If a driver needed to start working quickly, he could have his license expedited for a bribe of five dollars.[23]

The city hemmed, hawed, and replaced the agency head, but the scandal changed little.[24] Other matters were more pressing. In 1923, the city started feeling the effects of explosive growth in the taxi industry, fueled in part by a new middle-class prosperity and the declining cost of goods.[25] Whereas in the 1910s, taxis were only available to the rich and well off, the economy of the 1920s made them wildly more affordable.[26]

But the growth came with several unintended side effects. Competing taxi companies entered into cutthroat competition with one another, repeatedly slashing costs and making it difficult for the drivers to earn a living. Seedy drivers gained infamy. According to taxi scholars, "Cheating, hustling, false advertisement, stealing, and extortion became common."[27] Adding to the chaos, many cabs were painted yellow, making them so similar that it was difficult to distinguish reputable taxis from disreputable ones.[28] The industry became marred by horror stories of drivers mugging passengers and vice versa.[29] New York City periodically considered drastic measures, such as prohibiting passengers in the front seat and disallowing cabs at public parks after midnight.[30]

The cabs also created new heights of traffic congestion. In one year, the number of licensed cabs increased dramatically from thirteen thousand to sixteen thousand, several of which were constantly circling dense hot spots downtown. Many of them were racing each other to a curb the moment a customer needed a cab. Officials stated that the city could easily make do with only twelve thousand cabs, and newspaper editorials repeatedly called for reining in the supply. There was one problem: the roles of licensing and enforcement were split between two different agencies.[31]

For years the public complained about the surplus drivers, but the city was paralyzed. Two years earlier, in 1923, a taxi driver shot and killed two policemen, and still, nothing changed.[32] But the political magnitude of Dennis Kenny's shooting suddenly created enough momentum to revisit the issue.

The police pulled no punches to make a renewed push for the transfer of powers. The day after Leventine was arrested, they dragged both him and Kenny's date back to the scene of the crime to reenact the shooting and take official photographs. A large crowd gathered to watch, including reporters from *The New York Times*.[33] It was a staged press event, designed so the police department could send a single message: "The licensing of taxis should be transferred to us."

After the reenactment was finished, the police commissioner pointed directly at Leventine. "He had no license but a big revolver in his pocket," he said. "The Police Department, as I have said before, should have full supervision over all taxicab drivers in this city."[34]

Ominously, he then issued orders to determine how many more unlicensed taxi drivers were still operating citywide.[35]

Two weeks after the shooting, Dennis Kenny died at St. Mary's Hospital. Although he had initially been sent home to recover from the bullet wounds, he deteriorated after developing pneumonia, the combination of which "caused a general septic condition," according to *The Times*. In his last hours, he was rushed back to the hospital in an ambulance the family had donated to the fire department. But there was little to be done. A Catholic priest had already performed last rites.[36]

A few days later, Kenny's funeral procession was so well attended it was almost as if the mayor had passed away. The mourners included fire and police officials and multiple prominent members of Tammany Hall, including Governor Smith, who had brought his military staff in full uniform. News coverage stated that crowds lined the sidewalk as the casket was carried to the Church of St. Vincent Ferrer, where "great masses of flowers flanked the bier."[37]

The evening after Kenny's death, the NYPD took a dramatic step. The staff mobilized a massive blitzkrieg force to perform a citywide audit of the entire taxi fleet. The department pulled in five thousand officers and detectives from whatever they were working on, regardless of whether they were on duty, and deployed them to the streets to review every last taxicab and driver they could find.[38]

At each taxi, policemen ran through questionnaires, reviewed drivers' papers, and inspected their vehicles, keeping a special eye out for weapons or liquor. Their questionnaires were thorough, listing twenty points of review, and the inspections were especially intense. Taxi drivers were required to keep a long list of documents at all times: chauffeur's license, vehicle license, registration card, a hackman's license and badge, and so on.[39]

The vehicles were also scrutinized for even minor violations. Was the official rate card posted? Was the vehicle plate missing? Was the taximeter light lit? Were any curtains or shades installed to prevent a full view of the interior? If the police noticed a serious offense, such as having a weapon or failing to produce a valid chauffeur's license (or holding one that wasn't their own), drivers were arrested on the spot. Those who passed inspection had a blue sticker placed on their windshield to clear them for other police inspectors. Those who did not were issued a summons to explain themselves before a judge.[40]

News of the mass inspection quickly spread across the city. Reportedly, several unlicensed "nighthawk" cab drivers in Brooklyn hid their cabs in garages until it was over; police arrests there were notably lower than in other areas of the city. *The Times* reported one driver simply abandoned his cab as police approached and ran away on foot.[41]

The inspections continued around the clock with rotating shifts of police staff until the NYPD was satisfied they had combed all available drivers. Within two days, an astonishing eighteen thousand cabs had been inspected, and only one other driver was reported to have a gun.[42] All told, roughly fifty drivers were arrested and nearly a thousand issued summonses.[43] News of the department's audit spread to other media outlets across the country, including *The Washington Post*.[44] Kenny's family connections, combined with the police department's ambitions, led to one of the largest inspections of the taxi industry – an event rarely seen before or since.

As a political tactic, the NYPD's over-the-top demonstration was a success. The mayor openly supported the transfer of powers, and within a couple of months, it was signed into law.[45] John Leventine pled guilty to second-degree murder and received a sentence of twenty years to life in Sing Sing prison.[46] After his release in the 1940s, he returned to Hartford and led a relatively quiet life, marked only by the occasional arrest for administering an illegal betting operation out of his home.[47]

The environment Uber would enter nearly a century later was fashioned by events like Dennis Kenny's death. Left alone, taxis were too tempting to the under-skilled, too prone to corruption and abuse. Both regulations and market structures evolved around the need to make sure *someone* maintained vigilant oversight.

The great taxi audit reflected basic questions that regulators would tackle for decades. What rules were needed to keep the profession orderly? What steps could be taken to prevent bad actors from becoming drivers? What was the appropriate penalty for violations? Could regulators encourage independent owner-drivers, or was it better to make drivers accountable to taxi companies?

Early on, certain norms took hold nationwide that would last for generations. Maximum rates were legally set to prevent gouging. The general premise was that a passenger shouldn't be surprised with an expensive fare after the ride ended. And to ensure that taxi drivers couldn't cheat, taximeters were installed (and periodically checked) to automatically calculate the fare. Also, most cities required that cab companies distinguish themselves with starkly different color schemes. Yellow was the favored color because as originally conceived, it was the easiest color to spot from a distance.[48]

As taxis experienced explosive growth in the 1920s, safety issues became more of a priority. Several US cities began regulating taxis out of their police departments. Insurance requirements were passed, and where possible, drivers were vetted against existing criminal files.[49] Before long, police and civilian regulators learned to approach taxis from a strong enforcement perspective. The great taxi audit of 1925 became almost like a model operation. More and more, taxis were inspected in the field to verify their legitimacy.

But the most severe regulation – one that would fundamentally change the entire American taxi industry – came during the Great Depression. After the stock market crash of 1929, unemployed masses flocked to new taxicabs with the slim hope of making an income, which was preferable to the alternative of no hope at all.[50] Many of the new drivers were persuaded by the auto industry itself, which either owned or was heavily indebted by several taxi fleets. With a surplus of new cars and no customers to sell them to, the auto industry came up with a clever solution for their surplus inventory. According to taxi scholars,

> With sales sagging, automobile manufacturers saw the taxicab industry as a place to unload new cars. A manufacturer would "sell" cars to a taxi operator on favorable financing terms with low down payments. The cut-rate taxi operator would then lease the cars as taxis to drivers for three to four dollars per day.[51]

For the unemployed, the advantages were attractive. Being a taxi driver didn't require any specialized skill set; one simply had to know how to drive. There was also an immediate reward: drivers didn't have to wait until the end of each week for payment but could simply take home whatever cash they ostensibly collected each day.

Throngs of amateur drivers took the job, so many that police enforcement became impossible. It strained cities to their breaking points. One estimate stated the taxi industry enlarged to 150,000 cabs nationwide, only about half of which existed prior to the Depression.[52] By 1932, the growth was seemingly out of control.

Especially hurt was the electric railcar, the primary form of local public transit before automobiles. Since the early 1900s, the railcar had been adjusting to growing competition from buses and taxis, and since their routes were physically installed into the ground, it was too expensive to suddenly adapt with new ones.[53]

The railcar industry sometimes lobbied for relief. In the 1910s, they successfully pushed for onerous regulations against the brief but notable industry of jitneys, small buses that provided shared, on-demand transit.[54] With the uncontrolled growth of the taxi industry, the railcar operators once again complained loudly about the rise of a "new carpetbagger."[55] A few cities and states tried to help, but they couldn't protect them anymore.[56] Railcar problems weren't special. Everyone was suffering.

Preparing to act, New York City officials in 1930 took a census of the explosive industry and all of its problems. They counted approximately sixty-eight thousand drivers who took turns operating nearly twenty thousand cabs – another unwanted growth spurt since 1923. The industry took in $144 million per year including tips, which meant each driver earned roughly six dollars per day on average, not including expenses for gas, maintenance, or rental rates. After costs, most of the independent drivers were either making nothing or even losing money, and taxi companies fared only slightly better.[57]

Herding the taxis was like trying to herd fish. New York City was split by over five hundred cab owners, the vast majority of which held less than twenty-five cabs each. "Cruising," the practice of driving around looking for a street hail instead of waiting at a designated taxi stand, had not yet become socially acceptable. Nonetheless, thousands of taxicabs were driving around empty, adding wear and tear to the roads and clogging streets. Worse yet, taxis only made up 4 percent of all cars in the city but were still involved in one in six pedestrian fatalities and one in four collisions. The number of accidents spoke to the desperation of drivers, as if they had only learned to drive the day they'd rented a cab.[58]

Financially, the industry was eating itself. The Great Depression had already made passengers scarce, but new competitors led to renewed price wars. Several drivers pressured passengers for tips, and usually, they worked twelve to twenty hours per day.[59]

To remedy the problems, several cities nationwide began imposing strict barriers on the industry. In essence, each city declared that the taxis were a public utility whose market, when left alone, functioned poorly and created too many undesirable consequences.[60] Fundamentally, cities began raising barriers by asking themselves two questions. First, could they count on independent owner-drivers to behave, or did they want all drivers held accountable to a parent company? The answer generally depended on how much political clout independent drivers had and how much of a headache cities were willing to endure. But secondly, would they impose a specific cap on the number of cabs on the street or let the market's owners figure it out themselves?[61]

Cities could mix and match these answers as they pleased, but they tended to favor at least one of the restrictions. They could make it a company-only town, impose a supply cap, or more often than not, do both. With the notable exception of Washington, DC, nearly every city erected barriers.[62] If cities used a supply cap, the number itself was arbitrary, but it passed scrutiny as long as it sounded reasonable. In Seattle, it was one for every twenty-five hundred residents, and in Chicago, it was simply the number that existed roughly a month before the market crash of October 1929.[63]

If a city chose both paths – that is, placing a supply cap *and* only allowing taxi companies to operate – it usually took the form of a franchise license known as a "certificate of convenience and public necessity." Effectively, it granted taxi rights to a monopoly or oligopoly of owners. Much as the name implied, new taxi entrants were legally blocked unless they could prove that market conditions necessitated their arrival. For decades, this tool allowed many taxi companies to keep competitors out of their territory.

New York, the city with by far the most cabs, took longer to erect taxi barriers, but they would eventually do so with one of the most important tweaks to the industry. But first, they had to overcome several political problems created by taxis. While attempting to only allow for an oligopoly and do away with independent drivers, Mayor Jimmy Walker was caught accepting a bribe from a cab company.[64] It was the same year New York Governor Franklin Roosevelt first ran for president, and the scandal was so embarrassing to him that Walker was pressured to resign.[65] Fiorello La Guardia was elected mayor the following year, and the taxi mess was his to inherit.

As a new mayor in office, La Guardia faced a quixotic political problem. The city was overrun with independent cab drivers who competed for more business than was available to earn a living. To create market stability, they *needed* to reduce the number, but they couldn't figure out how. Which taxi drivers were worthy of their jobs? How was his administration supposed to choose winners and losers? More delays ensued.[66]

In early 1937, a narrow window opened to take action. As unemployment had steadily declined from its peak four years earlier (just before another recession), the number of drivers declined somewhat.[67] The city rushed forward. On March 9, the mayor signed into law the Haas Act, a bill that declared the taxi industry a "public interest" and capped the supply of taxis to the number in operation as of that moment. Any qualifying cabs not in use were deemed "abandoned" and effectively forfeited their license.[68] This meant that of the 16,900 issued, the number was effectively reduced to 13,595 licenses, and a short time later, drivers forfeited nearly two thousand more.[69] The city finally achieved its taxi stability.

But the speedily passed Haas Act also brought into play one of the most controversial aspects of the taxi industry's supply caps – the taxi medallion. Conceived as an immediate visual cue, the medallion was a simple piece of metal with a government emblem and a number. Owned by the government, it gave the bearer the legal right to operate a cab as long as the driver and vehicle met the basic regulatory requirements.

What Mayor La Guardia didn't realize was that over time, the medallion would develop into a transferable asset.[70] Those who owned a medallion could sell them to other cab companies, and after World War II, it turned into a commodity with its own secondary market. For the first time, the public policy of reining in the taxi industry was directly tied to a market price. Originally sold in 1937 for ten dollars apiece, the price on the secondary market slowly ballooned upwards to $7,500 fifteen years later.[71] Even adjusting for inflation, its value matured by a factor of nearly four hundred times in less than two decades. A medallion was an astonishingly good investment.

But it came with an important caveat, one that would later hurt the industry when Uber launched. To maximize their attractive investment value, medallions had to remain as scarce as possible. The ideal way to game this investment was simply to halt or slow the creation of new medallions over time as city populations grew. Thus, demand would continually increase while supply remained relatively restrained.

This was one of the first pressures on the industry to keep the taxi supply subdued, and thus began a decades-long tug-of-war between large cities and taxis. If lawmakers and regulators wanted to raise the number of cabs over time, the government had to fight the business interests of a commodity that, ironically, the government itself created. If the government was strapped for cash during a budget shortfall, it might resist and push back harder by holding a lucrative medallion auction. But more often than not, medallion owners got their way.

The pressure to keep the taxi supply low was shockingly successful. For decades after World War II, all the way through the 1980s, the number of medallions in New York City remained constant at 11,787 despite the city's dramatic leaps in population and density. Even during a rare auction, the total increase of new medallions was by less than a thousand.[72] As a result, by 1986, New York City's medallion price reached over $100,000, an inflation-adjusted gain of over twelve hundred times their original value.[73] Nowhere else in the United States were there as many medallions as in New York, but in every city that had them (or the equivalent paper permits), the pressure worked about as well. Any increases were sporadic and small.

By the 1970s, other developments were warping the business model and its incentives. Severe rifts began to form between labor and management in the taxi industry. As employees of a cab company, usually earning a forty-sixty split off of fares, drivers often complained of poor working conditions and depressed wages.[74] In response, cab companies often complained of expensive overhead costs. Labor disputes were nothing new for taxis, but they were turning especially heated and sometimes lethal.

In the '70s, inflation and unionization led to severe losses, and taxi owners apparently had enough.[75] Cab companies found a new way to earn revenues. Instead of employees, they would hire drivers as "independent contractors" and force them to pay an upfront leasing fee. Much like hairstylists or strippers, drivers would pay taxi companies for the privilege of using their facilities and equipment, and the driver would then keep all money earned on the job.[76]

For the taxi companies, this move had several advantages. They could save on the cost of employee benefits, and as a condition of their contracts, they could shift gasoline and minor maintenance costs to the drivers. Most critically, drivers assumed the entire risk for ups and downs in the business cycles. They would be responsible for collecting enough in fares and tips to offset the lease fee and make their own living. Whether the drivers succeeded or failed, cab companies still earned their lease fees.[77]

Once more, leasing was dependent on a restrained taxi supply. After all, the entire point was to extract from the driver an upfront fee, but in order for it to work, drivers had to believe there were plenty of fares on the streets to cover that fee. As a result, taxi companies would support mild, incremental supply increases and only if it added to their *own* supply. Conversely, if a city wanted to let a new cab company enter the oligopoly, the incumbents vehemently opposed it. New companies made it harder to compete for drivers and charge high lease fees; *existing* cab companies often insisted they reap the spoils. During hearings, they would often declare something like, "Market conditions are fine – there's no need for more taxis, and we should know."

Nationally, the shift to contract drivers was widely popular.[78] In New York City, after several taxi bankruptcies ensued following the 1970s recession, they argued it would bring stability to the local market.[79] Drivers' unions hated the new business model and fought it tooth and nail, even supposedly setting fire to an independent contractor's taxicab in Chicago.[80] But overall, they were powerless to stop it. As usual, lawmakers more or less gave the moneyed interests what they wanted. In a minor victory for drivers, many cities still required that operators provide workman's compensation for drivers injured on the job and insure against the risk of collisions and accidents. But those were the only silver linings.

Effectively, the role of the taxi company itself shifted. Although they had all of the leverage, they still needed to make themselves attractive enough to entice drivers to sign on, especially in cities where drivers could choose between multiple cab companies. Instead of specializing in collecting fares, they now specialized in dispatching calls to drivers to give them the most business possible, and thus charge them the greatest lease fee possible. Locally, the most lucrative company was often the one that first secured the yellow color scheme, as yellow cabs were the most preferred.

As New York legalized independent contracting in 1979, it also months later legalized medallion rentals. For a few years, some of the financially savvy medallion owners had acted on a "eureka" moment when a very basic thought crept in: "This lucrative asset isn't making me any money when it's not in use." Instead, it dawned on them that they could find someone who wanted to drive a cab but for whatever reason didn't have the time or money to acquire a medallion, and then simply rent them one. The idea was ingenious; renting the legal right to operate a cab created a brand new facet to the taxi industry and made medallions a more attractive investment.[81]

With the notable exception of Las Vegas, most American cab companies switched to leasing their cabs regardless of whether their city issued medallions. In larger cities, drivers had the double whammy of paying both medallion and lease fees, but their combined price was usually balanced enough that drivers didn't quit the job en masse. Still, upfront fees and independent contracting turned drivers' middle-class incomes into subsistence living. By the time Uber entered the picture in 2010, drivers typically earned $20,000 to $30,000 per year after expenses.

Since the taxi industry was still a public utility overseen by the government, these new business models dramatically changed the political landscape. Cab companies and medallion owners were regarded as rich fat cats, earning money without absorbing risk. Whenever local lawmakers felt it was time to raise the number of taxicabs on the street, independent contracting pressured drivers to oppose it aggressively. Drivers were typically dirt poor, taking home little more than minimum wage. More drivers meant more competition for the same low-wage pie. Adding more cabs almost always pissed them off.

For lawmakers, ignoring driver complaints was precarious. After the new independent-contractor model took effect, driver demographics radically changed from mostly white, lower-middle-class to a predominantly immigrant population.[82] Politically, drivers appealed more so to Democrats than Republicans as part of a unionized and immigrant-heavy labor force. It was easy to paint themselves as the victims of cold government regulations that benefited millionaires. And on any election day, there were more drivers at the polls than taxi owners.

Every time a city tousled the industry's bottom line, the divisions of labor and management created a two- or three-way tug-of-war. On one side were drivers suffering under the intense fees of cab leases and medallion rentals, on another side were the cab companies bearing the capital-intensive overhead costs, and where applicable, larger cities had a third side of medallion owners who simply didn't want to see their promised investment decline in value. They all generally opposed new competition, and drivers and medallion owners opposed any supply increases at all.

One of the side effects of using independent contractors was that service quality degraded. Since drivers were barely making a living wage, to compensate, they looked for ways to cut costs. Often this meant hanging around areas of town that were relatively dense with customers: usually downtown centers, airports, or nice hotels. As a result, other neighborhoods were often neglected, and since they were now independent contractors, taxi companies were legally prohibited from telling their drivers to roam around underserved parts of town.[83]

Unless they were pressured by regulators, the companies often didn't care about poor service quality. At slow times, a driver might simply idle in front of an airport or nice hotel. During peak periods, they did their best to avoid long trips across town where they would "dead head" without a customer for a return trip. Over time, as cabs began to enter the world of radio dispatching, a driver could use these same principles to either accept or reject a potential fare. If a customer called a taxi company to request a cab, a driver's arrival was far from certain because they could always say no.[84] It was not uncommon for a city to experience dispatch rejection levels reaching 10 to 20 percent of all calls.

Under these tense conditions, regulators often had a hell of a time just trying to keep the market stable. Most cities spent decades trying to find the right balance through trial and error. Cab company bankruptcies were not uncommon, especially during a sluggish economy. The downturns were compounded further by mismanagement and union disputes. It was ironic because the barriers to entry already gave companies overwhelming market control. Conveniently the barriers also corrected this problem, enticing an ostensibly better cab company to replace a defunct one by dangling the cheese of that overwhelming market control. In the space of one or two years, a taxi regulator might watch a company go out of business, panic about the lack of available service, and then successfully attract new operators.

Over the long run, this predictable cycle allowed taxi regulators to develop their own normal rhythm chiefly focused on enforcement and licensing. As long as the local market appeared sustainable, they devoted their attention to safety matters. Were companies insured? Did they honor workman's comp claims? Did they keep their cars regularly maintained? These were sleepy responsibilities, and as city governments grew bigger, most transferred them away from the police to a civilian agency, usually one in charge of local transportation or business licensing. The regulators themselves were often housed alone in small, cramped offices and with minimal support staff.

Even though most cities deemed taxis a public utility, they weren't necessarily overseen like one. For example, in a public utility like an electric company, the market is meticulously analyzed by government regulators to compare prices against supply and demand, while still ensuring a fair profit to the operator. Tucked into most electric bills are a fee to hire and pay well-educated staff who provide ongoing analyses of rates, costs, supply, and demand.

Taxi regulators didn't function this way. Taxis affected a limited number of people and weren't treated as "high art" in government circles. Analysts weren't hired to keep track of the changing cost of gasoline, oil, maintenance, and repairs and then make rate adjustments as needed. Nor in most cases did they closely monitor demand to track market stability. Market regulations were left on autopilot, and they were so infrequently analyzed that when they finally got around to it, regulators hired consultants to tell them the state of the market. The regulators spent time on less cerebral tasks like licensing drivers and companies, administering medallion transfers, reviewing franchise agreements, overseeing driver infractions, and pushing away unlicensed "bandit" competitors – anything that fit into the parameters of licensing and enforcement.

Technically the regulators *were* in charge of recommending rate changes and cap increases, but these tasks were usually treated in an ad hoc manner. Typically they only occurred when enough time had passed that someone said, "Hey, maybe we should increase the price," or "Hey, maybe we should put some more cabs on the road." It only happened when the timing felt right.

When they crafted fare rates, regulators came up with a simple formula. Take the total number of drivers, assume they all work full time, determine the number of miles driven per hour on average, and then between time waiting and distance traveled, calculate a rate that allows the driver to earn a fair wage based on the industry standard of charging per mile when travelling and per minute when idling (plus in many cases an upfront "flag fare"). If the result sounded reasonable, the rate was often imposed as the minimum and maximum.

Some of the assumptions in these calculations were more art than science. For nearly all of the twentieth century, regulators had little access to sophisticated databases of how far each cab driver was traveling or how much money they were taking in. Much of the data was self-reported from taxi operators, who kept the information in daily trip sheets. But even that data was shaky. Consider a city with only five hundred cabs, and assume each is filled by two drivers per day at twelve-hour shifts. That adds up to 365,000 trip sheets per year, all of which were on paper. Before computers, what government regulator in their right mind was going to have time to collect, review, and summarize even a statistically relevant sample? Even if they had wanted to, the cab industry was not stellar at maintaining records.[85] The prospect was dodgy at best.

When it came to deciding the number of cabs to place on the street, the number was almost always set to handle a city's *average* demand over the course of a month or a year. But that method was very simplistic. Like all traffic, taxis didn't encounter "average demand" at all hours of the day. Peak demand occurred during morning and evening rush hours, special events, adverse weather, or emergencies. Inevitably, peak demand led to taxi shortages, and thus, frustrated passengers. Cab drivers themselves might decide that if it ate too much of their time to drive near a special event, like an NFL game, they would avoid that area of town altogether, leading to further shortages. What's more, taxi companies were powerless to prevent it, and they had no incentive to do so. They had already earned their money before each driver turned the ignition.

Taxi regulators seldom had the skill set to fix the problem of low-supply periods. It was just a fact of life. Unless there was something on the scale of a Super Bowl in town, they didn't think about positioning drivers for busy periods. Most cities required that cab services had to be available twenty-four hours a day, seven days a week, and in response, most cab companies created simple shift schedules. As with buses or rail lines, shortages were just another public transportation challenge.

After roughly five decades of barriers, lawmakers grew tired of market controls in several industries, including taxis. By the 1980s, a broad nationwide movement aimed at lowering prices had spread like wildfire throughout the United States. Influenced by the Chicago school of economics, its basic argument was that by trying to control the market of a given industry, the government was hindering the price-lowering pressures of competition, creating unnecessarily high costs ultimately borne by the consumer.[86] Price fixing and barriers to entry might take good intentions and, over time, twist them into something unrecognizable.

Proponents argued that if a market could properly function on its own, goods could be cheaper if the government simply loosened some of its control. In many cases, they were right. Congress passed several bills lifting restrictions that, at least from price and choice perspectives, benefited consumers time after time. Historically the US Civil Aeronautics Board had made it painfully slow for airlines to change their fares or add new routes, sometimes taking years to do either.[87] That is, until their powers were stripped in 1978 by the Airline Deregulation Act. Railroad freight regulations, originally created to protect consumers from monopoly power, eventually forced railroads to operate at a loss.[88] That is, until the Staggers Rail Act of 1980 gave them more independence to set their own rates and routes. Bank loan interest rates, long-distance telephone service, trucking rates – all were reformed by federal legislation as a response to long-term market controls.

Because taxis were under state and local governments, Congress was powerless to change those markets nationwide. Nonetheless, cities still applied the same principles to deregulating the taxi industry, which seemed like an ideal market. It was as if lawmakers, under the comfortable lull of fifty years of market barriers, suddenly lifted their heads up and asked, "Why the hell were we restricting taxis again?"

In academic circles, two camps formed debating the merits of taxi deregulation, with the larger camp decidedly in favor.[89] Economists theorized that removing price controls, and perhaps even the market caps, would allow taxis to more efficiently charge passengers. For example, a customer taking a long trip from a hotel to a remote suburb could be charged a premium fare so the driver could recoup the costs of the empty return trip. Conversely, the price for a quick trip between, say, two downtown nightclubs could be lowered because demand in that area was already strong, and drivers were much more likely to grab another fare near the drop-off point. In general, economists predicted that with greater efficiencies, prices would decrease overall. In addition, quality would improve through competitive marketing, and with less oversight, cities could lower their administrative costs. Most importantly, if entry barriers were lifted, the supply of cabs that had been restrained over decades might finally meet demand.[90]

Beginning as early as 1965, and more so toward 1980, twenty-one cities in the United States pulled the trigger and took a hacksaw to their taxi regulatory schemes. They either a) abolished all their barriers in favor of an open entry system or b) simply created minimum business requirements for operating a taxi. Mostly they were mid-sized cities, such as Seattle, San Diego, Phoenix, Indianapolis, Kansas City, and Milwaukee.[91]

They didn't make the decision armed with technical analyses. It was more a leap of faith that the successes seen in other industries would replicate themselves in taxis. However, larger cities like New York and Chicago didn't jump on the deregulation bandwagon. It was still too experimental. They had more cabs in their markets, meaning there was more capital at risk, and the pressures to maintain supply caps were stronger. They were content to let smaller cities be the guinea pigs.

It turned out that larger cities were right to be cautious. Much to the surprise of most economists, taxi deregulation was anything but a success. Indeed, it enticed a number of new competitors, but in several cases, drivers merely stuck to the same hotspots existing taxicabs already circled: downtown centers, airports, and nice hotels. Taxicab-stand and dispatch-call wait times didn't improve in any meaningful way. Service quality deteriorated as both service refusals and the age of cabs increased. Small or independent fleets, which flooded the market, experienced service refusals upwards of 30 to 60 percent.[92]

Even more bizarre, prices went up. Here in this multicity experiment, the markets saw more competition, and in turn, they *increased* prices.[93] It was baffling, and it could only be explained from the customer's point of view.

In a city in the 1980s, well before the Internet age and armed only with the yellow pages and a handful of quarters, customers found it impractical to shop around for a taxi.[94] When a customer got off a plane and walked to the taxi stand, they didn't scurry alongside passenger windows, going from one cab to the next asking, "How much do you cost?" A customer simply took the first one available, and they were off. Likewise, on a busy downtown street, no one flagged down a cab, inquired about their prices, and then said, "Okay. Wait here for ten minutes while I shop around a little more." At a behavioral level, price shopping didn't exist. It wasn't an issue in heavily regulated cities because the rates were set by law – price shopping would have been moot. The great experiment demonstrated that regulated or deregulated, shopping for a taxi was simply infeasible.

Not only did the customer not shop around, but cab drivers weren't tied to repeat business. There was no reputation to earn or lose. Customers selected taxis at random. Once a passenger got out of a cab, the odds that they would see that same driver again were remote. Taxi drivers quickly recognized this pattern and realized that it wouldn't hurt them to raise prices. And because there were now more drivers to compete against, they didn't have much of a choice. Each cab's market share had become more fragmented. To keep food on the table, they collectively raised their prices to compensate. They could easily get away with it, too. Without consumer shopping, the market didn't punish taxis for bad behavior.[95]

The great deregulation experiment suggested that taxis could not survive in a free market. After a few years, most of the twenty-one cities that had experimented with deregulation reversed course, either fully or partially, and reinstituted market barriers.[96] Inside taxi circles, regulators who studied the industry used these experiments as a mantra to continue justifying the need for supply caps. "Deregulation doesn't work," they often said.

Outside of taxi circles, the experiment was largely forgotten. As population growth further widened the gaps in the taxi supply, frustrations continued to build. Newspapers and academics sometimes published articles wondering why the government had any business regulating taxi markets at all.[97] For outsiders who hadn't studied the problem, it seemed strange at face value. Taxis didn't look like a water company or an electricity provider. They were considered a public utility despite several characteristics of an efficiently functioning market: plenty of suppliers, a diverse array of customers, low capital requirements, a lack of technological superiority, and no price discrimination.

But if you applied some of the dynamics of taxis to a well-functioning product – toothpaste, for example – you could begin to see the chain reaction of a breakdown. Toothpaste cartridges are affixed to grocery shelves, available for comparison. If cartridges instead zipped around the store on a complex conveyor belt just barely within arm's reach, you'd have to grab one before someone else got it. The lack of price shopping might tempt sellers to occasionally jack up the price, which would tempt lawmakers to control the price in the name of public health.

Once prices were strictly controlled, it probably wouldn't even be profitable to invest in branding. The distinctions between brands would diminish. Rather than flashy boxes printed with creative fonts, buyers would see just a plain red cartridge marked "COLGATE" or a simple blue cartridge marked "CREST." Product improvements would require new capital, which is difficult to obtain under price controls. They'd probably have to wait until regulators forced improvements upon them. And in all likelihood, entry into the toothpaste market would have to be controlled so that untrustworthy producers didn't sell fake or inferior toothpaste.

The taxi industry wasn't born this way, but between the Roaring Twenties and the Great Depression, it got there quickly. Once medallions and lease fees came into the picture and turned each taxi into a high-priced, rent-extracting asset, the industry cemented its own flaws. All deregulation accomplished was proving the industry didn't know how to survive without strict barriers. Like a functioning alcoholic, it was addicted to them. Taking away barriers was like taking away a flask. There was no motivation for change, absent a novel market solution.

CHAPTER TWO

New Entrants

As the taxi industry kept the supply of cabs restricted, new players began taking up the slack of unsatisfied demand. Among the most important were limousines and luxury-class sedans called "black cars." Although high-end cars had been around for decades, they gained prominence in the 1970s, followed by a sharp increase in the '80s.[1] Patrons of the new business donned an aura of importance not bestowed in the past. Black cars were especially popular in New York, where in 1971 the police department's taxi oversight powers were permanently transferred to a standalone agency, the Taxi and Limousine Commission.[2]

In terms of regulations, the taxi industry wanted a clear dividing line between itself and the new class of cars. Very quickly, a simple compromise was reached where taxis, by law, would have exclusive right to the street-hail market (as cruising became socially acceptable after WWII) and black cars could only be summoned by prearranged appointment. For black cars, the fare had to be a flat rate set in advance, which they were fine with. Business was booming, and they were already charging a premium. Besides, their cars were either too dark to be hailed on the street or too large and bulky to wiggle through traffic.

The compromise was so congenial that, depending on the jurisdiction, black-car regulations may have been worded as a loose conceptual framework rather than a set of specific limitations. They might have simply said, "Luxury cars shall charge more than taxis," or "they will be summoned by prearrangement." It was generally unnecessary to be more specific. The luxury cars cost so much more that they *had* to charge larger fares. Many cities didn't even bother to specify what duration of time distinguished a street hail from a prearrangement, and in some cases, black-car rates were left up to the free market. For all concerned, it was a niche, low-priority market incapable of facing the same supply-chain pressures plaguing taxis. There was, though, an occasional friction. As the supply of cabs remained constrained over time, black-car drivers sometimes saw opportunities to pick up a street fare on a slow night, often by waiting outside a nice hotel for well-off customers.

It was a symptom of a larger problem. As a city's population grew far faster than its proportion of taxicabs, the industry began to see an increase in illegal operators infringing on their territory, known as "bandit" (or sometimes "gypsy") cabs. Bandit cabs were the natural response to a restricted market where demand constantly increased. Opportunities abounded to fill in the gaps, so many that they were too attractive for illegal operators to ignore.

Larger city governments responded to the threat with low-level sting operations. Bandits oftentimes drove plain vehicles, or perhaps even knockoff yellow-colored cabs without the proper signage and equipment. They were easy enough to spot, as they usually looked for high-value opportunities like popular late-night bars or clubs. If they didn't have the common characteristics of a cab, they had to either yell at potential customers from their windows or advertise themselves in want ads or on communal cork boards.

Administratively, sting operations required a fair amount of planning and were difficult to execute on a regular basis. In the course of a year, a city might only perform a handful of sting operations, which barely dissuaded bandits. Los Angeles, which arguably had one of the most active enforcement programs, made nearly five hundred impounds or arrests of bandit drivers from 1997 to 2006, and it still wasn't enough to move the needle.[3] In 2006, the LA Department of Transportation formally created the Bandit Taxicab Enforcement Program, with help from the LAPD. They had a front-row seat to watch how, just as during the Great Depression, the nation's financial collapse and economic downturn accelerated the rise of bandits to a new peak. In 2009 alone, LA saw twenty-two hundred arrests or impounds.[4]

The combination of low-regulation black cars and the soft pushback against bandit cabs created an opening that would allow aspiring entrepreneurs to finally fill the unsatisfied demand.

In San Francisco, the roots of what would later become "ground zero" for ridesharing companies stemmed from a massive corporate collapse in 1974. The Westgate-California Corporation declared bankruptcy, leaving up in the air the fates of several yellow-cab franchises, an airline, a tuna cannery, and the San Diego Padres. Its founder, C. Arnholt Smith, a wealthy financier and personal friend of Richard Nixon, had bought the United States National Bank during the Depression. Forty years later he pleaded no contest to embezzling from the bank to build his other businesses, which included San Francisco's Yellow Cab Company – the largest in the city. The resulting bankruptcy left hundreds of medallions up for grabs.[5]

At the time, the practice of medallion leasing that New York had so quickly embraced was culturally taboo in San Francisco, a city that empathized with taxi labor more than taxi management. Few wanted to end the practice, but the city grew weary of what it saw as the exploitation of its drivers.

The Yellow Cab bankruptcy presented a possible solution. In 1977, the city called for a public referendum, Prop K, which effectively froze the free-market sale of medallions. Aimed at cutting off the fat-cat lessors who relaxed comfortably in their offices, the measure ensured that no longer would medallions transfer to random investors while drivers sat behind the wheel for twelve hours a day. Under Prop K, no one could own more than one medallion, cutting off the chance to turn medallion ownership into its own business. Any further corporate ownership of taxis was prohibited, and if an existing corporate entity changed ownership by more than 10 percent, its medallions were forfeited back to the city. To possess a medallion from this point forward, an applicant had to be an individual person who demonstrated his or her intent to become a full-time taxi driver.[6]

To help Prop K pass, one of its compromises was that anyone who owned a medallion prior to its passage was grandfathered into a special permit that could still be leased to cab companies without any requirements that the medallion holders become taxi drivers themselves. In effect, they were legacy investors, some of whom had cleverly placed their medallion under corporate ownership at the last minute, allowing for more loopholes to transfer the asset upon death. Otherwise, regardless of when it was issued, whenever an owner died, the medallion was forfeited back to the city for redistribution.[7]

When Prop K passed, San Francisco effectively took a valuable taxi asset and loaned it free of charge for its holder's lifetime. The idea was that this would ultimately benefit drivers as a way of taking ownership over their careers. Pre-Prop K owners would eventually dwindle, theoretically leading to a utopia in which only drivers would own medallions, and when they weren't using them, they could lease them to other drivers.[8]

But the policy came with drastic unintended consequences. The legacy investors dwindled very slowly, hoarding their profitable medallions for as long as humanly possible. The city created a waiting list so that applicants could hold a spot in line for when the next medallion became available, usually after an owner had died. In 1978, San Francisco had 711 medallion permits, and after thirty years, fewer than half of them actually cycled back into the driver-only system. By 2010, the San Francisco taxi administrator estimated that "those people had earned about $800,000 over the last thirty-two years, and they don't really have to drive or manage the medallion." Meanwhile, the waiting list ballooned from three hundred names in 1984 (the first year it was created) to thirty-two hundred in 2010.[9]

The city still retained the right to create additional medallions, but due to strong political pressures, it only did so at a rate of twenty-five per year on average. Every time the board of supervisors (i.e., San Francisco's city council) considered adding more – usually one hundred to two hundred every few years – the drivers vehemently protested.[10] As in other cities, the board was only politically brave enough to increase the taxi supply in small increments, and there was plenty of reason to fear the opposition. Over the thirty years after its passage, the board of supervisors attempted several more public referendums to reverse Prop K, but voters shot them all down.[11] According to the city's taxi administrator, each campaign was presented as "a war between the big corporations and the working poor taxi driver," and the voters invariably sided with the drivers.[12]

At the slow rate existing permits cycled back to the drivers, the last applicant in the list of thirty-two hundred names would have to wait forty-two years to earn a valuable medallion, while also earning meager wages by leasing an existing cab in order to qualify. As a result, a number of drivers died before they could reach the front of the line.[13] It was strangely paradoxical – the very drivers who yearned for a medallion might not live long enough to receive one, but at no point did they want the total supply to increase because it would dilute their eventual payoff.

In the decades following Prop K's passing, everyone who needed to use a taxi suffered. It led to an environment in which the cab supply in San Francisco was more constrained than in most other major cities. At forty-seven square miles, San Francisco grew into the densest American county outside of New York City and came to appreciate space between buildings the way orthodontists appreciate space between teeth.[14] By 2010 there was only one medallion for every 630 daytime residents, the number of people estimated to work in a city during the day. By contrast, Manhattan, which had spent decades avoiding any increases in the taxi supply at all, had one for every 240 daytime residents.[15]

As a result, whenever San Francisco analyzed its taxi issues, it found demoralizing service problems. In 2005, the City Controller's Office surveyed residents from three distinct zip codes and found that 43 percent said they could only sometimes get a taxi, while 23 percent said they usually could not. The last time the respondents *could* successfully get a taxi, only 41 percent said it arrived within fifteen minutes or less.[16] Two years later in 2007, the San Francisco Taxicab Commission performed an annual public convenience and necessity review, where they found that half of all taxis summoned were no-shows, a rate that increased as they traveled further away from the Golden Gate and Bay Bridges.[17] Increasingly, it became harder and harder to get a cab.

Over the same period, personal time turned into a precious commodity as living in the Bay Area became increasingly expensive. A decades-old housing crisis stemmed from multiple supply problems: the lack of available development space, the city's rent controls, a prohibition of buildings over forty feet tall, and the relative ease with which residents could block new developments.[18] From the late 1970s to 2010, home prices increased by roughly 500 percent, and since the 1990s, San Francisco was practically in competition with New York to see which city could produce the most expensive one-bedroom apartments.[19] It was like the city was turning into an expensive resort town, minus the resort.

Residents commuted increasingly long distances or worked longer hours to afford the rising home prices. Increasing the taxi supply could have mitigated some of these problems but it didn't happen nearly fast enough. As with housing, demand for transportation was like a steel pipe violently shaking from too many pounds of concentrated steam. It was only a matter of time before the private sector would release a pressure valve.

As San Francisco boomed into a dominant tech hub, one of its most non-traditional tech conferences aimed at entrepreneurs and start-ups was the annual FailCon, a conference that branded itself as a safe space to admit that business failure is common in the tech industry. Instead of internalizing it shamefully, everyone was made stronger if lessons and experiences were shared. Eventually their motto became, "Embrace your mistakes. Build your success."[20] It was here that Travis Kalanick, one of the pivotal cofounders of Uber, once recounted his career path and confessed that he was the "non-luckiest entrepreneur of the year."[21] He wasn't arguing that he was unlucky in the sense of putting money on a blackjack table, and in every hand the dealer would land on twenty-one. It was more like he put money on the table, and then regardless of the cards, the dealer would punch him in the face.

In 1997, while a senior at UCLA, Kalanick and a handful of other computer science students helped form Scour, one of the first online peer-to-peer search engines.[22] Peer-to-peer (P2P) programs downloaded files in pieces from multiple other users, making sharing so diffuse and widespread, it was difficult to stop if licensed files were shared illegally. Scour was another iteration of the many P2P companies of the time, and in this program, users could download any format of searchable files, including music, videos, images, and PDF documents.[23] The practice had been brought to the forefront in 2000 when the music-sharing website Napster fought multiple lawsuits accusing it of copyright infringement.

Although exposed to heavy litigation, P2P companies were nonetheless attracting so many users that it was difficult to ignore the commercial potential. At Napster's peak, market analysts calculated it had roughly 25 million users, and a dedicated audience on a legally dubious platform was still a dedicated audience.[24] Well before the days of Netflix or Apple's iTunes, the industry believed that if it could adequately police the copyright violators, it could legally sell licensed music and videos in the relatively new manner of simply downloading them, a path Scour pursued.[25] Kalanick's company made strong inroads with distribution studios like Dimension Films, even exclusively releasing a promotional trailer for *Scary Movie*.[26]

As Scour ran low on money due to increasing server costs, they attracted the attention of a couple of aggressive financiers, including Michael Ovitz, the former president of Disney and founder of talent agency CAA. Considered one of Hollywood's most powerful figures, Ovitz was chronicled in *The Late Shift* negotiating David Letterman's historic move from NBC to CBS. Scour signed a thirty-day term sheet with Ovitz, which had a no-shop clause that prohibited discussions with any other financiers. According to Kalanick, Ovitz didn't provide any cash within the thirty days and exploited the no-shop provision to starve the company, freezing its negotiating power, and leverage for more ownership. At the end of the thirty days, Kalanick phoned Ovitz.[27]

"I had to call Michael Ovitz and say, 'Look, we're running out of money. You're not funding this. It's clear; I get that; that's okay. We got to go and find money.' And three days later, we got sued for – what was the reason? Oh yeah, shopping the deal…. The next day [the suit] showed up in *Wall Street Journal*. I wonder how that happened."[28]

Ovitz and Scour reconciled, but by July 2000, Napster's legal problems had spread to Scour. At the time, journalists noted that despite the company's attempts to remove bad actors from the network, it was still relatively easy to download bootleg copies of movies like *Gladiator* and *Final Destination*.[29] While in DC speaking with US senators about Scour's implications for intellectual property, company executives received a cryptic suggestion that they should talk with the movie studios. Kalanick was on a plane headed back to Los Angeles when Jack Valenti, head of the Motion Picture Association of America, announced plans for a massive lawsuit.[30] Scour was sued by "thirty-three of the largest media companies in the world" for a quarter of a trillion dollars, a figure that Kalanick often compared to the gross domestic product of Sweden.[31]

The suit never made it to court. Scour declared Chapter 11 bankruptcy, which delayed any ongoing litigation, and the thirty-three media companies, eager to score a victory, settled out of court for $1 million.[32] Kalanick tried to argue to partners that Scour had only filed for bankruptcy for strategic purposes, but in fact, the company was going out of business, a fight against reality he often referred to as "Fake it til you make it."[33] For Kalanick, this was a critical learning experience for future endeavors, a lesson that to succeed, empty rhetoric cannot trump the facts on the ground. Kalanick often publicly mentioned the profound experience of watching a company he spent over three years helping build from scratch sell in a court auction in less than thirty minutes.[34]

Immediately after Scour, Kalanick and another cofounder set out to form what he called a "revenge company" against the thirty-three litigants who had sued him. He called it "Red Swoosh," and at its core, the goal was to create a P2P product those same media companies could use to save money. Each was eventually going to either develop or interface with on-demand streaming websites where their media could be viewed. Kalanick took the peer-to-peer principles from Scour and built a program that, instead of illegally downloading a video from multiple sources, spread the viewing bandwidth among multiple shared sources.[35]

It was a clever concept. A server's bandwidth, like an electric battery, had a limited capacity, and supplying more to cover an expanding customer base was expensive. Red Swoosh proposed that instead of buying several car batteries worth of bandwidth, a company might quickly and easily borrow several dozen AA batteries from spare junk drawers that weren't in use at the moment. If an online video was pulled from several sources and reassembled as a single uninterrupted video for the viewer, media companies could save on their own bandwidth costs. Multiply those savings by thousands of videos, and the benefits became self-evident.

Although useful, the concept was several years early to the market, as video streaming was still evolving on the Internet. Kalanick started Red Swoosh in 2000, and the first YouTube video wouldn't appear online for another five years.[36] Still, he felt if he could build a quality program, the main business play would be to secure acquisition from the market leader at the time, a relatively small company called Akamai.[37] But a number of challenges and stumbling blocks got in the way. In their first year, Kalanick and his cofounder from Scour had a bitter falling out. Reports differ on what actually caused the acrimony, but the general sense is that the two had wildly different styles for running a business.[38] Kalanick stated the final straw came when he discovered his cofounder had sent an email to Sony Ventures soliciting employment, which led Kalanick to show him the door.[39]

Kalanick pressed forward under duress. The company was running out of money and desperately needed an influx of cash. He secured a meeting with the Akamai chief technology officer, who tragically was flying in to Los Angeles from Boston on September 11, 2001.[40] The plane was hijacked and became the first of two to crash into the World Trade Center. Eleven days later, Red Swoosh ran out of cash, the first time of several, and then soon after, Kalanick learned the company owed the IRS $110,000 in non-withheld employment taxes (accounts again differ as to what caused the oversight). To make ends meet, he had to forgo paying his employees on the promise of a future payoff.[41]

Kalanick often described these difficult years in the 2000s as the "blood, sweat, and ramen years."[42] They were marked by long-term roller-coaster swings of Red Swoosh running out of money, skirting the brink of bankruptcy, and then securing funding from a new customer or venture capitalist to keep the ride going. Each time he took in funding, Kalanick had to negotiate from a position of weakness, meaning he often had scant leverage with which to argue the terms of a deal, try as he might.

The financial strain was a blow to his self-esteem. Even when he could secure funding, he often used large chunks of it to pay his debts and employees first. He seldom could afford to pay himself a salary, and he lived at home with his parents, both of which led to "no ladies," as he put it.[43]

The Red Swoosh roller coaster came with a lot of motion sickness. At one point, his last engineer was near quitting, news which had leaked on *Fucked Company*, a website ruthlessly dedicated to reporting any small kernel of misfortune in the tech industry. The rumor aired right as Kalanick was near signing a long-form agreement, and the buyer backed out. This was the other source of heartache: as often as Red Swoosh neared bankruptcy, it also came inches short of success. Dallas Mavericks owner and venture capitalist Mark Cuban invested in the company, and to help cope with the ongoing years of stress and sinking morale, Kalanick relocated his employees to work on the beach of Thailand for two months. But later Cuban lost interest and pulled out, right as Kalanick had nearly secured a deal with the parent company of Dish TV. Once more, unsettling news about the company killed the deal. Kalanick said of Cuban's departure, "Maybe it was my off-shoring extravaganza that sort of upset him a little bit."[44]

After six years, his persistence finally paid off. In 2007, Akamai bought Red Swoosh for a sale price of almost $19 million.[45] The days of ramen and living at home had come to a quick end. The revenge company had triumphed.

Some of the anecdotes of this period, recounted in his FailCon presentation, certainly contained inaccuracies.[*] But what's clear is that Kalanick's fight from 1997 through 2007 to prove the profitability of P2P left his psyche battle hardened. "I will beat anyone as the non-luckiest person in the room," he said at FailCon. "Definitely not 'unlucky,' but damn I had to do some time." His failures made him a stronger and more aggressive businessman. Having already endured the battle scars, he became more fearless if forces undermined his business play.

---

[*] For instance, Kalanick stated he learned his last Red Swoosh engineer had quit through an online tweet. But *Business Insider* has since discredited this detail, since it occurred before Twitter existed.

Kalanick came away from Red Swoosh more focused and in a better position to explore new businesses. Exhausted from the multiyear struggle, he used his expertise and new fortune to hang back from the role of CEO and become a venture capitalist himself.[46] He bought a home dubbed the "Jam Pad" where entrepreneurs he was talking or working with could couch surf and trade ideas or war stories.[47]

He invested in companies like Kareo, a provider of medical-billing software for independent practices started by a former Scour cofounder. Other ventures included Formspring, a social network designed to let users share personal information through anonymously submitted questions, or StyleSeat, a booking website for making appointments with hairstylists.[48] His investments all shared common flavors. Most were geared toward either integrated tools for social media sites or streamlined business tools for niche markets.

During his stint as a venture capitalist, Kalanick could more clearly identify underhanded business tactics from the opposing corners of venture capitalist and CEO. He became a walking collection of great stories about the deceitful nature of the tech industry, some of which he shared with an audience when he was in an upbeat or excited mood. But beneath several of the narratives was a certain sense of bitterness and suspicion. "I'm deeply scarred," he once told an audience about his prior companies.[49] Everyone with leverage took actions that seemed clouded by ulterior motives, and to Kalanick, a savvy entrepreneur needed to learn to spot them as critical business risks. For example, he once summarized the relationship between CEOs and venture capitalists (VCs) as such:

"VCs tend to kill founding CEOs.... They're all so founder-friendly. They love founders. They exult them, put them on pedestals: 'They're beautiful people, we're just the measly VC.' It is in the VC's nature to kill a founding CEO. It just is. What it really comes down to is that CEOs that survive *are* CEOs. There are forces all around you – to take you out, and the ones that survive are the ones that are supposed to be there."[50]

Despite his pessimism and abrasiveness, Kalanick still garnered admiration in the industry for his intelligence, insight, and prior success. In December 2008, he attended the LeWeb tech conference in Paris, one which he attended frequently. He rented a large apartment and invited friends to stay with him, including Garrett Camp, cofounder of the online discovery engine StumbleUpon, which recommended personalized content for its users.[51] Camp and Kalanick had both accomplished parallel successes at roughly the same time in their careers. Camp had spent years building StumbleUpon to prominence and then sold it to eBay in 2007 for $75 million.[52]

According to Brad Stone's inside account in *The Upstarts*, Camp had already been developing the idea for a fleet of town cars that could be summoned by an app. He bounced the idea off of colleagues, including Kalanick, and even came up with the name "UberCab," registering the LLC shortly thereafter. At LeWeb, he talked more about UberCab with Kalanick, who reportedly became more excited after encountering a rude Parisian cab driver.[53]

In the months after LeWeb, Kalanick and Camp continued to press forward on the idea. At first, Camp wasn't thinking about solving a city's transportation problems but instead solving their own. The app was originally conceived for private use by themselves and a select group of friends.[54] They would travel in a higher class of transportation using luxury black cars to get around, because, as Kalanick frequently stated, "We just wanted to be baller in San Francisco."

They planned to acquire a parking garage and a small fleet of Mercedes S-class black cars and have drivers at the ready to come and grab them within five minutes, provided the user had access to the app. In a sense, this was like a "timeshare for drivers" in that ownership of the property would be split among a small group of people. While it was still in development, Camp called Kalanick and said, "Travis, I've got the papers for the parking garage," to which Kalanick replied, "Don't do it! *Don't* do it."[55]

Kalanick ultimately had no interest in owning the assets or employing the drivers.[56] It wasn't efficient, nor was there any guarantee that a small club of customers could keep it solvent. It was easier to just contract with existing black-car operators in San Francisco, who were already licensed by the State of California, paid their own insurance, owned the vehicles, and had the drivers ready. There was no need to duplicate their ownership and administrative headaches, and Kalanick still had a lingering burnout from his Scour and Red Swoosh days. He wasn't yet ready to jump back into the responsibility of running a company.

Camp began to develop the app "in earnest" in March 2009, but by the summer he had reacquired StumbleUpon from eBay and was once more its CEO, leaving only Kalanick with any time to work on the app. He prodded Kalanick with a "charm offensive" to temporarily run the company and get the product to prototype. It was likely the word "temporarily" that made the plan palatable to Kalanick, and he agreed.[57]

In those early days of 2009, it was nearly impossible to keep the app a secret. Kalanick and Camp's friends began meeting others who wanted to jump on it, too. "It started out for a hundred of our friends and ... we would be at restaurant and then, you know, there'd be new friends ..."[58]

The obvious signs that San Franciscans had unmet transportation needs were difficult to ignore. Still, the timing was a little bizarre. The prior October, the country had entered the Great Recession following the nation's financial collapse. Unemployment figures dealt California a body blow of 12.2 percent, one of the highest rates in the nation in 2009.[59] It spoke to the sad state of transportation that despite the terrible economy, a number of San Franciscans were still hungry for a ride from A to B, even if it meant paying a premium for a black car.

By early 2010, Kalanick was moving forward with turning UberCab from a side project into a more formal operation. They began beta testing the app in a handful of locations like New York City, preparing for a launch in San Francisco by that summer. When looking for a general manager, Kalanick put out a general call on Twitter under his handle, @KonaTBone, and announced to all of his followers,

> Looking 4 entrepreneurial product mgr/biz-dev killer 4 a location based service.. pre-launch, BIG equity, BIG peeps involved – ANY TIPS??[60]

He didn't know it at that moment, but Ryan Graves, three years out of college and working in General Electric Healthcare's IT management program, had been following him online.[61] Graves would later say it was because "I knew he was tapped in to what was going on in Silicon Valley."[62] Three minutes after the first tweet, Graves replied, "@KonaTBone heres a tip. email me :)" Kalanick loved the response, and a short time later, Graves flew out to UberCab's offices in New York and impressed Kalanick right away as a "super sharp guy" who had "the trifecta: hustle, emotional intelligence, and smarts."[63] The team was now assembled: Kalanick, Graves, Camp (as a partial owner), and a few engineers to help develop the app.

One of the early challenges was scaling the company so that enough black cars and drivers were on the system. This meant calling around to local limousine companies and persuading them to add their black-car fleet to the platform. According to Kalanick, "Three of them hung up, four of them were 'maybe,' and another three were super pumped."[64] It's not clear how UberCab specifically convinced them, but there were obvious advantages. Black cars couldn't roam the streets looking for someone to hold their arm up and wave them down. Nor could they actively solicit pedestrians. Instead, the drivers would sit by an office telephone waiting for the next customer to call and arrange a trip, which probably led to a lot of downtime. But if a black-car service could be motivated to roam the streets and wait for their next trip by smartphone app, they would earn more money even after costs. The companies would pocket 80 percent of each fare and UberCab would retain the rest. From a black car's perspective, there was little to lose and a lot to gain.

Even before launching, the team advertised their service as an alternative to the unreliable taxi market. The company began a blog on Tumblr, and in their third post, Graves, who was still transitioning from

Chicago to his new home in San Francisco, wrote about a recent experience trying to get to the O'Hare Airport. In a piece titled "Why Taxi's Suck," he vented about an attempt to find an empty taxi just hours before his flight.

> I finally found one, a lovely man that likely hadn't showered in a week, and decided to cut the cheese every 5 minutes or so. Eventually I decided regardless of the brisk Chicago weather to ride the rest of the way with the window down ... I'm pretty sure he knew why. Awkward.[65]

Graves arrived at the airport at the last possible minute before checking in, and the anxiety led him to post a whole series on the Tumblr blog, inviting anyone to submit similar horror stories.[66] In the weeks that followed, he posted a number of entries for anyone who followed their modest blog, painting the taxi industry in the worst light possible. Twitter users had taken his title and turned it into a hashtag: #whytaxissuck.[67] He reposted a photo from a recent news story of a New York taxi that had suddenly burst into flames, accompanied by the caption "SO NOT UBER."[68] He also posted a report from the NYC Taxi & Limousine Commission stating that three thousand taxi drivers regularly overcharged riders by quietly applying rates that would only apply outside the city.[69]

None of the negative taxi feedback was really a surprise to the UberCab team. In a way, they were banking on it. Before launching, they posted on their blog a want ad for a "rockstar engineer," explicitly stating they would expand "to hundreds of cities and 10's of thousands of cars around the world."[70] New York, where the company already had an office, was frequently on their minds. In the fights that followed in the years ahead, parties would often debate whether this new app was intended to supplant the taxi industry. But there's no question that at the very least, it was originally designed to compete with it. Graves described UberCab's advantage in the want ad:

> The ugly reality in the car services business is that if you need a ride to be on demand, you're screwed. Your option is a taxi that you can't find, is unreliable if you try to call, and takes too long if and when it actually arrives. In many cities across America, when you need a taxi, you come to terms with the possibility of being stranded. This industry is technologically

challenged, and has been propped up by a corrupt partnership between Taxi companies and local governments. This pain is our Uber opportunity![71]

All the vitriol aimed at the taxi industry also gave UberCab an early and obvious marketing goal. Creating a superior product was about not only the availability of luxury black cars but also the experience within the ride itself. They wanted it to be as smooth as possible, and they also wanted the passengers to associate deeply positive feelings with a black car that they wouldn't with a taxi. At one point pre-launch, the team reportedly brainstormed about potential ways to market the ride's experience with Kalanick's friend and venture capitalist, Chris Sacca.

> The initial ideas the group came up with were freshly baked chocolate cookies (DING!), and customized music playlists via Pandora/Last.fm.... scantily clad female drivers was also a hit ... patent pending.[72]

Finally, on May 28, 2010, UberCab formally launched in San Francisco.[73] A customer could download the app, summon a black car directly, and most importantly, watch the map as it arrived in real time. When the ride was over, they paid via a stored credit card and rated the driver on a five-star feedback scale.

Generally a black car cost 1.5 to 1.75 times more than a taxi, but its reliability was a stark improvement over the competition. Many were impressed with the ability to get a car within five minutes. UberCab spent the first few months slowly developing a loyal customer base, and the company marketed itself aggressively. By August, they had offered a Groupon stating that if they could get a hundred people signed up within twenty-four hours, everyone would receive half off all rides the following day.[74] In local tech reviews, such as *TechCrunch* (some of which were written by Uber investor Michael Arrington) and *True Ventures*, the response was positive overall.[75]

But despite the accolades, behind the scenes, the app did not function as efficiently as it could have. Originally, when it was built as a proof-of-concept for a hundred of Kalanick and Camp's friends, much of the code was developed in Spanish, which was difficult for new engineering staff to change. Most of the business functions like the website and blog were grouped together with the app on the same server, and the app itself took up a lot of memory.[76] Occasional glitches dispatched two drivers to the same customer.[77] Prior to the release of the iPhone 4, which followed UberCab's launch by nearly a full month, "the driver would go for two or three hours, and his battery would be dead."[78] Also, the estimated travel time was based on Google Maps, which was often inaccurate.[79]

And then there was the problem of expanding capacity. As their great reputation spread, getting new black cars and drivers onto the platform was difficult. According to blog posts, the customer base was expanding "sometimes 30% week over week."[80] UberCab encountered times when too many people would open the app to find no cars available. During a Thursday night gala sponsored by UberCab in late 2010, the number of zero-car moments jumped to twenty-five by 10:00 p.m.[81] High-volume nights like Halloween and New Year's Eve were even worse. It drove the company crazy. The app was supposed to be the reliable alternative to the taxi industry, not suffering from the same supply constraints that had plagued taxis for decades.

Such was the life of a fledgling tech company trying to find its proper footing. But when it rained, it poured. In late October 2010, UberCab was served joint cease-and-desist letters by the San Francisco Municipal Transportation Agency (SFMTA) and the California Public Utilities Commission (CPUC).

Years earlier, right as Kalanick sold Red Swoosh to Akamai in 2007, the City of San Francisco had discovered a way to remove the shackles of the entrenched Prop K ordinance. In 1998, the voters had approved a referendum to create a taxicab commission, much as New York and a few other cities had already done. However, the agency was generally regarded as powerless to effect any substantive changes. Reportedly, it was only good for airing grievances and generating the highest ratings on local government TV.[82]

Then in November 2007, a heated transportation referendum came before a vote: Prop A. Not aimed specifically at taxis, the new ordinance was a massive overhaul of transportation regulations, transferring most powers to the SFMTA. One new power buried in the ballot language gave the SFMTA permission to abolish the taxi commission and absorb its taxi-related oversight. Most importantly, it could adopt regulations that would "supersede all previously-adopted ordinances governing motor vehicles for hire."[83]

This meant that if it chose, the SFMTA could alter or do away with Prop K by a simple vote.[84] Several local taxi drivers noticed the provision and attempted to protest it, but it was to no avail.[85] Passing by a margin of ten points, Prop A was a radical and badly needed overhaul, San Francisco's second in less than ten years.[86] The city was apparently desperate to find a workable bureaucracy, and the referendum stripped away transportation policy from its elected board of supervisors. In short order, the taxicab commission was also dissolved.

One of the first taxicab administrators the SFMTA hired was Christiane Hayashi, a bright, dedicated attorney with tired eyes and messy blond hair who was adopted by her Japanese stepfather when she was young. She had worked for the city for several years but in 2001 got mixed up in a minor scandal at the San Francisco Department of Elections after it was alleged that thirty-six hundred ballots had gone missing.[87] It was a large number, considering that eighty-seven candidates ran in the prior year for eleven seats, most of which were decided in runoff elections.[88] Hayashi was placed on administrative leave for several months, during which time she performed volunteer work in a Mexican village. By coincidence, while there she ran into Aaron Peskin, a progressive-leaning supervisor representing San Francisco's northeast corner. Peskin was quickly impressed with Hayashi, who by December 2001 was cleared of any wrongdoing and by 2009 was recommended by Peskin to the post of taxi administrator.

Hayashi came into the job with no staff and only a simple order. "The only instruction I ever got was to reform the medallion system," she said. But the timing couldn't have been worse. In conjunction with SFMTA's new powers, the state and various city budgets in California were beginning to feel the imminent Great Recession. Unable to pass a plan in the legislature before a critical deadline, the State of California declared a fiscal emergency in 2009 to the tune of a $26.3 billion deficit.[89] At the same time, San Francisco was planning an annual budget already beginning $522 million in the red, and separate from that, the SFMTA had its own deficit of $129 million.[90] Everyone was in trouble, and no one had cash to spare.

Under pressure to make up the shortfall, the city quickly pulled the trigger on selling taxi medallions. Mayor Gavin Newsom argued that this asset had been historically underutilized, and he dubiously claimed that "if drivers had more of a stake in their industry, that could translate into better service for cab customers."[91]

Initially, drivers were furious. For many who had been waiting several years for their chance to earn a free medallion, their eventual prize had been taken away. But to soften the whiplash, Hayashi led open town hall meetings to formulate ideas and recommendations on how to smoothly administer the new program.[92] At each meeting, taxi drivers had to grind their teeth and opine on a plan designed to replenish the city's coffers at their expense. Although sold as reform, the move's primary goal was to generate $20 million. As Hayashi explained, "That was a difficult criticism to supersede. However, I was able to point out to everybody in the room that the reason they were all there is they wanted money, so ... fair is fair."[93]

Hayashi spent over 175 hours in meetings mollifying disgruntled taxi industry members.[94] They became like a second home. During one meeting near Halloween, she wore a yellow jumpsuit like the main character from *Kill Bill*.[95] Over time, the group painstakingly filled tall whiteboards and large sheets of easel paper with dozens of lists and notes, fleshing out the specifics.[96] Hayashi worked out the program details with an even-handed discipline and clarity and an astonishing level of creativity not commonly seen in government employees. She was like Leslie Knope of *Parks and Recreation*.

They settled on a premise that if the city had to sell medallions, then it should harm the drivers as little as possible. But it wasn't as easy as attaching a price tag to medallions. They had to adapt from an old market dynamic that had existed for three decades. There was no data available to help them understand its new impact, no local medallion "values" or driver income figures. To proceed carefully, they created a pilot program that would allow each taxi driver over the age of seventy to sell their medallion, essentially collecting a lump-sum retirement bonus. Fearing an auction would make the sale price prohibitively expensive, they imposed a flat price tag of $250,000 each and, just as before, only allowed drivers on the medallion waiting list to purchase them.[97]

The $250,000 value had two advantages for taxi drivers. For one, it made the medallion attainable if the proper financing was in place. The SFMTA reached out to credit unions and developed a clever arrangement where the driver could put down $12,500 as cash, the seller would put down $37,500 as an interest-bearing certificate of deposit (CD), and combined, they would have enough to meet the bank's required 20 percent down payment (the seller could cash their CD after the driver paid off 20 percent of the medallion).[98]

Secondly, although untested, it was believed that $250,000 was well below the market equilibrium. A driver who needed to could resell the medallion under rules yet to be adopted by the SFMTA. At the very least, it was unlikely the city would let the drivers lose money on their investment; otherwise, it would sour future medallion sales. A driver could feel reasonably certain they'd at least break even, plus however much they made leasing the medallion on the side.

After the pilot program was formed in August 2010, the SFMTA created the Taxi Advisory Council, a group of local taxi stakeholders assigned to monitor the pilot program and recommend improvements. In their third meeting in September 2010, members of the advisory council began noticing the existence of a strange new company offering black-car rides via a smartphone app. According to their minutes, a driver "reported that a new company called UberCab has opened. He read a newspaper article regarding the company and questioned the legality of it."[99]

A week later, another driver forwarded an ad to Hayashi from the SF section of *Thrillist*, where UberCab described itself as "a Tara-Reid-simple iPhone app giving you instant access to a fleet of a dozen way-better-than-a-cab Town Cars, Benzes and Escalades that'll cost you about $5-$10 more than your average taxi trip."[100] There was little doubt that this new service was intended to compete with taxis, and to anyone in the industry, UberCab was a bandit service.

In an interview years later, Hayashi recalled meeting UberCab's representatives. "There was an early meeting, I can't remember exactly when, but it was just as [UberCab was] launching. We pointed out these difficulties to them, and they pretty much just shrugged their shoulders and walked away, and we never heard from them again."[101]

The SFMTA took no action for over a month, and perhaps UberCab wasn't much of a threat at that moment. The black-car market was small, and before UberCab existed, two major smartphone applications, TaxiMagic and Cabulous, had launched and were already clearing a lot of business. Designed solely for the purpose of summoning a taxicab, these apps merely informed a taxi company's dispatch center that a customer at a certain location was requesting a ride, and then a dispatcher manually looked for the nearest available cab to send them. The apps changed nothing from the taxi driver's perspective; payment, pricing, and equipment all remained the same.

In San Francisco, because of the strained supply of cabs, the taxi apps were well utilized. Luxor Cab, one of the two largest taxi companies in the city, used TaxiMagic, and in April 2009, they had completed a thousand rides for the month, a figure that escalated to a thousand per day by March 2011. The taxi industry might have been nervous about UberCab, but for a brief moment, there were reasons not to panic. But then on October 15, 2010, *TechCrunch* reported that UberCab secured $1.25 million in an angel financing round, giving new life blood into the upstart company.[102] Five days later, the SFMTA and CPUC issued their joint cease-and-desist orders.

The reason *both* agencies issued letters is because they regulated different parts of for-hire business in California. San Francisco had jurisdiction only over taxis within its city limits, but the state had jurisdiction over all other for-hire vehicles such as black cars, limos, and tour buses. Since UberCab functioned as a hybrid between taxis and black cars, dual letters prevented UberCab from simply telling one agency they were supposed to be regulated by the other.

Between the SFMTA's new medallion sales program and UberCab's black-car service, the two forces were a cosmic mismatch destined to repeatedly butt heads like stags. On the city's instructions, Hayashi had already spent well over a year implementing the medallion program with a lot of care, forethought, and 175 hours of aggravating debate. She was invested in the taxi drivers' future, having already demonstrated she'd minimize their harm while the city collected its revenues. Legal or not, any bandit service was an inherent threat. Plus, even though the medallion sale price was artificially set by the SFMTA, its value still depended on a constrained supply of taxis in the local market. Once the medallion program was in place, the market principles of the previous thirty years would continue to guide them. That is, the total number of medallions might increase, but it would never rise sharply and risk destabilizing the taxis. Medallion values depended on not allowing any outside force to undermine or compete with taxis.

Toward that goal, the SFMTA's letter contained warnings against UberCab for every type of violation under the sun, even describing penalties beyond what it could enforce. But it was also confusing. The letter implied UberCab both was and wasn't a taxi service. For example, it was a city violation to operate a taxi service without a permit:

> Please be aware that the penalty for operating as a taxicab without a permit is $5,000.00.[103]

But then the letter implied UberCab wasn't a taxi service since it was a state violation for a charter-party carrier (one of the types of vehicles regulated by the CPUC) to represent itself as a taxi.

> As there are no taxis in your fleet, we demand that your company... cease calling itself UberCab, UberTaxi, or any other term with... Taxi or Cab in its name.[104]

UberCab charged customers rates for distance traveled and time at idle, which was problematic for a *limo* service.

> While these rates would need to be vetted by the State Public Utilities Commission, it is common knowledge that Limousines often charge a flat rate by the hour or a flat rate based upon a trip.[105]

Lastly, any device that charged for-hire customers by distance had to be inspected by a state weights-and-measures agency:

> You are clearly in violation of Type Certification requirements that are placed upon such devices by the Department of Agriculture.[106]

To sum up:

> The SFMTA demands that UberCab, LLC cease and desist all activities, operations, and advertisements related to car service in San Francisco.[107]

The SFMTA's letter was mostly a warning about what *other* agencies could do, and therein lay a strategic flaw. Although the letters made the government appear as a unified force against UberCab, they came from agencies with completely different motivations. Like that of its counterpart, the CPUC's letter made similar ominous threats of a $1,000 fine and/or three months of jail time for each day of operation.[108] But the CPUC didn't have a vested interest in the taxi industry, and they didn't share the SFMTA's priorities. The CPUC hinted that if UberCab obtained the proper permit, it could resume operations. For UberCab, this represented a clear path forward. If it dropped "cab" from its name, the SFMTA would have no ground to stand on, and they could deal with the CPUC one step at a time.

A day after receiving the letters, the company issued a blog post titled, "We've Always Been Uber, Now It's Official."[109] In an interview roughly a year later, Kalanick would say of the letters, "For me, [they] felt like a homecoming. I'm home now... I know how to operate in this world."[110]

CHAPTER THREE

New Engineering

In public Kalanick often acted as though Uber had modified its name and otherwise ignored the cease-and-desist letters, but at a rapid clip, it had in fact retained the counsel of San Francisco attorney Daniel T. Rockey, who had immense experience representing Internet technology companies. Although not a specialist in transportation, Rockey had closely followed how agencies like the Federal Trade Commission regulated commercial Internet advertising. Earlier that year, he wrote a legal article titled "FTC Investigates Ann Taylor for Encouraging Bloggers to Tout New Product Line."[1] Within days of receiving the CPUC's cease-and-desist letter to Uber, Rockey reached out to its author, and after a week, he had met with one of the senior investigators of the CPUC's enforcement arm, its Consumer Protection and Safety Division.[2]

Immediately, he addressed at least two of the division's concerns: 1) Uber's company name would no longer imply it was a taxi service, and 2) Uber would take stronger steps to ensure that its black-car drivers held valid permits issued by the CPUC, a change also noted on Uber's blog.[3]

But these were small potatoes compared to the CPUC's third and primary concern, namely that Uber was a "charter-party carrier."[4] Derived from the California Passenger Charter-Party Carriers' Act, a charter-party carrier was a legal term for a person or company that used non-taxi vehicles for hire, such as black cars and limousines. They were therefore subject to the

CPUC's basic permitting requirements: insurance, workers compensation, vehicle maintenance procedures, safety education, driver record checks, driver drug testing, and so on.

In his discussions, Rockey laid out the argument that, while the black cars dispatched under Uber's service were undoubtedly subject to these regulations, Uber itself was simply a software application. It owned no company vehicles, hired no employee drivers, and to date, had only engaged in partnerships with sixteen existing companies comprising a total of forty vehicles. Uber, he argued, was more like Orbitz or Travelocity, acting "as an intermediary between buyers and sellers."[5] Even customers who used Uber's app had to agree to the all-caps terms and conditions that further reiterated that Uber was not a transportation provider:

> THE COMPANY DOES NOT PROVIDE TRANSPORTATION SERVICES, AND THE COMPANY IS NOT A TRANSPORTATION CARRIER. IT IS UP TO THE THIRD PARTY TRANSPORTATION PROVIDER, DRIVER OR VEHICLE OPERATOR TO OFFER TRANSPORTATION SERVICES WHICH MAY BE SCHEDULED THROUGH USE OF THE SOFTWARE OR SERVICE. THE COMPANY OFFERS INFORMATION AND A METHOD TO OBTAIN SUCH THIRD PARTY TRANSPORTATION SERVICES, BUT DOES NOT AND DOES NOT INTEND TO PROVIDE TRANSPORTATION SERVICES OR ACT IN ANY WAY AS A TRANSPORTATION CARRIER, AND HAS NO RESPONSIBILITY OR LIABILITY FOR ANY TRANSPORTATION SERVICES PROVIDED TO YOU BY SUCH THIRD PARTIES.[6]

In a strange twist, Rockey also spun the intent of the Passenger Charter-Party Carriers' Act on its head. The Act stated that to qualify as a carrier, a company must meet *all* of the legal requirements, not just some or most. The wording was drafted into law to create a visible distinction between legal and illegal operators, and allow enforcement officials a basis for shutting down the bandits. Rockey argued that because it was infeasible to apply *all* the requirements to a company that owned none of the black-car infrastructure, the CPUC had no standing to regulate Uber.[7] It was somewhat of a stretch. A limo company couldn't argue that because it declined to purchase insurance, it wasn't subject to regulatory requirements. But then again, a limo company wouldn't argue that it didn't have any cars to insure in the first place.

Rockey and the CPUC were dancing around the question of who ultimately controlled this ecosystem. Through its smartphone app, Uber had successfully organized several black-car companies into an unprecedented virtual conglomerate, but that organization existed in the ether. Uber didn't place the black cars on the road in scheduled shifts; they were drawn there by a financial incentive. There was no person manually connecting passengers with drivers; the connection was made through an algorithm, and the driver could decline at any time.

At its core, Rockey's argument was that the Uber app was its own marketplace designed to better facilitate transactions, not unlike an art gallery. There were rules about participation requirements, how quickly the art was made, size and shape limitations, transaction requirements, and which artists were allowed to return. All the rules were designed to facilitate the gallery's brand identity and build a customer base. But the gallery didn't provide the materials or control the artists as employees, and if an artist was banished, they didn't stop selling their art. For the CPUC, the real question was if you took a regulated industry and placed a virtual marketplace in the middle of it, who was held responsible? The gallery owner or the visiting artists? The regulations were never designed to anticipate this question or even provide basic guidance. And as taxis and black cars existed under different agencies in California, there was little concern about how one market balanced with the other.

The CPUC said they would begin an examination of Uber's operations to assess whether it was required to seek a permit as a charter-party carrier.[8] Hayashi and her staff kept in touch with the CPUC, seemingly impatient to come up with at least a game plan to address the new company. In December, she instructed her office,

> It is time we came to our own decision about what to do, and to do it. If there is a factual record to review in what they submitted to PUC, then we should be reviewing it. If for some reason they cannot share it with us, we

need to move forward on our own ASAP with the information we have.[9]

But by most accounts, nothing moved forward. At the SFMTA, there were questions about whether they even had the legal authority to do so. In 2011 during advisory council meetings, which Hayashi usually led, Uber would sometimes pop up as a topic of conversation, and the meeting minutes would usually record something to the effect of:

> [A taxi representative] wants to know if the city can prohibit Uber cab.

> [An SFMTA employee] said that Uber cab can not be hailed on the street and they can not have a meter – that is how the city regulates them.[10]

In other words, it was legally out of their hands. The city had no authority to regulate black cars or limousines.

Meanwhile, the CPUC's Safety Division was already focused on a growing shit storm unrelated to Uber. In September 2010, across the 101 freeway from the San Francisco International Airport in a residential neighborhood of San Bruno, a massive natural gas explosion sent a thousand-foot fireball billowing through the air.[11] The fire immediately consumed several homes and burned for hours, as it took ninety-five minutes just to shut off the gas line.[12] Dozens of firetrucks and aircraft finally contained it the next day, but the explosion and fire ultimately killed eight people and completely destroyed thirty-eight houses, wounding several more people and causing property damage to a number of other homes.[13] In the aftermath, witnesses reported that some areas of the neighborhood looked like "a moonscape."[14] Federal investigators later determined that the explosion was caused by defective welds in a thirty-inch pipe owned and installed by Pacific Gas & Electric (PG&E) in 1956.[15] An electrical problem had sent increased levels of gas pressure through the pipes, exacerbating the defects and ultimately leading to the explosion.[16]

The incident was considered one of the worst pipeline calamities in US history, and the CPUC suddenly found itself under the scrutiny of a giant magnifying glass. Several had questioned how the safety division had not discovered, or caused PG&E to discover, the defects. Prior to San Bruno, there was another less serious explosion that could have led PG&E to reevaluate its safety reviews.[17] Several widely accepted methods within the pipeline industry could have detected the flaw, such as hydrostatic testing. That is, they could have pumped water through the pipe to see if there were any leaks.[18] The chairman of the National Transportation and Safety Board, which investigated the incident, said that the CPUC had placed "blind trust" in the companies they were overseeing.[19]

The new spotlight on the CPUC's regulatory lapse was so prominent that the commission itself hired a consulting firm to review its safety culture for shortcomings. An initial report revealed a division with massive cultural problems, almost as though it had been assembled from a random grab-bag of priorities. The commission lacked clear guidance, a long-term vision, established processes, and accountability. Initiatives could be easily dropped, as there was a "lackadaisical attitude toward follow through." Directives from upper management were often ignored because managers easily forgot about them later.[20] To characterize the CPUC Safety Division as ineffectual would have been an understatement. For all intents and purposes, it was constipated. It glossed over problems because it had no formal structure for resolving them.

For Uber, which was probably unaware of these shortcomings, it was an invisible blessing. The CPUC took no actions at all against the company in 2011, and even if the San Bruno explosion hadn't dominated the safety division's time and attention, there's no guarantee they ever would have moved against Uber. Rockey's brief encounter with the senior investigator sufficiently kept the matter at bay, not that it required a lot of effort. It was like jingling a set of keys in front an infant's face. The infant forgot what it had been looking at before.

Throughout 2011 Kalanick appeared for conference presentations and interviews where he would sometimes complain about the cease-and-desist letters, but he usually had little to say about Uber's response. At a *TechCrunch* presentation that year, he was asked about the penalties he was facing. The CPUC letter noted that for each day of violations, he could be subject to three months in prison. In a half-joking, half-nervous tone, Kalanick replied, "I think I've got, like, twenty thousand years of jail time ahead of me."[21]

For Uber, which was in the process of revamping its smartphone application and expanding to other cities, the safety division's shoddy organization was a wild stroke of luck, even if Uber didn't know it. To upgrade and expand, the company was going to need another round of investment capital, which would have been more likely to fail had the regulators actually shut them down. Had a better organized or more effective regulator stepped in, they might have asked a judge for a temporary restraining order, followed by heavy fines. With only forty black cars in its system, the long-term damage to Uber's future could have been devastating. Instead, it was in the most ideal start-up environment in which to plant roots and grow. Uber launched in San Francisco because of the city's tech-friendly culture, but operating in California was regulatory kismet.

Two months after receiving the cease-and-desist letters, Kalanick took over as CEO of Uber, effectively demoting Ryan Graves. It was by all accounts an amicable decision, and in a joint blog post, Graves even said he considered Kalanick a mentor and was "super pumped" that he was coming on board full time. *TechCrunch's* Michael Arrington poked fun at the blog post, writing a story about the change in leadership under the headline "Uber CEO Pumped about Being Replaced as CEO." Kalanick followed up on the blog, clarifying that this was now a partnership, not a replacement.[22]

It wasn't that Graves was doing poorly, but the previous six months in San Francisco had more or less been a test run to understand what worked and what didn't. The company now needed to focus on expansion, and the current operational model simply wasn't cutting it. It was unrealistic to plop down in a new city and hope the demand for black cars would grow in a steady, organic rate that wouldn't overburden their system and crash them into failure. Doing so would have been operating under the "fake it til you make it" mantra, which Kalanick hated. To compete with local taxi markets in each city, the app needed to offer service with a high degree of reliability and timeliness beginning on day one. They needed to control their deployment. Kalanick summed it up as a new phrase entered the Uber lexicon. "Two words: Supply. Chain."[23]

In 2011, Kalanick hired a variety of new top-tier staff. Chiefly, the first goals were to clean up the Spanish-written coding and develop a variety of models so Uber deployed in a city without sacrificing reliability or timeliness. Some of the first hires occurred after a bad day in December 2010 when Uber's drivers experienced serious malfunctions and many customers were unable to get a car. Kalanick quickly hired Curtis Chambers, a software engineer who had worked at Red Swoosh, Akamai, and one of Kalanick's angel investment companies.[24] Chambers' mission was to develop a more sophisticated and efficient software architecture for the application, and wasting little time, Kalanick immediately put him to work.

Just like at Red Swoosh, Kalanick brought back the beachfront workspace. As Chambers said in an interview, "Literally the day I joined, Travis and I jumped in his car, drove to LA, and rented a beach house for two weeks and just white-boarded, prototyped, built all these different things . . ."[25]

From a data-architecture standpoint, Chambers quickly intuited that building a peer-to-peer system for black-car rides was more or less the same thing as building one for video streaming. "Instead of bytes, it's a service," he once said.[26] Uber would now be based on a data framework similar to that of his previous peer-to-peer companies.

But to develop proper supply-chain management, Kalanick brought in a team of employees who would increase their understanding of city and passenger behaviors. The difficulty with planning rides for a city is that a city is not a static environment. If the goal was to ensure that a black car arrived at a given location in, say, under ten minutes using an automated program, then the company needed to study all the factors that could harm that deadline.

One way to think of this problem was like the video game *Frogger*, in which a digital frog merges with and crosses between streaming lanes of traffic. As the frog, the player has to anticipate the changing traffic patterns to move across the screen. Similarly, Uber had to predict traffic patterns, combined with the demand generated by hundreds or thousands of passengers, and then incentivize enough frogs (i.e., black cars) to those areas of town – all to ensure that drivers arrived at yet-to-be-determined pickup points within fifteen minutes. To add another layer of difficulty, software engineers had to mathematically implement those changing dynamics into a decision-making algorithm to match each passenger to the best available driver.

It was a monumental challenge, and to tackle it, Kalanick effectively hired a de facto mathematics department. He brought in specialists in statistics, economics, neuroscience, and above all, machine learning. When released into a city under a special beta-testing period, the app would use trip information to automatically assemble traffic data and learn route patterns, which would then be used to predict response times. In blog posts, the vehicles used during beta testing were sometimes referred to as "secret Ubers."[27]

Data analysis became one of the integral functions of Uber's math department. Bradley Voytek, a neuroscientist, began a tongue-in-cheek series on the company blog called "#UberData," providing an in-depth analysis of trends they discovered. In one of the first postings, Voytek pulled the results from the 2005 San Francisco taxi survey – the one covering the disappointed residents from three zip codes – and compared them against Uber's track record. Voytek created a bar graph showing that while only 27 percent of taxi customers were picked up in less than fifteen minutes, that number shot up to 94.62 percent for Uber. Also, Uber had been working to increase the percentage of people who were picked up in less than *ten* minutes, which Voytek demonstrated using a monthly scatter plot with an arrow pointed up and to the right. He had scrawled the word "MATH" atop it.[28] It was a way of poking fun at the taxi industry's relative laziness, since it had never thought in these terms before.

Over time the "#UberData" posts increasingly showcased social science that proved useful in prediction models and targeted marketing. Voytek looked for any correlation showing how customers used Uber, broken down at a highly granular level. He listed which neighborhoods passengers were traveling between, broken further down by gender, weekday or weekend, Android or iPhone, and the rating of the ride.[29] The company could then develop probabilities of where customers would travel, and thus, where their black cars would need to be positioned. In essence, Voytek sought geographic "personality" traits to anticipate how service changed in different neighborhoods. For instance, one neighborhood might have an active nightlife while another went dead after 5:00 p.m.

Sometimes, his analysis was borderline creepy and inappropriate. He wrote a post on the correlations between Uber demand and neighborhood crime rates, discovering statistically significant connections to prostitution, alcohol, theft, and burglary.[30] In another post, Voytek analyzed the number of people who appeared to be using Uber for their "walk of shame" the morning after a sexual encounter. That is, he looked for passengers who got a black car between 10:00 p.m. and 4:00 a.m. on a Friday or Saturday night and then requested a second ride four to six hours later within 0.1 miles of their previous drop-off point. Voytek dubbed it the "Ride of Glory" and even created color-coded city maps to show which neighborhoods it occurred in most.[31] It was an early sign that Uber didn't understand how its personality could be off-putting to the public.

As Uber grew, studying city neighborhoods became increasingly important. Behind the scenes, Uber staff had access to a function called "God View" where they could view each car on the platform and a live map of passenger demand. This was often represented as a heat map where "hot" areas represented high-demand areas that had not yet been "cooled" by enough black cars to pick up the customers. Uber also maintained data on the geo-location of every person who had simply opened the app, referred to as "eyeballs."[32] In cities where Uber was not yet operating, this tool was helpful in determining which future markets would be the most promising to enter. In early 2011, Voytek posted a national heat map of eyeballs, which included several pockets of activity in large cities Uber had not yet launched in, especially in Florida, Ohio, and Texas.[33]

The amount of data and forethought Uber put into play was staggering, and the taxi industry had never come close to using it in a similar fashion. Taxis may have beaten Uber to the punch in releasing smartphone apps to dispatch a car, but they weren't yet using them to improve response times or the distribution of taxis. Even in 2010 many regulators were struggling just to get taxis to accept credit card payments, as there was often disagreement about whether labor or management would bear the administrative costs. Some taxi owners would later gripe that Uber didn't deserve recognition as a technology pioneer since TaxiMagic and Cabulous launched before Uber did, but when it came to supply-chain management and service planning, there was no question Uber had leaped far, *far* ahead of them.

Aside from data analysis, another core component aiding their supply-chain management, which would become one of its most controversial among regulators, was the use of dynamic pricing that Uber had termed "surge pricing." Put simply, surge pricing allowed Uber to temporarily increase the price when the local demand heavily outweighed supply. Increased prices incentivized more drivers, "cooling" excess demand. It was a way for Uber to avoid what it called "zeroes," customers who would open the app and find a message informing them that no cars were available. By many accounts, Uber intensely hated it when that happened.

Surge pricing was somewhat of a taboo. In the taxi industry, pricing was strictly controlled by law and was not allowed to change unless approved by the local government. Generally, the premise was that since it was impractical for a passenger to shop for taxi service, the price was legally fixed in order to prevent gouging. Uber didn't originally build surge pricing into their platform, but they had grown so quickly that it was dearly needed. On Halloween of 2010, "95% of requests resulted in 'No Cars Available,'" according to a blog post.[34] Anticipating a strong demand the following New Year's Eve, they manually doubled their prices, which helped a little.[35] But Uber still needed to trigger surges at a neighborhood level, and software engineers began programming surge pricing into the algorithm. They put it into place beginning on Halloween 2011.[36]

For the first few years, it was difficult for Uber's customers to acclimate to dynamic pricing. In fairness, Kevin Novak, a data scientist who helped create the framework, acknowledged that the app's warning to customers was not well designed at first.

"If you originally saw the surge pricing screen . . . it was a wall of text," he said at a tech interview. "Like, it was size-twelve font, which to an engineer is like, 'Of course; I read text all day; I'm very detail oriented.' You're not thinking about customers and the . . . 'I've had three to six to twelve drinks, it's three in the morning, I'm not really reading all of it.'"[37]

Novak's mistakes taught Uber the hard way. Easily their busiest day each year was New Year's Eve, the biggest night when large swaths of people partied, drank, and needed a ride home. But it was also the one where Uber received the most complaints about surge pricing. Intoxicated passengers seemingly didn't care how much it cost to get a ride home when demand drove prices much higher than usual, but then they would be surprised when reviewing their receipts the next morning. The company was especially nervous about the New Year's Eve leading up to 2012, the first since surge pricing had been automated into the program. Uber tried to soften expectations by reminding its customers with emails and several tweets, but it was all for naught.[38]

On January 3, 2012, Kalanick published a blog post with photos where he appeared disheveled, tired, and unshaven, as he re-capped the disaster of New Year's Eve in a lengthy essay. Although the app didn't malfunction, the staff had watched in horror as surge pricing boosted to unexpected levels, reaching as high as 6.25 times normal pricing. It had been a mass of desperation, as customers sought *any* transportation option available. Kalanick compared the demand to a "tsunami that had a seemingly infinite amount of water behind it."[39] For one night, Uber was trapped between a rock and a hard place. People were paying ungodly sums for a black-car ride, which didn't help Uber brand itself as a competitive alternative to taxis. But if they had manually lowered the multiplier during the night, it only would have made the problems worse. Drivers would have had no incentive to head to high-demand areas, and customers would have had less success getting a black car at all. The lesser of two evils was to choose reliability over low prices.

Uber was trying to shift how people thought about paying for rides, and they acknowledged the transition needed to be smoother to avoid the "serious sticker shock," but the New Year's Eve drama wouldn't push them away from the concept.[40] A reliable ride required a system that maximized the number of trips, and there was no more efficient way to do that than with surge pricing. It was necessary. Period.

By the end of 2011, Uber had hired over forty employees and expanded to five cities in the United States, and to a handful of others internationally. In addition to San Francisco, it had launched in New York (May), Seattle (August), Chicago (September), Boston (October), and Washington, DC

(December).[41] For each city, Uber began to develop a "play book." That is, they developed a plan to market their app, attract customers, and, later on, face any regulatory hurdles.

Usually one of the first steps was to "pay homage" by throwing a lavish party at a four- or five-star restaurant, where Uber catered, provided an open bar, and invited influential members of the local tech community. And of course, it was the perfect excuse for guests to try out the app. In New York, for instance, they held a pre-launch party at Del Posto, a high-end Italian restaurant co-owned by Mario Batali of *Iron Chef* fame. Invited guests included columnists and editors for *TechCrunch, CNET, The Wall Street Journal, The New York Times,* and *The Huffington Post*; cofounders of Vimeo and Foursquare; and a person *Businessweek* once named the top angel investor in the tech industry.[42]

But despite the fanfare and local press, it often took months for any regulators to notice when Uber showed up to a city, and when they finally did, it was much like Christiane Hayashi's experience. Someone from the taxi industry would get a hold of their local regulator, make a complaint, and push for an enforcement action. If one were to bet money on which city Uber would have received the most regulatory resistance from after their expansion, an obvious choice might have been New York. Nowhere in the country were medallions more heavily priced, meaning that those who invested in taxi services had the most to lose from a bandit competitor.

But the launch in New York was timid compared to other areas of the country. At first, the city's regulatory agency, the Taxi and Limousine Commission (TLC), issued Uber a cease-and-desist letter. According to Brad Stone in *The Upstarts*, Kalanick initially resisted the idea of complying with any TLC regulations, in part because of his experience with Hayashi, but his NYC manager defied him and cooperated nonetheless.[43] Luckily the TLC's initial resistance was superficial. They didn't seek a shutdown the way the SFMTA had.

Uber enlisted Brad Tusk, Mayor Michael Bloomberg's former campaign manager, who was able to navigate the TLC and work out the kinks. According to Tusk, "We solved the problem with the TLC relatively quickly because I think they a) were generally friendly to innovation and new technology, and b) understood pretty quickly what Uber was and what Uber wasn't, and as a result, they were able to sort of work something out pretty quickly."[44]

Within two months of entering New York, the TLC had issued a couple of industry notices on Uber's presence.

> The TLC has received a number of inquiries regarding the status of smartphone application businesses that offer ... for-hire transportation services to the general public.... In particular, the Commission has received inquiries as to whether a Smartphone App is required to hold license [to operate from a base].[45]

Although somewhat arcane in the Internet age, transportation providers in New York City were required to dispatch vehicles from a central facility known as a "base," which was the TLC's main concern. A base was one of the main tools to distinguish licensed vehicles from unlicensed vehicles, and the TLC wanted assurances that a smartphone application wouldn't be used to circumvent that verification. After a few conversations back and forth, Uber satisfied the TLC that it was a legitimate service.[46] The cease-and-desist seemingly came and went with little more than a whimper.

Instead of a showdown in New York, regulatory panic more surprisingly popped up in Washington, DC, of all places, which was a little unexpected. Washington was one of the few major cities in the United States that had an open entry system. There were no limits on the number of cabs, nor were there any requirements that drivers affiliate with any company, but that was only because the District had no choice.[47] During the Great Depression, they would have needed an Act of Congress to erect market barriers, and even when taxis looked like an out-of-control crisis, it proved impossible.[48]

One wouldn't have anticipated a fight in DC. Not only were the taxi barriers lax, but so were the black-car regulations. Unfortunately, Uber's timing was inconvenient. Similar to San Francisco's situation two years prior, the District's taxi industry was in the middle of a revitalization.

Taxi rules in Washington were antiquated compared to other cities. Not only did they resist credit cards, but for decades, DC cabs didn't even use taximeters. They operated on a zoning system where a driver calculated the number of times he crossed between five separate zones of town and charged a fare accordingly.[49] In addition, there were several ancillary fees a driver could charge, such as luggage.[50] Although wildly confusing for tourists and not very common elsewhere in the country, zoning had the advantage of saving the independent drivers from purchasing expensive taximeter equipment, as many of them couldn't enjoy the economies-of-scale savings that a taxi company could for a large fleet.

The odd rules appeased DC's low-paid, working-class taxi drivers, who enjoyed a relatively large amount of political clout. To force any upgrades on them was akin to lighting their hair on fire. But by 2008, the mayor and city council had become so frustrated with the stagnant industry that they nonetheless moved forward with a series of modernization efforts. They began by installing taximeters, and over time they also pushed credit card acceptance and a medallion system to cap the local supply.[51]

The local drivers fiercely hated the new requirements, and the transition itself turned into a corruption scandal. Not long after a new taxi commissioner was appointed in 2007, an influential owner of a taxi repair shop anticipated how valuable the newly created medallions would become and offered the commissioner a $20,000 cash bribe to obtain a license to run a cab company. The commissioner, a former career police officer, immediately began working with local police and the FBI by frequently wearing a wire to determine how far the bribery extended. After a four-year investigation, they eventually caught an aide to one of the city council members as well as dozens of drivers who were part of the scheme.[52] The commissioner himself had not done anything wrong, but the taint of the corruption scandal made him politically unpalatable to Mayor Vincent Gray, who was sworn into office in 2011 and wanted a stronger figure in place.

Enter Ron Linton, a long-time DC resident who'd made his career in a lobbying firm for federal infrastructure contracts. At eighty-one years old, Linton was clearly visible in any room with his large girth, healthy posture, wide-eyed and spry demeanor, and semi-obvious toupee. Often wearing a light gray suit, he was alert and carried himself as though he were decades younger. Remarkably, he had also spent twenty-three years performing unpaid volunteer work for the DC Police Reserve Corps, working his way up to chief in 1994. He was then tasked with overhauling the reserve units. He was also very active in the District's economic development in the 1990s and periodically crossed paths with Mayor Gray's future city administrator. Linton was strongly recommended for the post of taxi commissioner as a highly effective agent of change. After an interview, Mayor Gray concurred he had the right temperament to take on an aggressive taxi industry resistant to upgrades. Linton took the challenge head on.[53]

Coincidentally, when Uber entered DC in December 2011, the city council proposed a bill to overhaul the taxi industry with most of the provisions they had been discussing for years: mandatory satellite navigation systems, credit card acceptance, vehicle age and mileage limits, fuel-efficiency requirements, and so on – everything except taxi medallions.[54] Still, the drivers hated the legislation, making Linton's job every bit as tense and difficult as advertised. In public hearings, he constantly encountered an incumbent industry resentful and suspicious of his motivations.[55]

In all likelihood, taxi reforms kept the industry distracted from Uber for a short time. *The Washington Post* wrote a puff piece on Uber upon their DC launch, and the reaction of regional taxi companies appeared mild. Linton was not even quoted, suggesting that no reporter had even brought the new company to his attention. One executive of a five-hundred-cab company in Montgomery County, Maryland (just north of DC) implied that Uber would face reliability problems because "it remotely cannot assure the same service quality" as local fleets.[56] Uber was still new to this space, but already there was a disconnect between expectations and reality.

The following month, in January 2012, Linton held a monthly meeting of the DC Taxi Commission where, during public testimony, several independent drivers made their customary complaints. One brought up Uber's entry into the local market, an issue that was apparently already on Linton's mind.

"I would tell you that in our reference of and review of their operations," Linton said, "they're operating illegally and we intend to take steps towards that end ... they will be dealt with."[57]

Notified of the "dealt with" comment by tweet, Uber turned it into a regional public relations campaign within just a few hours. They quickly published it in a blog post, which then instantly entered the public fray on sites like *TechCrunch* and the local news site *DCist*.[58] The latter interviewed Linton for an explanation, but in general, none of the sites were very sympathetic with the plight of the taxi industry, nor could they see an inherent logic as to why Uber was illegal. In a *Washington Post* article covering the fracas, Kalanick even said that before launching in DC, they had conversations with taxi commission representatives about DC's regulations.[59] On its blog, Uber insisted that they had read the regulations prior to entering and were legal, and they reached out once more to Linton's office to address his concerns.[60]

Whether deliberately or just by coincidence, Uber's use of the media in response to Linton not only galvanized support but also increased their brand awareness. As all of this was happening, the company began a Twitter campaign under the hashtag #UberDCLove to ask for the community's involvement. "We need your tweets, FB posts, blog posts and videos to show your support and so that we can put on display the positive impact we're working to make in DC," it emphasized in bold letters.[61] Several of the Uber staff got the ball rolling by tweeting the blog post under the same hashtag, and a local taxi watchdog group quickly offered their support, "as [Uber] provides consumer choices," it declared.[62]

Inherently, the company was asking the public to 1) vent their frustrations about Linton, and 2) publicly attest to Uber's advantages over taxis. It was the best kind of media: free.

Two days after the "dealt with" hearing, Linton upped the ante. He invited reporters to wait for him at 9:00 a.m. in front of the Mayflower Hotel three blocks from Dupont Circle.[63] Linton had summoned an Uber black car, which happened to be from Virginia. He got into the back and directed the driver to the Mayflower, where an enforcement team and media waited on site as the driver was ticketed and his black car towed. The driver was cited for not having insurance, charging a fare using both time and distance, and driving an unlicensed vehicle.[64] Uber employees were immediately called to the scene, where they were photographed by the press looking frantic.

Within a couple of hours, Uber once more took to Twitter. This time, at Kalanick's suggestion, he and several employees demonstrated their support by posting pictures of themselves holding a white piece of letter-size paper with the "#UberDCLove" caption.[65] Though the pic postings didn't quite catch on, the response was still overwhelmingly supportive. One Twitter user found Linton's cell phone number and posted it so others could call him to complain.[66] A transit reporter of the local news site *TBD* said of the Twitter reaction, "The level of response and depth of passion amazes me," which Uber employees immediately re-tweeted. *TBD* stated that several local personalities and business leaders jumped on the bandwagon, promising never to use local taxis again.[67] Kalanick also noted that their growth in the District was remarkably quick. They had accomplished almost as much in one month in DC as they had in nine months in San Francisco.[68]

Beyond Twitter, the number of media outlets covering Uber's DC presence suddenly expanded. In addition to the usual suspects, websites like *Slate* were equally confused about why regulations were quashing innovation. And Linton was getting his fifteen minutes of fame as a celebrity regulator, later even earning a disdainful reference in Newt Gingrich's book prior to his run for president.[69] Between competing stories, there were back-and-forth accusations as to whether anyone from Uber had ever contacted the DC Taxi Commission. Uber vowed to cover the cost of the citations and impounding and even provide a little extra cash to the driver who was out of work for three straight days, as the sting took place on a Friday and the following Monday was the Martin Luther King Jr. holiday.

Linton made little effort to hide the fact that he was trying to dissuade other drivers from using the service. In a local newscast later that day, he said, "We did it to send a message to drivers who are signing up with Uber that we are going to enforce our laws."[70] He couldn't go after Uber as a company, so he decided to make an example out of a driver instead. Depending on whom he was addressing, Linton sometimes walked back his comments and said it wasn't a sting operation as much as it was a "test" to see how the black-car service would perform.[71] But reporters have since confirmed that Linton invited them to wait for his arrival at the Mayflower that morning. It was clearly a sting.

Over the ensuing three-day weekend, DC Council Member Mary Cheh noticed the vitriolic public response and jumped in as a referee. Cheh was a progressive, wonky law professor who represented the District's upper-income northwest ward. She spearheaded the controversial taxi overhaul bill introduced the previous month, and she was also chair of the council's committee on transportation matters. As is common in city government, whenever an agency head has to report to their council, he or she is in fact responding to a de facto boss who oversees their agency. Not that a council member is usually empowered to issue orders directly, but no director who wants to keep their job ever pisses off their committee chair.

Cheh sent a letter to Linton requesting he soften his position on Uber:

> After last week's sting operation, many residents rose to Uber's defense and voiced their support for the company. The reason for this is because many residents view the District's taxi system as mediocre and unreliable, and see Uber as a convenient, dependable alternative.
>
> If our laws do not work for Uber's model of metered fares for limousine

service, then I hope that we can work together to amend District law to permit Uber and similar companies to operate legally here.[72]

Linton called off his dogs for the moment. For its part, Uber was convinced this was simply "round one," from which it had walked away unscathed. Before the end of January, the company placed an invitation on Eventbrite for anyone to attend a cocktail gathering at the upscale event hall Shadow Room, close to George Washington University. The event was meant to recap the previous two weeks and provide a loose plan for how they would persevere in DC, centered around continued community support. It also included a special guest from out of town. "As our way of saying thank you, please come join the Uber DC team and Uber co-founder and CEO Travis Kalanick for drinks on us." Anyone who used Uber to get there would also get five dollars off of their ride.[73]

At the event, Kalanick stood at the back presenting a slideshow as the capacity crowd watched up front. Dressed in a designer suit with the tech industry's traditional tie-free ensemble, he recapped the whole episode. Kalanick, who never seemed 100 percent comfortable in front of a crowd, appeared to be venting for his own sake as much as he was addressing the audience.

"There was a hearing January 11 – I can't believe this was only two weeks ago. I think I've aged five years," he said.[74]

He made forceful gestures toward the screen as he spoke.

"Anyways, January 11, Chairman Linton was at a public hearing about new taxi regulations and was very flustered because the taxi drivers were in a riot or something because there was a bunch of crazy stuff in there. And he then spouted off something, saying, 'Uber DC is operating *illegally*.'"[75]

In that split-second as he emphasized the word "illegally," the audience began to groan and boo, and Kalanick hissed loudly into the microphone. Blunt and acerbic, it was as if he was cajoling the audience. One spectator yelled out, "Fuck that guy!" to which the rest of the audience laughed.[76]

Kalanick transitioned into Uber's blog post and response. As he talked about the due diligence of researching the District's regulations and finding no conflict, he at times gripped the microphone with both hands for dear life as he held it in front of his face.

"We did our homework.... We made sure we were a hundred percent legal. And we *still are!*"[77]

He was upset, and he made sure his lubricated audience knew where to channel their blame. He was preparing them in a preamble for the next regulatory battles in DC, and he encouraged the audience to continue demonstrating public support. Kalanick noted that without it, Uber was going to be shoved out of the District one way or the other.

He ended by mentioning that on Valentine's Day the following month, Uber would hold a promotion where every woman who entered a car after 4:00 p.m. would receive a rose from the driver. It was also the same day that the Uber team would meet with Linton to try to work out their issues.[78]

"We'll be bringing roses *and* chocolates," he said mockingly.[79]

That same evening, Linton gave an interview to *NPR*, which covered the cocktail gathering.

"I find it a bid odd that they would have a big party – that I understand they're holding tonight – to celebrate, in their words, their victory over the rule of law in the District of Columbia. It seems a little arrogant to me."[80]

Linton had a point. Uber's actions weren't intended to persuade the taxi commission to its viewpoint but to politically force the regulators off their back. They may not have technically started the fight in DC, but once Linton ignited the match, Uber wasted no time turning it to their advantage. By pouring gas on the flame, they gained immense political leverage, dedicated customers, and increased exposure.

Up until this episode, Uber had operated with subtlety. When the CPUC issued a cease-and-desist, they quietly hired an attorney in response. When

New York issued their letters, Uber hired a lobbyist to work out the problems. But in DC, Kalanick was making a strong, forceful, and very public push to overcome regulatory resistance. It would be the first of several times Kalanick used such overpowering tactics.

Some have speculated that Kalanick deliberately crafted these maneuvers like a clever chess strategy, knocking an opponent off balance and positioning the pieces for a great conquest. In all likelihood, though, Kalanick made a forceful play in DC because it was a knee-jerk reaction that aligned with his aggressive personality. If his abrasiveness was only part of a strategic play, one might have expected to see someone less reckless and more mercurial, vacillating between the extremes of overbearing and gentle.

Kalanick simply didn't work that way. He didn't have much of a personal filter, and he was intensely competitive by nature. His former friend and early investor, Chris Sacca, once noted that Kalanick had astonishingly found time to become the second-highest ranked player in the world at *Wii Tennis* "while also being the CEO of Uber.... That is not a normal person."[81] Perhaps it was his competitive personality that allowed Kalanick to suspect, accurately, that this episode in DC was simply the first round.

Around the same time that Kalanick roasted Linton at Shadow Room, Linton happened to receive a visit from a pair of guests passing through the District on business. They were from the International Association of Transportation Regulators (IATR), a regulatory trade association that since 1988 had met once per year at an annual conference to discuss issues related to for-hire vehicles, especially taxis. Linton probably hadn't realized it at that moment, but he had made contact with the group that would become one of Uber's fiercest regulatory rivals.

CHAPTER FOUR
Rogues and Regulators

As a regulatory body, the IATR formed out of necessity. In each city, a taxi regulator operated alone in his or her own siloed world. If there was ever a question that needed an expert's second opinion, it's not as though they could walk across the street and speak to the taxi regulator in the next building. Each city typically only had one, and they were lucky if they had a large staff to assist them. For some, taxis were one among many other industries or transportation issues requiring their attention. Especially rare was the taxi regulator who had his or her own dedicated agency, as New York and DC did. The IATR's existence made sense, if for no other reason than taxi regulators needed peers to chat and compare notes with.

Throughout most of the 2000s, the IATR was a ragtag organization that was "international" in the sense that its members were mostly Americans but also included a few Canadians, plus the sporadic participation of one or two European countries. It barely had any operating income and lost roughly $10,000 each year as it hosted a conference at a budget hotel somewhere across the US.[1] The officers were all taxi regulators themselves, meaning their attention could be focused on the IATR only sparingly and second to their full-time jobs. They took turns electing presidents and presidents-elect, the latter of whom organized the following year's conference.

When Linton was visited by IATR officers, the association had dramatically changed. Its president was Matthew Daus, a former (and the longest-serving) chair of the New York Taxi and Limousine Commission (TLC). A Brooklyn native with a moderate accent and dark thick hair, Daus left government service in 2010 after his term expired and began developing a profile as a taxi expert. He took a position as partner for the New York law firm of Windels Marx Lane & Mittendorf, chairing the firm's transportation practice, and became a visiting professor at City College of New York.

In 2009, Daus had been elected president of the IATR, and after leaving the TLC, he became the first former regulator to head the organization in several years, qualifying only because of his academic association to City College. By most accounts, Daus remained president under a general agreement that he would bring with him the resources of his law firm, a first for the IATR. The association had long held in its bylaws a goal of sharing information and, when needed, educating communities on transportation regulation.[2] In practice, though, no one had time for such endeavors. Organizing an annual conference was difficult enough. In many respects, Daus's arrival was a relief, and after his election as president, his leadership remained more or less permanent with no serious challenges.

Once president, Daus began heavily reforming the IATR, in terms of both prominence and revenue streams. Instead of the organization losing money (or breaking even) each year, he worked to take in much larger funds. He had the IATR's website upgraded to appear more professional and focused more heavily on sponsorship from the taxi and limo industry. Non-regulators had always been invited to join the IATR in a non-voting capacity, but Daus pulled in companies like Verifone and Creative Mobile Technologies (CMT), the two main taxi credit card-processing vendors during his tenure at the TLC. Other sponsors included Ford and Chrysler, both of which manufactured taxi vehicles; the dispatching app company TaxiMagic; Mobility Ventures, a company that made wheelchair-accessible vehicles; VerifEye, which produced safety cameras to monitor taxi interiors; and Frias Transportation Infrastructure, a Las Vegas company that was developing a citywide taxi smartphone application.[3]

In January 2012 Daus was in DC for a transportation conference, and he was also meeting with congressmen to discuss upcoming legislation.[4] Since Daus had become president, the IATR had begun to take an active role in crafting legislation, which it had not done in over a decade. One of the bills they were beginning to float in Congress would later be titled the Passenger Safety and Security Act (PASS Act), a measure to turn the IATR into a clearinghouse for taxi background checks. Although taxi laws were under state and local jurisdictions, the federal government maintained one of the key databases for fingerprinting drivers and scanning for matching criminal records. A short bill, the PASS Act's only function was to give the attorney general the authority to grant database access to the IATR, even referring to the association by name.[5] In turn, the IATR could then obtain permission from state and local governments to perform fingerprint background checks of taxi and limo drivers. Daus would make the case that as "a central player in the ground transportation industry, [it was] the perfect fit for providing criminal background checks."[6] Daus told his membership this was their best opportunity to acquire a dedicated source of revenue, outside of conferences, to stabilize and hire a staff.[7]

While in DC, he made the rounds in Congress with Karen Cameron, a former taxi regulator from Calgary, Canada, who had been hired by the IATR to help plan the annual conferences. According to Cameron, they met with congressional staff in a board room, passing around business cards, and it was clear that for the staff, this meeting was one among several that day. "They're kind of getting their head wrapped around which meeting this was, and they realized this topic was on taxis." Then the staff enthusiastically replied, "Oh, we're going to a focus group on Uber tonight. We love Uber!" According to Cameron, the staffers were glowing about Uber and initially assumed the IATR was pro-Uber, as well.

Daus and Cameron met with Ron Linton, mostly as a pitch to encourage him to join the association.[8] Linton's predecessor, the taxi commissioner who wore a wire for the FBI, had also been an IATR officer (and reportedly attended one or two annual conferences wearing his wire). Linton signed up.

In New York, Uber began to appear as an issue closer to home for Daus. In 2002, Mayor Bloomberg entered office to find a taxi industry struggling to make ends meet and begging for a fare increase. Bloomberg agreed but wanted to implement a series of tech upgrades in return. By the one hundredth anniversary of taxis in New York in 2007, he wanted to see taxicabs accepting credit cards as a form of payment. Daus was put in charge of overseeing the program.

Throughout the 2000s, credit cards had been an especially contentious subject. Between expensive lease fees, maintenance, and fuel costs, drivers had been forced into subsistence living and had no interest in absorbing any more fees. Yet, cities were growing tired of the fact that taxis were a cash-only business. It not only made drivers more susceptible to violent crime and theft, but it was especially annoying for visiting tourists. To pay for a fare, a passenger had to either carry large amounts of cash or grimace as a driver took them to an ATM while keeping the meter running.

But as with all small businesses, the problem with credit cards is that they charge an interchange processing fee, typically a percentage of gross receipts. If a long cab ride cost, say a hundred dollars, the credit card company would keep roughly five dollars as its fee. For the taxi industry, the interchange fee could amount to several hundred thousand dollars per year, and labor and management could never agree who would absorb it. Was it the working-poor drivers, the cab companies that had all the leverage, or would they pass it on to the customers, who already paid hefty rates? Everyone treated it like a hot potato.

New York was one of the first American cities to break through the stalemate. In 2008 the TLC under Matt Daus's leadership implemented the Taxicab Passenger Enhancement Project (TPEP), which specifically mandated taxis would install credit card processors in the back of cabs and collect GPS data. To pay for the equipment, TPEP required that they also install small flat-panel monitors to sell advertising for the captive passenger. Two companies, Verifone and CMT, had won the contracts for processing credit cards in taxis, which is how Daus was able to later invite them to become IATR sponsors. By October 2012 credit card transactions accounted for half of all taxi trips, and the TLC reported customer surveys showed a positive response to the credit card equipment (although passengers found the advertising screens somewhat irritating).[9]

But once Daus was out of government service, his successors at the TLC became interested in taking technological progress a step further. New York still didn't allow for taxis to be hailed by smartphone application, meaning that apps like TaxiMagic and Cabulous couldn't yet operate in one of the biggest markets in the United States. TPEP started when the iPhone was first released, and four years later, the TLC felt they were behind the times and wanted to experiment with new services. They introduced pilot programs to allow Square card readers, which charged a smaller interchange fee than the existing vendors, into a handful of taxis.[10] They also announced a request for proposal (RFP) for a vendor that could provide a smartphone hailing application for taxis.[11]

The smartphone RFP apparently made the industry nervous. How would it be implemented? And what would it mean for a company like Uber that was already in this space and active in New York through its black-car app? Daus fired off an email to Christiane Hayashi in San Francisco, who had been an IATR member for a few years:

From: Daus, Matthew
Sent: Wednesday, February 15, 2012 12:19 PM
To: Hayashi, Christiane
Subject: square, uber etc

Chris – these issues are popping over here in NYC.. looking for any files or info you have on either of them here. I know there was a case involving Uber in that they were not operating per your laws? any public documents you can provide would be helpful

trying to get these guys for a case study at iatr this year if you are able to participate Matt

---

The IATR conferences were typically held around the fall, and more than half a year out, Daus was already making plans for Uber. Hayashi replied to him with a copy of the SFMTA's 2010 cease-and-desist letter.[12]

On Valentine's Day 2012, as Ron Linton's office met with Uber representatives, Linton's general counsel received an email from Christiane Hayashi in San Francisco. At the time, another taxi regulator in Toronto (and fellow IATR member) had just learned of Uber's plan to begin operating in their city. Not having followed any of the company's history, he asked Hayashi how San Francisco had brought Uber into compliance with regulations. Hayashi replied, cc'ing her response to Linton's general counsel,

> Uber has been contemptuous of all regulation and regulatory bodies in San Francisco. First they responded to our cease and desist order for calling themselves "UberCab" by issuing press releases to high tech and venture capital journals to the effect that we are just a bunch of fuddy duddies who don't know how to program our VCRs. They are still under scrutiny by the [CPUC], which regulates limousines (we don't), and towards which they exhibited the same contempt for regulation. Then they waltzed over the Mayor's Office of Economic Development and announced themselves as a new SF company and ask for City favors like permission to use transit lanes. I wish that our state Department of Weights and Measures would inquire into their use of cell phones for time and distance measurement.[13]

Inquiries like this one weren't confined to Toronto and DC. As Uber continued to expand, they were constantly appearing on taxi radars – especially as taxi companies sounded off more and more alarm bells. Before the end of 2012, Uber would launch in nine more US cities, including Los Angeles, San Diego, Philadelphia, Denver, and Dallas. Unsure how to regard them, most regulators panicked. For decades black cars and taxis were held functionally separate, but this strange new company appeared to be the bastardized offspring of both. The service looked like a black car but functioned much like a taxi. They found it unsettling.

Several regulators were desperate for more information. They learned what they could reading stories about Linton's experiences in DC. And much as Toronto had reached out to Hayashi, taxi regulators began sending out broad emails to other regulators across the country, many of whom knew each other from the occasional IATR conference. The taxi regulator from Dallas queried twenty-five different colleagues, many of whom were in cities Uber had not yet touched.

> I have been asked to do a little research on the company listed above (UBER). Does anyone know anything about this company and how it works. Also, do any of you or your agencies permit them and if you do how are they permitted (taxi, limo, shuttle, etc.).[14]

Uber launched in Boston in October 2011, and in the neighboring northeastern town of Cambridge – home to Harvard, MIT, and Red Swoosh benefactor Akamai Technologies – a town weights-and-measures official drafted an internal report in March 2012 noting several possible violations of Uber's services. It was a grocery list of concerns. There was no way to verify whether the dispatched vehicles were licensed. City regulations required an eight-hour advance notice on reservations for black cars, which Uber ignored. The city's minimum fare for black cars was forty dollars, and for Uber, it was fifteen. There were several consumer protection concerns, such as an unverified device used to calculate fares, no written receipt, and no clear warnings about how tolls and surcharges were assessed.[15]

Cambridge staff had also spoken directly with Ron Linton about his experiences, and they discussed how Uber was impacted by DC's existing ordinance for black cars. As the Cambridge regulator noted,

> Whether the law is good or bad, [Linton] believes public policy is a matter for their Council to decide, but the taxi commission has to operate in real time. This means regulating and enforcing the law as it is written.[16]

Another regulator in New Orleans had made a similar comment in private. New Orleans was to host the 2013 Super Bowl, and during planning the previous year, an official from Dell had passively asked a city tourism staffer whether Uber would be in town. The staff member reached out to the local taxi regulator (the last IATR president before Matt Daus), who replied,

> Although the technology is very good, it violates many jurisdictions laws. For example, taxicabs are the only universal "on demand" type transportation. All others operate on pre-arrangement. Uber makes those vehicles available on demand. As a result, these car services basically become taxicab operators.[17]

Their comments were especially telling about the mentality of taxi regulators. They looked at Uber solely as an enforcement issue. It didn't matter if it functioned better than the existing taxi industry. It didn't matter if Uber offered better reliability. It didn't matter if Uber was heavily desired by the local population. It didn't even matter if licensed chauffeurs benefited. Taxi regulators felt it was their sacred responsibility to insulate the local taxi industry from competition, and until legislators were willing to exert political capital to change the law, they saw no reason to suddenly become flexible. When ambiguity existed in the law, such as in San Francisco and DC, the regulators felt that a publicly regulated transportation service offered more assurances than a company that regulated itself.

It was a somewhat myopic viewpoint. There's no indication any regulator examined the root problems of their industry and questioned whether Uber's service could fix them. The reason supply caps existed in the first place was because customers didn't shop for taxis and open competition caused more harm than good. The reason taxis didn't reach underserved areas was because it was costly to do so. Uber offered a model that could alleviate some of the problems, but it didn't matter. A vehicle that functioned like a taxi *was* a taxi, and if you didn't follow the rules, what you brought to the table was irrelevant. You didn't fit into the paradigm. You didn't belong.

One theory about regulators' motivations, rarely discussed even privately, was the possibility that if any of them invited Uber to the table, it may have been career suicide. The taxi industry had been sustained by the momentum of market controls for decades. Any regulator assessing the political landscape knew that taxis had too much time and capital invested, too much skin in the game. To bless Uber was to upend the industry.

When asked about her motivations against Uber and similar companies, Christiane Hayashi replied, "Mayors have risen and *fallen* on transit-system issues." Working with Uber would have rocked the boat, and for taxi regulators, who were usually mid-level managers, it would have drawn a lot of unwelcome attention. Even if they were secretly interested in working with Uber, any regulator who either researched them in the news or sent an inquiry to Linton or Hayashi quickly learned there was little reason to go out on a limb for a guy like Travis Kalanick. It was clear he didn't work well with others.

Back in DC, Linton was having his fill of Uber. When he met with their representatives on Valentine's Day, he offered a compromise to allow them to operate. He wanted to give the taxi commission the ability to seal – that is, to inspect and close off from tampering – Uber's fare-calculating systems. In addition, the commission would establish minimum and maximum rates, and Uber would be required to provide a *printed* receipt at the end of each fare.[18]

After that encounter, Uber stopped meeting with the commission. They had consistently maintained they were legal from day one, and in all likelihood, they probably felt Linton had no leverage to "offer" such overbearing terms. Instead, they began meeting with Council Member Mary Cheh, the chair of the council's transportation committee who had previously broken up the fight between Linton and Uber, to see what more she could do.[19]

Linton was determined to prove that Uber was operating illegally, and if need be, develop the foundation for a criminal case. In May 2012, one of the local owners of a limousine company forwarded him a media advisory from the Taxicab, Limousine, and Paratransit Association (TLPA), the largest organization of taxi and limo owners and managers in the country. Ever since Uber first started operating in San Francisco two years earlier, the TLPA had no tolerance for them, and the email listed a link to a San Francisco news story about Uber's growing presence. It included a secondhand quote from Kalanick, who had once stated, "We are going to dominate every city we are going to go into." The email also said the CPUC was beginning an investigation into Uber, which was probably true only on paper since the San Bruno explosion.[20] A CPUC investigation had technically commenced in late 2010, but there was none actually moving forward.

The day after receiving the media advisory, Linton ordered one of his taxi enforcement officers, the same one who had been present at the sting operation the previous January, to execute a few more stings. His direction was simple.

"I want those two test rides done on Uber and then have the AG office move on them," he wrote.[21]

He was referring to the District's attorney general (AG), the equivalent of a city attorney's office. Linton wanted to use additional citations to demonstrate that Uber's presence in the District inherently facilitated illegal operations, so that the District AG would use its authority to shut it down. It wasn't clear whether the District AG had initially agreed with Linton's legal assessment of Uber's operations. At the rally in January, Kalanick said that Uber had made inquiries to their office, and the response had been generally apathetic. Linton was building ammunition to bring a stronger case to their doorstep.

Two weeks later Linton's enforcement officer sent him an after-action report of an attempted Uber pickup at the Pennsylvania Avenue Baptist Church in Southeast DC.

On Tuesday, May 22, 2012, I went on-line (uber.com) and registered for a pick-up ride with Uber (m.uber.com). I requested to be picked up in front of 3000 Pennsylvania Avenue, SE, Washington, DC. I received a text message saying that a driver, identified as TJ, would pick me up in 12 minutes. I then received a telephone call at 12:26pm from the driver TJ. He told me he was in route and would be at my location in 12 minutes. After about 15 minutes, I received a text message which read "Hi Sharon, TJ had to cancel your ride. We may have another Uber available! Please text your address with city to request again." I texted the address again and never received a response.[22]

Uber had apparently thwarted an attempted sting operation. The enforcement officer's name had appeared in *DCist* after the January sting operation, and presumably, Uber staff had canceled the ride after recognizing her name.[23] Although frustrating for Linton, the taxi commission executed another sting operation the following month from a Hampton Inn in the northwest part of the city. This time it succeeded. The driver was once more issued multiple citations, his car was impounded, and Uber itself was issued a $500 fine for "Permitting an Unlicensed Hacker."[24] After the sting, the enforcement officer reported that Uber had closed her account.

Since the sting approach was hit or miss, Linton began changing his tactics. The mayor's director of communications reached out to him about the company.

"Are they still operating in violation of DC laws?"[25]

Linton replied, "Yes, and we are moving on them. However, the solution will come when the pending legislation is passed and we create a new category of public vehicle for hire service called 'sedan' Uber will then have to comply or be subject to fines."[26]

In other words, if existing law was fuzzy as to whether Uber was illegal, the council was going to clarify the distinction by revising the ordinance in the taxi overhaul bill that was already moving through the council. A new class of vehicles would be created specifically for Uber so they could be regulated.

As the bill progressed, Council Member Cheh began considering an amendment to address regulations for Uber. Since black cars and taxis were now competing with one another in the District, it made sense to at least create a basic framework of safety and consumer regulations they would operate under. Quietly, Uber was lobbying for the least restrictive outcome with Cheh's staff, but the amendment they initially proposed was so light that even her own staff considered it "unworkable."[27]

In late June, Cheh's legislative director reached out to Linton with a draft of a proposed amendment expected to make everyone happy. They considered Uber as simply a smartphone app that summoned vehicles, like TaxiMagic, and in that vein, it made sense to exempt them from regulations. As the draft language existed up to that point, Uber would be exempt from regulation, provided it met a few simple requirements: the passenger would receive an estimate when the sedan was booked, the taxi commission would review and approve the smartphone app as a type of taximeter, the passenger would receive a receipt, and Uber would ensure that all sedans on its platform were licensed.[28]

Linton hated the amendment. He replied,

> Any exemption to regulation by the regulatory agency of a class of vehicles effectively neuters the agency. Within a matter of a few years most service will be on an electronic basis and this will allow the entire system to be undermined. I cannot support this amendment.[29]

Linton also reached out to his office's general counsel. "Please read what they are proposing and give me some advice on countering it."[30] His counsel responded with a long argument, but in general, the main difference between Uber and a taxi-summoning app like TaxiMagic was that Uber had a contractual relationship with the driver and a transactional relationship with the customer. In other words, between the black cars and the customers, Uber had the lion's share of control, and thus, *it* was the one effectively providing the rides. It didn't exist as a technological add-on licensed by the black-car industry the way TaxiMagic did for taxis.[31]

"Uber is not on the side lines simply providing connecting service," said

Linton's counsel. As it applied to Uber and the transportation market, the tail was wagging the dog. Linton's counsel suggested that Council Member Cheh should either a) exempt actual pass-through companies like TaxiMagic that didn't insert themselves in the middle of transactions, or b) create a new class of regulations for companies like Uber, "which may include minimum fares" and other regulatory controls over drivers, vehicles, and advertising.[32]

Cheh's office took another stab at the amendment to try to satisfy everyone. This time, in addition to the basic requirements, the District would legally segregate the markets between taxis and black cars. Literally titled "Part B – Uber Amendments," the new draft established basic regulations for "sedan" class vehicles, instructed the taxi commission to develop comprehensive regulations within a year, and required a minimum fare of at least five times the taxi "drop rate."[33] Sometimes called a "flag rate," the drop rate was the upfront fee taxis charged just for beginning a fare, and in DC, it was set by law at three dollars.[34] As Uber already charged a minimum fare of fifteen dollars (five times the drop rate), Cheh expected that Uber would be fine with the language.

Explaining the rationale for the minimum fare, the draft language stated, "These requirements would ensure that sedan service is a premium class of service with a substantially higher cost that does not directly compete with or undercut taxicab service."[35] But the explanation was a smokescreen. Passengers had already shown a strong willingness to pay for Uber's highly reliable service over a lower-cost taxi, and the language did little to change Uber's existing operations. Linton once more handed the bill to his general counsel for her analysis and reply.

"I am stumped," she said. "I do not understand the need for support from Uber, a California corporation, that has disrespected every jurisdiction it has invaded. But I will move on."[36] Hayashi's influence was beginning to shine through to Linton.

The DC Taxi Commission still felt the language was too soft, and Linton was getting desperate. In a last-ditch effort, he forwarded all of his counsel's damning critiques of the draft language, "strong and internal" though they were, to Cheh's legislative director.[37] He'd hoped to influence her office's thinking on the bill and explain why Uber needed to be more heavily regulated by the taxi commission. Cheh's staff thanked him but still proceeded forward with the amendment as-is.[38] On Monday, July 9, 2012 around 4:00 p.m., the amendment was placed on the agenda for a vote the following morning.[39] After addressing the amendment, the council also expected to place a final vote on the taxi reform bill.

Uber, which had been following the bill closely, saw the changes coming and panicked. Within a two-week period before the council's vote, two new competitors either launched or were planning a launch in Uber's hometown of San Francisco. One was the company SideCar, which offered a self-described "ride-sharing" app at market rates set by passengers. The app underwent beta testing for months before launching in late June, having already completed about ten thousand rides.[40] Then on July 5, *The New York Times* reported that the company Zimride, an online carpooling website with 350,000 users, was also launching an app-based version of its service called "Lyft."[41]

In an apparent response to these emerging competitors, on July 3, Uber launched a new service on the app: UberX. Not yet having anything to do with ridesharing or carpooling, UberX was introduced as a lower-cost alternative in which licensed limo drivers would now drive hybrid vehicles instead of luxury black cars.[42] Uber had apparently wanted to expand the new service to other cities like DC to maintain its destined market dominance. But the proposed fifteen-dollar minimum in Cheh's newest revision prevented any kind of lower-cost alternative. She publicly insisted that she had negotiated with Uber for several months, since around the time of the January sting operation when they first contacted her office, and that they were on board with the amendment's language.[43] At the last minute, though, Uber decided to shut it down.

Less than forty-five minutes after the amendment was formally proposed on July 9, Uber broadcast a series of messages to their DC users. As the July

4 holiday had just passed, Kalanick published an alarming blog post titled "Un-Independence" detailing the District's efforts to supposedly restrict Uber's service. In bold, underlined font, he emphasized that the bill would charge "**no less than 5 times a taxi's minimum fare**," which was a half-truth. It would have charged no less than fifteen dollars, which was already Uber's minimum fare. But Kalanick *did* emphasize this would harm their ability to offer lower-cost services in the future. To spur their supporters to take action, he published a link to a Change.org petition, informed them the amendment would be voted on the next day, and listed the email, Twitter handle, and office phone number of each council member. A similar message was emailed to all of Uber's DC users.[44]

Immediately hundreds of Twitter users posted a link to the blog post, and even though Uber staff had also posted it themselves, the message went viral on its own. It spread rapidly and exponentially. At 11:30 that night, the mayor's chief of staff emailed Linton and several others in the mayor's cabinet.

> What is the Council threatening to do tomorrow? I have heard from 2 people today saying, "don't let the Council hurt Uber." And who is behind it – Cheh?[45]

Linton, who was awake at 3:30 a.m., replied,

> Uber wants to be an unregulated operator. We don't know yet what cheh's final position is. If uber gets its way you will have jungle in the public vehicle for hire industry.[46]

Linton didn't quite understand what was transforming before him. No one did. Less than twenty-four hours after Uber's campaign began, more than fifty thousand emails had been sent to the council members, the Change.org petition had gathered forty-three hundred signatures, and thirty-seven thousand tweets had mentioned Uber. The Twitter-analytics website Topsy reported that exposure to the hashtag #UberDCLove was 4.4 million, and as the council neared its scheduled vote at 10:00 a.m., the term "Uber DC" had increased from two hundred thousand to 1.6 million Twitter exposures in less than an hour.[47]

The next morning, the public backlash scared the bejeezus out of much of the council. Any city council will usually tackle a few thousand issues per year, and to receive this level of public interest on one issue alone was exceptionally rare. At 8:00 a.m., Linton emailed a more complete update to the mayor's chief of staff. "CM Cheh has amendments one of which may exempt them from regulation, she is having second though[ts] but I don't know her final position yet...."[48]

During a council breakfast at nearly the same time Linton's email went out, two council members said they would introduce their own amendments to strip out the Uber language. Cheh then stated she would simply rescind the Uber Amendments and push them off as their own separate bill in the fall.[49] The public pressure also reached Linton, who told his enforcement officer to cease all sting operations targeted at Uber until further notice.[50]

A great coup for Uber, the press jumped on it as fast as possible trying to explain the chain of events that had built up to this moment. Cheh and Kalanick gave conflicting accounts as to *when* exactly Uber first protested the minimum-fare language, and between them, Kalanick's comments were more inconsistent, though few noticed. In one news site, Kalanick was quoted saying that Uber didn't know about the amendment until 4:00 p.m. the previous day. But when UberX was announced eight days before, a *New York Times* article quoted of Kalanick on the DC fight, "They want to keep our prices from going down, which is a very unusual price-fixing scheme."[51]

The council had a packed agenda on July 10, the last day available before the summer recess, and among the several issues remaining, they still needed to vote on the taxi overhaul bill with or without the Uber Amendments. Before their inboxes were flooded with emails, several of the members had barely heard of Uber and didn't have much clue what it was. But there was too much of a spotlight to ignore the issue now. The months of quiet political maneuvering evaporated overnight, and in a matter of hours, council members were scrambling to ask themselves and each other what the best regulation was to apply to this odd new company.

As the bill came to a final vote, the council spent roughly an hour trying to decide what to do about Uber. Some like Marion Barry and future mayor Muriel Bowser felt that it needed to be regulated like a taxi company. Council Member Barry even said he was a close political friend of the taxi industry and that several drivers had complained to him that Uber was harming their business. Another said it didn't make sense that ordinances should prevent Uber from operating.[52] In fairness, Cheh never actually tried to pass an amendment hobbling Uber's black-car service, but now that the issue was at the forefront, the taxi-friendly council members seriously considered it an option.

There was so much confusion and disagreement that it was too daunting to settle that day. In this spectrum of an up or down vote, a more moderate measure gained traction: a simple delay. Uber would be exempt from regulation until the council could revisit the issue in the fall or winter.

It was not an easy vote. The members were struggling to get their head around this concept in a short amount of time. In DC, taxis were barely a public utility since their supply was never capped. There wasn't as strong a need to protect the market from bandit competition. But here was a service competing with taxis that wanted almost no regulation at all, and the council debated back and forth about the merits of placing an unregulated service next to a regulated one, even if it was temporary. The more it became apparent there would be no consensus, the more a delay was pushed.

As the council chair finally started to call for a vote, one of the other members jumped in for a question. In frustration and impatience, the author of the extension amendment broke from his customarily professional tone and immediately slumped in his chair. "Oh, god!" he vented, a rare sight in a city council meeting. The interrupting colleague wanted to know about the implications of some of the amendment's wording. Ignoring the question, the impatient author sat up and went on a condescending rant to close the seemingly endless debate. Slowly, he patronized his colleague in a lecture.[53]

"What this does, or is *intended* to do, is to put the status quo in place so that Uber can continue to operate because without this, they are operating *illegally.* Mr. Linton went out and arrested people from Uber several months ago because they were operating *illegally.* He was told not to do that. But without this amendment, they will be operating illegally again. That's *all* this is intended to do is to buy some time to get us from here to [December 31]. That's it. Now we can nitpick this thing to death if you want to do that. But this is the best we could do in the time that we had to get this done. Because I, like you, have received over *five-thousand* emails from people who use this service."[54]

The colleague wouldn't let up with his question about the language.

"Then you vote no," the condescending author said, placing his hand on his colleague's shoulder.[55]

Even Cheh had a last-minute reservation, wanting to prohibit drivers from Maryland and Virginia from operating, a sensitive issue to drivers who sacrificed more money by living in an expensive DC home. It went over like a lead balloon.

"I assume if you put another restriction in place, you will get another four thousand emails tomorrow," the impatient member said.[56]

"I have capacity on my phone," Cheh retorted.[57]

Other members also became impatient and finally called a voice vote. The amendment passed, and Uber was in the clear for the rest of the calendar year.

Uber's political tactics in DC were extraordinarily overbearing. They had a great political ally in Mary Cheh, and regardless of how closely they had or hadn't worked with her office, she nonetheless attempted to get Linton off their backs. But as other competitors started to surface, Kalanick torpedoed that relationship to fix a minor flaw in the legislation. It was like swatting a fly with a sledgehammer, and politically, it was embarrassing. Council Member Cheh would later characterize Kalanick's actions as "berserk."[58] From her perspective, it probably also resonated as a severe trust issue.

It was as though Kalanick had thought back to all the anecdotes he had recounted at the FailCon 2011 Conference about when he had resorted to trust instead of leverage and it had cost him dearly. He wouldn't make that mistake here. The safest path was overwhelming force, even if it was overkill, even if it burned bridges. And it perhaps demonstrated how seriously Uber regarded its emerging competitors, SideCar and Lyft, and how much the company felt it needed to lower its prices to remain competitive in the future.

It's doubtful that anyone who emailed the DC Council was aware of any of these behind-the-scenes nuances. They took Kalanick's apocalyptic message at face value, which demonstrated Uber's immense political capital. No one who used the local taxi industry trusted it to improve. It was as much a vote of no confidence in taxis as it was a show of support for this new service. The Uber team realized they had a powerful political weapon at their disposal, one which pressured a city council so much that it practically drove them mad, one which they would keep handy for years to come. According to Brad Stone, after the DC incident, the tactic of cajoling a politician's constituents was officially added to Uber's playbook.[59]

After Uber's victory, the taxi regulator from Philadelphia sent IATR President Matt Daus, Christiane Hayashi, and a few other IATR members a link to the DC story.

"See link below. Uber is not going to go gently into that good night," he wrote.[60]

Across the country, taxi regulators were beginning to overlap one another in their efforts against Uber. Two days after the DC vote, a Philadelphia Parking Authority (PPA) deputy director sent out a mass email "to all industry members" noting that the authority had "conducted an investigation into an 'Internet transportation business'" it considered "an illegal service provider." The director warned, "Limousines may only be operated within Philadelphia by holders of a certificate of public convenience.... Any vehicle found to be operating in Philadelphia by a non-certified entity, is subject to a penalty, including suspension and revocation."[61]

IATR President Matt Daus then asked the PPA director if he was going to crack down on Uber.

He replied, "I think I will probably invite them to meet with us in the next week or so to discuss 'regulatory issues.' If any impounds of their vehicles occur in the mean time ... that's life."[62]

Daus himself began taking a more proactive interest in Uber, which had invaded half the cities of the IATR's officers and board of directors. But more than that, Uber was a symbol of panic for New York's taxi industry, where Mayor Michael Bloomberg had championed several upgrades, including the introduction of a smartphone app for hailing taxis. Bloomberg also wanted to do away with the classic Crown Victoria model of cabs that had been around since the 1980s and replace them with a newly designed "Taxi of Tomorrow," and he wanted to allow yellow cabs to accept street hails in boroughs outside Manhattan.[63]

The local industry hated the tech upgrades for fear the costs would cut into their profit margins, and spreading cabs over a wider area would distort their revenue streams. In short, the industry liked consistency. But as for smartphone apps, Uber was a fearful warning sign that an app could do serious damage to their market. For the city's former TLC Chair, Matt Daus had been laying the groundwork since at least February, when he'd contacted Hayashi, to find a workable middle ground where taxi-friendly apps could exist without hurting the industry's financial interests.

On June 29, 2012 he published a white paper on Windels Marx's letterhead titled *"Rogue" Smartphone Applications for Taxicabs and Limousines: Innovation or Unfair Competition?*[64] The paper made the argument that regulations, as applied to Uber and other companies, should be interpreted in the strictest possible light. Taxis and limousines should operate in their traditional, segregated markets.

Three days earlier, the IATR and Windels Marx sponsored a forum at Baruch College as part of the University Transportation Research Center titled "Taxi and Livery Issues of Today and Tomorrow." Daus moderated a discussion regarding several of Bloomberg's taxi reforms, and he brought in a state senator, state assemblyman, and city councilman, all of whom were protective of the taxi industry (and one of whom was a Windels Marx client).[65] When they discussed smartphone apps, Daus gave the impression he could develop a set of model regulations that, if implemented, would allow apps to work without disrupting the status quo. The legislator-panelists gave it their blessing.[66]

Daus immediately embarked on an extensive campaign to characterize Uber as a "rogue" service, a term he would repeatedly apply for years. To his thinking, Uber was no different than a taxi, save for the fact its service took place in a black car. Hailing a car by smartphone was just an electronic version of a street hail, which by law was reserved to taxis. Uber was "rogue" because of all the ways it deviated from long-held taxi regulations. Fares were non-standardized, GPS had not yet been approved as a legal form of a taximeter, and the app's terms and conditions circumvented liabilities that taxis normally absorbed as business risks. Furthermore, Uber allowed for service refusals, which many jurisdictions prohibited – taxis were supposed to pick up anyone and everyone who hailed them on the street. As proof, the Windels Marx paper alluded to an *Economist* article, stating that after a ride was over, not only were drivers rated, but the passengers were as well. Kalanick was quoted stating that a "driver can decline a fare if the hailer has a bad reputation."[67]

As the white paper examined various jurisdictions, it concluded that conditions were worsening as bandit apps were on the rise. News reports surfaced that Hailo, a new London-based smartphone app for taxis, was considering entering the New York market.[68] Most of the taxi companies disliked Hailo because instead of integrating with a company's dispatch services, as TaxiMagic and Cabulous had done, it was "direct-to-driver." That is, the drivers themselves could download the app and use it to pick up fares without informing their parent companies. Uber had launched a similar service, UberTAXI, in Chicago the previous April.

Since cab drivers were independent contractors who legally could not be ordered to destinations, taxi companies were powerless to stop it. But taxi companies made their money off of lease fees, and the best way to market themselves to drivers was to brag about their ability to attract dispatch calls from customers. Direct-to-driver apps undermined their ability to market themselves by cutting out the middle man. A decentralized dispatching system jeopardized their ability to charge high lease fees and attract new drivers.

Daus's white paper examined how the strictest regulations *should* apply to Uber in a handful of jurisdictions across the country. In most of them such as San Francisco, New York, Seattle, and DC, regulators or their city councils arguably weren't doing enough to shut down "rogue" operators. The paper didn't say why they hadn't done more, but there were plenty of reasons.[69] The California PUC was stuck with the San Bruno explosion, New York was moving toward experimentation with new apps, DC's Ron Linton was arguing with Mary Cheh's office, and in Seattle, the state legislature abruptly extended oversight over limo service to the city but without any funding.

The white paper was a renewed call for action on several fronts. Daus used it to create a new IATR "Smartphone App Committee" to develop model regulations that would bring Uber in line with "rational regulations."[70] Before 2012 ended, he would enlist taxi regulators from a core group of major cities to join: San Diego, Los Angeles, San Francisco, Denver, Toronto, Chicago,

Philadelphia, Boston, Montreal, DC, Houston, and Austin. Effectively, these regulators composed a web of resistance that, when possible, would coordinate with one another to keep Uber out of their cities.

In addition, Daus published the white paper on the Windels Marx website, and it quickly found its way into the hands of taxi operators, who then forwarded it to their regulators. It was a way to light a fire under the seat of any regulator who wasn't already moving in lockstep with the IATR on this issue. They could hand over the paper and say something akin to, "Hey, here's a taxi expert and industry leader who argues you should resist Uber. Instructions included."

At a regulatory level, 2012 was turning into a contentious year for Uber. While Linton and Daus advanced their campaign battles, others were unfolding simultaneously. The issue of using a smartphone as a type of taximeter – cited by Hayashi, Linton, and Daus – played out in a particularly strange way. In Seattle, taxi regulator Craig Leisy received an inquiry in August 2011, asking about Uber's legality shortly after they had launched there.[71]

Leisy was atypical for a taxi regulator. Wonky, easygoing, straightforward, and verbose, he managed both taxi *and* local weights-and-measures regulations. A sleepy regulatory function of state and local governments, weights-and-measures (w&m) regulators exist to protect consumers from gouging. If a commercial device measured some type of metric to calculate a consumer price, it needed to be inspected to ensure it charged customers accurately. If you pumped ten gallons of gas at a 7-Eleven, the pump needed to display ten gallons. If a jeweler weighed a twelve-carat diamond, the scale needed to register twelve carats. In 2015, New York City fined the grocery chain Whole Foods after w&m regulators discovered they were regularly overweighing several of their products, effectively bilking customers at large profits to the store.[72]

There were practical reasons for Seattle to merge this function with taxi regulations. Drivers developed an early reputation for tampering with taximeters in order to gouge customers. In the industry's early days in New York, customers often complained they would take the same route home and be charged a different price each time.[73] As regulations evolved, cities and states required that taximeters conform to national standards of testing and installation to keep the business honest. The equipment would first be inspected to make sure it charged accurately and then "sealed" to prevent tampering.

Leisy didn't panic at Uber's presence in Seattle. He didn't issue cease-and-desist letters, nor did he order any sting operations. Instead, as if his eyes had suddenly grown wide, he ignored Uber as a bandit service and focused on the company as an important advancement in the field of w&m regulations. Within days of receiving the inquiry, he started asking New York regulators, who used GPS to track taxicabs, how they regarded Uber's app.[74] Within two months, he had drafted a proposal to include GPS devices as a type of taximeter.[75] Leisy wanted it as a national standard.

The National Conference on Weights and Measures (NCWM), a nonprofit trade group, debated and voted on measurement specifications at biannual meetings. When new standards like Leisy's proposed amendment were agreed upon, the US Department of Commerce's National Institute of Standards and Technology (NIST) published them in a handbook. States could then choose whether they wanted to adopt the national standard, which was often the easiest choice, or adopt their own.

The NCWM even developed type-evaluation programs, giving regulators objective standards for testing a device. This was a complaint that Hayashi's office brought up in her 2010 cease-and-desist letter: UberCab's app had not been "type evaluated." But even if they had wanted to, the lion's share of w&m standards applied to physical devices, not ethereal programs that could only be viewed virtually. Leisy saw Uber's app as breaking new ground.

Craig Leisy felt strongly that regardless of how one viewed Uber, this new technology was a watershed moment, and it didn't matter if it involved complicated programming language. He believed GPS-enabled smartphones would eventually replace expensive taximeters, and if Uber could prove the concept, other measuring devices were sure to follow. If the NCWM and NIST didn't get on top of this, their role as weights-and-measures regulators would be marginalized, and he bluntly told them as much.

> I realize that the W&M community generally ignores taximeters whenever it can – preferring to spend time on "real" W&M work like scales and gas pumps. "Virtual taximeters" are just the first of many computer apps with wireless technology – who knows what will come next? ... In the case of new wireless computer app competing with old technology, NIST and NCWM risk quickly becoming irrelevant if they don't get in the game. [76]

The fact that Leisy focused on Uber as a regulatory advancement and not as a usurper of the taxi industry was stunning. At the time, he sat on the IATR Board of Directors, the inner core of taxi regulators who vehemently disliked Uber. In 2001, he had even written a paper detailing Seattle's experience deregulating and then re-regulating the taxi industry during the 1980s, a paper often passed around by taxi advocates. He was in the perfect position to understand and distrust Uber's impact on the taxi market, and although he had *some* concerns, Uber's presence didn't disturb him nearly as much as it did his peers. Uber's marketing director in Seattle even reached out to him for guidance on new state regulations for limo service, and Leisy was happy to offer a few pointers. [77] When a limo company complained that Uber unfairly competed with taxis (while also forwarding a story of Ron Linton's sting operation), he politely told them to take it to the state. [78] Unlike his counterparts, Leisy didn't proclaim with certainty that Uber was a de facto taxi service. He took the wonky, professorial view that he wasn't sure and wanted to explore the issue.

In fairness, Leisy was also resigned to the fact that limo enforcement in Seattle was more or less trapped in purgatory. In 2011 new laws allowed the city to take some of the limo-enforcement burden off of the state's shoulders, but it didn't come with any new staff.[79] Leisy's office was already too swamped to take it on, and then the state's budget for limo enforcement was gutted.[80] Seemingly no one in Washington State had the time or money to go after Uber, but Leisy didn't particularly care. The taximeter issue was more important.

Unbeknownst to Leisy, NIST had already assembled a small working group to discuss changes to taximeters as New York's cutting-edge TPEP program forced them to consider new changes.[81] Because w&m people had little interaction with taxi regulators, NIST still needed an expert who could bridge both worlds, and Leisy's enthusiasm made him the perfect candidate. Both NIST and the NCWM were glad to have him on board.[82] Matt Daus also invited him to join the IATR's newly created Smartphone App Committee, which he agreed to in order to help bring uniformity to the taximeter issue.[83]

In May 2012, NIST's US National Work Group (USNWG) on Taximeters held its second meeting online, and where before it was a quiet group with only a handful of participants, it had ballooned into a who's who of w&m regulators from across California, various taxi equipment manufacturers, and Matt Daus himself. Because there were so many new people, it was mostly an introductory meeting, but already they had a key question on their lips: Is a GPS device a form of taximeter?[84]

It was really a question about whether Uber's app was legally a taximeter. Although GPS had been used by the taxi industry, no one other than Uber used it to calculate a fare. The question they were all dancing around was whether they could use this standard against Uber, and they wanted a formal declaration from NIST. But like Leisy, NIST wanted to explore the issue and get more information on GPS. They would have to wait until the next meeting months later to even advance the discussion.

Meanwhile, two days after the USNWG meeting, regulators in

Cambridge, Massachusetts, the same seven-square-mile city that had reached out to Ron Linton for guidance, decided to answer that question. Cambridge didn't attend the USNWG meeting, but after talking with Linton months earlier, they wanted to emulate his approach of a sting operation – except, unlike Linton, they would push it chiefly as a w&m issue.

On a Friday morning in Cambridge, city staff hailed an Uber black car at a senior center across from city hall. The driver took the car roughly two hundred feet before his passengers asked him to pull over. A waiting police officer cited the driver for operating an unlicensed livery service and for using a "non-conforming device" and confiscated his iPhone as evidence.[85] A month later, Kalanick tweeted, "Cambridge, MA home to Harvard, MIT and some of the most anti-competitive, corrupt transportation laws in the country."[86] Uber appealed the citation, out of either a perceived necessity or Kalanick's hyper-competitiveness, and in all likelihood, the Cambridge staff were overjoyed. Uber was falling into their trap.

By law, the State of Massachusetts allowed anyone (outside of Boston) charged with a w&m citation to appeal it at a hearing before the Division of Standards, a state agency in the executive branch with quasi-judicial powers. Once more, Uber hired top-talent outside counsel, including a former Massachusetts deputy attorney general, to represent them. In July, on the same day that Uber's faithful in Washington, DC sent fifty thousand emails to their city council, Uber argued before the Massachusetts director of standards that GPS was a highly accurate measurement system that had been available for civilian use since the early '80s. Further, they used the loose argument (similar to their CPUC argument) that a phone wasn't a formal measuring device, and thus, taximeter standards couldn't apply. Cambridge simply argued it was irrelevant – unapproved devices couldn't be used in place of an approved one.[87]

A month later, in August, the director issued a decision agreeing with Cambridge's interpretation. However, because it took place in a state agency and not a judicial court, the hearing did more than just uphold a fine. In the same decision, the director ordered that Uber's devices must be discontinued statewide until NIST updated its taximeter standards and Uber's device was type-approved. Effectively, it was like a cease-and-desist order for the entire state of Massachusetts.[88] In DC, Ron Linton quickly received the news and excitedly informed Mary Cheh and the local Yellow Cab Company.[89]

The story broke in *The Washington Post* on August 10, and in it, a defiant Kalanick said that Uber was not shutting down. He hinted that it was the taxi industry that was behind the decision, and in response, Uber would explore both political and legal options. "You can imagine who are the loudest people questioning this," Kalanick told the *Post*. "It's not the riders, I'll tell you that much."[90]

The cease-and-desist story didn't gain wide coverage, though, until Kalanick turned it into another Uber blog post four days later. This one was uncharacteristically subtler than the DC post the month before. There was no call to action, no listing of government email addresses, and no Twitter hashtag campaign. There wasn't even a link to the Change.org petition created in response to the hearing's decision.[91] One news source hinted that Uber was trying backdoor channels rather than a political counterattack.[92]

Following the blog post, events moved almost as fast as they had in DC but in a more haphazard, deflated way. Uber supporters had no central point of focus for channeling their outrage. Some of the attention turned to neighboring Boston, where Mayor Thomas Menino announced his general support for innovative products and said his office would meet with Uber representatives. Users had taken to social media to voice their support but in smaller numbers than seen in DC. An independently created Change.org petition received twelve hundred signatures, whereas the DC one had received over forty-four hundred.[93]

Even when there was support, none of it was directed at any one entity or office. There was no obvious remedy. The Division of Standards considered the matter closed. It was like Uber's crusaders were complaining to the sky. With no other focus, the media spotlight simply turned the press's eyes toward Uber, and oddly, they didn't use the news coverage as a bludgeoning tool against anyone. It all suggested that something was quietly happening behind the scenes. And it was.

The day after Kalanick's blog post, Cambridge learned of a flaw in their apparent trap. Although the division was endowed with quasi-judicial powers, it wasn't insulated from outside political pressures. As part of Massachusetts's executive branch, the division shared the same boss at the top of the totem pole as every other agency: Governor Deval Patrick. And despite the relatively small and muffled outrage, there was enough persuasion to change the outcome in Uber's favor.

Around noon the day after Uber's blog post, Governor Patrick's communications director tweeted, "With all @massgovernor has done for the innovation economy, we're not shutting down [Uber]. Working on a swift resolution."[94] In a separate tweet, he also said that Uber was popular in the governor's office and he himself had used it the previous night after a Bruce Springsteen concert.[95]

Hours after the tweet, the governor's office issued a press release titled, "Massachusetts Gives Green Light for Uber Technologies." Attached to the statement was a modified hearing decision from the director of standards, reversing his prior decision. The director stated he'd recently become aware of a concurrent examination by NIST to evaluate whether national taximeter standards should be amended to include GPS.[96] It was the same "examination" advanced by fellow w&m regulator Craig Leisy. For whatever reason, neither Uber nor Cambridge brought it up during the hearing.

Cambridge learned of it no later than two days after the division's hearing because their w&m regulator called Leisy himself. Leisy discussed the proposed amendment with Cambridge's regulator in exhaustive detail, as he often did with anyone who mentioned Uber. He even said that the best solution to the Uber dilemma was probably the adoption by local regulators of an *interim* standard for GPS-based taximeters.[97]

Ironically, the Massachusetts director of standards said the same thing in his revised ruling. "The Division has historically allowed for a provisional type approval of unapproved devices pending the results of an ongoing study undertaken by NIST...."[98]

It was the perfect loophole Uber needed to continue operating. The director vacated the original citation against the Uber driver, and the governor's office apologized for the confusion.[99] Leisy probably hadn't realized it, but by promoting the taximeter issue at NIST, he had given Uber and Governor Patrick the means to overturn a statewide cease-and-desist order. It was the equivalent of regulatory judo, using one taxi regulator's efforts in Seattle against another in Cambridge.

The City of Cambridge attempted to sue in superior court to reverse the decision, which a judge denied.[100] After the incident, the USNWG on Taximeters spent years of sporadic meetings continuing to deliberate GPS. In the interim, other regulators would often mention that Uber's app was still not type-approved, often citing it as a point of complaint. But in any meaningful way, Cambridge was the one and only time regulators used it as a test case to shut Uber down.

It was also the first time a governor was brought into the picture to shield Uber from regulators. As the IATR's efforts mounted, it would prove not to be the last.

CHAPTER FIVE

Yours in Cronyism

Arguably, no other regulator was more motivated to rally against Uber than Christiane Hayashi of San Francisco. It wasn't just that Kalanick was an unlikable guy. Hayashi didn't want to see the city's taxi industry destabilized. The SFMTA taxi-medallion sales program was designed specifically to benefit both the city and the working-poor drivers, but to allow Uber or any other company to compete against taxis would dilute the drivers' investments. If the medallions lost value, they'd be trapped in an underwater investment, like a beachfront home in 2008. By 2012, Mayor Gavin Newsom, who had originally given Hayashi's office its instructions, was long gone. He'd won election as California's lieutenant governor in 2010. But the implied financial security of the medallions still carried forward, and Hayashi didn't want to see an industry upended.

Recognizing Uber for the competitive behemoth and efficiency zealot it was, Hayashi began a series of reforms to modernize the local taxi market and make it competitive. Almost all of the burden was placed upon her shoulders. According to an internal report to the SFMTA Board, "Currently the Deputy Director is the only resource available for all analytical work, outreach, legislative matters and complex drafting that is required of regulatory reform."[1] To say the least, it was daunting.

To augment some of the burden, one of the first steps was to hire a taxi consultant who could determine how many total medallions they should make available within the city. If the flood of reports about cabs not meeting demand hadn't convinced them to increase the supply, Uber's popularity was the cold splash of water they finally needed.

Hayashi also understood that for the average passenger summoning a taxi, it was inconvenient to download a different smartphone app for each of the city's many cab companies, which was how Cabulous and TaxiMagic operated. In early 2012, Toronto's regulator asked her how she dealt with Uber, and she replied,

> My response at this point is to develop an application like the one that they are using so that the cabs can compete with them. If people could get the same electronic hailing capacity at a lesser price I think the taxis would give Uber a run for their money.[2]

In other words, she needed to find a way to take all fifteen hundred San Francisco taxis and put them on a single app.

Credit cards were another issue. Nationally, much of the taxi industry still didn't require cabs to use credit cards because they were bickering about who would absorb the administrative fees. Not only had Uber jumped ahead by accepting *only* credits cards virtually, but other cities such as New York and Boston were beginning to see positive results with their new credit card hardware devices.

San Francisco had a trial program for such equipment. In 2010 the city integrated its federally mandated paratransit services into taxis, and 350 cabs were outfitted with credit-card monitors similar to New York's TPEP systems, which allowed passengers to slide a credit card and choose a tip amount from the back seat of the cab. Drivers initially protested them for a variety of reasons, including a fear of the radio waves the devices gave off. But before the end of 2012, the SFMTA ended the deadlock and required credit card acceptance of *all* cabs.[3]

In credit cards especially, Hayashi found new heights in her love/hate relationship with the industry. Initially, they required drivers absorb an interchange fee of 5 percent of the fare. In mid-June 2012, a group of drivers drove around city hall in protest. One of them held a sign, which Hayashi often remembered, stating, "CHRISTIANE GO LEAVE US ALONE."[4] She was forcing them to improve faster than they wanted, and it made her job all the more thankless.

In concert together, credit-card processing and a system-wide taxi app would make the taxis as competitive as possible with Uber. Among her peers, Hayashi was ahead of the curve. Most taxi regulators looked at Uber simply from an enforcement perspective, but she was beginning to see they needed to fight fire with fire by improving the experience for the consumer. But just as she was making progress, another headache loomed on the horizon. Between June and September, the very first ridesharing smartphone apps in California, SideCar and Lyft, had launched.

SideCar was the brainchild of Sunil Paul, a forty-seven-year-old entrepreneur who had amassed millions building and selling start-up companies, similar to Kalanick and Camp's career paths. His biggest claim to fame was Brightmail, a spam-filtering software for email clients that was sold to the anti-virus company Symantec in 2004 for $370 million cash. Immediately upon moving to the Bay Area in 1997, Paul saw the challenges of trying to hail a cab and started thinking creatively about how to address transportation issues.

"GPS as a commercial tool was beginning to arrive on the scene," he said. "There were 9-1-1 services that were beginning to perform cell-phone triangulation." Paul started to wonder if he could incorporate similar location-availability technology into phones. In 1999 he recruited a friend to explore the idea of building a transportation company but pulled the plug after two months. The technology wasn't yet advanced enough, there wasn't enough political will, and consumers weren't quite demanding it, yet. "Gas was ninety-nine cents a gallon, climate change was barely on the radar – no one had the imagination. It was a different time."

Still, Paul kept laying the groundwork. In 2002 he was awarded US Patent #6356838, which conceptually described requesting a ride by transmitting positional data to a server. He also continued to take active roles in clean technology and car-sharing programs throughout the 2000s. In 2010, after having invested in and run the car-sharing company Spride Share, Paul lobbied to change the insurance rules so that sharing one's own personal car wasn't considered a commercial activity (which might otherwise invalidate an auto insurance policy). The bill passed nearly unanimously and was signed by Governor Schwarzenegger.[5]

In 2011 Paul took notice of a small company, Shepherd Intelligent Systems, based out of the University of Michigan. Originally started as a school project, it had grown into a company able to cheaply use cell phones as portable tracking devices to predict arrival times for buses.[6] The company expanded into fleets of other vehicle types, including taxis and limousines, and Paul immediately saw the potential to bring their knowledge base into the world of shared rides. After Uber already entered the game with their black-car service, the idea seemed more tangible. Paul hired the Shepherd team, and SideCar was founded in 2011.

As they were building to launch in San Francisco, one of the original Shepherd founders was stranded in the Marina District after a late-night party. Unable to find a cab, he came across a pizza-delivery driver and paid him twenty bucks for a ride home. It was easy, almost effortless, and suddenly, SideCar's potential seemed self-evident.

The idea of using personal cars and drivers to provide rides in lieu of taxis was not unique to any one app. Other developers and entrepreneurs across the country saw the potential, which was even more of an indictment of the sparse, unreliable taxi industry. But chiefly, many entrepreneurs' goals were inspired by either environmental conservation or improved resource management. Logan Green and John Zimmer founded an online carpooling service, Zimride, in 2007 with both of those goals in mind.

At age twenty, Green had been appointed to the Santa Barbara Metropolitan Transit District with the hope of creating efficiencies in the public bus system. If more people rode buses, it would equate to less congestion and emissions. After a few years, he learned that public bus systems were inherently inefficient because they were heavily subsidized to keep prices low. "They're designed to lose money," he said in an interview, which made them impossible to scale upward. If the transit district attempted to increase bus prices even slightly, he found that one way or the other, the idea would get shot down.[7]

During Green's tenure he had also taken a trip to Zimbabwe where he came across an impressive discovery. "No one could afford to drive on their own," he said. Instead, people had taken a shared taxi system, similar to jitneys, that serviced on-demand rides around town. "I came back with my mind blown that here – one of the poorest countries in the world – had a more efficient transit network than we did in Santa Barbara." He started to think about a network that improved when more people used it, "essentially crowd-sourcing a public transit network."[8]

Green's future business partner, John Zimmer, had studied hotel management at Cornell University but in his senior year took a class called Green Cities. Zimmer was excited when during one class, the professor delivered an inspirational lecture on the history of transportation infrastructure and asked what would be the next step in its development. Zimmer started thinking about the answer using the main yardstick of success in the hotel school: occupancy. "I asked him, 'What is the occupancy of the seats in cars on our highways?'" The answer was a paltry 20 percent. In other words, 80 percent of seats in cars had remained empty. "In hotel," Zimmer said, "that's failure."[9]

The course made Zimmer think about the problem even more, but after graduating, he took a job at the Wall Street investment firm Lehman Brothers. One night in 2007, Zimmer came across a Facebook post by Green about a company he was building called Zimride, named after Green's influential trip to Zimbabwe. Zimmer was excited about the concept and reached out to Green through a mutual friend. The two partnered, and coincidentally, Zimmer left Lehman three months before it went bankrupt in the midst of the

2008 financial crisis.[10]

As it was originally created, Zimride was a Facebook-integrated website that allowed people to schedule shared rides with one another. It was extremely popular with colleges and universities, as the business aligned with every college's shrinking number of parking spaces and their dedication to environmental conservation. Although the website was profitable, they asked themselves in mid-2012 whether it was accomplishing the goals they originally had in mind. Arranged rides were all well and good, but they weren't filling empty seats to the degree they'd hoped. To scale upward, they decided to launch an on-demand smartphone app dubbed Lyft.[11] Just like SideCar, they beta tested for a few months and formally launched in early September 2012.[12]

Lyft created a hokey marketing gimmick in the form of a large pink mustache placed on each car's grill. Chosen because it was "whimsical and irreverent," it quickly became a visual cue as to how many such cars were on the streets of San Francisco. And it immediately infuriated taxi drivers. Uber's use of limousine black cars was at least *arguably* legal (and difficult to spot on the roads), but amateurs providing commercial transportation was inherently illegal. The drivers were not licensed, vehicles were not inspected, and insurance was dubious at best. To defend against the argument that they were a commercial service, drivers were prohibited from taking any street hails, and all fares for both SideCar and Lyft were optional as "voluntary donations."

For the better part of a year, Lyft and SideCar were chiefly Hayashi's problem. They were not yet on the IATR's radar in 2012, mostly because they were isolated in San Francisco, and Uber's tactics kept Matt Daus busy. SideCar expanded to Seattle in November, and although Craig Leisy was concerned, his hands were still too full to jump on it.[13]

Quickly, Hayashi was blocked from intervening directly against the new ridesharing services. Years later, the SFMTA was once asked why it never asserted jurisdiction against ridesharing companies, and Hayashi's boss said it was "fairly clear that City Hall didn't want us to step in."[14] When cab companies asked her why she never took enforcement actions, Hayashi told them, "The problem is in Room 200," which was the mayor's office.

Mayor Ed Lee, who took Gavin Newsom's place and then won election in his own right, positioned himself early on as strongly in favor of the sharing economy. With other board supervisors, he created the Sharing Economy Working Group to welcome such businesses to the city. He also assisted Airbnb, the online company that allowed homeowners to rent their homes and apartments as hotel rooms, which was controversial given San Francisco's housing shortage.[15]

Although Hayashi had no leverage to push them away, she still wasted little time and sped up her schedule on taxi improvements to keep the industry competitive. In early September, the SFMTA Board approved her request to issue an additional 150 to 200 temporary full-time taxi permits (i.e., medallions). Hayashi acknowledged that taxi service was unreliable in San Francisco, and it was generally believed the taxi consultant's upcoming report would recommend increasing the number of medallions. She was essentially asking for an advance. In her request, she even cited "services such as Uber, SideCar, Lyft, the new UberX, and numerous bandit taxis and illegal limousines" as her reasons to increase the taxi supply now rather than wait. Plus, the tourist-heavy events of Fleet Week and America's Cup were about to occur in October.[16] She knew that the longer they waited, the more the industry would suffer.

Ironically, Kalanick also wasted little time and scheduled a meeting to request an enforcement action from the California PUC. Located just a few blocks away from the SFMTA's offices, the CPUC was housed in an ominous building shaped like a quarter-circle wedge with a large inner courtyard. The building was five stories tall, and in an office at the top sat Marzia Zafar, the Director of Policy and Planning. Zafar, a longtime utilities professional who sported a Mohawk and dark, bold-frame glasses, had no power to issue citations. But she might be persuaded to develop an official CPUC position against Lyft and SideCar, which the safety division could then act on.

It was a clever maneuver, as Uber was still under a cease-and-desist order issued in 2010, which lingered as a back-burner issue for the safety division. Because the CPUC was so dysfunctional, the policy office of the fifth floor didn't interact with the safety offices on the second floor. They were segregated, meaning there was little threat in talking to Zafar. It was as though Uber had snuck by the infantry to chat with the generals.

According to Zafar, it was a bizarre meeting. She entered a conference room to find an entourage of Uber employees and outside counsel including Jeremiah Hallisey, a former campaign manager for Governor Gray Davis and commissioner of the California Transportation Commission. Kalanick sat at the middle of a meeting table, sitting in the opposite direction from everyone else. As everyone else stood to greet Zafar, Kalanick appeared oddly disinterested and continued staring toward the wall. Uber and their counsel explained their interpretation of Lyft and SideCar's illegal operations, and Kalanick insisted that the CPUC shut them down.

Zafar felt Kalanick was rude and demanding. No regulated entity of the CPUC holds a meeting to "insist" anything. But it was also strangely ironic. The taxi industry and their regulators had attempted to use the CPUC to shut down Uber, and now Uber was using the CPUC to try to shut down its new competitors.

After the meeting, Zafar briefed CPUC President Mike Peevey, who had no intention of shutting down either Lyft or SideCar. Peevey was not as committed to the sharing economy as Mayor Lee, but still, he felt there were benefits to the new, innovative businesses, and he wanted the free market to decide the outcome, not regulators.

"We regulate for safety; we regulate for customer choice," Zafar quoted of Peevey.

However, the message didn't reach the safety division, further demonstrating how segregated the second floor was from the fifth. In late

August the CPUC sent cease-and-desist letters to both SideCar and Lyft, which were generally ignored. From Lyft and SideCar's perspective, there was plenty of reason to consider this new batch an empty threat. It took a month and a half before the media even reported on their issuance, and Uber's 2010 cease-and-desist order was approaching its second anniversary without any follow-through.

Kalanick's public attitude toward Uber's new competitors was the complete opposite of the one displayed in his private meetings. In mid-September he attended *TechCrunch's* annual Disrupt conference, where he was interviewed in a fireside chat talking mostly about his regulatory battles to date. He gave recaps of the battles in DC and Massachusetts, and talking about it brought a scowl to his face. He was frustrated and at moments appeared flustered. As before, Kalanick insisted Uber was legal and that regulators were putting up unnecessary roadblocks. "If you put yourself in a position of having to ask for permission even when the rules say you can move forward, they will never ever let you make the city a better place." As the interviewer asked him about the reasons for the roadblocks, Kalanick steamrolled over her to elaborate further.[17]

"I have three principles that I've sort of honed it into. One is cronyism. They ultimately get a Stockholm syndrome with the folks that they regulate. They eventually feel like they're supposed to protect the people that they regulate. I had one regulator recently tell me that they view themselves as customer support for the folks that they regulate. Number two is control. If they don't have rules for something, they feel that it's illegal even when it's not. You have to have rules that you can enforce. You can't just say, 'We don't have rules, and therefore you're illegal and you must cease.' Number three is communication. They are incredibly sensitive to what's in the public view – what the optics are. They're more sensitive to the optics than the reality."[18]

As the interview shifted to the relatively new pink mustaches on the streets of San Francisco, Kalanick welcomed the competition. He hinted that

Uber might start its own ridesharing service as SideCar and Lyft had done.[19] His tone was different, enthusiastic. There was no hint he had attempted to shut down his new competitors.

"There's nothing wrong with providing value to a customer at a lower price because if you do that, you're going to win," he said.[20]

Uber's apparent goal now was to provide a more competitive product.

"I mean, competition is fun.... Let's have some fun and let's make the world a better place at the same time, but I'm bringing it. I'm not sleeping. If the other guy is sleeping, I'm going to kick his ass."[21]

Two hours after the fireside chat, *VentureBeat* reported the interview online in an article titled "Car Service Uber to Foes: If You Don't Evolve, I'm Going to Kick Your Ass." The article focused mostly on Kalanick's vitriol against regulators, and although it briefly mentioned SideCar and Lyft, it ended with Kalanick's "kick his ass" comment.[22] A couple of days later, IATR President Matt Daus forwarded the article to his Smartphone App Committee with the email subject line "Uber is going to 'kick the ass of us crony regulators?'"[23]

Daus had been busy. Two and a half months after creating the committee, he had recruited most of its founding members, including Hayashi, Linton, Craig Leisy of Seattle, and the NIST program manager who had led the USNWG on Taximeters. Letting the article speak for itself, he wrote to them, "Fyi...simply put – 'out of control'...."[24]

At nearly the same time, Daus sent a separate email under the same subject line to the IATR Board of Directors, some of whom also served on the app committee. As he had mentioned to Hayashi months earlier, Uber was going to be a topic at the IATR's upcoming November conference in Washington, DC, a location already decided before Uber's DC fight. Even though the app committee was already developing model regulations to block Uber, Daus's irritation reached a boiling point, and he began a back-and-forth discussion with his board members, all of whom were taxi regulators in their respective cities.

From: Daus, Matthew
Sent: Friday, September 14, 2012 7:18 AM

Hello folks - Now this is outrageous and truly out of control! Someone from Uber has asked to register for our conference. We need to do something about this! Simply unbelievable. M

From: Cohen, Mark [Boston]
Sent: Friday, September 14, 2012 7:49 AM

Dear Fellow Crony Regulators,

One school of thought might be to allow Über some access to our conference. As Sun Tzu said (or was it Michael Corleone?) "Keep you friends close and your enemies closer." It seems clear that Travis Kalanick sees some value in picking a fight with regulators (read: Big Government) and, likely, has little interest in understanding who we are, what we have accomplished or, more importantly, what our vision of the future might be. That said, if he is looking for a little competition, I like my team...

From: Daus, Matthew
Sent: Friday, September 14, 2012 7:52 AM

Lol maybe we can have him do some stand up or roast him
Yes, we should be inclusive... It will get interesting....any other thoughts?

From: Scott, John [San Diego]
Sent: Friday, September 14, 2012 11:43 AM

In California (the state regulates black car service) / San Diego UBER needs state or our approval to operate. On a somewhat similar issue We have a hearing coming up related to the ability of taxicab drivers accepting calls from unapproved dispatched services .

Regarding the conference ,is the interest to present to listen or both ?either way this could be an opportunity to obtain information and a show a united regulatory/industry front . The united approach could be something useful for actions(yet to be) taken by individual regulators later .

From: Hull, Malachi [New Orleans]
Sent: Friday, September 14, 2012 12:48 PM

We have not had UBER concerns, but I agree with John's assessment. Let's bring them in and show a united front.

From: Cohen, Mark [Boston]
Sent: Friday, September 14, 2012 6:45 PM

Might I also suggest that, if we decided to allow Uber to attend the upcoming IATR Conference, that, due to the "peak demand" for seats at the table, we institute "surge pricing" and charge them double to attend!

Yours in Cronyism,
Mark

From: Drischler, Thomas [Los Angeles]
Sent: Friday, September 14, 2012 6:46 PM

I recall that a driver's group attended the Seattle conference in '06. They were mildly disruptive, with the main problem being that they would weigh in during sessions with comments that were doctrinaire and off-topic. However, they didn't spoil the conference. I don't expect representatives from UBER would present us with any challenges we couldn't handle. We've all been playing hardball in the big leagues for many years. After some of the things I've been through at my commission and City Council over the years, I wouldn't find this self-aggrandizing hothead the least bit intimidating. Let's make sure they pay full price for their conference registration!

As for cronyism, I have to fess up. I'm a crony of the public. I'm a crony of passengers who should know their driver has passed a criminal history background check, who expect that the operator serving them is properly insured, who are entitled to know what rate they're going to be charged, who should have a means to file a complaint for poor service or overcharges, who want to ride in clean fuel/low emission vehicles and who aren't discriminated against because they are poor or disabled.

From: Daus, Matthew
Sent: Saturday, September 15, 2012 8:42 AM

based on popular demand and comments, we will welcome him with open

---

arms ...tell him we look forward to greeting him

At their core, the board members felt Uber wasn't getting the message about the historical reasons for taxi regulation, and having it explained to Kalanick one regulator at a time wasn't working. The "united front" they alluded to wasn't just among regulators but also among the regulated. Taxi companies were permitted to join the IATR in a non-voting capacity, and since Daus's presidency, many taxi vendors had participated as generous sponsors.[25] Perhaps Uber would get the message if every corner of the taxi industry expressed their viewpoint. Twelve employees from Uber registered for the November conference, including former senior vice president Ryan Graves.[26] Kalanick did not register, although he would pop in nonetheless.

Although Hayashi was not in on the board's conversation, she still received the initial "simply put - 'out of control'" email the app committee had received from Daus. Within a week her office met with the enforcement arm of the CPUC, as well as a commander in the San Francisco PD.[27] Yelling at SideCar and Lyft to cease and desist wasn't enough. She was pushing them to take action, especially as she was hobbled by her own city government.

Placing greater pressures on Hayashi, in October Uber released its UberTAXI product in San Francisco, the direct-to-driver app that connected taxi drivers with passengers while bypassing their parent cab companies.[28] As cab drivers at the San Francisco International Airport sat in the taxi queue waiting for a fare, someone had been handing them fliers encouraging them to download the UberTAXI app. One taxi owner then immediately contacted Hayashi:

> Are you guys going to do something about this?! Uber is now trying to use my business infrastructure to service their service calls.
>
> If we are not careful our entire industry will become deregulated. It already is starting to crumble. We need to act decisively and put an end [to] this nonsense.[29]

Hayashi forwarded the email to Daus.

"This is getting really bad," she told him.[30]

"Oh boy," he replied.[31]

More complaints reached Hayashi. Uber was harming each cab company's ability to market itself, but after exploring the legality of the app, Hayashi's hands were tied. "As drivers are independent operators, they are free to enter into contractual relationships that will expand their business opportunities," she told the taxi companies.[32]

In more blunt terms, the taxi industry had brought this on themselves. They were the ones who decades ago abdicated any risk for finding fares and instead simply charged drivers to use a cab. They had assumed the drivers would never have a better resource for finding fares than the cab companies' own dispatch systems. When the technology finally arrived to prove them wrong, it was like their legs had been chopped off.

Although Hayashi arguably cared more about the plight of the drivers that the companies, she still wasn't rooting for market upheaval. As she told one taxi manager, "We hope to address this issue in upcoming regulations governing smartphone apps."[33]

Matt Daus held firm that the new model regulations wouldn't be released until the November conference, in part because they were still being drafted. But some of the IATR Smartphone App Committee members were not interested in waiting. From September 2012 until the end of the year, IATR members would attempt regulatory pushback against Uber that only resulted in frustrating setbacks for themselves. Uber's fight with a regulator in one city would overlap with a fight in another, almost like the barrage of police the New York taxi industry encountered in 1925. Among government employees, Uber met far more enemies than friends.

In Chicago, where Uber had first introduced its UberTAXI product in May, the local industry was even more furious than in San Francisco. It filed a suit against Uber alleging a litany of consumer protection and fair-practice violations. It said Uber misrepresented it had been working with "fleet partners" when its app was direct-to-driver. Also, they took strong issue with the manner in which Uber earned revenue from its taxi app. Legally, Uber couldn't charge a fare different from a taximeter, which would have been an obvious violation of law. Instead Uber charged passengers an automatic 20 percent tip, of which it allegedly kept half.[34] Not only were cabs not allowed to charge "automatic" tips, but taxi companies had long since been prohibited from collecting even *partial* tips from drivers. Depending on whether one viewed Uber as a taxi dispatcher, it was potentially skirting regulations.

Chicago's taxi regulators (who were active in the IATR) were happy to let the industry's lawsuit carry the water. They were more concerned with Uber's black-car service. Initially working with the city, Uber obtained an appropriate dispatching license, but in late October 2012, local regulators quietly proposed a rule change that would not allow black cars to use any device that calculated fares based on time and distance.[35]

As drafted, the new rule insisted that black-car fares must be prearranged or such vehicles would be explicitly considered unlicensed taxicabs, subjecting them to penalties.[36] The regulation was meant to reflect a law passed the previous January in a massive regulatory overhaul put forward by Mayor Rahm Emanuel. A key provision in the January rules stated that black cars may not equip a meter "which registers a charge of any kind."[37]

Uber launched in Chicago four months prior to the January rules but had either not spotted the provision at the time or perhaps felt they could argue the term "meter" didn't apply to a smartphone. But the newest, more explicit rule change clearly would have criminalized their service. Uber initiated its customary media blitz to put a spotlight on the regulators, and within a couple of months, Chicago backed off.[38]

On a separate front, NIST held its second meeting in September for the

USNWG on Taximeters, this time in person at their offices in Gaithersburg, Maryland. According to the agenda, it appeared officials wanted to discuss updating the legal definitions of a taximeter. The attendee list ballooned even larger than before and now included weights-and-measures (w&m) staff from cities across the northeast, especially in Massachusetts. A Cambridge regulator who had participated in the March sting operation against Uber attended, and once more, so did Matt Daus.[39]

Unsurprisingly, their discussions again danced around whether the new language would legitimize Uber, which was tricky ground. Like most NIST definitions, a taximeter wasn't defined by its size, shape, materials, or model numbers. Instead, NIST used a broad series of concepts that, when brought together, matched the *function* of a taximeter. But some portions of the Taximeter Code hadn't been updated since the late 1980s, and since then, taximeter technology had evolved, becoming more digital and sophisticated. Large cities like New York were now using GPS to track their taxi fleets. It was hard to craft language that might allow for taxi upgrades but didn't have the unintended consequence of *also* approving Uber's smartphone app. They repeatedly questioned how to apply the right balance so the outcome was favorable only to traditional taxis.

Toward the end of their meeting, NIST also brought in an expert to answer a barrage of questions about the use of GPS, especially as a means for measuring the distance of a cab's trip.[40] But as most people in the room likely knew, it was a strategic ploy. No one within the working group had any intention of replacing traditional taximeters with a GPS system; they were asking whether there were any credible arguments to cast doubt on Uber's software.

However, the expert's opinion didn't help them very much. As he reported, GPS was extraordinarily accurate with little reason to doubt it. Between any two points, regardless of the total distance, GPS was accurate within one meter. He also said that the signal was usually strong, as most commercial systems updated their position five times per second.[41]

Instead, the group started to ask how the signal might be manipulated or distorted. Signal jamming was possible, but it would only have a significant impact if it was coming from within a cab. Finally, someone simply asked, "Can the GPS measurement be manipulated through the software application?"[42]

According to the minutes, the expert replied, "Software (any software) could be manipulated.... To change the measurement provided by the satellite position, it would be necessary to alter the signal (spoofing). This is very difficult to accomplish."[43]

The moderator asked the group whether GPS standards should be incorporated into the Taximeters Code or developed into a separate code. The group, seemingly defeated by GPS's near-infallibility, said it should just be incorporated into the Taximeters Code.[44]

After the meeting, the moderator noted in the minutes that there were several discussions about smartphone apps where the phone could be used for distance calculation and payment. Since GPS was more or less cleared, the next step was to determine how w&m staff across the country would review the software itself. Matt Daus specifically stated that on behalf of the IATR, he hoped the USNWG on Taximeters would address these systems and that it would not be in the public's best interest if this issue was ignored.[45]

The USNWG would continue meeting a few times per year, forming a subcommittee to determine whether GPS should be used to measure the distance of a ride. A deadlocked subcommittee, its unofficial purpose was to ceaselessly argue whether services like Uber, Lyft, and SideCar should be validated – and they would spend years trying to sort it out.

Meanwhile in DC, Uber's fight turned into a surreal public hearing featuring Travis Kalanick himself. Ron Linton's taxi commission took another shot at Uber, this time attempting to pass new regulations reflective of the taxi overhaul bill passed the previous summer. The overhaul had stripped away the Uber Amendments, but Commissioner Linton knew he could still affect the drivers under the District's newly sanctioned "Sedan" class of livery vehicles. In the draft regulations, he attempted to prohibit "demand pricing," require that passengers be issued both paper and electronic receipts, and mandate that sedan owners must have at least twenty vehicles in each of their fleets.[46]

Since Uber had entered the District, several limo drivers were teaming up to form limited partnerships, sometimes comprised of only two licensed drivers. The twenty-vehicle minimum would have made life especially difficult for Uber, and Linton knew it. The general manager of the local Yellow Cab Company contacted him about the dramatic flood of new operator applications over the summer, normally a dull period for taxis and limos. To help curb the influx of drivers, the DC Taxi Commission required that each driver already own their own sedan and not simply rent one on the side.[47] Later, Kalanick would allege that a chauffeur-licensing office had remained closed to stymie new licenses. Linton certainly tried to minimize the number of drivers available to Uber, and he told the Yellow Cab manager it was the best he could do until the new regulations took effect. Cab companies would simply have to market themselves better, he explained.[48]

After the regulations were proposed, Uber once more issued a media blitz, and just as before, the spotlight turned the situation in their favor and brought in a new wave of public invective against the taxicab commission. "Here We Go Again: DC Taxi Commission Proposes New Rules to Shut down Uber," their blog post was titled.[49]

In the process, Kalanick personally appeared a few days later before a meeting of the DC Council's transportation committee. It was a rare appearance for Kalanick in front of a legislative body, and he did not handle it well. He turned much of his ire to the committee chair, Mary Cheh, who agreed that some of the proposed regulations were onerous. In the hearing, she also attempted to reconcile any disagreements with Kalanick, move forward, and talk about the future of what sedan and taxi regulations should look like to foster both innovation and balance.[50]

DC was in an unusual situation. There were no supply caps protecting the local taxi market, but Uber's service was so effective it might still completely upend a heavily regulated industry. What was the right regulation? Should the council willingly jeopardize an industry that had existed for the last century? And if so, how would it be feasible politically? If the goal was to replace taxis, then Uber was effectively forcing the council to spend a lot of political capital on one issue.

For Kalanick, the correct response to Council Member Cheh's questions would have been to politely agree in principle, smile, and move forward. But just like at the *TechCrunch* Disrupt conference, he was agitated. He couldn't let the past go, and he began bickering with Cheh over revisionist history. They argued over how they came to the disagreement in the July 10 bill that led to the fifty thousand emails and whether Uber's representatives had or hadn't been in agreement with the initial language. And from there, it spiraled downward.[51]

"We're not in a fight with you. Do you understand that? I'm not in a fight with you," Cheh said.[52]

Kalanick contentiously replied, "When you tell us how to do business, and you tell us we can't charge lower fares off our high-quality service at the best possible price, you *are* fighting with us."[53]

Cheh moved on to let the next council member speak, slumping back into her chair in frustration.[54] Even as the committee tried to move the discussion forward, it was not easy for Kalanick to explain Uber's framework. Many of the members didn't understand how operational decisions were made, such as surge pricing. They didn't understand the machine learning and data mining that were programmed into the app.

It was up to Kalanick to educate them, but instead of assuaging their concerns like a thoughtful teacher, he behaved as though he were being cross-examined, as though he were maneuvering through a verbal minefield to avoid any criticism, big or small. He could have explained the social value of surge pricing, but he acted as though it was obvious and shouldn't be challenged. He could have explained why they didn't need to panic about Uber's impact on the taxi industry. Instead, he repeatedly accused council members of protectionist measures that would only allow the "rich" to use Uber's app.

At one moment in the hearing, the conversation turned outright childish. After the July 10 debacle, Uber had dropped its minimum price to twelve dollars for a one-month promotional period.[55] Uber's ability to drop prices so quickly worried another council member, a close ally of the taxi industry, who was concerned about the competitive impact. The council member was convinced Uber had sole discretion to set its prices, and he was trying to extract that answer out of Kalanick.

"Who sets the rates for Uber?" he asked.[*]

"We do it through discussions and negotiations with our drivers," Kalanick said.

"No, no, no, who makes the decision on what the rates are for Uber?"

"We negotiate with drivers when we first launch in a city."

"Do the drivers set the rate?"

"We negotiate with drivers when we first launch in a city."

"I don't think that – don't you set the rates for Uber?"

"We negotiate with drivers when we first launch in a city."

The audience laughed for a moment.

"I'm not sure how many more times I can say it," Kalanick said dryly.

"Well, you can say it a hundred times; I can ask it a hundred times."

The audience laughed again.

---

[*]   See second-to-previous citation for the following set of quotes.

"That's like '99 Bottles of Beer,'" replied Kalanick.

"The company sets the rates. The drivers are not setting the rates; the company is setting the rates," said the council member, attempting to answer his own question.

"We negotiate with drivers when we first launch in a city."

This was the general feel of the back-and-forth. The council wanted insights to craft a policy. Kalanick simply dismissed them. As his testimony concluded, Mary Cheh was still optimistic about Uber's operations. She told the committee she didn't think there would be "an obstacle to the full flourishing of these services."[56]

In other words, the message to Ron Linton was once more to lay off.

After that event, Kalanick would no longer testify at a regulatory hearing on Uber's behalf.

In 2012, Uber won more fights than it lost. During the two-month period before the November IATR Conference, there were only a couple of setbacks, both of which occurred in New York. The city did not allow taxis to use smartphone apps, and the RFP for a new taxi smartphone was still in progress. But apparently nervous over the announced entry of Hailo, the London-based direct-to-driver taxi app, Uber nonetheless pushed forward and began signing up taxi drivers to use its competing service, UberTAXI.[57]

This action violated several taboos in the heavily regulated New York taxi market. Strict requirements governed how cabs could accept credit card payments, and they were not yet permitted to accept prearranged rides, both of which UberTAXI ignored. Plus, there was Uber's automatic 20 percent tip, roughly half of which Uber pocketed.

More than that, Uber was jeopardizing a tenuous relationship with the city's Taxi and Limousine Commission (TLC). New York was a sacred market for Uber, the only one where it was willing to play along with local regulations. Uber skirted the line by offering a limited number of free UberTAXI rides, which temporarily made the commercial regulations inapplicable.[58]

But then it started accepting payments. Matt Daus noticed, and his law firm tested drivers to see if they were using the UberTAXI app. They then filed a complaint with the TLC. The Commission finally shut it down after a month of service, and Kalanick was remarkably less brusque about his agitation than he was in DC.[59]

"We'll bite our tongues and keep our frustrations here to ourselves," he wrote in the company blog.[60]

The other setback for Uber occurred in its black-car service just a couple of weeks later during Hurricane Sandy, which struck New York in late October 2012. Governor Cuomo and President Obama signed emergency declarations. Grocery store shelves emptied, and the bus, commuter rail, and subway systems all shut down.[61] With lots of demand for an Uber and limited supply, the app did what it was programmed to do: it charged surge pricing.

During public emergencies, state laws generally prohibited price increases that even *looked* like gouging. Several media outlets and the Twitter-sphere jumped on Uber. *PandoDaily* noted that in neighboring New Jersey, state law did not allow for goods to exceed 10 percent of their normal price. [62]Yet Uber's app was charging 100 percent more than normal.

After forty-five minutes, Uber made a temporary adjustment. To keep the incentives in place, surge pricing would remain active, but Uber would absorb the cost over 100 percent of the normal fare.[63] Still, it was difficult to get drivers on the road, and even *The Times* noted it took ninety minutes to get an Uber. On November 1, the company reinstituted normal surge pricing, stating it was losing too much money – upwards of $100,000 per day – but for the remainder of the emergency, it would give the entire fare to the drivers and remove its normal commission.[64]

Hurricane Sandy was an important lesson for the company. It showed them that during an emergency, customer expectations shifted dramatically and Uber was expected to behave more charitably. After that incident, Uber developed new policies to limit surge pricing during emergencies and donate its commission during those incidents to the Red Cross.

Not all of the regulatory actions against Uber were like the sharp blow of a sword. Some were slow, either by design or by circumstance. Local taxi regulators who struck at Uber were less likely to be effective. Time after time, sting operations had little effect. They were like an ant bite, a quick pain that inflicted little meaningful damage. Taxi regulators needed a camouflaged hole in the ground that Uber could be persuaded to walk over without noticing, one where a local city council member couldn't intervene and throw them a rope. As it happened, one was on the horizon.

In Denver, Uber encountered a city where regulators and the taxi community already had a close working relationship. In early 2012, local taxi and limousine companies were brought together with government representatives in a newly formed Denver Taxi Advisory Council. Their purpose was to coordinate industry improvements that the city could then bless in an ordinance, and it included representatives from Yellow Cab, Metro Taxi, and the Colorado Public Utilities Commission (PUC), among others. Colorado was unusual in that it was the state's PUC, not cities, that had the central authority to regulate both taxi and limousine markets.

Uber launched in Denver in August 2012, and once more, the timing was inconvenient. Yellow Cab, one of the two main taxi companies that controlled most of Colorado as a virtual duopoly, was using the TaxiMagic app.[65] The other cab company, Metro Taxi, began to deploy its own smartphone app that integrated GPS, dispatch coordination, and customer-tracking features with its fleet. Right as the upgrade was completed, Uber's entry into Denver was announced, weeks in advance, in the *Denver Business Journal.*[66]

Within a week of the announcement, the local taxi industry and state regulators were alarmed. Yellow Cab's manager sent a notice to PUC regulators warning of the supposed safety dangers of a company that avoided regulations whenever possible.[67]

"I believe we have a real issue coming to us in the Colorado market that may need some rule changes or legislative changes to clarify how phone apps can and should work with transportation," the Yellow Cab manager told the PUC. Along with his warning, he also forwarded a copy of Matt Daus's white paper on "rogue" smartphone apps as recommended reading.[68]

Both cab companies were already well aware of the potential threat Uber represented. Each one had strong ties to the Taxi Limousine and Paratransit Association (TLPA), the largest international association of taxicab owners and managers. The Yellow Cab manager was a member of the TLPA's app committee, similar to the IATR's committee to monitor Uber's expansion, and the owner of Metro Taxi had just served as the TLPA president in 2011.[69]

In response to the warning, PUC regulators appeared equally anxious. A week after the *Journal* article, one of the PUC staff informed the Colorado legislature's transportation committee about Uber.

"Just this last week, we've received word from both taxi companies, Yellow Cab and Metro, that there's a company called UberCab making its way to Denver.... It's right in between what we call a luxury limousine service and a taxi service. They haven't come to town, yet. So we don't know their model. All we've done is it was brought to our attention, so we looked at what they've done in other cities. But that's something- it's going to be interesting how that plays out this fall and into the spring, I imagine."[70]

"Interesting" was an understatement. The Colorado PUC already had a reputation for pushing away any perceived outsiders. Between 1994 and 2007, Denver's taxi supply remained constant. And in 2007, Metro Taxi and Yellow Cab paid for a report by Ray Mundy, a flourishing consultant widely described as one of the country's top taxi experts. In it, Mundy recommended the PUC approve taxi expansion only for well-capitalized cab companies with deep investments in management and technology. Only Mundy's benefactors, Yellow Cab and Metro Taxi, qualified.[71]

Since 2008, a group of taxi drivers who were tired of paying high lease fees had attempted to form a separate cooperative cab company. But like many jurisdictions, the PUC only granted permits under "convenience and public necessity," meaning it had the sole authority to decide when it was appropriate to allow more cab companies to enter a market. The PUC wasn't interested in granting a new franchise, and the new co-op spent years battling it out, even unsuccessfully pushing a bill in the legislature to overturn their decision.[72]

Even before Uber's entrance, some of Colorado's battles already had echoes of Matt Daus. Just before their launch, a local limo operator complained to PUC and Denver International Airport officials about Avis Rent A Car's WeDriveU program, where they provided a hired chauffeur with a car rental.[73] In 2009, the program had been quashed at LaGuardia, JFK, and Newark airports after complaints from the Limousine Association of New Jersey (LANJ), a group with multiple IATR connections.[74] After Matt Daus left the TLC, he would serve as the LANJ's general counsel, and its executive director, Barry Lefkowitz, would later become the IATR's hired lobbyist for the PASS Act in Congress.[75] After WeDriveU launched in Denver in 2012, Lefkowitz sent the complaining limousine owner some of the LANJ's WeDriveU documents, which were passed on to the Colorado PUC.[76] Between the limo industry and the taxi industry, the Colorado connections back to Matt Daus were pervasive and the barriers to entry formidable.

When Uber entered Denver, it also caught the attention of Denver Director of Excise and Licenses, Tom Downey. Although taxicab regulations were left to the state government, Denver still required drivers to obtain a local "herdic license" to ensure they knew the streets well enough not to get lost, and to make sure they behaved well in front of visiting tourists. Downey, a tall, husky figure with short, thinning hair and an easygoing smile, had thought of Uber in similar terms as he thought of the local pedicab industry, a growing issue often delegated to the local taxi regulator. As pedicabs had grown in Denver, they had become more independent, unruly, and prone to complaints. But overall, they were appreciated. Downey wasn't looking to do away with pedicabs but simply rein them in with a few regulations to hold them accountable. With Uber, it was no different.

"I called them twice," Downey said. "I left messages saying, 'Hey, I'm the Director of Excise and Licenses, and I have a very business-friendly approach.'"

He didn't hear back.

Downey was not a conventional regulator within the taxi industry. In Denver, Excise and Licenses covered a wide gamut of industries, the largest of which was alcohol, following by alarm services, taxis, and a short time later, recreational marijuana. He didn't know anything about the traditional taxi supply caps or the history of deregulation and re-regulation in the 1980s. But as chair of the Denver Taxi Advisory Council, he had an influential presence, and since Uber ignored his phone calls, he found it easy to join the group mentality that they needed to take some kind of action. He had also called Ron Linton in DC and begun asking about his experiences.

Meanwhile, in mid-September, transportation staff at the Colorado PUC had called and managed to get through to Uber's general counsel, Salle Yoo, who had been on the job for all of two months.[77] Yoo was previously a partner at Davis Wright Tremaine and had expertise arguing energy regulation in front of California's PUC, among other agencies.[78] She was aptly experienced to engage with regulators, especially at a utilities commission.

Yoo and a PUC transportation manager discussed alterations to Uber's app that would bring it into compliance with Colorado's regulations. Chiefly, their main concern was that the app should show a prearranged price before a black car was summoned.[79] Uber was already developing an updated 2.0 version of its app, and one of the newly planned features would allow passengers to obtain a fare estimate in advance.[80] Yoo informed them that Uber would release the new version on November 1.[81]

For the moment, the Colorado PUC was satisfied enough not to worry about Uber's compliance issues. But few others among the advisory council were satisfied. A Denver Airport ground transportation manager, still learning about the company for the first time, forwarded a Craigslist ad for an apparent unlicensed car offering rides from the airport to downtown for thirty-seven dollars. Mistaking it for Uber's service, he said, "I would think … limos trying to operate like de-facto cabs would be problematic."[82]

But from the PUC's perspective, Uber was violating little. State law required that limos schedule rides on a prearranged basis, but there was no time limit spelled out to clarify what that should look like. "As long as the limo is not negotiating with the [customer] at or near the point of departure, or parked in front of or across the street from a hotel … then there would not be a violation," a chief enforcement officer told other PUC and airport regulators.[83]

A week later the advisory council met again, and the Uber issue still had not been laid to rest. None of them could seem to make up their minds. The Yellow Cab manager insisted Uber was a taxi company, while a limo owner claimed they were a brokerage and communications firm. Tom Downey told them he would like to see the group discretely obtain an attorney general opinion on Uber. Another limo owner said Uber looked a taxi company to him.[84]

All that was clear was that they remained worried and uncertain.

Meanwhile, the Colorado PUC quietly geared up for a bait and switch to put Uber on the ropes.

CHAPTER SIX

Conference

About ten days before the November 2012 IATR Conference in Washington, DC, the Smartphone App Committee had one more conference call. They had held roughly three in total since the committee was formed in late June. The group was finally presented with a draft of the model regulations for vetting and final comments.[1]

As drafted, the regulations offered an à la carte menu of functional distinctions between taxis and limousines, and they prevented companies like Uber from using black cars to offer a taxi-like service. The rules made it clear that an immediate summoning of a car was no different than a street hail, a customer base most cities had legally reserved to taxis. Black cars could arrange trips through an app but only if they occurred at least thirty minutes after they were requested. No black car could use any device to calculate a fare of any kind, and all limo services needed to charge a minimum fare. Smartphone applications were obligated to obtain dispatch licenses and couldn't use their application as a taximeter until NIST had given its approval.[2]

The regulations also clarified what was and wasn't permissible for apps that dispatched taxis. Such apps would be required to integrate with a parent company's dispatching system, could not replace a cab's taximeter, and could not charge a customer for using the app.[3] Once implemented, these provisions were sure to benefit apps like TaxiMagic and Cabulous that already followed such rules, and they would certainly harm direct-to-driver apps like UberTAXI and Hailo, both of which the taxi industry hated.

Effectively, all the proposed regulations did was push apart taxis and limousines so that they did not interact with one another, preventing what the model rules referred to as "unfair cross-market competition."[4] They didn't ban smartphone apps altogether but to said that if they were used, then they played by traditional rules as the taxi world had known them. But there was no discussion in the model regulations about ways to improve the reliability of taxi service, as Hayashi had been attempting in San Francisco, which certainly would have been relevant.

When it came to reliability of service, most of the cities were all suffering from the same core problem: the taxi industry profited on supply constraints, strict market barriers, high rents extracted from indentured drivers, and resistance to credit cards. All were shortcomings that Uber's system exploited to encroach on their taxi rivals. Customers flocked to Uber because it was more reliable than taxis, a point that the model regulations never acknowledged. Nothing within them sought to change the taxi industry for the better so that Uber would be unnecessary. Instead, they simply raised the market barriers even higher so that Uber could not participate.

By all indications Daus's firm, Windels Marx Lane & Mittendorf, drafted the regulations and periodically vetted them to the app committee. Strangely, while reviewing them for the final time before the conference, neither NIST nor most of the eight cities in attendance had any comments to offer. It was as though they weren't familiar with them, and thus, were reluctant to say anything out of turn. Instead, most of them simply gave status updates related to Uber up to that point.[5]

Regulators in Philadelphia and Toronto had met with Kalanick earlier in the year. In Boston, there was no movement at all on Uber as an issue, and three months had passed since the Massachusetts Division of Standards fracas. Craig Leisy noted that Seattle had "a huge problem with the manner in which Uber calculates its fares," but more of a pressing concern was the introduction of a relatively new ridesharing company: SideCar.[6]

"Regulators should be cautioned that these types of companies are growing and will enter more markets," Leisy told them.[7]

As Daus offered aide to the industry by crafting a regulatory environment where taxi smartphone apps could thrive, New York regulators said very little. They would only comment that the model rules appeared consistent with the newly proposed rules for their smartphone app RFP. Also, they agreed that an automatic gratuity could not be generated.[8] Overall, New York's reaction was reserved, as though they didn't consider Uber a real threat at all.

The app committee also discussed the way the model regulations should be presented at the conference. Above all, they wanted to be clear that they were communicating the regulations in a "uniform voice," especially as "app companies and representatives will be in attendance at the IATR." But their uniform voice was only for the purpose of the conference. They were afraid that if they tried to explain their position in a public forum, they would be shouted down. It was decided that social media should be used sparingly because "it is best for 'opining' but it should not be utilized for 'understanding,'" as the minutes noted.[9]

Matt Daus also gave an update on the TLPA's opinion of the IATR's work. "Daus convinced the TLPA that the regulators are not the concern for the industry.... Although lawsuits have been discussed, the TLPA's intent is to fight back against Uber in the media."[10]

Indeed, the nation's largest association of taxi owners had been an active player in Matt Daus's crusade against Uber. The TLPA had formed their own app committee to study Uber, Hailo, and other apps it had issues with. Since July, Daus had been traveling the globe advocating against "rogue" smartphone apps that might take over their markets. The September meeting at NIST headquarters in Maryland was merely one of several stops. Daus had also flown to the TLPA's midyear leadership conference in Niagara Falls, the

TLPA Convention and Trade Show in Las Vegas, the Limo Digest Show in Atlantic City, and TLPA-like conferences in Abu Dhabi, Australia, and Germany.[11]

In Cologne, Germany, Daus attended the International Taxi Forum a week before the IATR Conference, where he gave a PowerPoint presentation using a dark, ominous picture of the city's cathedral. It was partly a practice run for his upcoming presentation in DC, as he'd reuse several of the slides at the IATR. A few slides would, however, later be replaced, such as one with the headline "Danger to Transportation Businesses." This slide elaborated:[12]

Collaboration with an unruly or rogue app could lead to loss of:
- Drivers
- Reputation with customers
- Goodwill (Its the app not the company that may matter with passengers in the long run)
- Total dependency to an app company
- Diminished service coverage to longstanding corporate clients
- Loss of brand

Another slide that Daus would leave out at the IATR Conference asked, "How Can You Protect Your Business?" It suggested that cab companies develop their own app (or contract with one that was already legal), carefully reviewing all third-party app contracts and being vigilant. Daus's presentation also offered hope to the taxi industry, noting that the IATR had created an app committee to develop a model code of regulations. The slides pointed out that the IATR's app committee had been working with the TLPA's app committee.[13]

This was the duplicity of Matt Daus's leadership at the IATR. If he was in front of regulators, he spoke about Uber in terms of danger to public safety. If he was in front of the taxi industry, he spoke about Uber in terms of harm to their business. Like the regulators he served, he aligned with the industry's self-interest to cushion against competition, their solemn belief that unmitigated competition only harmed taxis as a public utility and eroded the public protections that had existed for decades.

But regulators usually operated like referees, not partners. When they received complaints about Uber, they would then *tell* the taxi companies how they would work to fix it, regardless of whether they liked the solution or not. Instead, Daus directly partnered with the industry at the highest levels and enlisted their help to make sure they found the outcome favorable. Through the IATR, the line between regulator and industry dissolved so much that it was difficult to tell the difference between the two.

On November 16, 2012, the second day of the annual three-day conference at the five-star Four Seasons Hotel in the upscale Georgetown neighborhood of Washington, DC, Matt Daus finally gave his presentation on rogue apps titled "There's an App for That!" Dressed in a tasteful dark black suit and gold tie, with cufflinks and well-groomed hair, he gave the first presentation of the entire conference.[14] The room was filled with taxi regulators who had – or would soon have – conflicts with Uber. In addition to most of the Smartphone App Committee, it included Arlington and Fairfax Counties, Virginia; Austin, Houston, and San Antonio, Texas; Minneapolis; Portland, Oregon; Hillsborough County and Miami, Florida; and both the Maryland and Pennsylvania state utilities commissions. They were flanked on all sides by taxi companies, vendors, and a few academics.[15] Quietly sitting and observing from the back were about a dozen Uber employees, who were the target audience for much of the day. And although not registered for the conference, Kalanick was popping in and out as well.

Daus began his presentation trying to keep his tone light, offering brief levity with cheesy jokes. He talked about how several people had been calling him up that year asking about Uber, so much so that he began to be seen as the go-to app expert for the taxi industry. "Anyone here a *Seinfeld* fan?" he asked as he showed a photo of a New York vanity license plate that read "APPMAN."[16]

Daus then transitioned, framing the state of the world that had been turned upside down by Uber. As he had frequently stated before in his half-Brooklyn accent, he said that the taxi industry was in the "Wild West" thanks to apps. He put up a slide showing a sample of over fifty taxi-related app icons and scrawled over it in large lettering, "ALL APPS ARE NOT CREATED EQUAL!" He presented an *Oxford* definition of "rogue," emphasizing that it was "behaving in ways that are not expected or not normal, often in a destructive way." He then showed a picture of Sarah Palin.[17]

Reflecting much of the "rogue" smartphone apps white paper his firm had authored over the summer, Daus then went into the legal issues surrounding Uber, but instead of using their name, he simply referred to "rogue apps" generally. To speak of Uber anonymously was farcical. Nearly all of the "rogue app" controversies in 2012 pertained only to Uber, the model regulations were primarily designed for Uber, and everyone in the room knew which "rogue app" Daus was referencing.

Often holding his own smartphone in the air, he spent ten minutes listing all the ways their service could be abused, regardless if they were common issues or only potential dangers:[18]

- If a third party sent you a car, how would someone know that it had been properly licensed and insured? [Uber's black-car service had only worked with properly licensed limo companies.]

- "Service refusals... I mean, you could actually look at some apps on the tipping history and decide, 'You know what? This person didn't tip me too well, I'm not going to take them this time.'"

- There was NIST and the fact that smartphones had not yet been approved as a measuring device. In that vein, Daus also espoused the dangers of GPS signal-disrupting devices, which were not in wide circulation.

"So if you have an iPhone app that's operating with time and distance, you could actually shortchange the driver and rip off the driver. Can and *does* happen."

- There was dynamic pricing, the very core of Uber's supply-chain management.

"We've heard a lot about surge pricing. It's pretty much, pretty clear to I think all of the regulators that surge pricing is overcharging. It's illegal. It's ripping people off."

- One of Uber's more significant disruptions was that its business was so profitable to licensed chauffeur drivers that taxi drivers were fleeing their lease and medallion payments to become black-car drivers.

"The reality is that a rogue app in New York City is taking the passengers away from livery and taxi businesses and stealing the drivers of the black-car businesses. It's a real nice bait and switch. And I can guarantee you that that's the business plan of rogue apps in other cities."

- An area where the tech industry and transportation regulators collided with one another was the app's terms and conditions, also known as "contracts of adhesion." No taxi or limo company was ever permitted to waive its liability in the event of an accident, and despite having massive control over the transaction, Uber forced users and drivers alike to indemnify the company. This was common in the software industry, but integrated with a real-world car service, it made regulators extremely nervous.

"Someone gets killed or some gets hurt – 'We had nothing to do with it. So, you just sign your rights away as a taxi company, as a driver, or as a passenger, okay?' That doesn't happen in American or in any civilized country like our members. And it shouldn't happen."

Just like in the Smartphone App Committee, Daus then took a few minutes to spell out what the model regulations would accomplish. He ended his presentation by throwing down a gauntlet to the twelve Uber staff in the back.

"This is serious, okay? It's not a joke. We are going to pass these regs. The IATR ... is going to spend all of 2013 ... going to each and every jurisdiction that requests our help. If we have to testify, we're going to testify, okay? If we have to get [our lobbyist] ... we're going to lobby, okay? If we have to be subpoenaed to testify in lawsuits, we'll show up."[19]

Ironically, Daus then shifted to a calmer demeanor, asking "people" to tone down the rhetoric.[20] In reality, he was asking Kalanick to stop casting blame upon regulators.

"Let's all be cordial and nice. Let's turn over a new leaf. This is a new day. Let's put the rhetoric behind us, okay? I think we have, like, fifty reps from Uber here. Travis, thanks for coming. We're happy you're here. We want to hear what you have to say, okay? ... The regulators have an open mind and they're going to tell you exactly how they feel.... We want to do the right thing by everybody, but you need to understand, we're not cronies, okay? We're not in anybody's pocket. Believe me, [the regulators] aren't in anybody's pocket. They won't even take a cup of coffee from you if you wanted to. They're just doing their *jobs*.... People in the industry are very quick to point out, 'Well, you're not doing anything.' Well you know what, we're doing something today. Okay, so you can either get on the bus or you can chase after it. Thank you."[21]

The few regulators who had attended IATR conferences before Matt Daus became president could surely sense a changing aura. The association was fast becoming more lavish and extravagant. Money was becoming a prominent force. At the five-star Georgetown Four Seasons Hotel, the food and beverage bill alone was $110,000 (roughly $500 per head), more than the association *received* in conference fees, but they also brought vastly more in revenues than the conference had ever seen before Daus's presidency. In years past, they had often booked the conference room at a budget motel and secured a modest catering budget.[22]

The regulators were not more likely to attend because of the newfound extravagance. For them, the conference was mainly a means to keep up to date with emerging issues and convince their city governments that they were still in the loop with industry concerns. But the IATR Conference was also an opportunity for the taxi industry to rub elbows with their gatekeepers, to use the association as a conduit to gain influence with its members. And once they did, Matt Daus used every conceivable opportunity to extract revenues out of the sponsors, much as the taxi companies extracted fees out of their own drivers.

No stranger to insider influence, Daus was used to such horse trades. They had become secondary to his positions as both taxi expert and IATR president, an unspoken but continuous trading of favors back and forth. For example, as a taxi expert, he was influential in helping the Philadelphia Parking Authority overhaul new taxi and limo regulations in 2011.[23] But Daus was also general counsel to the Limousine Association of New Jersey, whose president was CEO of the limousine company Flyte Tyme.[24] Earlier in 2012, when Flyte Tyme performed a stock transfer with the Philadelphia company American Limo, Daus worked with the Philadelphia taxi regulator (who later became an IATR Board member) to ensure it went smoothly.[25]

Daus looked for any opportunity to reach beyond his regulator-members to dip a toe in the local taxi industry. Before Hayashi was given her marching orders to auction medallions in San Francisco for the first time in decades,

Daus had already talked to then-Mayor Gavin Newsom.

"I had a visit from Mayor Newsom," he said at one conference, "who actually came to my office and sat for a while and asked me, 'What's up? What's up with you, and how can we make San Francisco better?'"[26]

In another case in 2012, the IATR had just started issuing an award to the "Regulator of the Year," and some of the likely candidates were pushing hard to receive the honor. While finalizing the 2012 conference, Daus reached out to the Chicago taxi regulator and asked, "Any chance to get your mayor to come?"[27] The IATR had thus far booked Transportation Secretary Ray LaHood's general counsel, but to get Rahm Emanuel, President Obama's former chief of staff and Chicago's mayor, would have been a big coup.[28] The regulator replied that it couldn't hurt to ask. Daus then sweetened the deal.

"If you think it's a real possibility that your Mayor would come if the city gets the award, I will draft the letter. Thx," he wrote to her.[29]

"And if he doesn't, Chicago loses?" she asked.[30]

"No... but it will make the decision easier and put u over top with board," Daus replied back.[31]

This was the horse trading that Daus negotiated back and forth between regulators, the regulated, and their vendors. At the 2012 conference, Daus had even found a way to leverage the niche industry of transportation-related smartphone apps. He'd secured sponsorships from TaxiMagic, Cabulous, and strangely, Hailo, but he also had the IATR executive director, Karen Cameron, reach out to virtually any app company, including several smaller ones that were trying to carve out a market share, such as GetTaxi, Fleetbit, ZabKab, and FastCab.[32]

Many of them had something to gain from being sponsors. Several of the taxi apps were also applicants for New York's smartphone RFP, and included in the audience was New York's TLC chair (and Daus's successor), who was going to have a strong say in the matter.[33]

The carrot Daus dangled was more expensive than usual. In a typical year, the four levels of conference sponsorship were Bronze ($2,500), Silver ($5,000), Gold ($7,500), and Platinum ($10,000). But in 2012, he added a fifth level: Platinum Plus. For $12,500 a company not only purchased the ability to speak in one of the panel sessions, but on the first day, they could offer a "concurrent session" where they could present their product by tying it into a taxi or limo issue.[34]

On the very first day of the 2012 conference, the regulators spent the afternoon attending a variety of sponsored breakout sessions. The company VerifEye, for example, advertised its internal cab cameras by hosting a session titled "Safety Camera Programs – What Works, What Doesn't."[35] In effect, taxi vendors who were also presenters sold themselves to regulators as worthy experts, as though they had been handpicked and vetted by this regulatory association whose president was a taxi expert himself.

The reason Matt Daus waited until the second day for his "There's an App for That" presentation is because the first day was *entirely* dedicated to helping the association pay its bills. Taking advantage of the fact that they were in DC, the IATR organized a morning "Day on the Hill," where regulators traveled around congressional offices to lobby what would become known as the PASS Act, the bill to grant the IATR access to federal background-check databases.[36] After shuttling everyone back from the Hill, the afternoon was dedicated to the taxi-vendor workshops, and that evening, everyone was treated to a welcoming-reception gala at the Swedish Embassy, filled with even more sponsors, exhibits, and vehicle displays.[37]

Nearly every aspect of the conference was for sale. If a vendor wanted their name to ring out repeatedly, the IATR sold à la carte sponsorships. Name badges, portfolios, Friday evening's entertainment, Friday evening's dinner, refreshment breaks, an invitation-only cigar reception, a hospitality suite – all for sale because the IATR offered a captive audience of regulators.[38]

Sponsorship opportunities are not uncommon for regulatory

conferences. They're how such associations keep the lights on and their prices low, a cost of doing business. But in the days before Matt Daus's presidency, the IATR netted no more than $10,000 in sponsorships in any given year. They were much more modest affairs. They sometimes splurged for rooftop social events but not galas or sponsors' receptions. In a typical year they spent upwards of $70,000, most of which went to food, and still lost $10,000 after it was over. After Daus became president, the association got out of the red and became solvent, thanks in large part to sponsorships that increased nearly sixfold in his first year alone.[39]

By 2012, the change was staggering. Total revenues virtually doubled, reaching an astounding $200,000. But despite the dramatic increase, they usually spent almost as much as they took in. The association was still only netting $10,000 or less in most years, and in an unusual move, Daus comped thirty-one registration fees in 2012.[40] Karen Cameron, the IATR executive director and certified conference planner whose job was to organize the annual meetings, found it strange. They were already spending so much money that it seemed odd to subsidize attendees. She once asked a TLPA representative how many attendees they comped at their conferences and was told it was as many as three.

Subsidization was also a way to bring in new regulators, expose them to the IATR's philosophy, and then leverage their attendance. For example, in September 2012, while Tom Downey was in Denver still waiting for Uber to call him back, one of his fellow Excise and Licenses investigators, Larry Stevenson, encouraged him to attend the upcoming IATR Conference. Stevenson was a former employee of Metro Taxi, whose owner, Robert McBride, was a former TLPA President. Few knew it at the time, but Stevenson was still taking money from Metro Taxi, an illegal conflict of interest and misdemeanor charge he would plead guilty to years later.[41] Downey told both Stevenson and McBride that he couldn't attend the conference because there wasn't enough money in the city budget to cover the registration fees. In response, McBride suggested he ask Daus for a fee waiver, and Daus was happy to oblige.[42]

It wasn't unusual for a trade association to give new members their first conference for free, but Matt Daus had further intentions. Two weeks before Downey agreed to attend, Daus contacted Cameron.

From: Daus, Matthew
To: Karen Cameron
Sent: Saturday, September 15, 2012 8:31 AM

... 2 things - I got Tom Downey of Denver tlc to join. will get you info.....(2) please reach out to matt bellizia of mt data, and tell him robert mcbride asked you to call and lock in a sponsorship. mcbride is very involved with them and spoke to matt - i think mcbride is his no 1 customer

---

MTData was the vendor Metro Taxi hired for their fleet's smartphone app, which launched in August when Uber entered the Denver market. It's not entirely clear why Daus directed Cameron to pretend Metro Taxi's owner had reached out to her. But Downey's comped attendance certainly gave him a more compelling reason to do so. MTData would have one more regulator, the chair of the Denver Taxi Advisory Council, they could touch in a room full of like-minded taxi professionals. Effectively, Downey was being invited to his first taxi regulator convention so peers could help him discern which vendors and regulations were good or bad, and Matt Daus was the voice of authority deciding which was which.

The massive amount of sponsorships also distorted the conference in another way. In 2012, there were 198 registrants, and if anyone could look around the room and identify them all, they'd realize that regulators only made up a minority of this *regulator's* conference. Even excluding the twelve Uber representatives, regulators still made up less than 40 percent of the registered attendees. Nearly half were an amalgam of taxi companies, taxi app or equipment manufacturers, and other vendors. Capital One and Signature Financial, both of whom were active in medallion financing, also brought about ten reps between them.[43] But as long as the conference continued to address taxi regulation issues, no one openly questioned who it was the IATR was ultimately serving.

As Daus was giving his "There's an App for That!" presentation, ten feet to his left was a table filled with seven app vendors who had paid hefty fees to pitch the benefits of their services. After Daus finished, they rose to the podium one at a time to make their case. Some had to try harder than others. Among the presenters was Hailo, the direct-to-driver app that, ironically, would not fare well under the IATR's proposed model regulations. The sponsors also included the TLPA itself, whose president gave a surprisingly frank lecture about how the supply constraints of the industry had more or less created Uber.

"When Matt [Daus] says it's not the regulators' fault, I would disagree with that," the TLPA president said to the room. "It's really all of our faults – the proliferation of these apps. What is going on out there is that in certain situations, passengers simply cannot get transportation. And when that happens, that is the necessity that will breed the invention of an app."[44]

He hit the nail on the head and in a way that Daus had yet to acknowledge. Uber came to prominence because of the supply caps that had made taxi service historically unreliable.

"The supply of taxicabs in our industry has never been designed to meet the demand of every trip," he continued. "When you have an industry where the economics are that the driver must earn a sustainable wage, that means when you're dealing with peaks and valleys in demand, you are not going to be able to flood the market with taxicabs and suppress driver incomes enough to meet every trip."[45]

He was referring to the way a city calculates the number of drivers it allows on the road. If a city set the number of cabs to meet *average* demand, the result was a lackluster supply that Uber had exploited. "Average demand" was a flat calculation, and in reality, demand rose and fell throughout the day. In peak rush-hour periods, customers would have a harder time getting a cab under this model, and Uber filled that gap.

It was a refreshing identification of the taxi problem, but that's as far as it went. The TLPA president was only suggesting that more had to be done to increase efficiencies. In Los Angeles, for example, taxi companies were rated each year on how well and how quickly they responded to phone orders, and those with bad ratings were punished.[46] Regulators and the industry needed to work together to ensure that services like Uber wouldn't soak up the excess demand left on the table. But he left out one key obstacle. The financial incentives of everyone in the industry – drivers, taxi owners, and medallion owners – all depended on a constrained supply of cabs. Carrot-and-stick incentives would be an uphill battle, and even if successful, they would only be a partial solution. Uber hadn't just created incentives to maximize trips. It had programmed supply-chain management into its algorithm, and the taxi industry was still far behind in catching up.

After lunch, the panel sessions moved on to the perspective of the regulators themselves. Daus selected a panel from the Smartphone App Committee to speak briefly on their impressions of the model regulations. New and old members included Boston, Denver (with Tom Downey), San Diego, New York, Los Angeles, Montreal, and Austin. Most were enthusiastic. Tom Downey said he would take the model regulations to the Colorado PUC and say "please take these on, please adopt them; we think they're great." Downey would later recall that the model regulations made sense to him because of the consumer protections. He didn't inherently dislike Uber, but the company's unwillingness to talk scared him.

At the same panel session, the Austin regulator said simply, "We support the model regulations and look forward to moving towards implementation."[47] It was an omen of fights to come later in Austin.

But once more, New York's reticence stuck out like a sore thumb. Matt

Daus's successor at the TLC, David Yassky, would only thank the IATR for their hard work. Politely, he hinted that the model regulations were unnecessary in his city except for how they applied to yellow cabs.[48] In his mind, there was no need to alter the existing limo market so that Uber couldn't compete. It was one of a series of signals since the previous year that the TLC was not going to move against Uber. They would give them every benefit of the doubt and rein them in when needed, but they would not move to shut their app down.

Arguably, much of the sponsored presentations were for Yassky's benefit. Cabulous, Hailo, GetTaxi, Verifone, and Creative Mobile Technologies were all Platinum Plus sponsors and had all submitted bids for New York's smartphone RFP.[49] Nissan, whose model NV200 taxi had been selected for a lucrative, ten-year Taxi of Tomorrow contract, was entering legal and political mires in New York, and they also chipped in a $12,500 contribution.[50]

For the rest of the hour-long session, the panel took questions and comments from the audience. Among those who stood, it became clear they had not yet had time to read the model regulations and simply espoused varied opinions about regulating apps in general. In short, no one proclaimed any love for Uber. The running theme of their comments, which spoke to the taxi industry as a whole, was a resistance to change. Smartphone apps were scary not because they were a *technological* improvement but because they represented an ease of use that threatened their market dynamic.

Even adding new regulations to keep Uber away was in itself worrisome. A taxi operator from neighboring northern Virginia stood up to request that as regulators implemented the model regulations, they should "dance with who brung you. If you developed a local regulatory system – in our case, [public convenience and necessity] ... then don't uproot that in the interest of doing something new in order to accommodate apps coming into your market."[51]

Another speaker from Toronto said it more bluntly. "It seems to me the underlying concern here is self-interest, the protection of the existing regime. There is concern about this revolution that's taking place worldwide in the taxi industry."[52]

Much of the hour went on like this. Each speaker took a whack at the Uber piñata, begging regulators not to let "progress" undermine their revenues and offering small suggestions to shut out Uber a little longer. One of the perils they discussed was the potential of unlicensed bandit cabs to sneak onto an app as a de facto dispatch service. This was largely a criticism of UberTAXI and Hailo, as some wondered how the companies could prove that only licensed drivers used their platforms. And in all likelihood, they didn't realize they were also predicting a future iteration of apps already present on the West Coast: Lyft and SideCar.

Among the audience, only one speaker discussed some of the taxi deficiencies that made Uber more competitive. George Lutfallah, owner and publisher of the taxi publication *Chicago Dispatcher*, told a story about Uber's superior reliability (while breaking the unwritten rule of saying Uber's name aloud). Similar to what Ryan Graves had written in an Uber blog post years earlier, Lutfallah recalled needing a cab to the Chicago airport to fly to the TLPA trade show in Vegas but finding none available. In a crunch, he downloaded and used the Uber app. Although the car took twenty-four minutes to arrive, that was still faster than the local Yellow Cab. "Anyway, I got to the TLPA, and I got to hear about how awful Uber is when I got to Las Vegas," he told the audience.

Lutfallah was trying to use his story to point out why Uber was faster. Because each taxi fleet often used a different app, there were too many of them to compete effectively against Uber.[53] It was a valid point, although it did not seem to carry much weight with the audience. Trying to convince the taxi industry they needed to combine forces was futile, another resistance to change.

Aside from Lutfallah, no one had anything remotely positive to say about Uber. The response was nearly as unified as Daus had planned. For their part, the Uber reps spent most of the proceedings quietly watching from the back as an entire industry badmouthed them without saying their name (with one exception). They were watching an industry pushing against the tide.

On the surface, the industry might have appeared "unified," but deep rifts still permeated, and the hour-long session at times turned existential. Who was supposed to profit from the taxi industry? Owner or driver? Who was supposed to shoulder the costs of upgrades? Owner, driver, or passenger? Uber had landed in the middle of an ongoing regulatory feud, and the only thing the industry was certain of was the need to toss them out, or else none of the other questions would matter. Without a market to share, they'd all lose.

As the session came to an end, Daus gave an Uber rep the chance to speak. Rather than going on a rant, the rep invited all the regulators to a separate session – not sponsored by the IATR – at the end of the day. Uber had privately booked the Four Seasons' Algonquin Room, and Kalanick himself would be there. "Travis will have a few things to say on the topics. You guys can ask some candid questions, and we'll just have a frank discussion," he said.[54] A half-hour later, Uber even sent them an email reminder. "Appetizers and open bar will be provided. Look forward to chatting soon!"[55]

The vendors were upset. There wasn't supposed to be any separate session. They had spent several thousand dollars promoting themselves in front of regulators, and for the cost of a meeting room, Uber was effectively piggybacking on their conference. Furthermore, they were undermining the value and access sponsors attributed to the IATR. Still, there was little Daus could do to stop it.

Some of the regulators attended Kalanick's side session, while others were either uninterested or not allowed to attend any meeting in which booze was freely available. But by all accounts, it was simply a pitch by Kalanick, a plea to recognize the benefits of Uber's service. There was no dialogue about how regulations should be changed so that Uber could exist either alongside or as a competitor to taxis.

Kalanick probably felt that his service inherently benefited the public interest, but for his audience of regulators, the public interest was already defined by state and local laws. *Taxis* were the ordained service, and whether or not there were loopholes, there was nothing to indicate lawmakers intended to allow for a taxi-like black-car service. Market barriers were set up for a reason.

There was an underlying question Kalanick failed to address to the regulators themselves: If a superior competitor enters the market, should regulators care what happens to taxis? By all indications, he thought the answer was obvious: they shouldn't, because Uber was more efficient. The regulators also thought the answer was obvious: they should, because the law said so.

The IATR 2012 Conference came and went with game plans and hints of the future, but neither side had moved the other from their intractable positions. *The Wall Street Journal* and later *The New York Times* (the latter of which had attended the conference as an observer) covered the model regulations.[56] By coincidence, earlier in the week, the California PUC had finally acted on Hayashi's request to beef up enforcement and levied $20,000 fines against Lyft, SideCar, and Uber. It was the first major punitive action against any of the transportation app companies, and the media's interest intensified. Because of the citations, *The Journal* and *The Times* were looking at the model regulations as they pertained to ridesharing companies, even though that issue wasn't yet on Daus's radar. But as the app committee had predicted before the conference began, they weren't going to win this battle in social media.

After the stories published, Daus forwarded to the IATR Board a couple of examples of the negative feedback he'd received, which appear to have come from financial investors interested in Uber. They sent Daus pro-Uber complaints with subject lines like "GPS is good enough for the US military" and accused him of taxi protectionism.[57]

Daus wrote to the board, "I have received a slew of email from Uber people   totally ridiculous. i am happy to be a crony i guess."[58]

In a post-conference breakdown, he also informed the board, "Fyi ... btw, every single sponsor is upset we allowed Uber to be on our premises and to undermine our non-rogue sponsors."[59]

Karen Cameron, the IATR's conference planner, responded with her two cents. She was beginning to show signs of discomfort with Daus's relationship with the taxi industry and reported that Uber had spent so much money in registration fees – nearly $10,000 – that they were practically sponsors themselves.[60]

As for sponsorships, "IATR becomes vulnerable to undue influence of sponsors and industry participants the greater the levels of contribution," she reported. "We are dangerously close to the upper limits."[61]

Cameron had reason to be concerned. Although she was one of the IATR's few outside hires, much of the conference support staff were employees of Daus's law firm, Windels Marx. During the first night's reception at the Swedish Embassy, one of the taxi vendors had handed Cameron a document, mistaking her for one of Daus's legal staff. According to Cameron, it was a retainer agreement to hire Windels Marx as outside counsel.

The 2012 IATR Conference foreshadowed the regulatory battles heading into 2013, many of which the IATR would actively participate in. The Uber reps sitting in the back seemingly didn't notice Tom Downey say he was talking with his friends at the Colorado PUC about implementing the model regulations. PUC officials had previously negotiated with Uber a deal to at least move past the major issues if Uber installed a fare-estimate feature in its app. But the November 1 deadline passed, and Uber didn't release their revamped 2.0 app, which included the fare estimate, until December. When they did, the new feature wasn't exactly an estimate but a narrow range of prices the rider might pay. Unsatisfied, the PUC quietly moved forward with a strategy to push them out of the market by 2013.

At the same time, Austin, Texas, had entered the fight. Earlier in 2012, Austin saw its own version of an upstart ridesharing smartphone app, HeyRide, launch much in the same way that Lyft and SideCar had: without asking for permission, they simply jumped in. Austin, the largest city in America with only one interstate running through it, was prone to several congestion problems, especially during major festivals like South by Southwest (SXSW) or the Austin City Limits Music Festival. HeyRide's founder was inspired to create the program during the prior SXSW conference in March. Exhausted and unable to find a cab, he walked up to a normal-looking stranger in a Volvo and convinced him to give him a ride home in exchange for ten bucks. Together with a handful of programmers in a small office, he then created an app that, like SideCar, allowed passengers to announce their need for a ride digitally and select their preferred nearby car.[62]

HeyRide was the Austin taxi industry's first major bandit competitor in several years, and the local Yellow Cab Company was nervous. If Silicon Valley was where the tech industry developed products, SXSW was one of the prominent marketplaces where they were bought and sold. An app like HeyRide was likely to gain traction in a company town like Austin. Months before HeyRide even launched, Yellow Cab's president, Ed Kargbo, sent the local taxi regulator a copy of Daus's "rogue" smartphone apps white paper.

"This is the best work to date on rogue apps (as we discussed the other day)," Kargbo wrote to him.[63]

But Austin's Yellow Cab wasn't a typical standalone taxi company. Its parent company, Texas Taxi, Inc., owned the Yellow Cab fleets in Houston, San Antonio, Austin, and Galveston, making it one of the most lucrative taxi companies in the state.[64] The general manager for each fleet was more or less the ambassador for the parent company's interests. And as it happened, MTData, the same company working with Metro Taxi when Uber entered the Denver market, also created Texas Taxi's smartphone app. They called it HAIL A CAB and released it in October 2012, roughly the same time HeyRide launched.[65] In the world of smartphone apps with a taxi-like fleet, Texas Taxi now had a direct competitor running an unlicensed service.

That same month, as HeyRide started to gain profile and appear on the cover of local Austin publications, the Austin Transportation Department (ATD) sent them a cease-and-desist letter. HeyRide suspected that the taxi community and the ATD were working closely together. They had received a tweet from an Austin cab driver showing a photo of their cease-and-desist order before it was announced on the news.[66] HeyRide was right, but they didn't know the full extent of it.

Days before the IATR Conference, Ed Kargbo forwarded the ATD a copy of a private investigator's (PI) report. On the weekend of November 10, the PI had used the HeyRide app three times and provided detailed descriptions of each experience. "Laura D. appeared to have facial stud/jewelry," he reported of one driver.[67] The PI even forwarded a customer service email he'd clandestinely sent to HeyRide to determine on which type of smartphone their app was available.

From: [Private Investigator]
To: Support@Heyride.com
Sent: Friday, November 9, 2012 9:02 PM

Trying to download to IPAD and Android to use ride service. No luck. Here

---

for weekend while daughter at [University of Texas]. She is busy with school and I need short trips to see Austin and game. Can you help. Liked website and the donations being made to a worthy cause. Rather use your service than cabs.

Although Uber was not yet operating in Austin, HeyRide's unregulated presence was enough of a reason for both Texas Taxi and the ATD to join the IATR's fight against rogue smartphone apps. Texas Taxi registered for the conference as a Platinum sponsor and brought their CEO and two major fleet managers, including Kargbo, to the conference.[68] Along with TaxiMagic and Cabulous, they too presented their app, HAIL A CAB, app in front of the regulators. Austin's taxi regulator, Carlton Thomas, had also registered and joined the IATR's Smartphone App Committee.[69] As one of the regulator panelists reviewing the model regulations, he was one of the voices of encouragement who simply said, "We like the model regulations and look forward to implementing them."[70]

Kargbo relentlessly kept his taxi regulator abreast of HeyRide, noting instances when drivers were advertising themselves or when the company appeared on the radio or in the news.[71] On November 21, the ATD director sent the city manager a memo stating HeyRide's operation "very closely resembles that of a taxi franchise," and in Austin, franchises had to be approved by the city.[72] They threatened to issue citations to any drivers caught using the platform. HeyRide was the starter pistol of a years-long campaign Austin's transportation regulators had initiated against ridesharing, which would eventually envelop Uber.

In California, the taxi industry thought they had made some headway after the CPUC issued $20,000 citations to each of the three major companies a week before the IATR Conference. Uber's citation even referenced the case number that was opened in their 2010 cease-and-desist letter.[73] It took nearly two years, but the regulators had finally caught up with them.

Down on the second floor, the safety division had been gearing up for this moment. After the catastrophic San Bruno explosion, a new director was hired in April 2012, former Brigadier General E. Jack Hagan. A warm-spirited and highly disciplined former investigator of the California Bureau of Investigation, he'd sign his emails with the phrase, "No better friend – no worse enemy!" A licensed law enforcement officer, he transitioned to the PUC's San Francisco offices still holstering a gun and a knife, making some of his coworkers uncomfortable.[74]

As a Citadel graduate and career officer in the US Marine Corps since the Vietnam War, General Hagan had a die-hard sense of military organizational efficiency and a strong track record of applying it to new programs and disheveled agencies.[75] In 2003, he organized California's first homeland security readiness and response exercises. Then in 2010 as chief of investigations at the Department of Consumer Affairs, he tackled their overwhelming caseload problem and declining morale. Periodically between jobs, he also worked as a special agent at the California Department of Justice, even once surveilling Scott Peterson before his arrest.

Upon arriving at the CPUC in 2012, General Hagan found a safety division with a haphazard organizational structure that had evolved in a sloppy, ad hoc fashion. His deputy director for limousine enforcement had just retired, and the division itself was underfunded. "It was chewing gum and bailing wire," he said. "Everything was on paper, nothing was automated. One guy didn't return phone calls and didn't use email."

He renamed the division Safety and Enforcement (SED) and spent several months performing an overhaul. In one of the more prominent moves, he disavowed the concept of political capital in their decision making. His policy was that if his staff felt something should be done, then SED should just do it. Period.

According to General Hagan, when Lyft and SideCar launched in San Francisco, "limo drivers started to bitch about them," which was true. Even after the first round of cease-and-desist orders in August against Lyft and SideCar, a chief of staff for one of the CPUC commissioners received a phone call from a San Francisco limo company owner. "This competition is 'skirting the rules and not playing fair,'" the chief of staff quoted the limo owner. "He also tells me that he's tried to reach someone in [SED] Licensing but no one is returning his calls."[76] SideCar and Lyft had ignored the cease-and-desist letters, but from then on, the pressure to move harder had built.

General Hagan had no concept of the traditional regulatory structures between taxis and limousines, especially as limousine regulation only made up a small portion of his oversight duties. But Lyft and SideCar were trying to push the argument that they were an extension of traditional nonprofit carpooling, and General Hagan had enough experience to see through that argument. He remembered what carpooling actually looked like during the energy crisis of the 1970s. In DC, it was so pervasive that even a Marine general couldn't stop a soldier from catching a ride home off-base unless the general also arranged his transport. Despite the fact that Lyft and SideCar accepted money as "voluntary donations," a for-profit smartphone app was not traditional carpooling. At the encouragement of one of his staff members, the same one who sent Uber their original cease-and-desist in 2010, the general followed up on the letters with $20,000 citations.

The Friday before the fines were issued, a group of Bay Area cab drivers filed a class-action lawsuit against Uber, and although coincidental, the timing of the fines probably appeared coordinated.[77] All three of the companies were quickly defiant of the citations, and Lyft especially had rapidly spun them into a media blitz in several tech and San Francisco periodicals. As one reporter noted, "An email signed by John Zimmer and Logan Green ... has been making the rounds, popping into my inbox twice in the space of an hour."[78]

Publicly, General Hagan would only state, "This is a matter of public safety."[79] Still, while Lyft and SideCar were performing "ridesharing" services, Uber was only using licensed black cars, and it wasn't clear what the CPUC had in mind for them. But as it played in the media, it seemed the immediate goal was to reinforce the market barriers every taxi regulator in the country had tried hard to enforce. Daus even mentioned the citations in his IATR Conference speech, characterizing them as a step in the right direction.[80]

What the taxi industry didn't realize at first is that the citations were simply meant to get the app companies' attention. CPUC President Mike Peevey had no intention of shutting them down but instead simply wanted to rein them in. Even as the agency responded to multiple press requests the day after the citations, the CPUC's press officer reminded General Hagan, "We need to demonstrate ... how we are willing to work with the companies on the simple task of getting them properly registered for the safety of their passengers and drivers."[81] In other words, they could operate but not freely and unregulated. Under instructions from the CPUC executive director, General Hagan brought in each company in December to hash out settlement agreements.

In a preliminary meeting with Travis Kalanick, General Hagan found a CEO who was every bit as curt and arrogant toward him as he had been toward the DC City Council only a few months before. "He was an asshole, an obnoxious little shit," said Hagan. Kalanick met him in his office as they sat around a small conference table, and according to the general, the exchange did not go well.

"I don't even know why I'm here, you have no jurisdiction over me," Kalanick reportedly said.

"Why don't we talk about this?" General Hagan replied.

"Jack, I don't think I'm even going to stay," Kalanick said as he prepared to stand up.

"First off, I'm not 'Jack,' I'm 'General Hagan.' And you're here because of the $20,000 fine, and if we don't come to an agreement, I'll issue another one. And then I'll put every enforcement officer I have on the street."

According to the general, Kalanick then "blushed, fussed, and fumed," but he sat down and became more quiet and attentive. For the rest of the month, Hagan met with each app company separately and in occasional joint meetings, but that was his one and only encounter with Kalanick. For the remainder of the negotiations, Salle Yoo represented Uber. By comparison, General Hagan found Lyft distinctly more courteous despite his disdain for their so-called "ridesharing" argument.

While the SED got the ball rolling, Marzia Zafar's office on the fifth floor was beginning to organize a rulemaking session to address transportation smartphone applications. One of Hagan's staff reached out to Christiane Hayashi to invite her to participate; in turn, Hayashi offered him a copy of the IATR model regulations. "Would love to talk to you all about them," Hayashi wrote.[82]

Hagan's staff member replied, "Yes, but now is not a good time for me," as he was busy looking for more local regulators and stakeholders to invite.[83]

A few days before Christmas 2012, the CPUC announced the upcoming rulemaking hearings, stating their intent was "to protect public safety and encourage innovation ... by companies such as Lyft, SideCar, and Uber."[84] Publicly, it had now become clear that the commission was looking to legitimize these companies, not protect the taxi industry. The CPUC had become the first and, for years after, *only* regulatory body in the United States to embrace this new industry.

In January 2013, all three companies signed settlement agreements with the CPUC. The gist of the agreement was that they'd hammer out the specifics in the rulemaking sessions. Until those were finished, and provided they met a few basic requirements, the fines and cease-and-desist letters would be suspended and they could continue to operate unhindered by state regulations (except at airports, where they would need to obtain prior permission). If allowed by the DMV, they would enroll in a "pull notice" program that informed them when their drivers had committed a serious moving violation. They'd institute a zero-tolerance policy for drugs and perform national background checks on their drivers. Other than that, they needed to provide excess liability and property damage insurance, provide a contact person for consumer complaints, contact state weights-and-measures officials to have their app type-certified, and make their documents available for SED review.[85]

Uber did not go along with the settlement agreement easily. For them, this process was still strange. They only used black cars already licensed by the CPUC and viewed themselves as a middleman between drivers and passengers. But the roots of the 2010 cease-and-desist letter had still not been resolved, and the CPUC wanted to attack the "app issue" all at once rather than in a piecemeal fashion. In negotiations, Uber representatives were especially weary of the provision to allow the SED to audit their records unannounced. General Hagan only wanted enough access to ensure Uber was living up to its part of the bargain, but Uber was extremely protective of some of its records, considering them proprietary to their algorithm.

In the meeting, General Hagan looked at the Uber rep and said of the surprise audits, "I'll make you a deal; the only time I'll ever do it is if I bring a warrant."

"Oh, yeah; that sounds great," he recalled the Uber rep saying.

"Do you know how a search warrant works?" the general asked. "Well, let me explain. We'll have twelve guys wearing black vests marked 'police' come by, and we'll take everything. Every scrap of paper. Every billboard posting. Then we're going to go to your office and take everything there. Then we're going to hold you [the attorney] up against a door, and when you tell us that the information in your office is protected by attorney-client privilege, a little guy in a suit appointed by the court is going to review all of the alleged attorney-client-privilege documents and take all of *that*. Once we take all of those documents, I don't know when we're going to be done with all of them and return them to you. And did I mention the TV cameras waiting for you when you walk outside? ... Now, do you still want to do this?"

"No."

"Then why don't we just sign this piece of paper."

Travis Kalanick signed on behalf of Uber on January 30, 2013. Included in the term sheet was also one small recital: in the future, Uber's app might be used to connect riders to non-licensed commercial drivers, similar to Lyft and SideCar.[86]

CHAPTER SEVEN

Breadcrumbs

At the beginning of 2013, Uber found itself the target of the Colorado PUC, as the company didn't quite come through on Salle Yoo's promise of a fare estimate. In the 2.0 version of the app, it was just a range of potential fares, not a precise figure.[1] As the PUC executive director put it years later, "The range of the fare estimate didn't sit squarely into the four corners of limo regulation." Prior to the update, PUC Transportation staff had more or less decided Uber was legal (absent the fare-estimate issue), but as of January 2013, there was nothing to say that the regulations couldn't be changed.

In the midst of a scheduled review and update of existing transportation regulations (aimed heavily at tow trucks) PUC staff effectively severed its working relationship with Uber. Instead of improving on their compromise with Uber's general counsel, they quietly introduced new provisions designed to push Uber out of Colorado.[2]

As the rulemaking process generally worked, PUC staff submitted requested changes, and after a period of public review and comment, an administrative law judge (ALJ) would issue a final recommendation to the commissioners for approval, denial, or amendment. The idea was not to create new laws – that was the legislature's job – but merely to ensure that regulations reflected changing conditions. If, for example, a chapter of detailed regulations was created in the 1950s to oversee the production of wristwatches, it probably only pertained to analog models. As consumers moved to digital wristwatches, questions would arise as to whether the regulations were still relevant and applicable. In this respect, the PUC was ensuring its code kept up with the times.

But in Uber's case, the PUC Transportation staff saw a golden opportunity to close a loophole. In the United States, luxury black cars had remained comfortably segregated from taxis, and PUC staff were attempting to reinforce the traditional dynamic. Since the Colorado PUC was a state agency, there wasn't a city council Uber could pressure to stop the process. The three-member PUC commissioners were appointed by the governor in staggered terms, and although they were an executive agency, they operated more or less independently.

But attempting to regulate Uber was tricky; it was only the intermediary between riders and drivers. To broaden the scope of their reach, PUC staff recommended that the definition of "motor vehicles" under their purview "includes advertising or otherwise offering to provide transportation." In other words, if Uber simply offered to provide Colorado customers a ride in a black car, the new rules applied to them, too. They also gave the provision teeth by adding a penalty of $1,100 for each violation. Further, luxury black cars could only charge for a "specific fixed price" and could not pick up their passenger within thirty minutes of arranging the trip.[3]

The proposed revisions had hints of the IATR's model regulations, which Tom Downey said he would push the PUC to adopt. For example, one of the less relevant rules included a restriction that smartphone apps that used black cars couldn't confuse customers by using the words "taxi" or "cab" in their name, a situation which had only occurred in San Francisco in 2010 when Uber's name was still "UberCab."[4] Although the incident was never repeated, the restriction was pushed hard by the IATR, and it found its way to the Colorado PUC.

The proposed changes were published in late January 2013, and Uber responded publicly with its typical social media barrage. "Colorado PUC

Trying to Shut Down UberDenver!" read their blog post. Addressed to the "Uber-Faithful," it offered Uber's customary pairing of regulatory provisions designed to hurt its business model and a call for action, this time toward the Colorado governor, the PUC chair, and the PUC executive director.[5]

The blog post also marked a notable first in 2013, as Uber's Denver manager, rather than Kalanick, had authored it, and its tone was remarkably more concise and balanced than previous posts written in similar situations. There was no sarcasm or personal scorn inserted into the language. Rather than casting wild blame, Uber's Denver manager even stated, "We believe Colorado Governor Hickenlooper is a friend of small business & innovation and will be receptive to our cause."[6]

For those who might have been watching, Kalanick's role in Uber's regulatory fights was becoming somewhat more detached. With Uber's expansion across the globe, his numerous overlapping fights had made it more practical for local managers to absorb more of the burden and pen their own blog posts. Kalanick remained the figurehead and chief spokesperson for the company and would continue to speak out against regulators in the national press, but at a local level, Uber's tone used became more tempered, moderate, and restrained.

The day after Uber's blog post, the governor's communications staff responded on Facebook and Twitter rejecting Uber's claims of unfair treatment. But the governor's office also demonstrated they only had part of the story. Hickenlooper's staff stated that the main problem was that Uber did not have a feature providing customers with a fare estimate. This was the sticking point PUC staff had negotiated with Salle Yoo, and although Uber didn't come through exactly as expected, they *had* included a range of fares in their 2.0 update released the previous month, a detail the governor's staff neglected to mention.[7]

"In multiple meetings over the past several months, PUC staff has explained these requirements to Uber's attorneys and lobbyists," Hickenlooper announced on Facebook. "Uber insists, however, that its luxury limousine providers can provide transportation service without telling their customers what it will cost when the ride is arranged. Failure to disclose the price is contrary to regulations and the public interest. Complaints have been reported that actual costs have differed from what consumers were told."[8]

In the press, the PUC claimed that the rules were drafted only because taxi companies had complained that limo providers were providing taxi-like services. Uber was not targeted, they insisted, which was patently false.[9]

Uber's Colorado Twitter account told one user, "We promise we won't leave you."[10] They geared up for a fight, hiring as their representative the former PUC chair (through 2007). Also, they submitted public information requests seeking the alleged complaints against their service.[11] They found the original email that the Yellow Cab manager had sent to PUC Transportation staff back in August, which included a copy of Matt Daus's "rogue" apps white paper, and suddenly it became clear that Uber had been deliberately targeted.[12]

Over the next couple of months, both of the major Colorado taxi companies and the IATR stepped in to submit comments in favor of the proposed regulations. As he would do at several of these fights, Matt Daus sent around his prepared comments to the Smartphone App Committee for vetting.[13] In essence, it wasn't just Uber battling local regulators and taxi companies in Denver but also other taxi regulators nationwide via the IATR network. Daus had turned it into a group effort, both locally and nationally. He also told the committee he'd spent the weekend before "with the Mayor of Denver and meeting with regulators there, and it looks like rogue apps will be halted."[14]

In preparation for the hearings, Uber developed a visual aid from the complaints they acquired from their public information requests. They printed each complaint, categorized them, and sorted them on a table in four distinct stacks of paper labeled with handwritten sticky notes. "UBER SUPPORT" stood roughly two feet tall; "TAXI Complaints of Uber," roughly an inch thick; "LIMO Complaints @ UBER," roughly half an inch; and "CLIENT

COMPLAINTS @ UBER," zero pieces of paper.[15] It was a tongue-in-cheek way for Uber to emphasize that regulators responded to the incumbent industries, not customers.

In March, the PUC administrative law judge began the first of two hearings to review the proposed rules. Despite the fact that the PUC was the epicenter for much of this battle in Colorado, the ALJ showed no interest in taking sides. He was a neutral party, and he methodically went through the seventy-eight-page changes one section at a time. When Yellow Cab and Metro Taxi, who made no bones that the new rules were about Uber, wanted to speak broadly about the reasons for these hearings, he instructed them to address only the relevant sections under discussion.[16]

But further in the hearing, Matt Daus arrived personally to speak. Daus didn't say what specifically had brought him to Colorado, only that he was president of a group of taxi regulators, the IATR, that they had been working on this project, and that he was also a taxi expert.[17]

"We want to make sure that you, Your Honor, have the benefit of the expertise and perspective of the people that are doing government regulation around the world," he explained.[18] Interjecting himself in the middle of the judge's scheduled review, Daus went on for several minutes about the IATR's background with "rogue" apps, and the judge had difficulty placing the discussion back on track.

Daus passed out a copy of the IATR model regulations and confirmed that they had inspired the PUC's proposed regulations. "I applaud the Colorado PUC for actually taking a page out of the model regs in making this proposal," he told the judge.[19] Before the day was over, he gave formal comments reviewed by the Smartphone App Committee and delivered a condensed version of his "There's an App for That!" speech. He hit all of the high points, especially that NIST had not yet approved Uber as a taximeter, a delay Daus himself had contributed to.[20]

His arguments were overkill, and most were not relevant to the proposed regulatory changes. Still, Daus left no stone unturned. As the ALJ gave him a wide berth to speak, he emphasized the regulators' love of technology but warned of the perils of rogue services like Uber.

Despite Daus's appearance, the first hearing looked like an apparent victory for Uber. The judge strongly disliked the new definition of "motor vehicles" applying to anyone who so much as *advertised* transportation services. It was excessively broad and could apply to anyone who did as little as post an ad on a laundromat bulletin board.[21] Instead, the ALJ attacked the issue at its core. If Uber was simply a transportation broker, then that was the definition they should draft, which he said he would do before the next meeting the following month.[22] *The Denver Post* editorial board, which had supported Uber, urged caution, stating that the judge's approval of Uber's business model was not a certainty.[23]

Immediately after the 2012 IATR Conference, Christiane Hayashi went back to work trying to shoehorn systemic improvements to keep San Francisco's taxi industry afloat. A regional manager for Uber reached out to her asking if they could find a way to let the city's paratransit customers, who were issued government-subsidized debit cards specifically for taxi rides, use their cards with Uber's app.[24] The regional manager didn't attend the DC conference, but it showed the extent to which Uber's employees didn't quite understand the regulator mentality or that there was still a lot of baggage from previous fights.[25]

Hayashi replied with the equivalent of "you've got to be kidding me" and gave a long list of reasons why the answer was no. The SFMTA had several concerns about their service, and in this request, Uber was putting the cart before the horse. "For example, I have had it from eyewitnesses that UberTaxi is registering unlicensed, fake taxis through its service," Hayashi told him. Before the email, getting Uber to respond to the SFMTA was nearly impossible. Further, Hayashi hated their self-indemnifying terms and conditions, unregulated rates, mandatory tips, and use of unapproved smartphones as a form of taximeter.[26]

"I sent a message to Mr. Kalanick several days ago, inviting him to discuss these issues with us, as he said he would do at the IATR conference," she explained.[27]

Hayashi has since forgotten when between 2010 and 2013 she met Kalanick, but in a press interview, Kalanick described the experience as a severe berating. "Oh man, I've never ... She was fire and brimstone, deep anger, screaming," he was quoted.[28]

Hayashi, who often distributed Uber news stories like this one, told Matt Daus, "I'll cop to 'fire and brimstone,' but not to screaming like a banshee – that's just a lie. More of the same from Uber."[29]

Hayashi turned her attention back to the taxi industry. Still in progress was a report from a hired taxi analyst to provide the SFMTA the optimal number of cabs to put on the road. And Hayashi convinced the SFMTA Board to advance another 150 new taxi medallions, this time for the discounted price of $150,000 each.[30] Further, the agency was reviewing bids from a Request for Information (RFI), issued prior to the 2012 conference, to develop a citywide app that all taxi fleets would be required to use so that the industry wasn't split among multiple apps.[31] One of the IATR's more significant sponsors, Frias Transportation Infrastructure (FTI) from Las Vegas, had been working on such a product, but it had not yet been released.

The product Hayashi was asking for was largely experimental. It hadn't been developed before, and she was asking the industry who among them would like to take a crack at making it. In addition to FTI, several of the taxi industry's usual suspects submitted responses to the RFI, including the two prominent smartphone players, TaxiMagic and Flywheel (formerly Cabulous); New York's existing vendors, Verifone and CMT; and a handful of other taxi equipment manufacturers.[32] Bizarrely, the RFI bidders also included Hailo and Uber, two of the taxi industry's most hated app companies.[33]

Uber did not seem to appreciate the irony that it was applying for a contract Hayashi had created because Uber and similar "rogue" apps were severely damaging the local industry. The company submitted a response as though it was a normal applicant, but it was clearly a no-go for the SFMTA, which described their bid as a "step backwards for technology."[34] Also, Hailo did not take the bid seriously but instead used their application to politely tell the SFMTA that their RFI was wrongheaded. They should forgo a universal dispatch app and simply allow apps like Hailo to flourish, they argued.[35]

It was surreal. The two direct-to-driver apps most reviled by the taxi industry didn't seem to understand Hayashi's motivations. Or if they did, they had burned time and energy for the sake of a dry inside joke.

In January 2013, as Uber was negotiating its interim agreement with the CPUC, a *Wall Street Journal* article appeared titled "Travis Kalanick: The Transportation Trustbuster." It was another article lengthily describing Kalanick's background and the regulatory battles to date, except this one went more in depth into Kalanick's personality with a firsthand interview. The reporter started asking him about the regulatory conflicts, and he described Kalanick appearing agitated by the question, pacing around his office with a golf club in hand. Consistently, any reporter who ever talked to Kalanick about the subject seemed to rile him.[36]

She asked him if he had simply ignored the original cease-and-desist letters in 2010. He responded, "The thing is, a cease and desist is something that says, 'Hey, I think you should stop,' and we're saying, 'We don't think we should.' The only way to deal with that is to be taken to court, and we never went to court."[37] Of course, one of the ways they avoided court was throwing regulatory staff off the app when they were spotted, as had happened in DC.

Kalanick continued to allege a great deal of cronyism and corruption in the taxi industry. It was pointless, in his mind, ever to ask for permission to operate, save for New York City. Although Kalanick was not a pleasant person, he had a point. Regulatory systems like the taxi industry had chiseled monopolistic rules into stone, and like honor-bound samurai warriors, taxi regulators defended them without question. As Kalanick put it, they "disincentive innovation." Asked what advice he had for other entrepreneurs, he said, "Stand by your principles and be comfortable with confrontation. So few people are, so when the people with the red tape come, it becomes a negotiation."[38]

This was the heart of his regulatory strategy: if you get into a fight with the government, then make it as loud a fight as possible. What was implicit in his argument was that if your principles are backed by massive amounts of constituents, then the fight becomes increasingly uncomfortable for the government. Drawing attention to it gives you leverage, as had happened in DC, San Francisco, Massachusetts, and Chicago.

Daus reported to the Smartphone App Committee that he was "getting a lot of complaints from our members about this article."[39] In fairness, the article *was* one-sided, never mentioning the reasons taxis were regulated in the first place. And it served only to further irritate the IATR. Some of the members were beginning to bemoan Uber's constantly positive press coverage. They felt it was unfair. But the few times Daus or others were quoted, they put their argument in terms of public safety. They seldom, if ever, talked about the fact that regulations *were* protectionist.

In the few days after the *Wall Street Journal* article, the media coverage began to heat up even further. A few outlets reported that Uber had hired one of Facebook's public policy managers, Corey Owens.[40] Uber had finally realized that their fights were not going to diminish, and they needed a public policy team to attack them proactively instead of reactively. Of the new hire, Daus said to the transportation staff at his law firm, "Now this is problematic."[41]

Also, after Kalanick signed the CPUC settlement agreement, the term sheet leaked and several outlets excitedly reported that Uber was moving into the ridesharing space with Lyft and SideCar.[42] The news sent ripples of panic throughout the taxi industry. The president of the San Francisco Medallion Holder's Association told Hayashi, "Undoubtedly, like yourself, I am being contacted these days by many concerned, near-panicked taxi drivers regarding the rogue operators."[43]

Furious, Hayashi lashed out at Mayor Lee's transportation adviser, Gillian Gillett, for standing idly by:

From: Hayashi, Christiane
To: Gillett, Gillian
Sent: Sunday, February 3, 2013 12:02 PM

I can't tell how deeply disappointed I am in in the Mayor's Office. This is not about stifling competition or attracting venture capital. It is about protecting individuals who get into the cars of strangers late at night without safety protections. It appears that the Mayor's Office has chosen what is important to the to the Mayor's Office for its own purposes. That will be the last word you hear from me on the subject but I need to communicate how deeply offended I am by the "City's" priorities in this matter.

She also told Daus, "Consider my public resignation a strategic option available to IATR."[44] Hayashi was so passionate she was willing to be a martyr for the cause.

Uber was indeed moving into the ridesharing space, but what most reporters didn't realize was that Uber only wanted to use one brand to represent their low-cost alternative to taxis and black cars: UberX. But UberX already existed in three cities, including San Francisco, as a service where licensed limo drivers picked up passengers in a hybrid-fuel vehicle. Moving into ridesharing meant they would have to wind down the existing service. Any drivers who may have purchased a hybrid as a business investment could move over to the revamped service, but they were no longer in a class of drivers unto themselves. Either way, they were stuck with their hybrid cars.

To some extent, Uber also suspected that ridesharing was going to saturate their platform, which meant there was no point in flooding their system with more black cars; they would still be available as a service called "UberBLACK" but not needed as much. Effectively, Uber's services were now competing with one another. The professionally licensed UberBLACK drivers were only going to see a fraction of their regular business from this point forward.

In March, a group of former San Francisco drivers protested. Uber had already generated ill will, and for many of them, the transition was the last straw. Drivers were summarily dismissed with no avenue for appeal or reconsideration.[45] According to one lawsuit's complaint, Uber's alleged method for taking low-rated drivers off of their platform was to tell them there was something wrong with the smartphone issued by the company and they needed to bring it into their offices for service. When a driver arrived and handed the phone over, they would simply put it away and inform the driver they'd been removed, leaving them shell-shocked.[46] The drivers also complained that Uber had been gradually lowering its prices to remain competitive but effectively taking money out of their pockets.[47]

The drivers felt used, discarded, and unappreciated. The protest group alleged that Uber had taken five hundred drivers off of the platform in February, perhaps in the buildup to their new ridesharing platform. Kalanick stated that the number was false, but the protest still suggested that Uber was cleaning house.[48] Daus celebrated the protest with the Smartphone App Committee. In the subject line of an email, he wrote, "Happy St. Patrick's Day to all – and to Uber- whose drivers are now on strike in San Fran!"[49]

Meanwhile, as California's proceedings moved forward, the rulemaking hearings took a similar form to that taken in Colorado's PUC. In California, the process allowed interested parties to tediously submit written comments, followed by several written replies to written comments. Collectively dubbed "New Online-Enabled Transportation Services" (NOETS), Uber, Lyft, and SideCar had few allies among the respondents.[50] Every taxi company, limousine service, and taxi affiliate hated the idea of legitimizing these services. In their arguments, they tried to build a case that the ridesharing companies were misleading and untrustworthy.

Lyft and SideCar gave the taxi industry an opening by pushing the idea that their services were extensions of "ridesharing," a term for traditional carpooling. But since carpooling was by law a nonprofit activity, it was laughable and clearly a smokescreen, a way to wedge themselves into the only legal framework that *might* allow them to operate. Even if they only accepted "suggested donations," Lyft and SideCar were clearly not The Salvation Army. The donations were intended for commercial profit.

Further building distrust, the anti-ridesharing coalition noted that none of the apps were willing to share their internal processes with regulators. None would share the results of their background checks for drivers or hand over proof of insurance, proof of drug testing (if any), proof of driver training (if any), or proof of vehicle inspections (if any).[51] And all three guarded their ridership data like lionesses guarding newborn cubs.

Government agencies, including the SFMTA, were less overt in their opposition. They emphasized their love of technology and the need for public safety but stopped just short of stating the apps were harming the taxi industry. When it *did* come up, they would only hint at it vaguely. "Taxi service is an essential component of San Francisco's transportation system," an SFMTA brief stated.[52]

The politics of ridesharing trumped the regulators' ability to oppose them solely because of mistrust. However, playing bad cop to the regulators' good cop, the IATR submitted much more damning comments in partnership with Hayashi, the taxi regulator of Los Angeles, and the rest of the app committee. To their credit, Hayashi and the LA regulator both disclosed their IATR affiliation during the hearings.

Lyft and SideCar encouraged the CPUC to look beyond the letter of the carpooling laws and recognize the benefits of their service. But Uber's comments were resentful, and they characterized the hearings as unnecessary. Even though they clearly demonstrated their intent to enter ridesharing, Uber still treated the hearings as though they only applied to their black-car operations. Since black cars were already regulated, they made it seem as though they'd been dragged into the hearings kicking and screaming. "Any Commission regulation of Uber would be redundant and does not advance any public interest," they claimed.[53] At their core, Uber's argument reflected statements Kalanick frequently made about whether they were directly providing the transportation or just arranging it. Once again, they claimed it was the latter, which was why the regulations were "redundant."

For the first time, Uber also cited the federal Telecommunications Act of 1996, which, among other things, required the federal government to take a laissez-faire approach to the then-burgeoning Internet. Unless otherwise already regulated, the law told the feds to keep their hands off commercial transactions that strictly took place online. In a 2002 example, which Uber alluded to, online auction company eBay was named a defendant in a class-action lawsuit alleging a ring of sports-memorabilia autograph forgers were using the auction website to sell fake collectibles, a violation of California law. However, the courts ruled the Telecommunications Act gave eBay immunity, as it merely created the online platform but did not create the transaction itself.

California passed a state version of the Telecommunications Act, which took effect in January 2013, and Uber similarly argued to the CPUC that their company had created an online infrastructure but not the transactions themselves.[54] For all intents and purposes, Uber told the CPUC, they had no right to regulate their company.

Perhaps worried about Uber's entrance into the ridesharing market,

SideCar CEO Sunil Paul decided it was time to expand into new cities. In October 2012, the company raised $10 million in venture funding specifically for expansion, and after the CPUC signaled it wouldn't take enforcement actions against them in January 2013, they pressed forward.[55] In February, SideCar acquired the Austin-based HeyRide for an undisclosed amount, the same company the local Yellow Cab Company had worked with a private investigator to surveil.[56] For SideCar, it was essentially an "acquihire," the purchase of a company to acquire its staff. Paul had been impressed with HeyRide's user interface and wanted to bring that same skill to his company.

The same day they acquired HeyRide, SideCar announced they would immediately begin service on Friday and Saturday nights in six cities across the US: Los Angeles, Boston, Chicago, Brooklyn, Philadelphia, Washington, and Austin. Paul stated that in Austin, the company would be fully functional in time for the following month's SXSW conference, a prominent venue for showing off new software.[57] Paul knew about HeyRide's difficulties, and he retained a lawyer specifically to fight any upcoming regulatory battles. Paul pushed the idea that, unlike the emerging UberX redesign, SideCar was truly a "rideshare" operation because a passenger could select their own driver, rather than have one dispatched to them.[58] Also, drivers were not supposed to earn above the cost of the car's upkeep.[59] In any way possible, he wanted to tread in the legal gray area of traditional carpooling.

The day after the announcement, the Austin Transportation Department (ATD) instantly cracked down and sent SideCar a cease-and-desist letter.[60] As far as the ATD was concerned, SideCar was no different than its predecessor, HeyRide. The ATD was already worried about HeyRide's presence at the upcoming SXSW conference, apparently fearful it would take up some of the taxi industry's business during the week. Within two weeks of the cease-and-desist, the ATD convinced the city council to give them additional powers to impound taxi-like vehicles.[61] The council fast-tracked it as an emergency issue and placed the bill on their consent agenda, meaning it was passed among a package of bills without argument.[62]

Ten days after the announcement, SideCar was also targeted in Philadelphia with a plain-clothes sting operation.[63] At least three drivers were each fined $1,000 and had their cars impounded.[64] SideCar itself was fined $7,000.[65] It was the same jurisdiction whose regulator said to Matt Daus a year earlier about sting operations against Uber, "That's life." And for SideCar, it was also confusing. According to Sunil Paul, their company was invited to the city by the mayor's office. However, the local taxi regulator was the Philadelphia Parking Authority, an agency whose board answered to the governor and legislature. Much like in San Francisco, the mayor's office and taxi regulator were not in sync, but in Philadelphia, the mayor's office couldn't order the taxi regulator to stand down.

Attempting a tactic similar to Uber, SideCar responded to both Philadelphia and Austin with its own blog post, email campaign, and Twitter hashtag, #DefendSharing, but the movement didn't catch on.[66] SideCar didn't yet have the street cred of Uber or the pink-mustache recognition of Lyft. It was still a small player in the smartphone app space, and there were no "SideCar faithful" to speak of. Instead, they quickly changed tactics. In an attempt to gain a customer base in Austin and Philadelphia, they paid "ambassador" drivers out of their own pocket to give customers free rides, hoping the brand awareness would spread – especially in Austin, as SXSW was looming around the corner.[67]

Just before the SXSW conference began, events began to take a bizarre turn. An especially wonky Austin City Council member offered a resolution essentially asking (via the city manager) that their taxi regulator, Carlton Thomas, explore ridesharing regulations in other cities and make recommendations on whether it should be allowed in Austin.[68] Generally, most city councils were too busy to follow these battles. "Uber" and "SideCar" were names that meant little to them, unless a council member happened to be fascinated by these new companies.

Once more, the taxi community panicked. They were concerned Austin was sending a signal that SideCar could operate and that the cease-and-desist would not be enforced, just like in San Francisco. In a hearing, Ed Kargbo, the Yellow Cab president who sent Austin's taxi regulator several warnings about HeyRide in 2012, came forward to address several concerns. A stocky and charismatic former college athlete, Kargbo noted that regulators in both Philadelphia and San Francisco had ordered SideCar to cease operations, a tactic common to both regulators and taxi industry officials.[69] That is, if someone of authority in one city told a rideshare company to cease operations, then regulators or taxi companies in another city would point it out so they could take comfort in doing the same. They essentially made the don't-rock-the-boat argument of consistency.

Kargbo colored his argument as a public safety issue, despite acknowledging that SideCar was only using an ambassador program to promote itself. The taxi industry didn't want to give SideCar even an inch. "Their ambassadors are promoting illegal and criminal activity," he said. He passed out articles quoting regulators in Philadelphia and San Francisco, including a quote from General Hagan after his November 2012 fine against SideCar and others. "This is a matter of public safety," Hagan had said.[70]

Kargbo threw every negative connotation against SideCar that would stick, but there was one issue about ridesharing that stood out above the others: if allowed to operate, ridesharing was potentially a noninsured activity.[71] Most ridesharing drivers were not likely to obtain expensive commercial insurance policies, and *personal* auto policies excluded commercial activities. If a ridesharing driver got into an accident, there was a serious threat that no insurance would cover it. SideCar might have *excess* liability insurance to cover accidents, but using it was a precarious process. If a claim was denied, there was a cumbersome administrative process to overturn it, filled with several levels of appeals and potential lawsuits. It wasn't clear when a ridesharing company's excess policy would kick in.[72] Some of the city council members suddenly realized the seriousness of the issue, and the Austin mayor even commented that the city could be culpable if they authorized ridesharing in the first place.[73]

The wonky council member who had sponsored the resolution jumped into the conversation and emphasized that the purpose was not to take a position on SideCar. "It simply recognizes it is an issue we need to tackle," he told them. As apps were beginning to expand across the United States, he felt it important to examine whether they were a viable alternative to Austin's traffic woes. "I don't think it does anyone any good to look the other way and pretend these things aren't happening," he said.

Still, council members felt it important to give assurances several times over that this gesture was not a green light for SideCar. They even amended the resolution to direct the city manager "to use whatever legal and effective means are available to discourage use of peer-to-peer ridesharing *for compensation* until the public safety and other regulatory concerns have been addressed" (emphasis added). And even after the amendment, the resolution only passed by a vote of 5–2.[74]

In the wake of the Austin and Philadelphia incidents, SideCar announced in a blog post on March 2 that they'd met with officials of both cities and received assurances there would be no fines or impounded vehicles under the free ambassador program.[75] Regardless, the taxi industry was still nervous. Rumors began to swirl that this was the beginning of the end. To her fellow regulators, Hayashi spelled out doom. She emailed the Smartphone App Committee to give an update about the California PUC hearings.

From: Hayashi, Christiane
Sent: Tuesday, March 05, 2013, 7:14 PM
To: [IATR Smartphone App Committee]
CC: Daus, Matthew, et al.

...

Based on the proceedings so far, I anticipate that the CPUC will ignore regulatory concerns in favor of "cool new technology" and allow, as it has already inexplicably allowed in the interim, the continued operation of these entities notwithstanding evidence on the record that some of these services do not include the benefit of auto liability insurance, among other safety concerns. If that is the outcome, we will be forced to go to the state

---

legislature to make a case to fix our broken regulatory structure. Meanwhile, I hear through the grapevine that other jurisdictions, such as Austin and Philadelphia, have gone ahead and authorized these operations. I am writing to request your help in the form of some notice or discussion in this group when a jurisdiction intends to allow these operations so that the rest of us know what deals have been cut, what terms have been agreed to. Otherwise I fear 1) our position in California before the CPUC and the state legislature will be seriously undermined by many other jurisdictions agreeing to allow these dubious services to continue, and 2) all of us will be at a disadvantage in our own jurisdictions over not knowing what has been agreed to elsewhere and why. This is the biggest issue that I have experienced in my nearly 5 years in this position, dwarfed even by credit card processing. It has reached the point here in SF that nearly every other car on the street has a pink mustache and our taxi industry is, no joke, looking to be on the verge of collapse. . . .

These businesses are a small presence in your jurisdictions so far, but unless you want all your taxi drivers to throw off all the costs of regulation and start driving their personal vehicle with a pink mustache around your town, I would very much appreciate your cooperation in providing some advance notice to this group of your intention to settle with these operators for the benefit of the rest of us.

The next morning, Austin taxi regulator and app committee member Carlton Thomas replied to all:

From: Thomas, Carlton
Sent: Wednesday, March 06, 2013, 9:20 AM
To: [IATR Smartphone App Committee]
CC: Daus, Matthew, et al.

Greetings from Austin!

Please do not believe the "grapevine". Speaking for Austin, we have not approved the operations of rogue apps in our jurisdiction. However, we are aware of a blog post by Mr. Paul of SideCar stating both Austin and Philadelphia have "assured" them that we will not cite or impound their vehicles. Although I cannot speak to what the regulators in Philadelphia have expressed to SideCar, Austin has made no such assurances. A cease and desist order has been issued to SideCar and it remains in effect. Attached is a copy.

> As I'm sure most of you are aware, the developers of these rogue apps are not beyond stretching the truth or even out-and-out lying if, in their opinion, it furthers their platform. While we continue to work towards exploring a space for legitimate apps that compliment multimodal transportation options in a regulated environment, we have no intentions of authorizing rogue apps.
>
> ...

Much as Thomas had "no intentions" of helping SideCar, neither did Philadelphia. Their regulator also replied to let Hayashi know they would continue to perform undercover sting operations to make sure SideCar's ambassador program didn't charge passengers. In exchange, SideCar informed Philadelphia they'd come up with a plan to come into legal compliance. The regulator said they were "very dubious about the possibility that they may be successful in achieving it."[76]

The day after the Austin City Council passed their resolution, Daus emailed the Smartphone App Committee a simple quote: "Rogue ridesharing is just deregulation in disguise." Further, he said, "We should put it into some fortune cookies at our next iatr conference."[77]

SideCar's expansion across the US was rather inspiring to Uber. In the middle of the CPUC hearings, Uber took a bold step. On April 12, 2013, Travis Kalanick penned a blog post titled "Uber Policy White Paper 1.0," the company's formal announcement that it was entering the ridesharing space. It was, in part, an apology, a way of explaining why they had let nearly a year go by as SideCar and Lyft went otherwise unchallenged by competitors.[78]

Kalanick explained that before, there was too much risk as neither traditional commercial insurance nor licensing had existed for ridesharing.

But regulators had shown a willingness, at least in California, to let it slide. And in large markets like New York, Boston, Chicago, and Seattle, they didn't take immediate action against SideCar's entry, suggesting there was an opening to gain a foothold. Kalanick called it a "massive regulatory ambiguity."[79]

Kalanick's paper attempted to segregate the motivations of taxi companies from those of their regulators. When describing the "incumbent taxi industry," he denounced them for being "corrupt" and said they petitioned regulators to protect them. He said taxi companies sought to "shut down Uber," a phrase which included a hyperlink to the *Wall Street Journal* article about the 2012 IATR Conference. It was as though he were implying it was the taxi *industry*, not its regulators, that had pushed for the IATR model regulations.[80]

Regarding regulators, he acknowledged that Austin and Philadelphia had moved against SideCar but expressed optimism of a "mixed" reaction nationwide. A "lack of enforcement [elsewhere] shows at least some embrace of this kind of transportation innovation," he said. It appeared Kalanick thought regulators were open minded about the idea, when in fact only a tiny handful of them were. But he also pointed out Uber hadn't taken advantage of the lax enforcement. SideCar and Lyft had effectively bet that "regulators for the most part will be unable to act or enforce in time to stop them before they have a critical mass of support," a bet Kalanick felt was already paying off. They needed to get into the game.[81]

At the end of the paper, Kalanick presented a policy for Uber's expansion. "Uber will roll out ridesharing ... in any market where the regulators have tacitly approved doing so," he wrote. He defined "tacit approval" as any *competitor* operating in that city for thirty days without an enforcement action. In other words, Uber would let Lyft or SideCar test the waters, and in any market where it looked like they were getting away with it, they'd jump in, too.[82]

Seemingly unable to show any more surprise, Daus spread the white paper to the IATR Board of Directors, writing only, "holy cow you believe this one?" The email thread showed that Daus had been notified of the blog post by a retired former CEO of Texas Taxi, Inc., who had also sent it to other Texas Taxi and TLPA executives.[83]

Back in Denver, two weeks after the first rulemaking hearing in March, the ALJ delivered his proposed definition of a "transportation broker," and as *The Denver Post* had warned, he turned Uber's momentary victory upside down. In the new draft, a luxury limousine had to wait at least forty-five minutes before arriving to fill an order.[84] Even more damning for Uber, the judge created a definition which said that a broker cannot offer to provide transportation service.[85] He was effectively telling Uber that in the argument of whether they were Expedia or American Airlines, Expedia didn't advertise its own plane tickets. Neither could Uber offer the rides it supposedly brokered.

It was a clever solution to a question other jurisdictions struggled to answer. How can a broker have most of the control in the transactions it facilitates while also claiming its role is too small to be regulated? The ALJ's response was that it can't, and if Uber was genuinely a brokerage, it had no need to advertise the rides.

In addition, the new version also prohibited limousines from using any kind of taximeter or any other device that calculated a fare based upon time and mileage except for a clock.[86] Uber had argued that its system was more flexible than conventional limo services. If, for instance, a passenger wanted to make an impromptu detour or change their destination, a preset rate wouldn't cover that situation. The judge responded by telling Uber to just charge by the hour and add more time to the bill.

"It's not up to me to ignore the statute that governs this service," the judge said. "It's a time charter. And, so, I can't ignore a time charter and say, 'Well, we're going to provide point-to-point service.'"[87]

Economically, Uber's argument was sound. For the limo companies, the cost of a twenty-minute trip during rush hour was different than the cost of a twenty-minute trip on a Sunday morning. But the ALJ felt that state law based limo service on a charge for time, not distance, and it wasn't his role to craft any new laws.

While reviewing the newest draft rules at a second hearing, speakers lined up to present an onslaught of opinions favoring either taxis or Uber. The ALJ showed increasing impatience toward the political narrative. He didn't care about taking sides. In later correspondence, he would tell colleagues that the hearings were "somewhat hijacked by Uber issues."[88] He just wanted to move forward in a way that reflected existing state law.

Predictably, Uber's representative wanted to water down the new changes, while Matt Daus, who was overjoyed by the ALJ's modifications, requested even more stringent language. At one point, Uber's rep got into a somewhat heated back-and-forth discussion with the judge about the taximeter issue, and the rep quoted a passage from the first hearing. The judge replied, "First off, that's in the first round when I read those – considered those; and second, don't read me something in my record."[89] The judge was getting punchy.

In certain ways, the second hearing felt more like a political campaign than a dry rulemaking session. One of Uber's few allies, the US Federal Trade Commission (FTC), sent in arguments in favor of any new service as long as public safety was not at risk.[90] For decades the FTC had had a contentious relationship with the taxi industry and even sued a couple of times in the 1980s to try to remove some of the market barriers to entry.[91] They were glad to support a market agitator like Uber that fostered competition.

Lining up behind the taxi industry, the TLPA submitted comments against Uber, followed by a handful of industry members from the Denver Taxi Advisory Council. The owner of Frias Transportation Infrastructure, the prominent IATR sponsor designing a citywide taxi app in Las Vegas, also appeared.[92] Yellow Cab brought in a longtime Colorado taxi attorney who for decades had defended the industry from competition.

Oddly, in a blink-and-you'd-miss-it moment, the taxi attorney addressed Matt Daus as "counsel," although he never said whose counsel he represented.[93] Daus himself said he was there representing the IATR.

In his typical overkill approach, Matt Daus also asked the judge to preemptively prohibit ridesharing, which hadn't yet launched in Colorado and was far outside the scope of the hearings. "Every single one of our regulators believes it is a just a form of deregulation and a way around the rules," he explained.[94]

As a whole, the campaign was lopsided against Uber, and the Colorado hearings made for an uphill battle. The judge showed little sympathy to their position, and by most signs, Uber walked away defeated and only waiting for the ALJ to issue a formal recommendation prior to a commission vote. Daus couldn't have been happier. "Looks like Victory for IATR in Colorado!!!" he wrote to his board of directors.[95]

A week later, Travis Kalanick was interviewed by CNN anchor Jessica Yellin at Google's DC offices, where he was once more asked about regulatory battles. Kalanick decided to paint part of the blame on the Colorado governor, even calling him out by name.

"The governor of Colorado and his Public Utilities Commission put out regulations that are essentially trying to put us out of business," said Kalanick.[96]

"Hickenlooper?" Yellin asked.

"Hickenlooper, straight up."

"He seems so technology friendly," Yellin said.

"He's an entrepreneur, and he's technology friendly, and he embraces innovation every step of the way until he *actually* has to."[97]

John Wright Hickenlooper Jr., a folksy, amateur politician and Democratic former mayor with a gangly appearance and a boyish haircut, first ran for Colorado governor in 2010. It was the year of the Tea Party's rise, and he narrowly won with 51 percent of the vote, with the conservative ticket split between two candidates.[98] During and after his campaign, Hickenlooper made innovation a forefront issue.[99] Like the rest of the country, Colorado was mired in the downturn of the Great Recession, and he was convinced the state's economy could rebound if they attracted the tech sector.

After taking office, Hickenlooper expanded tax credits to angel investors of tech companies, developed the Colorado Innovation Network, and sponsored a statewide innovation challenge.[100] "Innovation" might have become an overused buzzword in Hickenlooper's administration, but the message was clear: Colorado was inviting the tech sector with open arms.[101]

That's why Yellin expressed surprise when Kalanick told her that Governor Hickenlooper was unfriendly toward their company. In all likelihood, the governor had little to do with the PUC's proposed regulations, but Kalanick's comments cut like a political dagger nonetheless.

"You have places like Colorado and Hickenlooper – he's talking about innovation on one side but trying to embrace the taxi side at the same time, and you can't do both," Kalanick told Yellin. "You just can't."[102]

Kalanick's comments caught the attention of *The Denver Post*, which published them a few days later.[103] Whether he liked it or not, the issue was now on Hickenlooper's doorstep, and a reelection campaign was only a year away. His administration's innovation push had placed him in a tight spot, and he now had to prove just how much he supported the tech industry vis-à-vis Uber. In the space of one interview, Kalanick had effectively transformed "innovation" from a political buzzword into a double-edged sword.

While Uber was miserable in Colorado, SideCar was having an equally bad time in Austin. Eager for any kind of leverage during the SXSW conference, company representatives took meetings with city council members and the ATD, none of which went anywhere. At least one council member told them they were crazy for trying to take on the taxi industry. At Carlton Thomas's office they negotiated for a temporary pilot program, but the ATD reportedly withdrew it after initial conversations. Desperate, SideCar filed a half-hearted suit against the city for punishing what they argued was an extension of carpooling.[104]

The court denied an injunction against Austin, and the suit was dismissed within a month, but SideCar representatives were concerned it left a bad taste in the council's mouth.[105] However, most of the council members were too busy to care. The issue barely commanded their attention; to them, SideCar was little more than a pesky housefly. In Austin, as in many cities, the taxi industry was an easy source of campaign funds for *all* of the council members, even the sponsor of the ridesharing resolution. Taxi employees might donate as much as 5 percent of a candidate's annual war chest – not an overwhelming sum but decent enough not to risk alienating the taxi industry, and especially not for a company that had no roots in Austin. For all concerned, SideCar was easy to ignore.

SideCar came away from SXSW having given away a lot of free rides but changed few minds. After the festival ended, Carlton Thomas and Matt Daus began efforts to shore up more barriers to entry and further insulate the city's taxi industry. Thomas's office convinced the city council to change limo rules to require a thirty-minute prearrangement.[106] In May, Daus prepared a new white paper specifically to address Lyft and SideCar titled "Ridesharing Applications: Illegal 'Hitchhiking-For-Hire' or Sustainable Group Riding?"[107] Just like in the previous white paper for Uber's black-car service, he floated a new model definition for "ridesharing" that reflected the traditional definition of nonprofit carpooling, which Thomas was actively seeking.[108] On May 10, Daus's law firm sent the Smartphone App Committee a draft.

> *Rideshare*: The traveling of two or more persons by any mode of private passenger vehicle, including, but not limited to carpooling, vanpooling, buspooling, to any location incidental to another purpose of the driver, without charge, fee, or payment, for which a gratuity is neither accepted, collected, encouraged, promoted and/or requested, and for which the primary purpose of the driver cannot be profit or revenue based.[109]

Four days later, the ATD introduced a nearly identical definition at a city council transportation committee meeting.[110] Effectively, Carlton Thomas and Matt Daus worked together to cut off SideCar's legs by removing the ambiguity from its fuzzy carpooling argument. (Hayashi and the Los Angeles taxi regulator also said they would take it to the California legislature, although no such bill was introduced.[111])

Throughout May, SideCar's opposition grew on multiple fronts. While the ATD prepared its report on whether ridesharing should be implemented, IATR members wasted little time ganging up on SideCar in Austin. Independently, Hayashi wrote a letter to the Austin City Council, "which I didn't exactly have permission to send," she told a colleague.[112] In her rogue letter, she went through the grocery list of regulator concerns, such as questionable insurance and an "opaque" fare structure.[113]

But Hayashi also slammed SideCar for frustrations she'd witnessed in San Francisco, a warning of things to come if Austin approved of SideCar. During CPUC hearings, SideCar claimed that their service reduced greenhouse gases via reduced car usage, but the taxi fleets in San Francisco already consisted of nearly 100 percent hybrid vehicles. There was also increased hostility: Lyft cars, with their hard-to-miss pink mustaches, experienced tense confrontations with taxi drivers. And then there was the declining taxi industry, as taxi drivers jumped ship to become rideshare drivers so they could make more money without paying lease or medallion fees.[114]

She wrote,

> It is simply not possible to manage a regulated fleet like our taxi system alongside an identical for-hire vehicle service that has no controls. The proposition represents de facto deregulation of the taxi industry, and it is toxic to the highly managed municipal taxi systems that taxi regulators struggle to maintain.[115]

It was bold of Hayashi to say so. Even in California, her office's briefs to the CPUC were watered down so that while they characterized taxis as "indispensable," they weren't willing to outright call for Uber, Lyft, and SideCar's banishment. Also, it was unusual. As an argument, taxi regulators rarely cited the need to protect the taxi industry from competition. They brought it up tepidly and only if they had no more cards to play. Ridesharing and taxis were like fire and ice. Few believed they could coexist, and if regulators had to pick, they preferred the industry that could remain accountable to the government. But their refusal to say so publicly – and instead focus on public safety – showed how politically inconvenient the argument was, especially given the taxi industry's deficiencies. Regulators were effectively asking cities to choose heavily supervised taxis, which were not likely to improve service or ever meet public demand, over the more efficient, convenient, lower-cost, and nearly unregulated ridesharing industry.

It was an impossible argument to sell, and more so in the face of Uber's populist tactics. Few regulators would ever want to appear as though they were picking the transportation winners and losers, though they clearly *were*. To her credit, Hayashi was one of the few active regulators willing to state openly and as a matter of public policy that the disruptive bandits needed to be driven away. She was one of the few willing to have an honest discussion.

Later in May, at an Austin committee hearing, Matt Daus was scheduled to make a presentation titled "Going My Way? The Proliferation of Rogue Ridesharing Services." However, he got sick at the last minute, and Yellow Cab president Ed Kargbo presented it in his place. The gist of the slideshow was that SideCar was simply a peer-to-peer taxi-like service. It was not a nonprofit carpooling service, which was an easy argument to attack. Kargbo deftly sifted through SideCar's terms and conditions, pointing out all the ways the company treated itself as a for-profit business. But more than that, Kargbo (and presumably Daus) denounced the larger ridesharing industry in general, listing the indemnifying terms and conditions of Lyft and the expansion of Uber, neither of which had yet launched in Austin (though Uber had been operating for the week of SXSW).[116]

Kargbo told the committee, "I heard conversations about a potential pilot program. I don't know that that's necessary when you consider that they're claiming they've done a hundred thousand trips in San Francisco. Why do we need a pilot program in Austin when if they truly have that data, they can share that, and it'll demonstrate that drivers are providing services just like taxi drivers?"[117]

A couple of weeks later the ATD presented their initial report on ridesharing, which took the most one-sided viewpoint possible. Instead of assessing how attitudes toward ridesharing apps were changing nationally, it looked at the issue through the lens of how apps violated taxi regulations. The question, the report underlined, was whether "the use of an application is designed for or promotes compensation that exceeds the actual cost of the trip."[118] In other words, were apps acting like traditional carpooling or unlicensed cabs?

Using Carlton Thomas's connections from the IATR, the report discussed the cities that had stopped SideCar to date. "Based on staff research, only in California is there confusion related to the entry of smart phone dispatch applications in to the market," it said, referring to the CPUC hearings still underway.[119] "Confusion" was a cynical and dishonest characterization. Thomas knew full well from Hayashi's emails that the CPUC was leaning toward approving ridesharing.

Looking to peer cities around Texas (the same ones where Texas Taxi, Inc. owned a Yellow Cab fleet), the report noted San Antonio had passed an ordinance requiring transportation apps to be licensed, and Houston had started crackdowns against smaller apps. The report didn't mention Chicago, Boston, or Seattle, none of which had yet taken action against SideCar. It didn't mention that in several cities, attempts had been made and withdrawn to obstruct Uber's black-car service, suggesting some flexibility with apps competitive to the taxi market.[120]

Near the last page, the report included an appendix of sting operations the ATD had conducted against "Smart Phone Enabled Rideshare Applications," chiefly during the week of SXSW. Using emergency powers granted by the council, police impounded drivers' vehicles due to issues such as "check engine light was on," "exterior damage," and in one case, a driver with a breathalyzer-activated ignition.[121]

It would have made for a damning case against SideCar, except the report failed to acknowledge SideCar was still giving away free rides via its money-losing ambassador program. It couldn't have been charged for most of the infractions listed, such as lacking an operating permit or a chauffeur's permit. Since the report didn't specifically list which companies the drivers worked for, it implied that all the citations were issued against SideCar's drivers – except they weren't.

If anyone had pulled the citations for a closer examination, they would have seen that of the ten issued, two were written against HeyRide before SideCar acquired them. In another two, the drivers listed their "employer" as Uber – one for a 2011 Nissan Versa and another for what appears to be a 2000 Honda CR-V, neither of which were luxury black cars.[122] Although Kalanick's "White Paper 1.0" wouldn't formally announce Uber's entry into ridesharing for another month, the company had apparently beta tested UberX during the SXSW conference. Ironically, because neither the city nor Uber had disclosed it publicly, SideCar received the brunt of those two extra citations.

Like Ron Linton in DC, Carlton Thomas tagged along for several of Austin's sting operations. Most of them were for drivers who described themselves as "self-employed." In only one case was a SideCar driver ticketed, for the mild infraction of accepting a gratuity after the free ride was over.[123]

With everyone ganging up on SideCar, the ATD's ordinance to define ridesharing using Daus's definition was moving its way through the city council. Effectively, it would have prohibited any ridesharing company's for-profit operations. The council, however, kept delaying the bill, pending the outcome in California.

Colorado, Austin, and California were the hallmark battles for the IATR in 2013, though not the only ones. Milder ones were beginning to take off in Maryland, Rhode Island, and Portland, Oregon. But seemingly wherever they occurred, Matt Daus made an appearance or sent a letter. In both articles and the IATR website's "President's Updates," he went into detail about his efforts in the Colorado hearings, noting that "several Uber representatives testified, including its general manager, a very articulate alleged average customer of Uber who was trotted in with cameras in low to testify, and a couple of drivers who bungled their testimony."[124]

It was like Daus was everywhere, even in cities where regulators hadn't asked him to participate. In late April, New York finally cracked down on SideCar as officers performed sting operations against two female drivers while wearing bulletproof vests. Sunil Paul denounced the tactics, stating on SideCar's blog that these were ordinary women – a grad student and a Lutheran charity employee – just looking to make a few extra bucks. Paul said that his company had been in active contact with the New York TLC since beginning operations the previous month, implying a strangeness of the sudden change of heart.[125] Matt Daus stated it was because the IATR had intervened. He wrote in one of his updates, "Representatives acting on behalf of the IATR contacted and complained to the TLC's Deputy Commissioner for Enforcement, who immediately conducted a sting operation based on the information communicated."[126] After the citations, a judge ruled that SideCar couldn't even offer free rides as part of its ambassador program, causing it to leave New York altogether in early May 2013.[127]

It was difficult to explain Daus's intense motivation. Some of the regulators he represented, like Christiane Hayashi, strongly disliked ridesharing services, while a small few were ambivalent. None of the regulators in New York were asking for his intervention. There was no obvious pattern to explain his attacks, but there were subtle hints, breadcrumbs of information not publicly discussed. And at least a handful of IATR members knew what those reasons were.

Much like the IATR, the TLPA held their own app committee meetings to discuss monthly updates on the proliferation of "rogue" apps. In May 2013, Matt Daus's firm provided a brief to the TLPA to inform them how the transportation frontier was changing. At the top of the report was the introduction:

> Windels Marx Lane & Mittendorf, LLP ("Windels Marx") has been retained as outside counsel to the Taxicab, Limousine & Paratransit Association ("TLPA") and its smartphone applications committee (the "App Committee"). Pursuant to the parties' retainer agreement, we submit this Monthly Report which summarizes the latest updates on regulatory activity, litigation, and other matters regarding "rogue apps" across North America for the month of May 2013.[128]

The report detailed regulatory fights and issues for SideCar, Uber, Hailo, and Lyft, with a heavy emphasis on the taxi app fights in New York.[129] It was strikingly similar to one of the IATR President's Updates of the following month, even covering several of the same jurisdictions.[130]

Two months later, Daus's involvement was further described by the owner of a large taxi company in Connecticut (who would later become a TLPA president) to both his state regulator and one of his competitors. The owner forwarded with his message a copy of the IATR's model regulations, which were going to be finalized at the 2013 conference.

From: Scalzi, Bill
To: King, Dennis; Marco Henry
Sent: Wednesday, July 31, 2013 11:12 AM

Dennis, Marco:

Attached are the draft regulations that are being proposed by the International Association of Transportation Regulators (IATR). Although in draft form, this document has already been released in many areas of the country due to the imposing threat of the rogue apps....

Matt Daus is the current President of the IATR and it is his law firm that has assembled this document. Matt is also the immediate past commissioner of the New York TLC and held that position for 10 years. **Also, he (his law firm) has been retained by the TLPA to combat the rogue app companies on behalf of the taxi and livery industries.***

May I suggest that you both take some time to go through them and then we schedule a time to meet and discuss. I also have another document that fully explains the ride-sharing apps that I will be forwarding soon.

Best,
Bill

---

*bold formatting added

As the email made clear, in a massive conflict of interest, Matt Daus straddled both sides of the taxi world. He represented both the regulators and the regulated.

One of the tenets of government regulation is that regulators do not share a financial interest with the companies they oversee. It's considered a violation of the public trust because it gives way to biased decisions in favor of private interests, whether they benefit society or not. Had any of the taxi regulators taken money from the industry, they would have been fired from their government jobs.

Matt Daus was no longer a regulator, but in leading the IATR, he placed himself in the next-best position to affect taxi regulations. He had access to a wide variety of regulators who, otherwise isolated, needed to collaborate with their colleagues and determine nationwide "best practices." The IATR brought the mountain to Muhammad, and as president, Daus could push policies like the model smartphone regulations on an international scale. Effectively, the taxi industry channeled their wishes through Daus, who then channeled them as best he could through IATR regulators, like when he fed the new ridesharing definition to Carlton Thomas of Austin, who then offered it as a new city ordinance.

Conceivably, the model regulations may have been created not for the regulators' benefit but for the industry's. And it may explain why the IATR was willing to pay for extravagant five-star conferences and comp the registration fees of many of its attendees, like Tom Downey of Denver. It helped shift regulators' opinions about these services from "on the fence," as Downey said he was, to the groupthink of strict enforcement. Plus, the more influential the IATR was, the more Daus could entice vendors and companies to sign on as Windels Marx clients.

It also may explain why an attorney during the Colorado hearings referred to Daus as "counsel" and why IATR Executive Director Karen Cameron was handed a retainer agreement at a 2012 conference party. Most importantly, it explains all of the TLPA events Daus attended, why he pitched Uber as dangerous to their business, and why the TLPA participated in the IATR's Smartphone App Committee.

It's difficult to know who all within the IATR knew that Daus was working for taxis, but it seems apparent that many who attended a conference were, at the very least, suspicious. Some figured it out instantly, and others said it wouldn't have surprised them. Hayashi was exposed to the TLPA connection because San Francisco's Yellow Cab manager, who was on the TLPA's app committee, sent her a copy of the May 2013 Windels Marx report, which explicitly stated that Daus's firm was working for the TLPA.[131] She then passed it out to a handful of other regulators, none of whom replied with any sense of shock or outrage. Nor did Hayashi herself identify it as a conflict of interest.

Many of the core regulators Daus represented hated the ridesharing industry. And to anyone not looking too closely, it might have appeared he was simply crisscrossing the country to attend regulatory hearings and campaign on *their* behalf – and that's exactly how he often represented himself at hearings related to ridesharing:

- "I am president of an organization known as the International Association of Transportation Regulators, also known as IATR. It is a group of regulators from around the world."
  - March 11, 2013 – Colorado PUC [132]

- "And my last hat is a volunteer hat. I've been pro-bono president of the [IATR]. It's a group of-- it's a nonprofit organization, which is comprised of transportation departments, PUCs, including recently the State of Rhode Island. Thank you for joining."
  - April 30, 2014 – Rhode Island PUC [133]

- "My name's Matt Daus. I am the president of the International Association of Transportation Regulators. We're a non-profit government group. We represent taxi commissioners all around the world."
  - July 29, 2014 – Public Transit Commission of Hillsborough County, Florida [134]

Usually, Daus also disclosed he was the partner of a law practice where he led transportation matters. At best, it was a hint that as an attorney for Windels Marx, he represented the industry as well.

Others sidestepped the connection. Asked whether it concerned him when Texas Taxi, Inc. paid hefty sponsorship fees to the IATR, Carlton Thomas softly replied, "They're members." Also, during the initial weights-and-measures hearings of 2012, Daus sometimes attended with fellow Windels Marx staff. A NIST manager pointed out to one of Daus's co-workers that while Daus represented the IATR, his colleague represented the law firm, and by extension, its clients.

"We are of the understanding that your firm may at any given time period represent various individuals or groups having vested interests on [taximeter] issues," the NIST manager told Daus's colleague.[135]

Perhaps it was just the way of the taxi world. The industry and its regulators were so closely aligned on the survival of taxis as a public utility that in several cities across America, they collaborated with one another to push away "rogue" apps. For them, it changed little that at the top of the food chain, the IATR president represented both sides. When requested, Daus provided a wealth of support for what they already believed in principle.

Still, others kept their heads in the sand. Traveling with Daus to various taxi events in 2013, Karen Cameron continued to receive retainer agreement after retainer agreement for Windels Marx. She routinely handed them over to Daus's staff without connecting the dots. She didn't want to know. As far as she was concerned, she was just there to help plan an annual conference.

But throughout 2013, she would become increasingly concerned.

CHAPTER EIGHT

Reversals and Appeals

In early 2013, as the California PUC hearings were taking shape, Hayashi's efforts to modernize the local taxi industry were running into a brick wall. The SFMTA had finally selected a finalist for the Electronic Taxi Access System, the plan to place all of San Francisco's cabs onto a single smartphone app.[1] They went with Frias Transportation Infrastructure (FTI) of Las Vegas, and Hayashi asked the SFMTA Board to approve code changes and give their blessing.[2]

But the local taxi industry bucked. The selection of FTI, owned by Mark James, was somewhat scandalous. A former Nevada state senator and Clark County commissioner, James became CEO of one of the three largest cab companies in Las Vegas, Frias Transportation Management (a separate company from FTI), in 2007 after its owner died. James took over and was made partner by the former owner's widow, giving him 48 percent of the company. But during his tenure, a lawsuit over a consulting contract emerged and allegations were made left and right that James had engaged in drug abuse and hired prostitutes. The suit wasn't dropped until the former owner's widow stepped in and pressured James to settle.[3]

Whether the allegations were hype or real, they were enough to plant the seeds of doubt in the San Francisco taxi community. "We didn't trust Mr. James," said the general manager of one of the larger taxi fleets.

But more than that, the cab companies didn't want to share their data with a government entity for fear that it might become publicly accessible. As with Uber, the ability to dispatch a vehicle was a taxi company's bread and butter. If competitors could access the data, they might learn how to undercut their rivals.

The larger taxi companies were also uncomfortable being placed on a level dispatching field with smaller companies. The basis of charging higher lease fees to drivers was their ability to funnel more dispatch calls than the other guys. With every cab company on the same smartphone app, their competitive distinctions would have eroded. After a few months, the cab companies convinced Mayor Lee to rescind the Electronic Taxi Access program. Taxis were still required to use at least one taxi app, if not the same one.

In late March 2013, the taxi consultant finally presented its report on the state of the taxi industry. It touched on Uber and the new ridesharing industry, even including a section titled "Is Uber the Solution?"[4] It spoke of these new competitors as lower-quality services, implying that as they became cheaper, it was because their safety standards, and thus overhead, were lower.

"We do not want to reach the state where a San Francisco resident or visitor unintentionally requests a ride through *kidnapme.biz*," the report stated.[5]

Pandering was the political reality of the handful of taxi consultants in the United States. Even if they secretly liked Uber and ridesharing, it would have been career suicide to do anything but admonish them. Neither taxi regulators nor taxi companies liked these new services, and to win contracts, taxi consultants had to dance with the ones who brought them. But dogma only went so far. Correctly, the report pointed out that the reason Uber was so successful was that its reliability was far better than taxis.

The most anticipated recommendation in the report was the optimal number of cabs that should be placed on San Francisco's streets. The consultant recommended between six hundred to eight hundred new cabs, added slowly over three years to soften their impact.[6] Local cab companies had eagerly awaited this special number for several months, which was a little odd. Usually, the desire to expand was instinctively counterintuitive; increasing the number of cabs diluted medallion values and expanded the already-competitive driver pool. But these were special circumstances. Uber and ridesharing ate into their market share because of a low taxi supply, and politically, taxis might strengthen their hand if they could show there were now enough cabs on the street to render "rogue" apps unnecessary.

But after the report was presented, the strangest thing happened. In a moment frozen in time, taxi managers walked outside, and as though they were looking at a car crash in slow motion, a cold and chilling fact overcame them: There was no way they could add more cabs to the streets. No way at all. Although they had been dying to do so, the idea was now clearly absurd. The damage had been done. Uber, Lyft, and SideCar had added so many taxi-like vehicles to the streets that between them and the *actual* taxis, adding cabs to the system would have done more harm than good.

For decades, the option to add more cabs to the streets was always on the horizon, within arm's reach only when pressures mounted to a critical mass. But now it was gone, a mirage in the desert. The market once seemingly capable of never-ending growth had reached its zenith. The SFMTA issued more medallions, but no one wanted to buy them. They simply sat, stale and undesired. San Francisco's taxi market was frozen and could no longer mature.

Hayashi had done everything in her power. All that was left were the California PUC hearings. Despite Uber's defiance of any regulation, the CPUC never backed off from its position that it wanted to encourage these new apps to operate. In the beginning, several parties, including Hayashi, had strongly requested that they perform evidentiary hearings, similar in structure to a trial.[7] Parties could file discovery and obtain expert testimony. According to the CPUC's policy director, Marzia Zafar, such hearings would normally require a past regulatory record. There was none in this case. Instead, in mid-April, the CPUC hosted a two-day workshop in one of its auditoriums to discuss how these new services should be regulated.

By this point, the scourge of "rogue" apps had spread in California well beyond the Bay Area. Lyft, SideCar, and UberBLACK had all launched in Los Angeles.[8] UberBLACK was also in San Diego, Sacramento, and a few stretches of beachfront towns along the coast.[9]

In preparation for the workshop, Zafar's staff laid out four options: the apps should be regulated 1) like taxis, 2) like limousines, 3) in a third, yet-to-be-defined way, or 4) not at all by the PUC.[10] According to Zafar, CPUC staff didn't take option #1 seriously. In any city that embraced such a structure, Uber, Lyft, and SideCar would have been required to obtain an operating permit and justify the need for more "taxis" on the road. Option #1 would have effectively shut them down.

As the hearing began, Zafar laid out the ground rules. This was not a hearing for public comment, she told them (the commission already had hundreds of pages of public comment on file) but for advancing any of the four options in a way that "protects public safety" and furthers the CPUC's mission of "encouraging innovation." Wearing a black polo SFMTA shirt, Hayashi sat up front studiously taking notes and quietly watching.

The audience wasn't having Zafar's rules. Only a small fraction of the auditorium's seats were filled, many by members of the SFMTA Taxi Advisory Council, followed by a small contingent from the disability community. By and large, they were there to oppose these new services, and they didn't care about the prohibition of public comments.[11]

The proceedings went off the rails early on. Zafar had invited Uber's

Bay Area general manager to the podium to briefly summarize their services. One of the taxi representatives interrupted him to ask a question, and the GM agreed to answer when his speech was over. Like many of the audience members, the questioner found it difficult to remain brief, and Zafar had to cut him off. But because Uber received more speaking time than anyone in the audience, a local taxi union official rose to object to the "special treatment," as though the company was being treated like a show pony. Several others joined in, protesting the format. They wanted to change gears and discuss why Uber should be treated as a taxi service. Zafar felt she was giving them an equal opportunity to speak, but from that moment forward, it was difficult to maintain civility.[12]

For much of the two days, the conversation turned into an intense cross-examination of one of the three app companies. It was as if the taxi and limo community saw themselves as the district attorney in a courtroom TV drama.

"When you charge my credit card, on my statement, it says 'Uber.' It does not say anybody else – true or not true? Is it true or not true?" pressed a limo representative.[13]

It even turned *Jerry Springer*-esque. At one point, a taxi driver called a Lyft representative a "dumb bitch" and was asked to leave.[14]

As they ignored Zafar's workshop questions, several in the audience focused on the illegitimacy of Uber's business model more than anything else. Zafar had little choice but to endure it. She usually held a microphone in front of them, letting them speak for two to three minutes before cutting them off to move on.

According to the agenda, the hearings were not specifically about Uber but the broader scope of regulations for any company that might follow in Uber's footsteps. For her part, Hayashi understood this better than most and picked her fights. She contributed by focusing on the intent of state law in the face of a changing transportation landscape.

On the second day, Hayashi asked for permission to deliver a prepared speech at the podium. Speaking on behalf of both the SFMTA and the IATR, she was insightful, fiery, and dogged. She attacked the rulemaking process itself, telling the CPUC that promoting competition and innovation were not referenced in its governing state laws. Listed there instead was the need to promote the public interest and mitigate congestion. Further, she pointed out that with almost no transportation enforcement staff, the CPUC was in no position to make sure any of the app companies would follow any new rules.[15]

"You seem ready to dump thousands of personal vehicles on *my* city streets, to troll for-hire [vehicles], to profit by the transportation business. But it seems apparent that there is no will or resources to take responsibility for the consequences to *my* pedestrians. To *my* bicyclists. To *my* public transit system.... *My* air quality. The cost of liability waivers and uninsured or underinsured vehicles to *my* hospitals and *my* general fund."[16]

As she spoke, her voice sometimes quaked with emotion. Her arms periodically crossed, she was clearly passionate but trying hard to suppress her indignation, as though she'd hoped her words, not her tone, would carry the weight of her message. But as she talked about the potential damage to San Francisco's 312,000 paratransit trips per year, which the city provided through its taxi companies, it was too much. Many other cities provided paratransit through a special van service, which Hayashi argued was less flexible.

"Why do we care about that? Well, here's an example. We had a wheelchair customer whose mother was dying in the hospital. And the paratransit taxi provider, who was a frequent provider for that particular customer, arranged to drop off the passenger that they already had in their van, and pick up this person and take them to the hospital before their mother died." Her voice suddenly cracked. She was fighting through tears. "Is Lyft going to do that?"[17]

Although her temper was running high, Hayashi had a valid point. There *were* larger public policy considerations the CPUC was glossing over.

Already, Lyft and Uber were dropping off customers at the San Francisco airport without permission, in violation of their settlement agreement. Insurance issues had yet to be resolved. As General Hagan had confirmed, the CPUC had almost no transportation enforcement staff. And the CPUC was stretching its authority to allow for these new services, undermining local control of taxi-like services, inefficient though they were.

Fundamentally, what the CPUC was debating was whether new ridesharing apps were an all-or-nothing proposition. Taxi regulators took the position that if ridesharing didn't perfectly match all of the taxi safety and public policy aspects, then by comparison, they were inferior and unworthy of consideration. Marzia Zafar and the CPUC disagreed. They believed they could build a *foundation* of ridesharing regulations and amend or add to them as needed.

The workshops concluded with the audience members having contributed little to the discussion except that the ridesharing companies were just bandit cab services. In written briefs, the pro- and anti-ridesharing parties continued to trade arguments back and forth. Despite formally entering the ridesharing space in April, Uber continued to denounce the hearings as redundant and unnecessary.[18] Likewise, SideCar jumped onto the argument that they were also immune from regulation under the federal Telecommunications Act.[19] Lyft, on the other hand, wasn't trying to escape regulations altogether and was willing to accept a modest framework to protect public safety, which gave the CPUC a modicum of political cover to move forward.

"If it hadn't been for Lyft, it would have been a much longer hearing," said Zafar.

In June, the hearings turned more aggressive. The Taxicab Paratransit Association of California (TPAC) filed a discovery request against the three app companies, including information considered proprietary. TPAC sought nineteen sets of documents and the answers to fifty-nine interrogatory questions. All three companies objected strenuously, and the CPUC moved forward without addressing the motion.[20]

On June 24, Tom Drischler, the taxi regulator from the Los Angeles Department of Transportation (LADOT) – who publicized his affiliation as an IATR Board member – sent cease-and-desist letters to all three app companies. Although the CPUC had already provided its blessing and theoretically superseded Los Angeles's authority, Drischler claimed they were under the purview of the *city's* taxi regulations, not the state.[21]

Los Angeles's letters also appeared to have connections to the city council's Transportation Committee, which oversaw LADOT. They came days after the committee chairman filed a council motion to determine whether ridesharing fell under the city's taxicab regulatory authority. The motion noted that "they should be subject to all the rules and regulations applied to taxicabs."[22] The TLPA president, whose own cab company was based in Los Angeles, applauded the chairman's efforts.[23]

The timing was also conspicuous since the letters were issued one week before LA's new mayor, Eric Garcetti, was sworn into office. App companies were seldom, if ever, mentioned in the LA mayoral campaign, but there were early hints Garcetti held a favorable opinion.[24] On July 1, the day Garcetti was inaugurated, those suspicions were confirmed. To address its cease-and-desist letters, LADOT was scheduled to release a press statement, which the mayor's office then canceled. Further, Drischler was prohibited from speaking to the press, and Garcetti made a statement in favor of the app companies.[25]

Ultimately, LA's letters came too late. The app companies continued to operate unfettered, and LADOT jumped into the CPUC hearings as a late party, barely having time to file a single brief of comments.

A month later on July 30, the CPUC issued its proposed decision. Doing away with the "NOETS" acronym, the commission developed a new term that would become a national standard: Transportation Network Companies (TNCs). A surprise to few, the commission found a regulatory justification to allow for the new apps to operate.[26]

Zafar's staff dismissed the notion that any of the apps were extensions of traditional carpooling, as SideCar had pushed. It was one of the few issues in which they were in agreement with the taxi industry. TNCs were clearly for-profit entities. Further, while the apps and their software might have been immune from regulation under the federal Telecommunications Act, the drivers and their cars were not. Cars were physical objects, not coded software, and the consequences of their actions were very real and already under the CPUC's governing jurisdiction. Also, the TNCs had the market power to guide their decisions. Immunity, the CPUC proclaimed, only extended so far.[27]

With the carpooling argument knocked out, the next step was to determine whether and how they were prearranged. By law, the CPUC's authority only extended to prearranged non-taxi services. Although not specifically defined, the traditional definition usually applied to an advance order of at least thirty to forty-five minutes. Instead, the commission was "guided by the plain meaning of 'prearranged' as something arranged in advance." This was a suggestion advocated by both Lyft and Uber. By downloading the app, the customer was already making the arrangements "in advance."[28]

However, in the proposed draft, the CPUC erroneously noted one additional characteristic of prearrangement: a customer *must* input their trip destination before requesting a ride.[29] Zafar's office had slipped up. This condition was only true of SideCar, and if passed, it would have solely given their company ridesharing authority, leaving Uber and Lyft in the cold.

SideCar loved the proposed condition and asked the CPUC to repeat it in other sections of the decision.[30] Uber and Lyft hated it. Lyft asked the

CPUC to clarify this aspect, assuming the commission did not intend to "micromanage the design and implementation of software applications."[31] Zafar's office realized the mistake and later redacted the trip-destination requirement.

As a whole, the proposed decision set up a basic framework of regulations. TNCs would be required to obtain a CPUC operating permit, and to keep it, they would have to maintain a minimal set of safety requirements, including excess liability insurance, criminal background and driver record checks, a zero-tolerance policy for drugs and alcohol, a driver training program, nineteen-point inspections of each vehicle, and a vehicle emblem or other "trade dress." The regulations fell silent on any issues of price regulation or supply limits – neither was addressed. In addition, since it was still experimental, the CPUC wanted the TNCs to turn over reports on the number of rejected ride requests and the number and percentage of rides provided for disabled passengers. To cover the cost of the new regulations, TNCs would pay a quarter of a percent of gross revenues.[32]

On paper, LADOT and the SFMTA were generally pleased with the decision, but in private, each one's taxi regulator hated it. In LADOT's response, they politely requested the CPUC grant cities the authority to impose additional restrictions.[33] Also, the day after it was announced, Christiane Hayashi sent a lengthy email to the IATR Smartphone App Committee that began with, "Why do we have minimum prices?" It was an essay about the need to distinguish and separate luxury transportation from taxi markets. She was pointing out that setting minimum prices was a way to keep the taxi market healthy so that black cars and limousines couldn't compete in the same sphere and impact services such as paratransit.[34]

In a strange twist, Hayashi and Drischler weren't alone in their agency's duplicity. On their blog, Uber also announced they were "pleased" with the proposal, but in further CPUC briefs, they continued to criticize it.[35] They still hated the idea that the CPUC would begin to regulate their service and not solely the drivers. Obtaining a permit to operate was effectively a leash they did not want to be tethered to.

They replied, "In the same way that Google did not become an energy utility by developing the Google PowerMeter software application, Uber does not become a transportation company by developing the Uber software application."[36]

Part of their resistance was related to the company's organizational structure. Uber's wholly owned subsidiary, Rasier, LLC, was the entity that entered into contracts with drivers while the parent company focused on software development. It was likely a structure designed to further Kalanick's Expedia-vs-American-Airlines argument. Uber could argue its app operations didn't commingle in the same world as its drivers. Thus, they countered, the parent company was still immune from regulation under the federal Telecommunications Act.[37]

The proposed decision had something for almost everyone to hate. Uber hated sending reports that even hinted how many total rides they might be providing, information they considered a trade secret. They likewise hated paying a fee as a *percentage* of gross revenues, which also might illuminate the health of their business. Also, for reasons bordering on the nit-picky, they hated asking their drivers to carry any kind of trade dress, as it implied Uber employed the drivers or owned their vehicles.[38]

The CPUC spent another month and a half sifting through indignant reply comments and replies *to* reply comments. Zafar kept tweaking the draft, making minor edits before the commission formally voted. In the final version, they removed the trip-destination requirement. And since they scheduled a review of the new rules for a year later, they also dismissed TPAC's earlier request for discovery documents. [39]

Marzia Zafar also took a perverse joy in replying to Uber's "Google PowerMeter" argument. The comparison was not appropriate, she wrote, since Google's tool didn't take money from customers.

The Commission elects to use a more appropriate analogy involving Google.

Google Search is an app and a software platform, and uses that software to provide a product: search listings. In 2011, Google agreed to pay a settlement of $500 million for allowing fraudulent pharmaceutical advertisements. In the case of pharmaceutical listings, Google Search was connecting people with products that were harmful or fraudulent, and which represented a threat to public safety. The people selling the illegal drugs had to be held accountable, but so did the software platform that connected people with the illegal drugs. The same is true with Uber.[40]

As a company, Uber needed to be held accountable, Zafar argued, especially since their insurance requirements were questionable at best. A TNC operating permit further ensured that Uber was not leaving anyone in harm's way. "I particularly enjoyed writing that section," Zafar said.

Uber showed little appreciation for this unique victory. Nowhere else in California or the rest of the country was a regulatory agency as welcoming of their luxury-car or impending ridesharing services. Even as the CPUC spent over nine months looking for ways to legitimize all of these app companies, Colorado, Austin, San Antonio, Philadelphia, Los Angeles, and New York all worked to make life harder for them. In the coming years, no regulatory agency would extend the olive branch the way California had. Instead of saying thank you, Uber quibbled over trade dress issues and parent company distinctions. Mirroring Travis Kalanick's personality, Uber was being handed a rare and valuable gift but complained that it wasn't wrapped properly. They were ingrates.

On September 19, 2013, CPUC commissioners voted 5–0 in favor of the proposed decision.[41] According to President Mike Peevey, who had led the charge, a couple of the commissioners were skeptical toward the beginning of the process but ultimately changed their minds.

"I think they saw this [new service] as a liberating thing," he said.

For the first time, Uber, Lyft, and SideCar were now legal in an entire state, and it gave each of them a foothold in the rest of the country. Shortly after the vote, both Lyft and SideCar abandoned their "voluntary donation" model in California.[42]

Uber was still resistant. Ironically, both they and TPAC filed appeals for a re-hearing to argue (for opposing reasons) that the CPUC had exceeded its authority. They spent months waiting as ridesharing took off internationally, and Uber's re-hearing request more or less fizzled out. TPAC tried an additional appeal to the California Supreme Court, which was denied.

The last to consider a formal challenge was the Los Angeles City Council, which was incensed by the CPUC decision. A month after it was issued, the council deliberated on whether to begin appealing the decision, the first step in filing a lawsuit against the commission. The motion lost by one vote, and instead the council voted to ask the CPUC to amend their decision in the continued hearings a year later.[43] Although more California fights would arise, the CPUC's decision had become ingrained.

Culturally, one of the lasting effects of the hearings is that they literally gave new meaning to the term "ridesharing." Even though it originally referred to nonprofit carpooling, the media continued to apply it to TNCs in the months and years after California's decision. In the beginning, Sunil Paul used it to argue that SideCar *was* a carpooling app, and even though that argument failed, the term stuck nonetheless. Perhaps because it sounded similar enough to the burgeoning "sharing economy" that now included TNCs, its meaning shifted. City transportation agencies hated it, claiming it was a term created to deliberately confuse TNCs with nonprofit carpooling. But like the TNC industry in general, it was beyond their control.

In August 2013, between the CPUC's proposed decision and the final commission vote, the City of Austin finally put their SideCar issue to rest. The ATD released an addendum to their May report on how other cities treated ridesharing. They included more updates on how New York and

Philadelphia had already shut down SideCar's operations. In June, after SideCar's ambassador program failed to gain any public relations victories, they left Philadelphia. The updated report also included cease-and-desist letters the City of Dallas sent to Uber for their black-car service. It was the first time the report was willing to mention how other cities were treating Uber's luxury car service, but it did not include any of the several instances in which cities had ultimately given them their approval.[44]

When the report turned to the CPUC's proposed decision, it cherry-picked with laser focus Marzia Zafar's singular argument that TNCs were not an extension of carpooling, the same argument SideCar was attempting in Austin. In bold formatting, the report emphasized that the CPUC "firmly believes that TNCs ... do not meet the rideshare exemption and actually are for-hire transportation services." It continued quoting the proposed decision for roughly a paragraph, reflecting the importance of regulating for public safety. Then, in a quiet whisper of an afterthought, the paragraph ended with the single sentence "The proposed decision suggests creating a new category similar to charter services."[45] It was the only sentence in the report in which the ATD noted that California legitimized SideCar (among others) and wasn't "confused" as the original version stated. The first state in the nation had given ridesharing a green light, but in its report, the ATD buried the lede, as though it were hoping no one would notice.

Carlton Thomas's office recommended against any pilot program for SideCar, and the following day, the Austin City Council voted to strengthen its carpooling ordinance so that SideCar could not operate.[46] The new law used a ridesharing definition similar to the one that Matt Daus provided to Thomas, and the council placed the ordinance on the consent agenda without argument. That same day, a Windels Marx staff member sent an update to the IATR Smartphone App Committee. Noting the contributions of Austin's taxi regulator, she wrote, "Special congrats to App Committee member Carlton Thomas of the Austin TD who was integral in pushing this new rule through."[47] The following year, Thomas would receive the IATR's "Regulator of the Year" award.

With few other options, SideCar discontinued it ambassador program and closed up shop in Austin within a couple of months, making Austin the third major city to push them out. Giving away several months of free rides hobbled the company. SideCar had expanded nationally before they could acquire a strong marketing advantage. Lyft had the pink mustaches, and Uber dominated in name recognition. SideCar had nothing comparable to either.

Sunil Paul wouldn't say specifically how much money had been lost in its 2013 ambassador program, but the amount was painful. For the next couple of years, as Uber and Lyft competed voraciously for new cities, SideCar struggled. It would only expand to a couple of California cities and a few more nationally in which Uber had already cleared a regulatory path. In Seattle, it contributed to a joint political campaign with Uber and Lyft but only with a fraction of the funds. The company slowly dwindled to obscurity.

Paul felt that if the company had more money to endure the tough times, they might have had a shot. "I think in hindsight, not having capital was the biggest mistake" he said. By December 2015, he announced the company was shutting down, and a month later, it was sold to General Motors.[48] At the time, Paul placed much of the blame on Uber's cutthroat tactics. "We failed – for the most part – because Uber is willing to win at any cost and they have practically limitless capital to do it," he wrote in a blog post.[49]

SideCar, the first major TNC to conceive of and launch a ridesharing app, had gambled and lost. It had bet heavily on an early national expansion and a dubious carpooling legal argument, both of which backfired, and it hadn't effectively built a base of followers who would come to its defense. SideCar needed political leverage in the face of regulatory resistance, but few ever emailed a city council member on its behalf. For much of the Austin City Council members and their staff, they were an unremarkable blip. In interviews three years after leaving Austin, several council members struggled to remember who or what SideCar was.

"We weren't ready," said Paul.

In July 2013, after Travis Kalanick denounced Colorado's Governor Hickenlooper, the two finally met for the first time at the *Fortune* Brainstorm TECH conference in Aspen. Hickenlooper delivered the welcome remarks at the first night's dinner, and Kalanick was scheduled for a public one-on-one interview.[50] The two spoke briefly, and according to the Colorado governor, it didn't go well.

"He's very quick and can be witty. He's intentionally abrasive," the governor said of Kalanick. Before his political career, Hickenlooper came from restaurants, having owned a brewpub. "In the restaurant business, no matter how unreasonable someone is, you will do anything so that the customer doesn't leave upset. I tried to maintain that attitude. There's no margin in making enemies."

At the meeting, Hickenlooper and Kalanick sat at a table with a few other tech bigwigs, including (reportedly) James Murdoch, chairman of 21st Century Fox and son of Rupert Murdoch. According to Hickenlooper, Kalanick unloaded his frustrations on the governor in front of their conference peers.

"I didn't react or shout back at him," said the governor. "I was more bemused. As we were leaving, at least one of [the other bigwigs] – they looked more horrified than I was."

The next day, Kalanick publicly described the conversation during a fireside chat. "What I got from Hickenlooper was that I think he gets it," he told the moderator. "I think he gets it. He knows that tech progress matters and that making Colorado a place for tech entrepreneurs and for technology, et cetera, is a good thing. And it's not just good policy; it's also good for the people of the state. So, he made it very clear that he was not the one that was trying to put us out of business, but actually, it was *his appointees* at the PUC that were trying to put us out of business."[51]

Kalanick was starting to acknowledge the divisions of authority in a state government. Governors oversaw state agencies, but often without giving them day-to-day orders. When told that Kalanick spoke positively of their meeting, Governor Hickenlooper replied, "He's very mercurial."

About a week later, the Colorado ALJ finally released his proposed decision. Mostly as expected, it prohibited "transportation brokers" from advertising their services unless they also pulled the miracle of obtaining an operating permit from the PUC, and it prevented any luxury limousine service from using any type of meter other than a clock. It also created a minimum buffer of distance between luxury limousines and taxicab stands (if the limos weren't in the middle of a prearranged trip). The judge summed up his reasons, stating, "To permit authorized carriers of one type of service to provide a different transportation service would be contrary to the Legislative intent, unless permitted by statute."[52] In other words, state law for regulating black cars was clear, and he wasn't interested in deviating from it.

The judge also expressed some concern at Uber's terms and conditions, noting a proviso in which Uber reserved the right to change the price at any time. "Please note the pricing information published on the website may not reflect the prevailing pricing," it read. The judge was concerned that without a more concretely prearranged price, "the provision creates a substantial potential for abuse."[53] It was another instance in which the app's voluminous terms and conditions scared the regulatory community.

Before it could be approved, the judge's decision still required a vote from the three-member commission, which was not scheduled for a few weeks. Uber quickly began considering its options. Although Kalanick and Governor Hickenlooper had at least developed a cordial understanding a week earlier, Uber didn't rely on it. Quietly, they submitted a public information request seeking communications from all PUC staff related to Uber.[54] They were fishing, looking for the slightest hint of impropriety that might disqualify a bad opinion.

A few days after their submitted request, Governor Hickenlooper broke his seven-month silence and went on record to the press against the proposed decision. "Attempts to micro-manage limousine services constitute an overreach, are unnecessarily complicated and are not in the public interest," he said in an interview. It appeared as though the political pressure was too much for him to ignore. *The Denver Post* noted that the Internet Association, a trade group of major Internet companies such as eBay and Amazon, had sent him a letter protesting the proposed decision.[55] Governor Hickenlooper had made his political bed on the future of the tech industry, and now he had to sleep in it.

"Because of the importance of this issue to Colorado's economy and tech-friendly reputation, the governor's office plans to formally comment on, and take exception to, certain parts of the proposed rules," he was quoted.[56]

Uber was now attempting a two-pronged attack. In case the governor's intervention didn't hold sway, they also tried to attack the proposed decision on procedural grounds. Their public information request found that the ALJ had discussed the hearings with a colleague at the California PUC roughly a couple of months after their *Jerry Springer*-style hearings. The two colleagues met at an administrative conference, and their emails showed them blandly trading notes on how existing laws treated companies like Uber.[57] The emails, Uber argued, were illicit because they were ex parte communications not included in the procedural records.[58] It was a weak technical argument, but it bought Uber a few more weeks to continue objecting to the proposed regulations. During the interim, the IATR continued to file its own redundant replies, repeatedly harping on the lack of price controls and the fact that NIST had not yet approved of the app.[59]

For Uber, the delay tactic was successful. Their most powerful Colorado frenemy stepped in. The governor's office filed a letter in support of a modified decision, which turned the outcome in Uber's favor. It also came on the heels of a similar letter from the Colorado Technology Association.[60] The commissioners took the hint and changed the ALJ's proposed decision. They loosened the prearrangement definition "to allow the use of innovative methods of communication" and let Uber charge its own fares as long as a "reasonable estimate" was provided beforehand.[61]

On the issue of price controls, the PUC – effectively the taxi regulator for the entire state of Colorado – broke with a long-held practice of distinguishing between taxi and luxury car markets. "Participants and commenters advocate that consumer protection is a prominent policy interest, and we agree," the commissioners wrote with a slight dusting of sarcasm. "Another important policy interest is removing unnecessary impediments to formation of contracts and allowing the market to function efficiently."[62] In so many words, they told the taxi industry they had a new competitor, market segregation be damned. State law didn't specify price distinctions between taxis and limousines.

Not wanting to drag it out any longer, they dismissed Uber's arguments regarding the judge's emails with the California PUC.[63] It was a way of telling Uber they got what they wanted, and it was now over. Let it go.

Two days later, Lyft entered the Denver market, opening a completely new can of worms.[64] The ink wasn't even dry on the PUC decision for Uber's black-car service, and now the most prosperous ridesharing app to date had entered Colorado. The PUC had a brief encounter with another ridesharing operation in 2012 before Uber first entered Denver. A student-run start-up company called "Rideorama" charged people for trips provided by ordinary, nonprofessional drivers to the Denver airport. Within two months, it was shut down after the PUC found fliers posted at the airport.[65] But unlike Rideorama, Lyft was well-capitalized and battle-hardened by regulatory fights in California. Plus, Governor Hickenlooper's make-or-break commitment to innovation gave them an ideal opening.

Dipping their toe in uncertain waters, Lyft started by offering rides paid only by voluntary donation.[66] For Uber, it was clear there was no time to lose. Instead of waiting a full thirty days, as Travis Kalanick said they would in his

"White Paper 1.0" blog post, they launched the competing UberX service two and a half weeks after Lyft.[67]

Colorado proved to be a case in which Kalanick's harsh, public criticisms of the governor, combined with the governor politically painting himself into the "innovation" corner, had allowed Uber to turn the tables. Whether by design or simply as a result of Kalanick's competitive personality, it was effective. Uber became an ambassador of the larger tech industry. For better or worse, the way an elected official treated them bled over into the tech community, and no politician wanted to be perceived as anti-technology, especially when the technology in question had large populist appeal.

For the taxi industry, it was a harsh lesson to learn. They often argued that Uber's use of software was not new, that public safety trumped the appeal of a seemingly hip, well-marketed software favored superficially by millennials. But they missed the larger point. It wasn't that the software was new or hip; it was that it was an improvement over taxi service. It was reliable and timely. It had included additional incentives to ensure the experience was satisfactory. All taxis could argue in response was that they better secured the public's safety. In some ways, it was true. Their liability insurance, for example, carried less uncertainty in the event of an accident. But the argument didn't hold popular appeal. As long as Uber and Lyft were *perceived* to be safe enough, then few cared about the holes in public safety. Their efficiencies outweighed any downside. The more traction Uber gained across the country, the fewer legs the taxi industry had to stand on.

In September 2013, as the PUC announced a reversal of the ALJ's proposed decision, the IATR's annual conference was only days away. Robert McBride, the owner of Colorado's Metro Taxi and former TLPA president, canceled his conference registration. However, one of Colorado's PUC transportation staff did register.[68]

Throughout all of the regulatory battles of 2013, there was a small but growing dissension in the IATR's ranks. Executive Director Karen Cameron found her perspective on Uber changing. In her late forties with light copper-brown hair and a perky smile, Cameron was a well-seasoned veteran of Canadian transportation systems. She had built much of her career working on Calgary's transportation for disabled communities. And in 2002, she transitioned to licensing and enforcement for the city's taxis and limousines. She understood taxi regulations, but after leaving Calgary in 2007, her career shifted more toward conference planning and association management, which she performed as a hired consultant.[69]

At the IATR, she was one of the few hired staff whose main role was to organize the annual conference, but she also assisted Matt Daus as needed. She attended meetings on Capitol Hill and often followed Daus on his excursions to TLPA and related conferences. After the 2012 IATR Conference in DC, Daus decided it was wise to at least keep an open dialogue with Uber, a task he assigned to Cameron.[70]

After Uber hired Corey Owens, Facebook's former public policy chief, he and Cameron were introduced in April 2013. They hit it off well, and Owens spoke of "resetting the relationship" with the regulatory community.[71] As much as taxi companies and taxi regulators saw Uber as a threat to the industry, Uber employees often didn't understand the regulatory community's deep resistance. As far as regulators should have been concerned, they felt, Uber was simply an additional competitor to the transportation industry. Perhaps they weren't fully beyond regulations, but the way they facilitated rides was straightforward enough that regulators should not have felt a need to push them out of any jurisdiction.

Even before speaking to Owens, Cameron could begin to see their perspective. She became especially interested in the FTC's pro-Uber argument that Colorado's proposed regulations were inhibiting competition, and she passed them around to other IATR Board members.[72] But the more she spoke with Owens, the more silent rifts were forming with Matt Daus.

In June, after New York, Austin, and Colorado had each taken actions against either Uber or SideCar, Cameron sent Owens a copy of the IATR President's Update titled "The Ride Stops Here – Regulatory Pushback Against Rogue Apps." It celebrated the jurisdictions where the app companies were meeting resistance, mirroring much of the summaries Windels Marx had already written for the TLPA.

"I imagine you will have reactions to the President's Update below," she wrote to Owens. "I had reactions to it too. I remain hopeful that we are working toward an opportunity to improve the quality of regulatory responses to new offerings in the market."[73]

Owens replied, "As you can imagine, I have many reactions to the various sections, not the least of which is that several of them contain outright (and what appear to be malicious) factual errors... I likewise hold out some hope for improvement of the relationship, but I confess emails like this significantly limit my enthusiasm for dialogue."[74]

"I too have many concerns with what is currently happening," she told Owens.[75]

Karen Cameron continued to dig in, hoping to bridge some middle ground between IATR regulators and Uber. In the 2013 conference that soon followed in St. Louis, an idea was floated to hold a debate between the app companies and the regulators. And as a show of good faith, she offered to craft a rebuttal to many of Daus's arguments. She shared few of the IATR members' views that the taxi industry needed protection and insulation from competitors. Rather, she thought of them in terms of whether "historical provisions and safeguards are still appropriate, and what the right regulatory response is in the new world."[76]

She started studying Uber, watching any video she could find online in which Kalanick or someone else had given an interview. In July she forwarded a list of videos to the IATR Board of Directors as "must view research."[77] But for Daus, the tone had already changed.

"Uber has no credibility in my eyes as I have seen them lie right in front of me to public officials and to the media," he told the board. "Other apps are great, but many regulators have grown tired of Uber's antics."[78]

Cameron forwarded another President's Update to Owens, which was equally as inflammatory as the last. Owens replied that he was "utterly dismayed" as the IATR continued "to do premature victory laps for advocacy on behalf of the taxi industry, revealing itself not as an independent peer group of regulators but an organized lobby for certain incumbent operators." The temporary detente was breaking down. Owens further told Cameron he was "fast approaching a point" where he couldn't maintain any credibility arguing there were "reasonable actors within IATR."[79]

Days before the IATR's annual conference in September, tensions were reaching a head. It was held at the four-star Hilton Hotel in downtown St. Louis, just a few blocks from the Gateway Arch, and Uber reps had once more been invited to attend and find a unified force pressuring them to back off of their business model.[80] But Daus instructed Cameron not to allow the Hilton to give Uber access to a separate meeting room. He didn't want a repeat of the 2012 conference in DC, when Uber promoted their app to the regulators. This was one of the few times of the year a large group of taxi regulators gathered in one place, a key opportunity for any company that wanted to promote itself through the IATR, which was normally done by sponsorship. Uber was undermining Daus's business model.

"It was embarrassing last year and disrespectful, and should not happen again," Daus told Cameron.[81]

Cameron immediately asked Corey Owens if they were going to book a room again. "I can say you won't be surprised by anything we have planned this year," Owens replied to Cameron. "If Matt wants us to do what we do in the hallway instead of a room, I suspect that will cause more of a stir, not less."[82] Uber reserved a room for the second conference day at 5:00 p.m., after the meetings had ended and at the least disruptive time they could manage.[83]

Daus was pissed. "She was instructed ten times not to do this," he discretely told a board member.[84] Later that evening, he reported another board member calmed him down. "Live and let live we can't let them get to us – because then they win!" Daus wrote.[85]

The day before the conference began, Daus forwarded to the Smartphone App Committee a copy of a report on taxi deregulation in the 1980s and the subsequent re-regulation. It came just after the CPUC's vote to legitimize Uber, Lyft, and SideCar, which Daus frequently characterized as "defacto deregulation." Cameron criticized the report and called it outdated, which quickly led to an online debate via email.

"We have to ask ourselves – have regulated markets become worse than deregulated markets for the consumer?" said Cameron. "That's what Uber is telling the elected officials and it's hard to defend against it."[86]

But her arguments were falling on deaf ears. No one else among the IATR membership shared her viewpoint. Ron Linton told her that if left unfettered, unsavory elements would intercept the public vehicle-for-hire industry, leading to spikes in fraud and identity theft. In that scenario, he said, the industry "will devolve into chaos and public safety will get compromised."[87]

Karen Cameron was alone.

To make matters worse, she learned of some disturbing news. On the first day of the conference, Karen, her husband, and some of the Windels Marx staff were manning a few of the IATR tables. One of the Windels Marx interns was "flapping his lips about all kinds of Windels Marx and IATR things in front of my husband," she said.

According to Cameron's husband, the intern further told him, "The IATR conference was about generating more business for Windels Marx. That's what its job was."

It was a revelation, one that should have seemed obvious much sooner but wasn't until she was hit over the head with it. Matt Daus was leveraging the IATR to bring in more business for his law firm, of which he was a partner. Instead of simply feeling ideologically isolated, Cameron was now beginning to feel repulsed.

On the second day, wearing a dark suit and striped tie, Daus gave a customary "State of the IATR" address from a podium at the front of a conference room. When he spoke, none of the growing tensions between him and Cameron surfaced, and in fact, Daus praised her more than once.

"Karen has been really the backbone of our group for many years," he told the audience. "She's our executive director ... she's been committed 100 percent, doing a lot of pro bono work, as I have for the group for many, many years. And I think we owe you a round of applause, Karen. Why don't you stand up again?"[88]

Daus continued on, giving many of his typical annual updates. He pointed out the accomplishments of a few specific regulators and talked about ongoing projects and goals the association was working on. But then he turned to the topic of IATR's past year of advocacy, where his tone shifted to one more serious, more frustrated. He pointed out that at their 2009 conference, a few regulators were floating the idea of hailing a cab by smartphone, before any of the "rogue" app companies had launched.

"We were the first to have the idea, not *you*," he said knowing that Uber staff were in the audience.[89]

He was clearly upset over California's recent decision. "You cannot deregulate an industry and have people flying around on the fly, picking up people and fist-bumping each other without licenses," Daus said, referring to Lyft's practice of encouraging drivers to greet passengers with a gentle fist bump. "People are going to get killed. This is serious stuff. It's not a joke, you know? So for those people that are forcing the envelope, please, just hear us out. We're not here to stop anything. We just want some sanity to prevail, okay?"[90]

It was a striking difference from the Matt Daus who only months earlier stood before the Colorado PUC asking a judge to issue new rules prohibiting ridesharing services like Lyft from operating. But Daus digressed. He returned to advocacy, noting how he'd met with Miami's mayor to prevent Uber from spreading there. He offered his services to any regulator who was being "railroaded by the press" or silenced by their mayor, a reference to LADOT's Thomas Drischler, who was silenced by Mayor Garcetti's office.

Daus's advocacy speech was less a public policy agenda and more a rallying cry. He proclaimed that the IATR would not be silenced or intimidated "by powerful lobbyists or ethically challenged legislators, overzealous government agencies, or well-financed and manipulative social media campaigns."[91]

In many other ways, the 2013 conference was characterized by conflict and angst. At Karen Cameron's suggestion, the IATR invited FTC Director Andy Gavil, who had filed remarks against the taxi industry during Colorado's hearings. Daus had previously characterized the FTC's participation as "an unusual and suspicious development."[92] And they now had more reasons to be suspicious. Uber had brought to the conference DC attorney John Thorne, a specialist in anti-trust and intellectual property law, who coincidentally attended law school with Gavil.[93] And now Gavil arrived to their conference to imply that taxi regulations had strong potential for anticompetitive behavior.

"All I can say is I hope I have my ass with me when I leave today," Gavil said in his opening remarks.[94]

After his presentation, Gavil received any icy reception during the Q&A. Several challenged the fairness of a private enterprise competing with a regulated business, and Hayashi once more connected the ridesharing threat in San Francisco to the city's paratransit community.

"It's not that we're just trying to keep competition out," she told the FTC director. "It's that we know that we need to maintain this service and that's, frankly, in jeopardy at this point."[95]

Other panel discussions were equally cold. Some had moments of bickering. In one session, the owner of Hailo, who was still trying to make regulatory inroads by sponsoring the IATR, was accused by the TLPA president of "operating outside of the regulatory framework," which he sternly rebuffed.[96] In another session, Mark James, the owner of Frias Transportation Infrastructure, the company awarded the SFMTA's short-lived Electronic Taxi Access program, was insulted by a fellow competitor from Creative Mobile Technologies (CMT). The competitor accused James of using his thirty-minute discussion on "big data" simply to advertise his own company. "Is this panel going to discuss big data?" the CMT rep asked.[97]

The barb rang true for Karen Cameron, who only a short while ago had been told that the IATR was more or less a commercial extension of Windels Marx. According to Cameron, it was in that moment that her frustration peaked and she decided she would quit.

The tension spiked again after the IATR formally adopted the model regulations for smartphone apps it had first proposed in 2012. Although Daus had already spent much of 2013 pushing for them in Colorado, Austin, and California, he wanted the association to formally ratify them, and the conference was the only time of year when the membership gathered. Corey Owens obtained a copy from Karen Cameron a few days beforehand. [98]

Owens was as aggravated as Cameron, and after spending the better part of a year watching these regulatory battles, he'd had enough as well. In the middle of the conference, he released an Uber blog post titled "On Consumers, Competition & Collusion," wherein he compared the taxi and limo industry to music and e-books, positing what the world would have been like had the government formed a commission consisting of book publishers and entertainment studios. If such a commission set minimum prices and wait times for downloads, he explained, it would inhibit the free market.[99]

"This laughable scenario is frighteningly real in the fight to revolutionize urban transportation," he wrote.[100]

Only the week before, Owens had been in Portland, Oregon, requesting changes before the city's taxi authority. He encouraged them to change the rules so that Uber could operate. "I was requesting these changes of a regulatory body made up of taxi companies and their allies," he said in the blog post. He noted that the authority was a "self-interested regulator" made up of commissioners from taxi and limo companies, which made his request futile. The fix was already in. "I'm here on behalf of Radio Cab, and I'm asking the board member from Radio Cab to please protect Radio Cab," he wrote mockingly. He went on to talk of similar "marriages" in Dallas, Colorado, and also St. Louis, where the IATR Conference was taking place. "This is regulation by the taxi industry for the taxi industry," he wrote.[101] He then turned his attention to the conference:

> Today, a group that generously refers to itself as the International Association of Transportation Regulators issued model regulations that would drastically limit consumer choice and transportation options if widely adopted. IATR counts regulators from cities like Portland, St. Louis, Denver, and Dallas as members ... and fills its treasury with contributions from taxi and shuttle companies.
>
> IATR has proposed that you only be able to pay for a ride using Uber in one-hour increments. Only take a 15-minute trip? Too bad, you're charged for the unused 45 minutes. IATR thinks it should be illegal to measure the length of a sedan trip using a GPS device. Ignoring for a moment that GPS has been used for things like defining national borders and navigating aircraft carriers for nearly 20 years, this newfangled technology can clearly not be trusted to measure the length of your ride home from work. And IATR says you should only be able to arrange a ride through Uber way in advance. Sixty-minute rules are in vogue; so better order your ride two or three drinks before you need it.
>
> The IATR model regulations are indeed a model. They are a tried-and-true model of anti-competitive and collusive policymaking. They are a model of serving producers instead of consumers. And they are an excellent model for cities looking to find themselves on the wrong side of history. That said, consumers ultimately will not be denied. Better, safer, more reliable transportation made possible by new technologies will prevail.[102]

The blog post was released shortly before Kalanick's end-of-day side meeting with regulators, which some have reported was tense and argumentative – possibly because much of the IATR viewed the blog post as a slap in the face. Although he'd been previously talked down, Daus was again upset about Kalanick's private meeting with regulators. According to Karen Cameron, he became very rude and hostile to hotel staff, and the Hilton manager felt so bad for her that he had lunch with Cameron and Owens at the rooftop terrace restaurant.

After the conference ended, Cameron shared a ride with Corey Owens to the airport, which she believed was an innocent gesture. It earned her ridicule from Daus, who criticized her for not showing enough loyalty to the IATR.[103]

The *San Francisco Business Times* immediately spotted Owens's blog post and quickly interviewed Daus, who called it "childish" and "defamatory." He said that if Uber did it again, the IATR would be "getting lawyers." It was likely a tense moment for Daus: he had to defend *both* the IATR and himself. On the allegations of cronyism, he said all the work he had done for the IATR was pro bono, though he declined to name any of the transportation companies Windels Marx represented.[104]

As he often did, Daus forwarded the article to the IATR Board to initiate a conversation. Christiane Hayashi had now been appointed as a board member, and LADOT's Thomas Drischler was its new chair. "I thought you would like to see the outrageous comments they made about us and [the St. Louis regulator] in our own backyard," wrote Daus. He then suggested the IATR permanently change their relationship with Uber and send them a cease-and-desist letter against any further "defamatory and libelous statements." He sought feedback from the rest of the board.[105]

Cameron, who was only cc'd the message, immediately responded, trying one last time to change the board's enforcement-only thinking toward Uber.

> Here is where we have our pants down around our ankles. Developing

model regs was not the right starting point. We should have started by producing an analysis of how technology changes the market failure premise on which regulation is based. We should have enabled a discussion about whether the suite of new market oriented policies are appropriate to for-hire transportation.[106]

Cameron specifically asked them to seek a middle ground between operator-focused enforcement and consumer-oriented economics.

"Uber isn't trying to deregulate the industry – they are trying to deregulate regulators and OUR self-interested strangle-hold on consumer 'over' protection," she wrote. It was too much to ask, and she knew it. "I know this response may not sit well with some of you, but I feel it is my job to protect our member regulators – even if it is from themselves."[107]

For all intents and purposes, she was proposing a sudden 180-degree turn in taxi policy after Corey Owens had publicly embarrassed them. Cameron felt she had nothing left to lose. If they fired her, so be it. She already intended to leave. If she was going out, it was in a blaze of principle and condemnation.

"Perhaps I need to be Matt's regulator!!" she wrote half-sarcastically.[108]

Daus replied to all that he was carrying out the wishes of the Board. "If you cannot see the distinction between the individual antics of the company itself versus virtually 'the whole world and their legitimate tech competitors' - I don't know what to say." He also accused Cameron of developing the sponsorship model Owens had used against them in his blog post and that Daus suddenly said he'd "always been uncomfortable with."[109]

For someone so discomforted, it hadn't stopped him the previous year when he'd instructed Cameron to extract a sponsorship out of MTData on behalf of Colorado's Metro Taxi. It hadn't stopped him from traveling to speak against SideCar in Austin, where an executive from a prominent IATR sponsor took his place when he got sick. Also, Windels Marx had made clients out of the TLPA and the app company Cabulous, both of which were IATR sponsors. Aside from this one email, Daus seldom, if ever, acted "uncomfortable" with sponsorships.

While the rest of the board remained mute, the St. Louis regulator stepped in and told them to knock off the back-and-forth.[110] Cameron broke off from the email chain and started conversing privately with Daus and Chairman Drischler, some of which she also forwarded to Hayashi and Seattle's Craig Leisy (another board member), neither of whom intervened.[111] When asked about this episode years later, Hayashi held her hands above her shoulders and replied, "I was only a member for the conferences."

Daus instructed Cameron to have no further conversations with Uber and asked her to hold off on emails until a board meeting the following week.[112] Regardless, Cameron was still defiant, saying she would only stop talking if Daus handed over a list of his firm's clients to Drischler. She accused him of using IATR funds for personal benefit, such as by channeling sponsorship funds to bring regulators for free. She told him via email,

> I was at the TLPA in San Fran when you were schmoozing [Connecticut taxi owner] Bill Scalzi to engage you to negotiate a deal with the MTA. So is he a client? And if he is, is it kosher for you to get him to be a bronze sponsor so that the money can be used to pay air fare, hotel, and registration for HIS regulator. Either way, that practice is wrong.[113]

She told Drischler she was concerned the IATR was imploding under Daus's indefinite leadership. "IATR has become a shallow gene pool with this new governance structure. The experiment has failed by any measure," she said to the chairman.[114]

Two weeks later, Cameron was officially fired from the IATR.[115] The board didn't hold a conference call to discuss her termination or call for a formal vote.[116] Instead, Drischler simply phoned or emailed each member individually. A couple of board members protested, but likely tired from the conference, Drischler said he needed to focus on his LADOT day job.[117]

In the months that followed, Karen Cameron tried to launch her own pro-Uber regulatory association called "the Regulators' Forum." Much as she had discussed with the IATR Board, it was dedicated to reexamining taxi regulations from the perspective of consumers, not the industry. On its website, it promised a "rethinking of for-hire vehicle regulation, grounded in sound economic theory and scientific research." The goal was to focus on measures of consumer satisfaction, coupled with public safety.[118]

Daus and other IATR Board members quickly took notice. Cameron sent regular news snippets, identical to a service provided by the IATR. But instead of articles discussing how cities were pushing out Uber, the headlines were more like "Taxi drivers ignoring dispatch requests a third of the time: report." As an association, the IATR suddenly had its own competitor, which Daus privately called "highly disturbing."[119]

For the first half of 2014, attorneys for the IATR attempted to negotiate a settlement with Cameron. She was still owed $20,000 for her conference planning services but also retained some of the IATR's internal files. The board also believed she had used IATR resources to create the Regulators' Forum LinkedIn account, which Cameron denied was anything but her own personal account. In exchange for her remaining payment, the IATR wanted all her files and the LinkedIn account, plus assurances she wouldn't publicly disparage or compete with them or divulge any of the IATR's trade secrets.[120]

For a number of reasons, Cameron felt she couldn't sign the agreement. The LinkedIn account was her own, she insisted. She wasn't turning it over. Furthermore, one of the settlement's more alarming confidentiality provisions held that if a law enforcement agency ever approached Cameron to inquire about the IATR, she was required to first give the association notice *before* cooperating with officials.[121] The parties were deadlocked. In June 2014 both sides walked away, each washing their hands of the other.

After her departure, Daus and much of the board renounced Karen Cameron's title as "Executive Director," since it was only an informal expression. After her termination, they would refer to her only as a former "contractor," minimizing her relevance. Not long after, Cameron abandoned the Regulators' Forum and went to work for taxi expert Ray Mundy, followed by various Canadian transportation associations. Once or twice, she asked

Uber for a job, which didn't go anywhere.

Cameron was the archetype of a regulator who could step back and evaluate Uber dispassionately, the one who asked questions about how ridesharing *could* fit into the transportation infrastructure, not whether it was compatible with the existing taxi industry. Hayashi protected taxis because she believed it was her solemn responsibility, as did most other regulators. Daus protected taxis because he saw a way to earn the industry's business as clients. But Cameron was possibly the only person in the regulatory community (at least through 2013) who asked whether the proven market failure of taxi deregulation still existed in a smartphone world, whether Uber was truly a usurper or simply a competitor of the taxi industry. Few other regulators of note had any interest in asking such questions. For them, the issue was simple: taxis were sacred, and Uber was an unregulated taxi service. Although she had tried, Cameron was unable to bridge the regulatory gap.

For Uber, the IATR's model regulations were a naked and brazen attempt to push away TNCs, although they rarely again called the IATR out for it. One notable exception was a 2015 lawsuit with St. Louis's taxi authority, where Uber would allege the local regulator, who was also an app committee and board member, conspired with the IATR and the TLPA to draft the model regulations. They even cited a comment overheard during the 2013 conference in which Daus reportedly wanted to "get a critical mass of cities buying into the restrictions, to adopt them, so there would be safety in numbers."[122]

There were hints Uber continued to keep tabs on Daus. A few months after the 2013 IATR Conference, an attorney from the same law firm that attended with Uber made a public information request to the City of San Antonio. One of the first cities to erect barriers against Uber and Lyft, San Antonio wasted little time making TNCs illegal. The attorney seemed to be hunting for signs of a grander conspiracy – connections that others already knew of or suspected. The attorney's request was broadly scoped to fish for any written correspondence connecting Mayor Julián Castro, the city council, or the police chief with Matt Daus, the IATR, the TLPA, or the local Yellow Cab Company (which was owned by Texas Taxi, Inc.).[123]

Years later, in 2017, another Uber attorney made a similar public information request in the Tampa area, where Daus served as a consultant to the local taxi regulator. The attorney asked for any and all files Daus or his law firm handed over.[124]

None of these fishing expeditions lasted very long. Uber had more important matters to address.

CHAPTER NINE

Coalitions Weak and Strong

In December 2013, the reality of a legalized Uber was starting to hit California's local taxi regulators in the face. Christiane Hayashi, Tom Drischler, and a few others traded despondent emails as though they were crying over their beers about the state of the industry. As Hayashi informed colleagues, "We are starved for taxi drivers, many taxis are going un-leased for lack of drivers – who figure why pay a taxi lease fee and live with all of these regulations when they can drive their own car for free." It was so bad, San Francisco was recruiting taxi drivers from neighboring cities "on an emergency basis," she reported.[1]

In Los Angeles, de facto deregulation was taking form. With a barrage of new TNC competitors, several taxi companies compensated by illegally raising their lease rates and charging high "administrative" fees for credit cards. Drischler informed his peers that his office had difficulty catching them in the act since his budget had been cut.[2] Still, in private, he finally acknowledged some of the service problems his city faced, writing to the others,

> Consumers … are left with a choice of a competitively priced, timely, cheerful TNC sedan service or taxi service offered by surly drivers, many of

whom smoke in their cabs, talk on their cell phones in a foreign language, overcharge and refuse credit cards and short trips.[3]

Some of the regulators were beginning to have a come-to-Jesus moment. Historically, Daus had blamed Uber's success on gimmicky marketing and millennial appeal. But at least in California, they were beginning to evaluate taxis from the passengers' point of view. There was a reason so many customers defected to the app companies. It wasn't solely about good marketing but also better service.

"They clearly have to improve their game," Drischler wrote. "Credit/debit card acceptance shouldn't even be an issue."[4]

At best, it was a fleeting and momentary change in their assessment of the battlefield. But they weren't changing their feelings about TNCs. A few weeks later on New Year's Eve, their consumerist sentiment quickly vanished when a ridesharing driver struck and killed a six-year-old girl.

Around 8:00 p.m. on December 31, 2013, an Uber driver near the intersection of Polk and Ellis in San Francisco – about four blocks from the CPUC – turned right without yielding to the pedestrians in the crosswalk. He struck a family of three recent Chinese immigrants: a mother and her five- and six-year-old children. The mother reportedly suffered a skull fracture and her son severe cuts and abrasions along the face.[5] Her daughter, Sofia Liu, died at the scene.[6]

In the for-hire vehicle industry, tragic accidents were a fact of life. No one ever ascribed blame to the parent company as long as it had done everything in its power to mitigate the calamity. For Uber, it was not the first physical injury caused by a driver, but it *was* an untested insurance case that scared the hell out of regulators. When it happened, the driver's Uber app was active but he had no passenger in his car, nor was he in the middle of picking anyone up.

In the world of ridesharing, Uber and Lyft generally provided excess liability insurance, which could only kick in when all other insurance failed.

But the insurance addressed three separate periods of operation:

> Period One: A driver's app is on but the driver is not carrying any passengers, nor have they accepted a ride request.

> Period Two: A driver has accepted a ride request and is on the way to pick up the passenger(s).

> Period Three: A driver has accepted a ride request and is transporting passengers in the vehicle.

Uber's excess liability insurance only covered Periods Two and Three, and the driver who hit Sofia Liu did so during Period One. Nothing from the CPUC's new regulations covered an incident like this. Drivers were required to have their own insurance, but all personal auto insurance policies in America excluded commercial activity.

The accident raised an uncomfortable question. If someone simply drove around in their own car with the Uber app open, and there were no passengers or accepted ride requests, were they performing a commercial activity? It was impossible to prove one way or the other. Maybe they were hoping to earn money, or maybe the app was just one of several open on the driver's phone while heading to a grocery store.

The scenario was a nightmare Matt Daus had predicted only three months earlier. Taxi drivers also had fatal accidents, but taxi companies were required to cover them with expensive primary coverage. Ridesharing played by a different set of rules.

IATR regulators immediately scrambled for more information. At the time, Uber's background checks were thought to be little more than simple searches conducted on weak background-check websites. The insurance situation was scary, but they also wanted to know if the driver was a convicted felon. They wanted political leverage.

Hayashi reported to the app committee that she was educating reporters who contacted her about the insurance situation.[7] On January 3, the Chicago regulator replied to her.

> We dug up a possible criminal driving record on the driver – from Florida. It's from 2004 – so don't know how much good it does you. But if we can find it in a simple search – it goes to show that Uber didn't even try![8]

The driver had been convicted of reckless driving in the Florida Keys, leading to a fine and probation.[9] His conviction was more than seven years prior to UberX's launch in San Francisco, which was generally the legal limit of private background checks, but the CPUC's regulations said that drivers couldn't have been convicted at all for certain offenses, including reckless driving.[10] What's worse, the CPUC had no transportation enforcement staff available to make sure Uber followed the rules. It was an intolerable situation. The regulations weren't rigorous enough to head off a fatal collision, and the insurance coverage was questionable at best. "The tide is turning in the press," Hayashi told the App Committee.[11]

Daus and Hayashi also used the issue to try to help with the IATR's PASS Act. Their lobbyist, Barry Lefkowtiz, reported, "Senator Reid's staff recommended that we reach out the family to ... see about having them testify before Congress. They feel this will give us the right type of publicity to help move the Bill."[12]

By the end of the month, a *New York Times* reporter was conducting a video interview of Travis Kalanick, whose facial expression appeared visibly cautious and inhibited. He wasn't aggressive, acerbic, or defiant as he'd commonly been before. His tone was unusually docile.

"If the regs say, 'Uber needs to work with folks who are insured,' and they *are*, then we say, 'Okay, accidents happen and they're not good, and ... our hearts go out in certain situations, cause they can be tragic.' But ... at the end of the day, it's, 'What was Uber's part in that accident?' is the question that I think has to be answered."[13]

Uber offered no mea culpa for the accident. Regardless of whether they should have, it followed an ongoing pattern of Uber abdicating responsibility for any problems that arose. The more Uber dominated markets, the more off-putting it seemed when they took no responsibility for their actions. The company's supposed grief came off as hollow and unconvincing.

In California, the incident ignited a new wave of resistance to ridesharing. In March the state's insurance commissioner convened a hearing, which Hayashi attended, to explore coverage gaps with TNC insurance.[14] A few weeks later, Hayashi and the CPUC's policy director, Marzia Zafar, appeared before a San Francisco Board of Supervisors committee to answer tough questions about whether the city should supplement state regulations with its own policies. It was a less-than-subtle opportunity to voice their discontent with the CPUC. Hayashi was lobbed softball questions while Zafar was strongly criticized for not gathering data or holding evidentiary hearings. One supervisor told Zafar, "It's mind-boggling what the CPUC did."[15]

Hayashi also reported that several cities were "scratching their heads" trying to figure out what to do about ridesharing.[16] And she was right. Since the summer of 2013, Lyft and Uber had been fighting a nationwide war for market-share dominance. Quickly abandoning the guidelines Kalanick laid out in his "White Paper 1.0" post, Uber took the initiative and started expanding to cities that neither Lyft nor SideCar had ever set foot in, such as Atlanta, Indianapolis, Tucson, Oklahoma City, Minneapolis, and Detroit. They weren't waiting for their competitors to test the waters and see if local regulators would punish the ridesharing industry. From 2013 to 2014, Uber and Lyft raced each other to jump into new US cities and command the local market share before the other could catch up.

Sometimes Lyft could get there first, but Uber was usually on their heels. Lyft launched in Baltimore on October 17, 2013, and then UberX launched five days later.[17] Later that year, on December 6, Lyft launched in Nashville, and then UberX launched four days later.[18] With only a handful of exceptions across the country, Uber was seldom more than a week behind Lyft.

As they expanded, Uber and Lyft demonstrated strategies similar to that of tortoise and hare. Through 2015, Lyft only operated in the United States, while Uber spread across the globe like wildfire. Lyft was also only entering large metropolitan areas, usually with a local population of at least three hundred thousand. Over time, UberX launched into small pocket-sized cities with fewer than a hundred thousand residents, where Lyft took much longer to follow. They were competing over the big fish while Uber captured the minnows.

The rapid expansion also changed the political nature of the fights. Taxi regulators still played an active role in the regulatory battles, but they were no longer the lead decision makers. Uber and Lyft were now appealing directly to local city councils for authority to operate, many of which had never heard of Uber or Lyft before they launched in their cities. Nor did they know or care about the heavy resistance from the taxi-regulating community in the years leading up to 2014. It was as though Uber and Lyft were starting from scratch and making their case to brand new audiences.

Because of the rapid expansion, the IATR's role diminished drastically. As Uber and Lyft grew so quickly, Matt Daus had neither the time nor resources to keep up his advocacy, although he tried in a handful of cities. But also, many of the IATR Smartphone App Committee members exited their jobs. Exhausted with the politics of the taxi industry, Hayashi elected to retire in mid-2014, and Ron Linton stepped down from his office in early 2015, passing away a few months later at age eighty-six.[19] Tom Downey left the City of Denver to enter private practice, and a deputy of the New York Taxi and Limousine Commission quit to take a job with Uber, stoking outrage from the local taxi community.[20]

Some no longer qualified as IATR members after their own cities pushed them out. In 2013, Boston's taxi regulator of thirty years was caught up in a scandal after the *Globe* Spotlight team – the same group that broke the Catholic Church's sexual abuse scandal in 2002 – performed an in-depth investigation of the local taxi industry. Against the backdrop of impoverished drivers, they found frequent incidences of petty bribes, illegal overcharges by taxi companies, and a missing city-administered $75,000 bereavement fund for drivers killed on the job.[21] The Boston regulator resigned from the IATR the following January.[22]

In New Orleans, the local taxi regulator, who was the last IATR president before Daus, sent a cease-and-desist letter to Uber shortly after the 2013 conference.[23] At the time, Uber was recruiting local drivers but had not yet launched.[24] Later, the regulator was investigated for poor oversight over his taxi investigators, a couple of whom assaulted a driver and a tour guide[25]. As the investigation progressed, the regulator spoke out against ridesharing at city council meetings. City investigators, some of whom reached out to Karen Cameron after she was fired from the IATR, cited him for negligence and poor oversight. He was fired for cause and later attempted to sue the City of New Orleans, claiming he was fired because of his opposition to Uber.[26]

In all likelihood, it would have made little difference had Matt Daus followed Uber and Lyft across the country. The desire for ridesharing was so strong that political pressure mounted well and above taxi regulators or the IATR. For example, after several weeks of intensive and transparent public sessions reviewing ridesharing, Seattle's city council passed a pilot program to cap the number of TNC vehicles on its streets. It was intended as a thoughtful and balanced compromise, allowing ridesharing to operate but in small enough numbers that it wouldn't overwhelm the taxi industry. In response, Uber, Lyft, and SideCar joined in a united campaign to overturn the cap. Due to intense public pressure, they ultimately succeeded.[27]

In what amounted to one of the greatest moments of schadenfreude against the IATR, UberX launched in Cambridge, Massachusetts, in early 2014. Cambridge, which had lost its lawsuit to overturn the 2012 Division of Standards decision in favor of Uber, tried again. The executive director of the city's licensing division attended the heated 2013 IATR Conference, and in June 2014, her agency introduced a set of regulations that copied and pasted the IATR model regulations nearly word for word.[28] When Uber spotted it, they provided one of their customary media blitzes, although they never pointed out the IATR connection.[29] At hearings, droves of taxi and Uber supporters crowded the city council's small basement meeting room, so many that they overflowed into the stairwell.[30] Within a week the executive director's boss backpedaled, stating that Cambridge had no intention of "stifling innovation" or "removing transportation options."[31]

The IATR continued to hold its annual conferences, and Daus popped up in an occasional hearing across the country. But they were now one voice diluted among several others.

In the middle of their expansion, Uber experimented with a new strategy. Although they fought against California's PUC decision, the outcome demonstrated a simple truth: in a single fight, they had earned the legal right to operate in an entire state. There was no need to go city by city and ask permission. If Coachella Valley didn't like that Uber was siphoning their taxi business, it didn't matter. Local regulators could complain to the CPUC for all Uber cared. The law sided with the TNCs. What's more, the CPUC created a basic framework for statewide regulations. Instead of continuing to fight the CPUC's oversight authority, it donned on Uber that the framework could serve as a model elsewhere.

In Colorado, Uber found itself with a problem that required them to test whether the California model could be replicated. Days after Governor Hickenlooper intervened in the 2013 hearings to deliver Uber a favorable outcome, both Lyft and UberX launched back to back in Denver, igniting an entirely new battle altogether. Colorado's new PUC regulations didn't say anything about ridesharing, nor did state law, and agency officials responded that they were (slowly) considering an investigation.[32] In reality, they were preparing for a second regulatory fight.

Drawn to the front of ridesharing's opposition in Colorado was Doug Dean, the PUC's executive director. A Republican, former Speaker of the Colorado House of Representatives, and former insurance commissioner, Dean arguably held more political clout than the three relatively nameless commissioners he served. Considered by fellow colleagues of both parties as gruff and aggressive, he cooled off somewhat after leaving elected office in 2001 and working in the executive branch a few years later.

"When he was Speaker, he was a son-of-a-bitch," said one legislator who didn't want to be named.

After Uber launched their black-car service in 2012, Dean was regularly informed by his transportation staff of updates. It's likely he was the one who decided to proceed with new regulations to push Uber out of the state. But after Lyft and UberX began operating in late 2013, he became much more public about his opposition.

"If the legislature doesn't pass a bill, make no mistake about it, we're going to be forced to put these guys out of business," he told reporters.[33]

Uber took his threat seriously and got to work. As the new legislative session began in January 2014, their lobbyists started assembling a team of legislators who would support a pro-ridesharing bill. One of the first was Senator Cheri Jahn, a Democrat from the Denver metro area who was familiar with taxi service problems and their control by an oligopoly of companies.

"Yellow Cab kills legislation every year," she said. "When I have disabilities people tell me that cabs don't show up, or there's a snow storm, or they're two hours late, that's not acceptable to me." With little convincing needed, she was eagerly on board.

But Senator Jahn seldom wanted to carry a bill alone; that wasn't her style. In principle, a bill builds momentum the more legislators who sign up as its sponsors. She turned to Senator Ted Harvey, a Republican who in years past fought unsuccessfully to end taxi oligopolies in Colorado.

"I was asked to come to a luncheon just before the session started," he said. "I came and some of the founders of these companies explained what it was about. It was absolutely fascinating."

Doing a little field research, Senator Harvey took several rides to get the drivers' perspectives. He found a health insurance salesman who paid off his debts making $1,600 a week. His next driver was an immigrant dry-cleaning employee.

"Any problems with other cabbies?" Senator Harvey asked him.

"Of course not, this is America," he replied.

Then there was a public bus driver, also an immigrant: "This is what America should be all about," he told the senator.

His rides reflected all the best aspects of Senator Harvey's free-market, job-creating ideology. A fellow senator later told him his constituency considered ridesharing the most important bill in 2014.

Meanwhile in the House of Representatives, a chance meeting allowed Uber to recruit Dan Pabon, a soft-spoken Democrat and Speaker Pro Tempore, the second highest-ranking position in the House. Speaker Pabon was talking with a close friend who was also an attorney and lobbyist.

"I've got this company called 'Uber,'" his friend told him. "We're looking for some legislative solutions. Who do you recommend in the lobby corridor?"

Pabon replied, "Come talk to me."

For Speaker Pabon, who represented a neighborhood in northeast Denver, the issue wasn't about politics but traffic congestion. Denver, a metro area that held over half the state's population, always had its share of traffic problems. But taxis weren't getting the job done. Pabon knew of Uber and tried it out once or twice in 2013.

"[My support] was pragmatic. How do you move a bunch of people?" he asked rhetorically. "This seemed like a good solution."

Senators Harvey and Jahn and Representative Pabon were in. Pabon convinced House Assistant Minority Leader Libby Szabo to join on as a sponsor as well. Szabo, a Republican, was the mother of a lobbyist for the Colorado Technology Association, which had joined with Governor Hickenlooper the previous August in opposing the proposed PUC regulations to outlaw Uber.

Together, they were a mod squad, the four primary sponsors of SB14-125, aka the Ridesharing Bill: half Republican, half Democrat; half House, and half Senate. The early culmination of strong bipartisan support was impressive. SB14-125 wasn't some fringe bill designed to fail just so a legislator could add it to the "issues" section of their campaign fliers. This one had political credibility behind it. This one had legs.

As introduced, the Ridesharing Bill was in many ways identical to California's PUC regulations. It borrowed the term "Transportation Network Companies" and allowed UberX and Lyft to carry excess liability insurance, conduct their own background checks, and oversee their own vehicle inspections. Each company would have to obtain an operating permit from the PUC and pay an administrative fee, but the PUC's oversight would be relatively light. Unlike with taxis, the commission would not have the TNC market control to set rates or regulate the number of vehicles.[34]

Instead of taxis, what quickly turned into the primary issue and would define the lion's share of Colorado's political battle was insurance. "Insurance was *the* issue in the Senate," said Senator Harvey. Although Sofia Liu's death in San Francisco was still fresh news, the legislators were not well aware of the story or its implications. Instead, it was Doug Dean sounding the alarm bells. A former insurance commissioner himself, Dean would use the issue to push back against TNCs – and he had allies.

Ridesharing made the insurance industry itself extremely nervous. They were represented in Colorado by the Property Casualty Insurers Association of America (PCI), a major political player in most states that could seldom be ignored. When the PCI was nervous, legislators grew nervous, too. The insurers weren't against ridesharing in principle, the way that taxis were, but they still hated the ambiguous Period One coverage, and they didn't care if it was a deal-breaker for TNCs. The PCI had the power to touch many state legislators and potentially kill the bill. Effectively, Uber could now add to their growing list of legislative opponents taxis, unions, Doug Dean, and the PCI.

Riding the wave of insurance fears, Doug Dean wanted Uber and Lyft to carry expensive *primary* commercial insurance on its vehicles, just as the taxi industry did. He also asked the legislators to increase the TNC liability insurance requirement from $1 million to $1.5 million, making the primary coverage even more expensive.[35]

In early February, the Senate held a customary hearing to review the bill for public comment before the Senate Committee on Business, Labor, and Technology (affectionately referred to as "BLT"). As one of the first to speak, Doug Dean listed at length several issues the PUC had with the bill. Many of them were relatively tame: being able to take complaints to the PUC, limiting each driver's continuous hours behind the wheel, fees, penalties for infractions, and so forth.[36]

But on insurance, he hammered the issue hard, pointing out there was no coverage for a Period One accident and explaining Sofia Liu's death as a non-theoretical example. "Uber is denying all responsibility for that claim," he said. "The driver's personal automobile insurance policy is denying all liability for that claim.... This issue needs to be fixed."[37]

He noted that the insurance industry was beginning to talk of a policy rider for auto coverage that drivers could purchase themselves, but it was still hypothetical. For the time being, the only product good enough was primary coverage.[38]

Although he focused on insurance, Dean couldn't avoid the topic of how

TNCs might affect the taxi industry. Ending his nearly twenty minutes of testimony, he delivered a dramatic speech about how taxis could soon fade into darkness.

"The passage of this bill may in fact lead to de facto taxi deregulation.... Suppose for a second you are the owner of a cab company, and this bill becomes the law. Would you decide it's in your best interest to become a transportation network company? There's nothing the PUC could do to say, 'No, you have to stay a cab company....' You wouldn't have to paint your vehicles anymore.... You wouldn't have to have vehicles of a certain age.... You would no longer have to serve your assigned territory. You could serve statewide.... You'd no longer have to accept all riders.... You no longer have to serve neighborhoods that you don't want to serve. You no longer have to provide service 24/7. You'd no longer have to purchase expensive meters for your vehicles. You'd no longer be subject to the PUC's limitations on the number of vehicles you can have out there.... You would no longer be subject to the Commission's rate regulation. So why would you stay a cab company under that hypothetical?"

"And I'm not claiming with a certainty that the cab companies are all going to do this. But we recently discovered that one San Francisco cab company has been unable to fill 25 to 33 percent of their shifts lately just in their first operation, and they attribute that to the drivers moving to the transportation network companies. But if our cab companies do decide to convert to a TNC model, people without smartphones and credit cards – and that's not an insignificant portion of our population – are not going to be able to avail themselves of these services."[39]

It was a speech worthy of Christiane Hayashi, and it was one of the rare times a taxi regulator publicly admitted their resistance was based on a desire to protect the taxi industry. Outside of the legislature, Dean was so worried about de facto deregulation that he was already carrying through on a backup plan. He'd sent cease-and-desist letters to the ridesharing companies, along with a show-cause notice.[40] If the legislature didn't pass a bill, he could use the PUC's hearing process to move against Lyft and UberX.

After Dean finished, the hearing also elicited a handful of speakers from the ridesharing community. Uber's general manager for Colorado, Will McCollum, showed up to discuss the "tremendous tragedy" of Sofia Liu, which Dean had mentioned. Lyft cofounder John Zimmer also flew in from San Francisco to give public comments. Throughout the legislative process, each company had their own lobbyists working behind the scenes, but Uber seemingly had an army not only of lobbyists but also consultants. The former PUC chairman who represented Uber in 2013 appeared, along with drivers they asked to speak on their behalf.[41]

There were so many lobbyists and consultants that it was difficult to spot them all. At the committee hearing, one of Uber's consultants was a pollster who had surveyed the Denver metro area on ridesharing. According to his poll, only a small portion of the population had used Lyft or UberX, but taxis weren't popular, either. But the pollster saved his biggest bombshell for last. As part of his survey, he'd conducted a push poll, describing ridesharing and then asking respondents if they'd voice their support or opposition of it to their legislators. Easily, most of them were supportive. But what surprised the pollster was that ridesharing had zero partisanship among passengers, making it a tempting bipartisan issue.[42]

"I've done a lot of polling over the last twenty-five years," he said. "I'm not sure I've ever seen anything that got 72 percent support *across the board*. Republicans: 73. Democrats: 73. Unaffiliated: 72. Same across male/female, young/old, high income/low income, all races, taxi users, and taxi non-users. All very high."[43]

The committee chair joked, "Thank you. And I believe 72 percent of the voters emailed me yesterday and asked me to support this bill."[44]

Uber had been busy with its social media campaigns.

Per procedure, the BLT held another hearing a few days later to consider amendments and the bill itself. They went back and forth, trying to wrap their heads around the basic issues. Senator Harvey had difficult questions to answer. Most of the BLT supported ridesharing, but their support left them wondering why they would force taxis to continue enduring tough regulations their new competitors didn't have to suffer. They also still weren't sure how insurance should apply during Period One. Harvey said he had looked into whether drivers could carry their own commercial livery insurance, a recommendation from Dean, but it would cost $4,000 to $8,000 per driver per year. No one believed any driver would pay that amount.[45]

Doug Dean, who had been invited to the second hearing to answer ad hoc questions, argued that a coverage gap existed. In Colorado, most resident drivers carried auto insurance that covered them if they were hit by an uninsured (or underinsured) motorist. Dean spelled out a dark scenario where if a wave of TNC drivers got into accidents (especially since so many more of them would be on the road), and if their personal coverage didn't apply, then insurance companies would shift the cost of those accidents to the rest of the state's residents. Put simply, the price for uninsured-motorist coverage would increase. As accidents increased, insurance prices would climb, effectively forcing Coloradans to subsidize Uber's and Lyft's insurance. But Uber and Lyft refused to solve the problem by providing primary coverage. The cost was too high.[46]

Senator Harvey dismissed the insurance gap as a nonissue. It was based on the theory of a dramatic increase in the number of accidents. Ridesharing had been around for nearly two years, Harvey argued, and Dean's apocalyptic scenario had not yet increased insurance prices anywhere else. Harvey's argument was convincing, but only narrowly. The BLT voted 4–3 to exempt ridesharing from Period One primary coverage.[47]

After dealing with insurance and a few other amendments, the BLT voted the bill out of committee by 5–2.[48] But the process didn't mollify Doug Dean.

"We were moving forward and delivering 99 percent of what he wanted, and he continued to be obstructionist," said Senator Harvey.

Harvey wasn't wrong. It would take another two months for the bill to work its way through the Senate and then start its first hearing in the House. During the interim, the campaigns on both sides intensified. Doug Dean sent a letter, cosigned by the sitting insurance commissioner, stating that if the current version passed, ridesharing would increase auto insurance prices across the state.[49] Uber had hired a *former* insurance commissioner, who sent a letter suggesting otherwise.[50] Much of the debate rested on a set of assumptions about how many accidents TNC drivers would cause. There was enough wiggle room so that experts could conclude one way or the other, and legislators were left with doubts on both sides.

Although the BLT deliberated the issue, the insurance question was far from settled. Statewide insurance providers grew more nervous. Unexpectedly, Senator Harvey received a call from a new ally who wanted to quell the collective fears, Senate President Morgan Carroll.

"She wanted to solve the problem," said Harvey. "She really did her homework and delved into all of the policy aspects. She came to us and said, 'This is what we're going to do.'"

As the bill was nearing a full Senate vote, a floor amendment was passed forcing insurance companies to cover TNC drivers under their personal policies during Period One. It also allowed insurers to pay for it by adding a surcharge on personal auto policies for TNC drivers.[51] With drivers absorbing the cost of covering Period One, the bill passed the Senate by 29–6 and headed to the House.[52] Effectively, if Uber and Lyft were unwilling to pay for Period One, then the best compromise was that their drivers would have to. Take it or leave it.

Five days later, Uber announced in a blog post that they would expand their *excess* liability insurance to cover Period One. Not intending it as a slap in the face to the political maneuvering of the Colorado Senate, the company cited the negative press coverage since Sofia Liu's death.

"There has been much written about the 'insurance gap,'" it read.[53]

Uber was trying to calm the growing fervor nationwide. Insurance was the one regulatory roadblock that all sides considered an honest concern. Even *The Denver Post*, which published scathing op-eds about Doug Dean's opposition to TNCs, referred to it a "legitimate issue."[54]

But Uber's and the Senate's attempts to calm fears fell flat in Colorado. Excess coverage wasn't good enough, and the idea of adding a rider to personal auto policies wasn't ready because there wasn't enough data. Insurance prices weren't based on random guesses but on detailed actuarial tables that calculated future accidents based on historical trends. Ridesharing was still new. They had no historical data to tell them how often TNC drivers got into accidents, and Uber and Lyft definitely weren't going to grant them access to their internal records. No one was mollified.

As the Ridesharing Bill approached the House, other political opponents began to emerge and start their own campaigning. The banking industry, represented by Doug Dean's wife, didn't want TNC drivers using their personal vehicles if there was a chance they would do so uninsured. Otherwise, if a driver who couldn't pay his auto loan got into a bad accident, it would be difficult to repossess and sell his damaged car.[55] Unions, represented by the AFL-CIO, stepped in because they were prevalent in several taxi companies.[56] Robert McBride, the owner of Metro Taxi, penned an op-ed stating that any argument that taxi companies opposed the bill to protect their turf was a "red herring" (though it didn't stop them from working closely with Matt Daus in 2013).[57] And then there was the House Transportation & Energy Committee chairman himself, Representative Max Tyler.

Tyler, a Democrat in his mid-sixties, had spent part of his early life as a taxi driver and founded a company in the 1990s that provided computer network support services. He wasn't alienated by technology, and like Senator Harvey, he had tested Uber's app a few times. But instead of seeing it as the inspirational "American dream" experience, Tyler was concerned and suspicious. He understood the regulatory merits of taxis better than most:

making sure they picked up all customers indiscriminately, making sure the drivers were insured, and making sure the cabs were in good working order. At the time, Lyft had their vehicles inspected by peers, not mechanics.

"Cool, dude. Thanks!" Tyler said mockingly. "That was their version of safety." The more he learned, the less he trusted TNCs. "When I talked to a driver, they were really happy to make $10 per hour, but that doesn't include costs. That bothered me."

Still, Tyler couldn't stop the bill in its tracks and keep it from progressing. Governor Hickenlooper wanted it passed, and Tyler received his marching orders from Pabon's boss, the Speaker of the House. "The instructions I received were to pass the best bill I could," he said. In other words, he could amend it as much as his committee would allow. But he couldn't kill it outright.

Uber had an uphill battle in the House, and they knew it. They asked their customers to send emails to Tyler's committee the day SB14-125 was passed by the Senate, nearly a full month before he would hold a hearing.[58] Uber had good reason to be nervous.

By the time Tyler's committee reviewed the bill in April, not only was insurance unresolved, but enough time had passed that more difficult issues had arisen. State representatives, who were more skeptical than their Senate colleagues, were dissecting and reexamining the merits of longstanding taxi policies. They then tried to use that understanding to evaluate TNC regulations. To what extent did they want to require TNCs to pick up disabled passengers, some of whom have medical equipment that may not fit into a car? Taxis had to carry workman's compensation for their drivers, but why didn't TNC's? Before there was a competitor to taxis, there had seldom been reason to bring these issues up.

Lyft, more so than Uber, was willing to answer the tough questions directly. A Lyft representative was asked why their drivers don't undergo medical exams.

"If we overdo it, and we impose very difficult burdens of people becoming drivers," he said. "Then the business will not survive. Drivers will not join the platform.... We need as many people to become drivers as soon as possible. When you put something like a medical in front of someone becoming a driver ... they don't do it."[59]

The Lyft response was phenomenal for a few reasons. For one, it explained for both Uber and Lyft why they opposed regulations others viewed as common sense. They were trying to avoid what Silicon Valley often referred to as "friction." That is, any requirement that made it difficult for TNCs to on-board new drivers made it more difficult to ensure enough drivers were on the road. In their regulatory approach, Uber and Lyft were trying to remove as many of those obstructions as possible.

Secondly, the response hinted at the competitive strategy between Uber and Lyft. Both companies used some form of dynamic pricing, the fare increase that kicked in when there weren't enough drivers to meet local demand. Neither company was willing to remove dynamic pricing from their algorithms, but the comment suggested they wanted to grow large enough to suppress it. The more drivers they could add to their platforms, the less often surge pricing would activate. In that sense, the more drivers they could add, the more competitive their prices would be with one another and others.

Thirdly, it contrasted the strikingly different political styles between Uber and Lyft. Lyft was willing to speak plainly about their intentions, but Uber was not. Once more Uber's Colorado general manager, Will McCollum, was the company's telegenic pitchman. When McCollum spoke, he evaded frank answers and focused instead on highlighting the positives of Uber's service. Like a presidential candidate, he told a story about a "mother of two who was earning $8 an hour managing a Philly cheesesteak restaurant" but could now make ends meet driving for Uber part-time. But when tough questions came up, he seemed evasive. For instance, when McCollum was asked about the workman's comp issue, he avoided specifying whether the bill *should* require it of TNCs, saying only that Uber didn't.[60]

At one point, McCollum was so focused on pitching Uber to the committee that he let slip a confidential insight. He had looked to see which among the representatives had used the app. "I know that only three of the committee members here have actually tried out the Uber app," he said. "I took the liberty, and I wanted to see who's actually familiar with using UberX."[61]

The "God View" feature, Uber's internal ability to review in great detail where and how each user had interfaced with the app, wasn't completely a secret. Kalanick had mentioned it several times, usually only in front of adoring tech crowds. But until this moment, privacy issues had seldom come up. In the previous four years of Uber's public policy issues, privacy was often an afterthought behind surge pricing, insurance, background checks, and impact on the local taxi industry.

One of the skeptical committee members asked McCollum to elaborate on their privacy and confidentiality. McCollum backtracked, saying he didn't reveal specifically who among the committee had used it and who had not. He then pivoted back to his pitchman tone, reminding them they had an opportunity to engage with the app "without all the noise, without all of the lobbyists" (some of whom Uber had hired). Unsatisfied with his non-answer, the skeptical committee member repeated the question. McCollum, seemingly confused in the moment, pivoted back to the website's terms and conditions and then asked her if she had a specific question.[62]

The committee member was now irritated. "It seems like you have done some research on us to discover whether we have downloaded the Uber app, which raises questions for me. What data *do you collect* and how do you use it on your riders? And I'd like to know specifically what kind of data – and I don't want to be referred to your web page, sir – I want to know specifically what data you're collecting on your riders."[63]

Getting the gist of the question, McCollum emphasized that Uber did not sell its data but used it to increase dispatch efficiency. More than that, he also emphasized that market forces didn't allow Uber to violate the social norms of Internet privacy.

"Imagine that front-page *Wall Street Journal* headline," said McCollum. "We have market pressures that dictate we take privacy and security extraordinarily importantly. And so when I say that, it's not necessarily these questions that we're afraid of. It's losing the trust of the riding public.... It doesn't pass the 'WSJ test' if we don't have confidence in our security."[64]

He ironically foreshadowed events to come later in the year.

The committee took public comments for seven hours, and a handful of government employees also spoke, though their motives were at best ambiguous. Larry Stevenson, a Denver city employee from Tom Downey's former office, informed the committee that there were active investigations of TNCs.[65] The following year, Stevenson would plead guilty to misdemeanor conflict-of-interest charges for simultaneously working for the City of Denver and for Metro Taxi, costing him his city job.[66]

Also, Doug Dean commented once more, but his tone took a 180-degree turn from his Senate testimony. For example, he called the TNC ratings of drivers "adequate" for monitoring vehicle conditions. He was no longer making apocalyptic predictions about the taxi industry, even though the House committee would have been more receptive to them. Instead, he vigorously emphasized that the PUC's position on the bill was "neutral," and he conceded that the insurance situation had improved since Uber was willing to cover the Period One gap. Perhaps most telling about his new attitude, he also emphasized that Governor Hickenlooper's office supported the bill.[67]

A week later, Chairman Tyler's committee deliberated the bill's amendments in an exhausting six-hour session. Representatives Pabon and Szabo as well as Doug Dean were on hand to answer questions. In a breezy half hour, the committee first passed a series of amendments without objection to address several of the minor issues.[68] To level the regulatory playing field, taxis could elect to convert to a TNC model if they found it beneficial to do so.[69] And TNCs couldn't disclose personally identifiable information without consent.[70]

For the remainder of the long evening, Tyler's committee delved into the chaotic policy minefield of insurance, anti-discrimination provisions, and general operating requirements. On many of these tense issues, the committee would consider pairs of similar amendments where one version was the strictest form of regulation while another was relatively light and agreeable to the TNCs.

But the path to less regulation for Uber was tricky. The committee's five Republicans (one of whom kept hopping in and out of the hearing) were dependable enough to vote for the softer versions. Of the eight Democrats, four (including Tyler) usually favored the greatest restrictions. That meant for the TNCs to get their way, at least two (or sometimes, three) of the four moderate Democrats were needed to either pass or kill each amendment. The success of a single amendment could depend on the mood in the room.

From the start, the Democrats were united in distrust and skepticism. On a minor amendment to allow the TNCs to handle complaints internally, they unanimously killed it.[71] If the relatively simple issue of passengers' complaints invited distrust, Pabon and Szabo likely sensed they were in for a long night.

The committee moved on to anti-discrimination. Neither Uber nor Lyft had any problem prohibiting discrimination based on race, gender, sexual orientation, and so forth. But the one "friction" issue was a requirement that TNC's pick up disabled passengers. Despite local requirements passed after the Americans with Disabilities Act of 1990, the taxi industry had been sluggish in providing accessible vehicles to disabled passengers. The disabled community had complained about service refusals for years, and it wasn't until the late 2000s that taxis started making improvements by purchasing ramp-accessible vehicles.

Uber and Lyft were not yet ready to accommodate disabled passengers, especially since they couldn't guarantee that a personal vehicle could store heavy equipment like a motorized wheelchair. They didn't know how to guarantee service to the them. But the eight Democrats weren't feeling generous about giving TNCs regulations so light they left disabled passengers in the cold. Also, some of the skeptics kept pointing to each company's terms and conditions, noting that they already prohibited discrimination broadly. The Democrats weren't sympathetic and again voted for the stronger requirements.[72]

On the tortured issue of liability insurance, the committee wasn't happy with the Senate's version, and Tyler was concerned that Colorado was replicating California's loose regulations. Despite the new regulatory framework created the previous year, the California insurance commissioner had announced there were still coverage gaps. In Tyler's eyes, the safest way to avoid the same problem was simply to require the TNCs to provide coverage themselves during Period One, a measure Lyft and Uber hated. For a brief moment, the committee hesitated over which agency would administer it. Pabon and the Republicans argued that the PUC was not friendly to the TNCs, which was true. But ultimately, it didn't matter. The Democrats didn't want personal auto insurance policies to pay for it.[73] They voted unanimously for the stricter version.[74]

Despite their disagreements, the committee members were generally respectful to one another, and Chairman Tyler deserves credit for keeping the tone civil and the proceedings fair. But as the long hours of debate wore on, their mental focus faded. They'd spent large chunks of concentration on insurance and disability issues. One of them said that it was nearly past their bedtime. Another said that if the hearing went past 10:00 p.m., he'd cry. An adjournment looked far off. Committee members began audibly crunching on snacks between comments, and at times, some seemed to lose track of what they were voting on, perhaps looking to others for signals.[75]

To Uber's benefit, as the committee members began to tire, the party coalitions started to fray. The committee went through a litany of TNC operational requirements, voting on them one at a time. On a vote as to whether TNC vehicles should be required to show an exterior trade dress, the amendment passed, although one of the more skeptical Democrats voted no. "Interesting," Chairman Tyler said after tallying the result.[76] They then voted on whether drivers should be required to obtain a fingerprint criminal background check from the PUC. Surprisingly, three of the Democrats voted no, killing the amendment.[77]

After the vote, Chairman Tyler declared, "So, we are not asking for a fingerprint criminal background checks of TNC drivers."[78]

"We are not?" asked one of the Democrats who had *just* voted on the amendment.

"No, we're not," another replied.

"I think I owe the committee drinks after this, I'm pretty sure," Speaker Pabon interjected.[79]

Chairman Tyler moved on to an amendment that would have given the PUC autonomy to determine a TNC's permit fee. Although the fee itself wasn't heavily contested, it was still a thorny issue. There was some expectation that after the bill passed, SideCar and other companies would join Uber and Lyft in Colorado. They wanted a diminishing fee structure that didn't allow the PUC to become cash-rich if, say, suddenly ten new companies entered the market. Designing it to be both flexible and limiting proved too tricky, though. They considered giving the PUC the ability to adjust as new companies launched, but the committee felt they were giving away too much authority.[80] They voted against it by 6–7.[81]

"Jesus," one representative muttered under their breath.[82]

"I won one!" Representative Pabon jokingly mocked.[83]

As the night moved along and the Democrats grew increasingly tired, they sided more with TNCs over their own chairman. At one point, Tyler introduced a poison-pill amendment that would have given the PUC power to regulate "surge pricing" (a phrase that only Uber used), which would have crippled the ridesharing business model. The committee voted it down 3–10.[84] Another poison pill would have given the PUC to determine each TNC's geographic area and maximum number of drivers. It died 2–10, and even Tyler himself voted against that one.[85]

Approaching 9:00 p.m. after six and a half hours, the committee finally voted 12–1 to pass the bill with its amendments.[86] Exhausted and slightly giddy, Representative Pabon thanked the committee with a brief speech.

"Esteemed members of the committee, you did *some* work today. I'm not sure what this bill does or what it looks like anymore."[87]

True to his word, Pabon took the committee members to the City Grille, a popular burger joint next door to the capitol, and bought them all a round of drinks.

The next day, Pabon and Szabo had a problem. Not only did the full House have to vote on SB14-125, but because it had been amended, the Senate was also entitled to a second vote. Ordinarily, once a House and Senate committee each took a crack at amending a bill, its language was more or less final. Any differences between the two versions were worked out in a committee of conference. But the two versions were completely opposite in nature. On insurance, the most controversial topic, the Senate version placed Period One coverage under a driver's personal insurance policy while the House version made Uber and Lyft pay for it. Not to mention that the House version required workman's compensation and for drivers to accommodate *any* disability equipment.

Uncertain as to what he could successfully amend on the House floor, Speaker Pabon took it to his co-sponsors in the Senate for their input.

"Okay, kill the bill," Senators Harvey and Jahn told him.

"Wait; what?" Pabon replied.

If the bill died, the Colorado PUC could then shut down Lyft and UberX. But Harvey and Jahn were so adamant about removing the points of friction that they were willing to let it die. Even though they were allies, the senators' threat was a way of drawing a line in the sand. Harvey and Jahn liked this new business model, and they didn't want TNCs so encumbered that they couldn't operate efficiently. Better to shoot the horse than let it run with a limp. In essence, the threat signaled to Pabon that he *had* to fix it on the House floor.

Besides the Senate threat, Pabon and Szabo faced more obstacles. Insurance concerns were still echoing through the House chamber, and no one was quite convinced they were resolved. Before the bill went to the House floor, it had to undergo routine votes before a couple of House committees to assess its impact on the state budget. In back-to-back committees, members had the same non-budget question.

"The biggest concern I've heard about this bill is the insurance issue," they were told in Finance.[88]

"I heard there was an issue as far as insurance," an Appropriations member said.[89]

Pabon could put them at ease temporarily but still needed a way to keep the coalition of TNC opponents from ganging up on him. The opposing side had formed a strange alliance of insurance, banking, taxi companies, and unions. Historically, unions and insurance were about as compatible as orange juice and toothpaste. They dreaded one another, but on this issue, their enemy's enemy was their friend. Pabon had to find their kryptonite.

First, he sought a new ally. Both the pro- and anti-TNC coalitions lobbied the disability community to join them. To keep them from becoming enemies, Pabon solicited the support of the National Federation of the Blind.

Not only were TNCs more reliable at picking up stranded passengers, but those with vision problems were more vulnerable to taxi gouging with hidden charges or "scenic routes." Plus, the blind disliked handling cash. TNCs solely accepted credits cards, and their apps made it difficult for the drivers to cheat them. It was an easy sell, and Pabon's coalition suddenly looked stronger and more credible than before.

Like Pabon, the opposition also designed their own series of consensus amendments they wanted included when the bill arrived on the House floor. They wanted to make sure that TNCs still provided primary insurance coverage, handicap accessibility, and safety inspections performed by a certified mechanic. But the group made a misstep. Their amendments were packaged together, not separately.

"I asked them, 'Which one is your most importance piece?'" Pabon said. "They hated that question because they couldn't agree, and it made their coalition collapse."

Taxis and unions wanted TNCs abolished, but bankers and the PCI simply wanted them more tightly regulated. If they couldn't agree on the outcome, then their package of amendments was infeasible.

"It was easy to go to the Speaker and say that they won't prioritize," said Pabon. "Their stubbornness caused them to fracture."

He cleared the political path to his floor amendments. And to be sure, he structured them as compromises that appeased everyone who wasn't interested in killing Uber and Lyft. In the newest version, TNCs couldn't turn down disabled passengers, but if a driver couldn't accommodate mobility equipment, they'd have to find a replacement car that could. The workman's compensation requirement was stripped out.[90]

On Period One insurance, a TNC's excess liability was acceptable but only until January of 2015. By then, either the driver or the TNC had to purchase primary coverage. However, insurance companies were explicitly *not* required to create any new insurance products.[91] Effectively, the legislature gave Uber and Lyft a deadline to work with the insurance companies and figure out a solution on their own. Otherwise, the TNCs were on the hook.

Pabon's gambit was effective. The amendments passed with little resistance. In late April, SB14-125 passed the House 60–5. Max Tyler and one other from his committee were among the handful of "no" votes.[92] Senators Harvey and Jahn also found the amendments acceptable, and the Senate concurred (without a conference committee) by 32–3.[93] In early June, three weeks after receiving the bill, Governor Hickenlooper signed it into law.[94]

When Hickenlooper passed the bill, one of its sponsors found it odd that there was no signing ceremony in front of any cameras. Colorado had just become the first state in the nation to pass a TNC law (as California had only passed regulations in 2013), supporting the governor's vision of promoting innovation. It was nearly beaten by Arizona where only a few weeks earlier, Governor Jan Brewer had vetoed a TNC bill.

It was strange. There were plenty of reasons to take credit. Not only was the Ridesharing Bill a bipartisan political accomplishment, but it had passed during Hickenlooper's first reelection year as governor. Four years earlier, he'd won because the conservative vote was split between a moderate Republican and a Tea Party ally. But the field had since changed. The Republicans had already nominated a decent challenger, former congressman and prior gubernatorial candidate Bob Beauprez. There was no prominent third-party conservative on the horizon to split the vote. Although it would only have been a small gesture, a signing ceremony would have cost little time or resources for Hickenlooper's campaign. Yet, it didn't happen.

According to the governor, although it passed with strong bipartisan support, it wasn't all smiles. There were "a lot of ruffled feathers," as he put it. He said, "A lot of people felt these new tech companies were getting an unfair advantage.... If we had maybe another six months to educate the public, we would have been more celebratory."

Also, before Hickenlooper unceremoniously signed SB14-125, other odd ripple effects took form. The day after the bill passed the legislature, PUC Executive Director Doug Dean passed an emergency regulation lowering taxi liability insurance to $500,000. Dean had frequently advocated that TNCs carry coverage of $1.5 million – the same as taxis – and vigorously insisted that it be purchased as *primary* insurance, arguing that they were a high-risk industry.[95] The legislature ultimately set TNC insurance to $1 million and gave Uber and Lyft time to sort it out with the insurance companies.

But there was no reason for the sudden change to taxi regulations that had anything to do with risk. It wasn't as if overnight, taxis suddenly became safe enough to dramatically cut their normal insurance by two-thirds. Once more, it looked like Dean was playing favorites by granting taxis a special favor. Editorials in *The Denver Post* implied it was a bait and switch. Dean fought back with his own op-ed, insisting he gave advance notice to Chairman Tyler and other legislators.[96] But the main sponsors – Harvey, Jahn, Pabon, and Szabo – who spent untold hours working the bill were not among them. They were shocked and outraged when they found out about the new rule.[97] If Dean told Chairman Tyler, he did so quietly, and Tyler, who supported the taxi industry, had little incentive to tell the sponsors.

Shortly after the bill passed, it took a little time for the Denver Police Department (DPD) to acclimate. They had apparently been so used to sting operations that shortly after TNCs were made legal, an Uber driver was pulled over on an empty expanse of highway near the airport. The passenger in the back happened to be a *GeekWire* reporter, who was told by the patrolman that TNCs were illegal. The police were apparently unaware of the new legislation. After a rude confrontation, publicly confirmed by the police chief, the *GeekWire* writer published the account, and the DPD quickly issued a public apology.[98] The incident revealed that the enforcement mentality embraced by taxi regulators carried a strong momentum. Reversing it was like trying to reverse an aircraft carrier in the water at full speed. Enforcement against non-taxis was the norm.

After the 2014 legislative session ended, Chairman Tyler cashed in his efforts and took a large haul of donations from the Ridesharing Bill's opponents. It's not clear who approached who first, but in two separate meetings in June and July, several of them donated to his campaign, many of whom were owners or managers of taxi and limo companies.[99] A couple of donors, including Robert McBride of Metro Taxi, had already given money the previous November just after Lyft and UberX launched in Denver.[100] All told, Tyler raised a little over $5,000 from the opposition, a good score considering state-representative candidates could only receive up to $400 from individuals.[101]

Looking back on it in 2016, Tyler reflected that it was simply part and parcel of political fundraising. "I've done that before," he said with a boyish smile. "A few years ago, there was a big battle over beer in Colorado. When it was over, I went to liquor stores and said, 'I helped you out; maybe you donate a few bucks.'"

Surprisingly, the donors also included Doug Dean and his wife, the principal representative of a state banking association.[102] Few had noticed that Dean was among the donors, which was a little odd since he was a Republican who usually donated to Republican candidates. In fairness, though, it was not uncommon for bureaucrats throughout Colorado to give money to legislative candidates. But no one questioned the potential conflict of interest, given that Tyler's committee had oversight over legislation that could affect the PUC. Tyler insisted that it was not a quid-pro-quo but Dean simply donating to someone who shared his political views over taxis, which was quite plausible.

For all intents and purposes, Colorado was a battle on two fronts. For the first time, it showed that a state legislature was willing to ignore taxis' pleas for market protection. Several of the Democratic lawmakers had been so intensely dissatisfied with their unreliability that they were willing to take a chance on Uber and Lyft. The barriers to entry no longer made sense.

It was also one of the most prominent insurance battlegrounds for Uber, but far from the only one. Before, during, and after Colorado, insurance was a disputed issue in nearly every jurisdiction they entered. Throughout 2014, state insurance commissioners across the country warned that ridesharing may not be fully covered and that something should be done about it.

In California, it was such a tense issue that in the summer of 2014, one state legislator attempted to require that TNCs provide primary coverage at the urging of the insurance industry. In response, Uber pulled one of its most cutthroat political tactics. The legislator was a state assemblywoman with her eye on a more prominent state senate seat. Uber's lobbyists sent attack-ad mailers to voters in both her home district *and* the state senate district she was interested in. According to multiple reports, the assembly's Speaker stepped in to warn Uber they had crossed a line and created more backlash than goodwill.[103] Still, the California bill passed with the insurance requirements the TNCs wanted.

Throughout 2014, equally heated insurance battles were fought in Virginia and Illinois. Unlike taxi regulators, the insurance industry was a lobby so powerful and well-funded that it even included the National Conference of Insurance Legislators, a trade group made up of state lawmakers who oversaw insurance-related bills. Taxis couldn't hold a candle to the insurance industry. Uber had the resources to make lawmakers turn against taxis, but insurance had more influence than anyone else they had ever fought against.

In late 2014, Uber, Lyft, and the PCI were all so exhausted from the year's insurance fights that they quietly began negotiations. With little argument, an amicable deal was struck. The PCI would give up the ghost on holding TNCs accountable for comprehensive and collision coverage. In exchange, Uber had to find a way to cover Period One with primary coverage.

In Colorado, just before the January 2015 deadline to implement primary coverage, Uber and Lyft solved the problem. The state's insurance companies developed a rider to personal auto policies, allowing TNC drivers to purchase affordable primary coverage for a few extra bucks per month.[104] At no cost to themselves, Uber and Lyft legally cleared the Period One hurdle.

Two months later, Uber announced their agreement with the insurance industry to standardize TNC policy coverage nationwide.[105] From that point forward, if a regulator or lawmaker ever had a problem with insurance requirements, Uber and the PCI could easily diffuse it. The issue would still pop up occasionally, but where it was once a severe bludgeoning tool, it would now only have the sting of a Nerf dart. In a rare feat, and counter to Kalanick's go-it-alone mentality, Uber had made peace with one of their enemies.

Thanks in large part to Colorado, Uber and Lyft developed a legislative model that they could later take to lawmakers across the United States. But for the remainder of 2014, as they rapidly expanded across the country, their fights were mostly with city councils.

And when city councils needed expert guidance, they often turned to their taxi regulators.

CHAPTER TEN

Reputational Angst

By far and away, Uber earned most of its infamy for the activities of 2014 – beginning with city councils. Uber and Lyft barged into cities, trying to out-compete one another with generous incentives for new drivers. But in the process, neither company asked local officials for permission. Although, they quickly learned there was little point in asking. The fines a regulator could issue to drivers were chicken scratch compared to the revenues from the instant craze of an alternative to taxis. Plus, Uber promised to pay every last sting-operation fine a driver received.

In all likelihood, had Uber or Lyft asked for permission before entering a city, officials would have delayed their approval. They would have negotiated against the ridesharing business model, insisting on concessions to ease the pain to taxi drivers. Even in Seattle, a mecca for the tech industry, the thoughtful city council tried to cap the number of TNC vehicles on the streets, and it went over like a lead balloon.

More commonly, a city may have simply told the TNCs no, which happened in Portland, Las Vegas, Miami, and several other cities. But by invading, Uber and Lyft quickly amassed armies of political supporters. If they received resistance, they had a large, instant base of local drivers and passengers to protest and push back on their behalf. Effectively, TNCs politicized their own existence.

Kalanick realized that as their fights became increasingly political, they needed a campaign manager. It wasn't enough to have talent like Corey Owens or Salle Yoo. In August 2014 they hired David Plouffe, who ran Barack Obama's 2008 presidential campaign in concert with David Axelrod.[1] Plouffe was a savvy political strategist who knew how to leverage limited resources to achieve the greatest effect. He became a strong asset, a liaison and voice of credibility to skeptical city Democrats who often supported taxi drivers.

As the TNC invasion spread across the United States, the demand for them immediately impacted the political landscape. Few mayors wanted a reputation of booting Uber and Lyft out of town, and they avoided that impression whenever possible. However, city council members weren't as restrained by their constituents to fight back against what they often viewed as an aggressive, self-interested enterprise. But when they fought, they often had to cite public safety concerns. Each TNC's background checks and insurance still had holes that were not yet plugged, soft spots that city lawmakers could attack – and the taxi industry vocally supported those who did.

But safety concerns only made up half of the arguments. More and more, the taxi industry in 2014 promoted the phrase "level playing field" when talking about ridesharing. They avoided any argument that they were protecting their own bottom line, focusing instead on issues of fairness and public safety. To address both problems, they wanted TNCs to purchase expensive insurance, as they did. To conduct fingerprint background checks, as they did. To seek permission for the number of cars in service, to have their pricing set at minimums and maximum, and to otherwise let regulators dictate their service as they saw fit, all as they did.

At its heart, "level playing field" was a disingenuous argument. Had Uber and Lyft agreed to it, the result was obvious: they would transform into de facto taxis. If the taxi industry truly cared about regulatory equality, they could have argued that instead of more restrictions on TNCs, they needed matching freedoms. For example, they could have requested an easing of price controls and supply caps. Except that price controls and supply caps were the bread and butter that had for decades allowed them to get rich by extracting rents from taxi drivers. When Uber and Lyft launched in a city, taxis never argued for matching freedoms. They didn't want equality as much as they wanted lawmakers to protect their own business model. Although there *were* safety concerns about ridesharing, their argument was ultimately self-serving.

In addition to barging into cities uninvited, Uber also gained a negative reputation for the extent it was willing to undercut its competitors. In San Francisco, Lyft drivers received fliers offering generous incentives to switch to Uber: a $50 gas card, commission-free fares for at least three weeks, and a $500 bonus if they could pick up twenty drivers during the same period.[2] In New York City, Uber staff also went after an on-demand, black-car competitor, Gett, by requesting over a hundred rides and then canceling each of them at the last second. In the process, Uber staff would also acquire the cell phone numbers of Gett drivers, who would later receive texts asking them to join Uber.[3]

Uber apologized for its tactics against Gett, but throughout 2014, the battles with Lyft intensified. Both companies cut into their own profit margins to entice the other's drivers. In August, Lyft reported to *CNNMoney* that over five thousand of their rides had been requested and then canceled within a few blocks of their destination.[4] At the time, anecdotal data pointed to independent recruiters taking advantage of Uber's rich incentives. In a project referred to internally as "Operation SLOG" (Supply Long-term Operations Growth), Uber put bounties on Lyft drivers, offering $750 referral bonuses to anybody who got one to switch to Uber. Often, the recruiters ordered Lyft rides to make a pitch to the drivers and then got out after a couple of blocks.[5] Ostensibly, some of them may have intentionally canceled rides to frustrate drivers and encourage them to switch. In the press, Uber denied any employees or drivers were instructed to cancel rides.[6]

Still, by all accounts Uber was unyielding, and as their competition with Lyft intensified, a bizarre triangle formed. Taxi regulators would often step in to push both companies away, forcing Uber and Lyft to cooperate (or at least not disagree publicly) with one another when fighting back. But neither one was usually willing to stop or slow down even when there was a serious threat on the horizon.

For instance, when both companies entered Pittsburgh in early 2014, neither were legal, the Pennsylvania PUC fined both companies $1,000 per day, and several of their drivers were issued fines.[7] Little changed. Then the PUC allowed the local Yellow Cab Company to operate its own ridesharing service, using a trained driver's personal car, called "Yellow X" (later renamed "Yellow Z").[8] It barely made a dent. PUC administrative law judges finally approved cease-and-desist letters.[9] But all that did was build political pressure against the PUC. State legislators began filing bills and resolutions to either encourage or legalize ridesharing.

Again, taxi regulators inserted themselves into the legislative process.

From: TLD@philapark.org
To: Taxi & Limo [mailing list]
Sent: Tuesday, September 09, 2014 12:25 PM

To All Philadelphia Taxicab and Limousine Industry Partners:

Attached for your review are four Pennsylvania House of Representatives Bills authorizing so called "Rideshare" companies such as Lyft and Uber X to operate in Pennsylvania under certain terms and conditions.

Only one of these four Bills excludes Philadelphia from this authorization: Bill No. 2445. Of the four, Bill No. 2445 provides for the smallest degree of impact to existing providers of call or demand and for-hire transportation services in Philadelphia.

You are urged to contact your elected representatives at the state level including those listed as sponsors of these Bills and members of the Consumer Affairs Committee immediately to register your support for Bill No. 2445 and your opposition to Bill Nos. 2446, 2453, and 2468. Votes on

---

this legislation may be taken as early as Monday, September 15, 2014.

James R. Ney, Director
Taxicab & Limousine Division
Philadelphia Parking Authority

No pro-TNC legislation passed in 2014. But still, under intense scrutiny, Pennsylvania's PUC unanimously approved an emergency petition to allow Uber and Lyft to resume operations, followed later by formal permits.[10]

Even in California, where the CPUC had gone out on a limb to legalize ridesharing, Uber and Lyft were reckless. They competed so intensely that they bit the very hands that fed them. Both companies were operating at major airports without permission, in violation of their agreements. Taxi regulators, especially the SFMTA, complained that the companies were also violating several local traffic laws. Neither was willing to turn over trip data as they had promised. With CPUC President Mike Peevey gone, the new leadership fined both companies for hoarding their data. Lyft quickly acquiesced, while Uber fought it tooth and nail.

All the negative press was beginning to catch up to Uber. In September 2014, as part of an annual tradition, Kalanick was interviewed by *TechCrunch* writer and Uber investor Michael Arrington. Although it was a friendly interview, Arrington probed heavily to understand some of Kalanick's driving forces.

"Some ... have called you sort of a Darth-Vader-figure in the startup world," Arrington noted. "Do you feel as though that you're like Darth Vader or possibly worse?"[11]

Kalanick attributed it to a "scrappy fierceness" he'd acquired at Red Swoosh, the company he founded prior to Uber that kept him impoverished for years before its eventual sale. When Red Swoosh teetered on bankruptcy multiple times over, Kalanick ultimately succeeded because of his relentlessness, he argued.

"That last inch is the difference between – let's call it 'epic failure' and making something happen. Pulling a rabbit out of your hat."[12]

Although Kalanick was trying to replicate Red Swoosh's successful tactics, the press was more sympathetic when he was the underdog. As Uber quickly grew and gained dominance, public perception changed. A combination of intense leverage and a "lone wolf" mentality churned into a sense of discomfort and alienation. Uber was tolerable because of its efficiencies but unloved because of its methods.

"As you get to a place where people perceive you as the big guy or 'the man,' you have to approach things differently, and you have to communicate differently, and we're not there, yet," Kalanick told Arrington.[13]

Within a couple of months of the interview, Kalanick began a public relations campaign intended to soften his – and by extension, Uber's – aggressive attitude. In November, several of the company's beat reporters were invited to a private meeting in New York to hear the beginning of a "charm offensive," as it was coined.[14] But only a few days after the meeting, public perception took another pitfall after a private, high-end dinner. Uber's senior vice-president of business, believing the entire dinner was off the record, suggested in front of a *BuzzFeed* reporter that they could spend a million dollars to perform opposition research on reporters who had covered Uber negatively. The VP focused especially on Sarah Lacy, a former *TechCrunch* columnist (who'd once interviewed Kalanick) and owner and editor of the tech news website *PandoDaily*.[15]

A month before the dinner, Lacy had criticized Kalanick for sexist and misogynistic incidents, which were easy to tie in with his aggressive personality. Lacy followed the trail of crumbs. Kalanick once referred to the women who hit on him as he became rich and famous as "boob-ers." When incidents of sexual assault were reported in Uber rides, the company condemned them but didn't strengthen its security measures. In Lyon, France, Uber ran a promotion that coupled its rides with an app for model services, connecting passengers with stunningly gorgeous female drivers advertised in lingerie (which was immediately discontinued after *BuzzFeed* reported it). For Lacy, all these incidents pointed to a cold indifference toward women, amplified further by a tech industry whose workforce was 70 percent male. Varying degrees of misogyny were the default culture, and Uber was simply the latest example.[16]

In gender issues and beyond, Lacy's articles often connected the tech industry's profit motives with moral apathy. Her prose read as insightful indictments, and Uber was as culpable as its peers. When the company made mistakes, its quick but limited reactions seemed less like genuine concern and more like halfhearted damage control. At the dinner, when the executive suggested opposition research against the media, it looked as though Uber were trying to draw attention away from its own dirty laundry.

What became even more incriminating was the implication of *how* Uber would dig up dirt. The VP said that the million dollars could be used to hire four researchers, partly to "prove a particular and very specific claim about [Lacy's] personal life," according to the article's unquoted text.[17] One treasure trove of research was Uber's database of trip logs to see where customers had traveled and when.

The day after the initial story, *BuzzFeed* published another about Uber's "God View" tool. God View was not a secret – Kalanick had mentioned it publicly before – but it was not widely known how easily it could be abused. Anonymous sources reported that Uber staff had easy access to track each passenger's rides. Also, reporters and investors described incidents when Uber insiders bragged to them that they could see their rides in real time.[18]

Both of the *BuzzFeed* stories spread like wildfire, not just in tech news sites but also in newspapers in cities where Uber was operating and had gone through tough regulatory fights. Suddenly, the "WSJ moment" about privacy violations that Uber's Colorado manager had mentioned only months earlier seemed to be coming to life. If the public wasn't aware of God View before, they were now.

The company rushed to get on top of the stories. Uber clarified its privacy policy in a blog post, and Kalanick published a thirteen-tweet apology for the VP's remarks.[19] But in the headlines, the damage had already been done. *PC Magazine* published a piece titled "Today I Deleted Uber: Here's Why You Should, Too." Similar articles emerged, such as one from *CNNMoney* titled "Opinion: Four Other Ways Uber Is Ethically Challenged."

It completely nullified Kalanick's charm campaign. His credibility was stretched too far. Uber had chased after market domination with such blind zeal that an apology seemed empty after getting caught red-handed, just another insincere moment of damage control. Before the year was over, Uber's chief political strategist, David Plouffe, would tell reporters the company had caused "reputational angst."[20]

In the aftermath, US Senator Al Franken, who chaired the Senate Subcommittee on Privacy, Technology, and the Law, sent them both questionnaires on their privacy policies.[21] Franken wielded enough influence that neither company could afford to ignore him. Uber replied that it had added access restrictions to God View and hired IBM's former chief privacy officer to conduct an audit and review of their privacy practices. Senator Franken replied that he was concerned about Uber's lack of detail in their response, characterizing it as "disappointing."[22]

At the same time, Uber had just closed another round of financing, raising $1.2 billion, and more than doubled its valuation from the previous summer, from $17 billion to an eye-popping $40 billion.[23] The scandal was damaging in the press alone.

Throughout 2014, busy city council members tried to form an impression of the company that had just dumped ridesharing on their doorstep uninvited. They were looking for hints of character traits. If they gave Uber legal legitimacy, how in turn would they respond? Would they follow the rules laid out for them? For some, the news stories they dug up in online searches were enough to convince them it wasn't worth it. Better to side with the inefficient taxi industry they knew than an aggressive usurper they couldn't trust.

In a handful of cases, those council members simply picked up the ridesharing ball without realizing they were adding to an already-rich history of regulatory battles. Texas, for example, was an extreme version of city councils that had rushed to push away ridesharing early on. Texas Taxi, Inc., an IATR sponsor, had dominated three major cities with its fleets of yellow cabs: Austin, San Antonio, and Houston. In early 2013, San Antonio had already passed legislation in anticipation of Uber by requiring smartphone transportation apps to obtain a license.[24] That same year, both San Antonio and Austin passed ordinances establishing reservation-buffer times for limousines, which made UberBLACK's instant service illegal.[25] Even in Dallas, taxi lobbyists strongly encouraged local police to perform sting operations against UberBLACK.[26] And of course, in 2013, Austin taxi regulator Carlton Thomas joined with the IATR to help push away the state's first major ridesharing providers, HeyRide and SideCar.

But in 2014, the groundswell of ridesharing attracted customers eager for Uber and Lyft to launch in their towns. Austin, a strong tech hub with severe traffic problems, began to envy other cities that already had it. In March, during the SXSW Festival, Uber all but planted a flag. They returned to Austin in defiance of their continued ban and offered rides through black cars.[27] Their return was anticipated as a temporary nuisance to regulators, only expected to last during the festival week and then leave again for another year. Although they *did* only operate for a week, they also started a Twitter hashtag campaign, #AustinNeedsUber, and asked followers to await further updates.[28] It looked as though Uber had its eye on a permanent presence.

During the festival, a tragic event broke in Uber's favor. One evening around midnight, a young man was spotted downtown by police driving erratically without his headlights on. When they tried to pull him over, he took off in a high-speed chase, traveling toward one of the festival's music venues. A line of eager fans had built outside after the rapper Tyler, the Creator tweeted that more customers would soon be allowed inside. Traveling at about 50 mph, the driver careened through a barrier and struck a couple dozen people in line, killing four. Witnesses reported that bodies horrifically flew through the air upon impact. The driver's blood-alcohol level measured 0.114 after his arrest, and he was later convicted of capital murder.[29]

The incident forced community leaders to confront a known-but-seldom-addressed alcoholism problem. One of Austin's longtime allures was a nightlife scene densely packed into a string of adjacent downtown neighborhoods that allowed for door-to-door bar hopping. Located only ten blocks away from the University of Texas, one of the largest student campuses in the country, the string of bars was a popular tourist trap ideal for SXSW. Without question, alcohol had a defining role in Austin's culture, but signs of a problem were mounting. Earlier in the week before the collision, Jimmy Kimmel took his late-night show on the road, filming in Austin during SXSW, where he half-joked that the real reason he was there was "because this is an intervention. You have a drinking problem, Austin. You need to stop."[30]

After the four deaths, a local paper analyzed alcohol sales and found that the Austin area sold more booze per person than any other county in the state, "and it wasn't even close," the article noted. One downtown zip code alone sold $1.5 billion worth of alcohol over a decade.[31] Effectively, it was a call for increased safety. The SXSW drunk driver had pushed the impression that taxis and other transportation options weren't getting the job done. An advocacy group called "ATX Safer Streets" immediately formed to push for more late-night transit options and even called for the legalization of Uber and Lyft.[32]

After SideCar's departure from Austin the previous summer, the embers of ridesharing were kept alive with periodic discussions but little more. Chris Riley, the policy wonk and city councilman who passed the 2013 resolution asking Carlton Thomas to report on how other cities were addressing ridesharing, felt it was finally time to move forward. "The number of taxicabs on the road actually *decreases* during peak periods late at night because a lot of drivers have no interest coming down to drive drunk kids," he said. Riley, a skinny, late-forties man with thin-framed glasses and short, silver hair that naturally jetted upwards, had not owned a car since 2008 and was inherently a supporter of alternative transportation. He partnered with Councilman Bill Spelman, a tall, equally wonky specialist in municipal police programs who liked the idea of improving transportation with technology. Together, they set out to design a brand-new ridesharing ordinance.

The pair of lawmakers couldn't simply introduce a bill legalizing ridesharing and expect it to pass. For one, neither of them would get any support from Carlton Thomas or anyone else at the Austin Transportation Department (ATD). In the council-manager form of government, which Austin had adopted, a city is run by an unelected manager, and the mayor effectively serves only as chief spokesperson and head of the city council. But absent a resolution or ordinance passed by the council, a manager is not obligated to act on the whims of its elected officials.

"Staff hated it," said Riley. "With Austin's council-manager form of government, one thing you get is a bureaucracy that can get very entrenched. You get all of this inertia. And in particular in the Transportation Department, you get very competent, qualified staff who are very good at enforcing the *existing* regulations."

Nor were they going to receive any support from the taxi industry, which had a small but notable voice within local politics. Most of the council, including Riley and Spelman, had for years routinely accepted taxi donations. And most of them were sympathetic to the worries of impoverished taxi drivers.

Instead of legalizing TNCs, the two tried something more incremental. In May 2014, they passed resolutions to develop a stakeholder working group for TNCs. The thirty-three-member group, which included taxi members, TNC representatives, city staff, and local community members, would develop recommendations to create a TNC pilot program.[33] But to show that the council wasn't trying to put taxis out of business, an additional working group was created so that Carlton Thomas would consider specific suggestions to make taxis more competitive.[34]

Generally, the taxi suggestions fell under the headings of either "difficult" or "non-starter," such as requiring the nearest driver pick to up a dispatch call or allowing drivers to use dispatch apps. They were also instructed to consider "a transition toward employee drivers" and a universal dispatching system across all companies, both of which taxi companies hated.[35] The hope was that each working group could develop a consensus so that no one was harmed by Uber's entry.

The council set a deadline for the working groups to report back within six months, and Uber appeared willing to patiently wait it out. But Lyft, sensing a shift in attitudes, launched in Austin within two weeks without seeking permission.[36] Thomas's office was incensed, threatening citations and car impounds.[37] Lyft hired a local lobbyist who called Council Member Spelman's staff and apologized profusely for the inconvenience. But they weren't backing down, and it all but guaranteed that Uber would follow suit within days.

"I had a phone call with an Uber representative," said Riley, "and I was trying to persuade them to hold off. I thought it would muddle the whole discussion, and I thought it would be a lot cleaner if we could get it worked out by regulations. And Uber said that based on their experience with other cities, they needed to start operating because that would help their customer base. To increase political pressure to get final approval. That people would become so accustomed to the service that it would be necessary to keep them around one way or another."

Uber launched in Austin five days after Lyft.[38]

As Uber had predicted to Riley, both companies followed what had become TNC standard operating procedures. Beginning with free promotional rides, they built a loyal base of customers, competed for the market share of drivers, and paid all fines for sting operations. Thomas's office worked with the Austin Police Department (APD) to issue citations to illegal Uber and Lyft drivers, an assignment that an APD union official characterized as a "waste of resources."[39]

It ran counter to their anti-DWI efforts. Not only was it a waste of the police's time, but there was nothing to show for it, no sense of accomplishment. The city seemed powerless to stop TNCs, and life simply continued on.

During the summer, frustrations continued to build. The TNC stakeholder group became as pointless as the sting operations. The thirty-three-member group met at an annex and was guided by a professional moderator. At each meeting, they would float a new policy topic: driver safety, insurance, data requirements, and so forth. They all agreed on basic issues. There should be *some* kind of background check. There should be *some* type of insurance in place. But once they delved into specifics, they couldn't agree on what the regulations should look like.

Depending on whom you asked, either Yellow Cab President Ed Kargbo or Uber's lobbyist created heated moments.

"From Day One, Ed was almost Trump-like. Everything he said you knew was a crock, but he totally believes it," said one working group member.

"One of the Uber reps was young and brash, creating a lot of tension in the room," recalled another.

By all accounts, there was no consensus on any of the important issues. Word got back to Council Member Riley, who was growing impatient with the stalemate.

"There was never going to be a 'kumbaya' moment where they had settled on something everyone could live with," Riley said.

Outside of the meetings, Ed Kargbo continued to voice the unfairness of tolerating TNCs. He argued that companies that violate the law shouldn't be rewarded for it, and he continued to press the safety concerns of insurance and background checks. In one venue after the other, Kargbo implicitly argued that taxi companies willing to tolerate strict regulations were entitled to their sanctioned monopolies.[40] Uber and Lyft had no right to reap their rewards.

Unofficially, one of the TNC working group's functions was to hold the issue at bay until after an upcoming November midterm election that had every sign of stress and drama. Years earlier, in 2012, the council voted to reorganize its structure.[41] For decades, the six council members (and mayor) took turns running in sleepy, citywide races during odd-year May elections. Since few voters showed up, the outcome was often predictable. There was a sense the election process was rigged and didn't represent the city's true demographics. To remedy the problem, candidates would now run in ten brand-new districts, and they would do so during a much larger voter-turnout season.

Because the upcoming November 2014 midterm was the first election under the new structure, all ten races, plus one for a new mayor, would be held at the same time. Dozens of newcomers had already thrown their hats into the ring. In all, nearly eighty candidates registered for ten council districts and a mayor's race. Only Riley and one other were running for a council member seat, both in the same district. At a minimum, the new council was guaranteed at least nine new members. Local pundits could only guess what the outcome would look like. And it also meant that the TNC working group's six-month deadline, set to coincide with the November election, was pointless.

"No one took it seriously," said one council staffer.

With a stressful election looming and no progress being made in the working group, Riley and Spelman saw an opening to push the issue. Although some council members still had misgivings about TNCs, they were popular with voters citywide. Two of the sitting council members were running for mayor. Also, Riley and his main opponent were running in a newly created downtown and university district. As Riley noted, anyone who depended on the downtown community for votes – such as four of the seven council members running for office – would have a hard time voting against the pilot program. Between the seven of them, all Riley and Spelman needed were two more votes of support, and it was a good bet they'd get at least three.

In mid-September, Riley held a press conference to introduce an ordinance legalizing TNCs under a pilot program. He was joined by the president of the local police union, a downtown business alliance, and ATX Safer Streets.[42] Modeled similarly to an ordinance passed in Detroit, the program would allow Uber and Lyft to operate virtually unfettered for at least a year. Just as in California, all of the provisions were tailored so that neither company would be bothered by regulators.

Most of the TNC working group was caught off guard, feeling as though the hours of meetings they'd dedicated were all for naught. Riley showed up at the following meetings to smooth over tensions. And although it wasn't strictly necessary, Uber and Lyft continued to show up for meetings, too.

By introducing the ordinance in mid-September, Riley and Spelman had effectively set a timer. Most ordinances needed at least six weeks to pass through the council, if not more. But as they approached November, the majority of the council had to spend more time on the campaign trail. They needed to phone bank and block walk, pitching themselves to voters and asking for support. Riley and Spelman were gambling that not only would a majority of the council be too afraid of their constituents to vote against the TNC ordinance, but they would be too afraid to delay it, either. If the bill stalled or failed before the election, Uber was likely to make sure the voters knew who was to blame, as they had in other cities.

Now under the gun, the behind-the-scenes TNC politicking intensified. Spelman's staff, tasked with the policy legwork, had to move quickly to ensure that all angles, including insurance, background checks, data sharing, and surge pricing were well addressed. Riley's office would work with stakeholders to build a coalition. They both also needed Uber and Lyft representatives available to answer tough questions and build a rapport with the council.

But in an odd twist that would cause problems for years to come, Uber's local lobbyist refused to be helpful to the process. Self-assured of their imminent victory, he didn't see a need.

"The Uber lobbyist was a pain to work with," Spelman said. "Everything was work, and it turned into a tonal issue. They'd basically say, 'Our business model is so obviously superior you should just let us do our job.'"

Spelman and Riley saw past Uber's attitude problem. But for some council members, the lack of bedside manner created a massive sense of distrust. Kathie Tovo, a former writing professor, and Laura Morrison, a former Lockheed engineer, were already deeply suspicious. It was bad enough that Uber and Lyft had barged into town uninvited and that the ordinance was placed in the middle of an election season, forcing their hands and speeding through a complicated issue. But Uber's obstinate lobbyist was the cherry on top of a sundae that, to them, reeked of misgivings and corrupt influence.

"[The Uber representative] was extremely arrogant," said Morrison.

Kathie Tovo, who was Riley's main opponent in the upcoming election, had been suspicious of ridesharing well before the proposed ordinance. She was one of two votes against Riley's 2013 resolution asking Carlton Thomas to report on the state of ridesharing nationally.[43] And she was closer to the taxi industry than any other council member. Executives from Texas Taxi viewed her as an ally, having already donated $2,400 to her war chest a month earlier.

But more fundamentally, both she and Morrison believed in the protective power of regulations and, much like Christiane Hayashi, hated that these new companies were crafting their own. A "regulation-lite" version of taxi ordinances was little more than undeserved preferential treatment, they felt. Every time Uber or Lyft referred to their services as "ridesharing," it irritated them since the traditional definition related to nonprofit carpooling. To them, it was all a campaign of gimmicks and tricks meant to pull the wool over everyone's eyes. They couldn't trust it.

By contrast, Lyft's lobbyist was more than willing to guide council members through the issues.

"Lyft's lobbyist was lovely to work with," said Spelman. "They would say, 'I wish we could do this, but we can't, and let me explain why.' Lyft was *terrific* for government relations."

The personalities of each company's leaders – Kalanick's aggressive competitiveness and Green and Zimmer's compassionate community-building – transcended the lobbyists they deployed. Both companies wanted the same outcome, but their approaches were radically different. Unfortunately for Lyft, any gains they made did little to mend Uber's broken relationships. They were like the "good cop" to Uber's "bad cop."

Against the backdrop of the election, the TNC issue also created tensions that were unusual for the Austin City Council. Although the members didn't always agree with one another, they were usually civil. But those courtesies started to erode. If Riley and Spelman were perceived by Morrison and Tovo as TNC cronies, then Morrison and Tovo were likewise viewed as taxi mouthpieces. No one threw chairs or shouted at one another – at least, not openly – but tempers were running hotter than normal. Uber was not only disruptive to markets but also to existing political relationships.

In public, both taxis and TNCs each tried to create the appearance that the public overwhelmingly supported them. Taxi proponents would often show up to council meetings filling the seats to capacity while wearing neon-yellow T-shirts with large-print statements like, "LICENSED, INSURED, LEGAL" or "ALWAYS THERE, ALWAYS FAIR."

Per standard operating procedure, Uber cajoled their users to send hundreds of emails to council members, a tactic that wasn't as effective as it used to be. Each council member had set up Outlook rules to filter the emails to other folders and simply watched them tally up. Watching it was fun, almost whimsical, but it didn't faze them. Like in Colorado, the real political pressure instead came from the local tech industry.

"It's not like I had Uber people sitting in my office and twisting my arm," said Riley. "There was a lot of talk about this whole issue in the tech community and that Austin was not embracing innovation that was consistent with its reputation."

On the flip side, as a skeptic of TNCs, Tovo felt similar pressures. "Any attempt to seriously regulate them, and you're suddenly painted as 'anti-technology,' 'anti-consumer,' or 'pro-drunk-driving,'" she said.

The other standard Austin held itself to was how this issue was being addressed in neighboring Texas cities. Since the beginning of 2014, ordinances legalizing TNCs had been proposed in Dallas, Houston, and San Antonio. And although each city was like its own flavor of ice cream, they were similar enough that if one city legalized TNCs, it was more difficult for another to justify why it wouldn't. By the time Riley and Spelman proposed their pilot program, Houston had already given the green light to TNCs.

But in Houston, the playing field changed. They didn't pass Uber's standard set of light regulations. In a rare and unprecedented concession, Uber agreed to a package of regulations designed by the city's taxi regulator, who was an IATR Smartphone App Committee member, including a demand that drivers obtain a fingerprint background check through the city.

In most jurisdictions, both Uber and Lyft considered fingerprint scans a deal-breaker because they created "friction," decreasing the chances that vital part-time drivers would complete the enrollment process. Normally the TNCs would only agree to conduct their own private background checks to keep the sign-up process simple and quick. The only other city where they had agreed to fingerprint background checks was New York, a market made up entirely of professional chauffeur drivers whose fingerprints were already scanned. Lyft outright refused to operate in any other city where fingerprint checks were mandated, and when the Houston ordinance passed, they soon left the market. But Uber said they would stick it out.

In public, Uber wouldn't explain why they had agreed to this one exception in Houston. Most likely, their city council wouldn't have legalized TNCs without the provision, and Uber wouldn't see a dime from the city's two million customers. Even after Uber agreed to it, only ten of the seventeen council members voted in favor of the bill – and they narrowly avoided calamity along the way. An amendment to cap the number of TNC vehicles to 250 per company, which would have frequently triggered surge pricing, narrowly failed in an 8-9 vote.[44]

But in Austin, all that mattered was Houston's final product. Council members like Tovo began to ask, if fingerprint checks were good enough for Houston, why not perform them in Austin, too? Uber's reluctance to talk about it turned the issue into a weakness.

Riley could only counter that his proposal was similar to how the California PUC regulated TNCs. Still, he had difficulty subduing the criticisms. In council meetings, Morrison relentlessly offered her own series of amendments, many of which were designed to "level the playing field" with taxis, even if they infringed on the TNC business model. Riley would try to point out that TNCs needed a free hand to improve for-hire services that taxis had poorly provided.

In response, Tovo would discredit that premise by turning to Carlton Thomas, who disliked TNCs, as an expert staff member. In public, Thomas was like a champion poker player. He stared straight ahead with a calm and reserved demeanor, never raised his voice, never showed any emotion, nor even so much as flinched. His tone was always professional, like a cop on a witness stand, the perfect resource for Tovo.

In one instance, Riley discussed a provision requiring Uber and Lyft to make outreach efforts to areas of town underserved by taxis. Tovo then turned to Thomas and said, "It was my understanding that taxicab drivers have a responsibility of taking the calls that come in regardless of where they originate."[45]

Thomas replied, "We are not aware of any predominantly underserved areas in town. That has just not been brought to our attention." He almost sounded like a neutral observer.[46]

But his statement was ludicrous. Thomas essentially told the council that all parts of town were serviced by taxis more or less equally, and there was plenty of evidence they weren't. The original HeyRide app was created because the founder couldn't get a cab when he needed one. Uber and Lyft were intensely popular because of taxi service problems. But since those problems were seldom reported, Thomas wasn't "aware" of it.

During council hearings, Tovo and Morrison proposed several amendments that were offered for the sake of fairness to taxis but also had the effect of constraining TNCs: limits on surge pricing and requiring expensive commercial insurance, for example. Most of their amendments failed, but the greater question legitimately puzzled the council as a whole: How does a public utility, whose prices and supply are strictly controlled, compete with a free-market enterprise offering a similar service? Few were comfortable with the possibility that the local taxi industry could go out of business.

At one point, Morrison asked the ATD how they would reconcile this problem. An assistant director replied that they envisioned an approach similar to Colorado, where taxis could switch between taxi and TNC regulatory models.

"So we see a future where the three taxi companies register as TNCs," the ATD deputy said. "So it may be that they have an application where they could get surge pricing, and it may be that if someone calls them on the phone, they use the taximeter. Or with [street] hails, they use taximeters. So, we may have kind of a hybrid system here until it actually gets in operation."[47]

The ATD would later abandon their proposed "hybrid" taxi future. But since the council was entering a period of sharp transition, few would notice.

To further ease some of the political strain, one of the more critical provisions of the bill was a measure instructing the TNC working group to continue with its recommendations and instructing the council to reexamine the ordinance six months after its passage. It emphasized that the pilot program was only temporary, that the issue was still undergoing review, and it gave the council extra incentive to move past Tovo and Morrison's amendments. After a while, whenever they expressed concerns, Riley or the mayor would simply tell them it wasn't worth worrying about. Other cities already had these regulations in place, and besides, the ordinance would have a short half-life. Insurance issues? They would be addressed in six months. Background checks? Six months.

As Spelman sat back in his council chair and watched these conversations about a level playing field and what was acceptable in one city versus another, he suddenly had an epiphany.

"The insurance issue wasn't about what's best for Austin," he said. "It was about Uber getting as sweet a [regulatory] deal everywhere else."

For Spelman, this explained a lot about Uber's odd behavior. Across the United States, Uber was trying to secure a patchwork of local regulations across several dozen cities. Each one looked to others for regulatory cues. If Uber was willing to accept an especially rigorous requirement in, say, Nashville, perhaps it would then take hold in Memphis. Before long, Uber would face a domino effect.

"When that light bulb went off, I suddenly understood why they were such asses," said Spelman.

There was also a deeper aspect of the regulatory arbitrage Spelman may not have realized. Namely, the more that taxi regulators across the country guided city councils with expert advice, the more likely Uber would be regulated as a de facto taxi company. Whether Spelman or Uber could sense it, the TNCs were right to be weary. As large Texas cities encountered the TNC issue at roughly the same time, Carlton Thomas regularly emailed taxi regulators from Houston, San Antonio, Fort Worth, and Corpus Christi, most of whom were IATR members.

They kept tabs with one another to gather inside information by tracking how each city was addressing the issue and offering the occasional moral support. "Sending positive thoughts," one of them told Thomas on the subject of TNCs.[48] None of them were thrilled about Uber and Lyft, but neither were they willing to confront their own city councils. Instead, they took a subtle approach, offering assistance that might nudge elected officials in a pro-taxi direction. For example, during the Austin City Limits Music Festival, which was attended by over seventy-five thousand people per day, Uber publicly claimed that they were so popular that they had provided a hundred thousand trips.[49] Since Uber was never going to share that data, a Houston regulator asked Thomas for the taxi ridership data during that period.

"A review of the taxi data may be the only way to cast a new light on the claims.... We may be able to use the information to ensure we all establish best practice regulations," she told Thomas.[50]

Thomas himself was no stranger to nudging the Austin City Council. When it came to the TNC pilot program, he was curiously absent when Riley and Spelman needed help drafting the ordinance. "My department has played no part in it," he told a Houston colleague.[51] However, he *was* happy to help Tovo and Morrison craft amendments making life more difficult for Uber and Lyft. It was a strategy similar to when Thomas's office penned the 2013 report unfairly painting SideCar in a harsh light. He had been skeptical of

TNCs at least since his first IATR Conference in 2012. Except now his pro-taxi sentiments had spilled over into the lawmaking process. Want to assist council members friendly to TNCs? Thomas was a ghost in the wind. Want to help skeptical council members draft amendments that *constrain* TNCs? He was Johnny-on-the-spot. And when the TNC working group couldn't reach a consensus, the recommendations simply reflected the ATD's sentiments.

Curiously, no one from Uber or Lyft ever expressed concern over or even mentioned Thomas's affiliation with Matt Daus and the IATR. Nor did the council seem particularly bothered that Thomas straddled dual roles as both the local vehicle-for-hire expert and a surreptitious taxi advocate. After all, he had to maintain a good working relationship with taxis on a daily basis. To council members, his job required him to appease two masters.

By mid-October, just a few weeks before the election, the ordinance passed more or less as Uber and Lyft had wanted, by a vote of six to one with Morrison as the lone vote against. Riley and Spelman's bet had paid off. On the night of the vote, one council staffer remembered seeing a look of shock come over Carlton Thomas's boss in the audience. In news articles, a couple of reporters seemed surprised Tovo had voted in favor of it.[52]

"It was a flawed ordinance, but we wanted to have some parameters in place rather than none at all," said Tovo. "It was better to have the ordinance."

Two weeks later, Uber held a party at one of the higher-end downtown music venues to celebrate the victory. Riley attended and was featured in an Uber blog post, listed in a photo credit as "Champion Councilman Chris Riley."[53]

Locally, Riley earned a lot of recognition for his support of TNCs, especially in neighborhoods near the university. Late-night transportation was an important issue to student communities. "I spent a lot of time around UT, and it was as very big deal to them," said Riley. Around campus, political ads dressed as faux movie posters hung in kiosks. Sketched as cartoon renderings, they featured a toned, smiling Riley, sitting on touring bicycle, wearing aerodynamic shorts and a blue jersey with an R-shaped Superman emblem. Behind him sat two white cars, one with a pink mustache affixed to the hood. The banner read, "If District 9 Had a Superhero, IT WOULD BE **CHRIS RILEY**," and in the tagline, "GOING GREEN JUST GOT GREENER."

While campaigning, Tovo also found strong student concerns about TNCs. "When I was knocking on doors and talking to students, many of them knew nothing else [about the council] except who was standing next to Uber and Lyft," she said.

Although it was important for downtown voters, the TNC issue was not prominent in the 2014 Austin City Council elections, which were otherwise a chaotic free-for-all. The local ballot was jam packed with higher priorities and strange distractions. A $1.4 billion bond issue to create a downtown "starter" rail line turned into a high-profile losing battle. And the Democrats made a more-serious-than-usual push in the gubernatorial race with an all-female ticket.

Whereas in years past the May council elections were sleepy affairs, they had transformed into bitter oddities. In one district, the two frontrunners were brother and sister, casting family divisions and rumors of suspicious motives. In another district, a frontrunner's newspaper endorsement was retracted because an audio tape leaked expressing her belief that the 9/11 terrorist attack was a government plot.[54] As far as most voters cared, there was no reason to revisit the settled issue of TNCs.

In the downtown district, divided chiefly between Riley and Tovo, Riley had taken 40.4 percent of the voters against Tovo's 49.1 percent.[55] Because neither candidate had obtained at majority of the votes, a runoff was required on December 16. But many suspected, accurately, that runoff elections would draw far fewer voters, mostly diehard politicos who identified farther left or right than their district as a whole, which was a bad omen for Riley. The university students, nearing both finals season and a winter break, were unlikely to return to the polls in December. Plus, there was little question that downtown diehards would favor Tovo.

Easily doing the math, Riley withdrew three days after the general election.[56] He wasn't the sole loser among the council's Uber supporters. The two sitting council members running for mayor both lost against a popular outsider. When it was over, in the shift from a 6–1 (as in six members and one mayor) to a 10–1 council, Tovo became the one and only holdover. Spelman returned to academia, and Riley took a sabbatical to Brooklyn.

Two weeks after the election, *BuzzFeed* broke its stories about Uber's VP contemplating digging up dirt on reporters and their "God View" tool. Riley and Spelman had timed their ordinance even better than they could have expected.

Regardless of whether they held office, they took it on faith that the pilot program would build its own momentum. Since TNCs performed more efficiently and reliably than cabs, there was every reason to believe that, absent a scandal, political strength would organically flow to the best service. As the ordinance was written, Uber and Lyft were guaranteed an operating agreement for at least a year, with a TNC review to begin halfway through.

But there were no more policy wonks on the council to defend Uber and Lyft in Austin. Nor was the taxi industry sitting back and letting events unfold organically. Their expiring franchise agreements with the city needed to be renewed by the following August. To make friends, taxi owners and managers donated a total of over $35,000 to nine council candidates, four of whom won their districts. TNCs on the other hand, donated only a few thousand dollars to a few candidates across the entire United States, to say little of Austin. By staying on the sidelines, they were now more vulnerable.

What few also noticed was that although the pilot program created a framework for TNCs in Austin, it didn't address the day-to-day life of the city's remaining for-hire providers. It treated TNCs as though they lived in a bubble separate from everyone else. Taxi drivers were still required to obtain chauffeur's licenses. Uber and Lyft were not. Limo services were still required to charge high minimum fares. Uber and Lyft were not. Even pedicab and horse-and-buggy operators were required to obtain a fingerprint check. Uber and Lyft performed their own checks. And with the TNC working group still moving forward, the ATD saw it as another opportunity to nudge the new council.

On all sides, a bubble of political resentment was forming.

CHAPTER ELEVEN
Couched Conversations

By February 2015, with the Austin City Council's six-month review of the TNC pilot program on the horizon, Carlton Thomas wanted to change the regulations as soon as a reasonable opening formed, and cautiously, he waited for the right moment. San Antonio's taxi regulator shot him an email. "Do you know when the plan is to take the new proposals to the Council?" he asked.

From: Thomas, Carlton
Sent: Wednesday, February 11, 2015 6:08 PM
To: Gary Gilbert (SAPD)
Subject: RE: TNCs

Gary,

We changed from 6 at-large council members and a Mayor, to 10 single-member districts and an at-large Mayor. 10 of them are newly elected and only one incumbent. Taking things to council at the moment is touch-and-go.

I really don't know.

CT

As it turned out, Thomas didn't have long to wait. As the new council was organizing itself, someone emerged who would challenge Uber and Lyft's unfettered autonomy in Austin: Council Member Ann Kitchen. An attorney, health benefits consultant, and former state legislator, Kitchen had been well ingrained in local Democratic politics.[1] Her husband, a notable campaign consultant, had worked for several of the former council members, including a position as Kathie Tovo's campaign manager in 2011.[2]

Since taxi donations tended to gravitate toward strong Democratic candidates, Kitchen was an ideal recipient. A network of local donors contributed $4,000 to her election on the very same day the council passed Riley and Spelman's pilot program.[3] It was not the most money they had given to any single Austin candidate, nor was it sizable compared to the $125,000 her campaign spent that year. But the taxi industry was trolling for new allies, and in Kitchen, they had definitely found one who, if nothing else, was sympathetic to the labor force of low-income taxi drivers.

Early in 2015, the council created a new Mobility Committee to address transportation issues and assigned Kitchen as its chair. In March, they held their first meeting and discussed TNCs at length. During the opening public comments, several speakers, including Ed Kargbo, came forward to complain that TNCs were allowed to operate on an uneven playing field. Some claimed they were losing drivers to a service that didn't require a chauffeur's license.[4] Of course, none of the taxi representatives were asking for fewer restrictions on prices or the number of cabs on the road, anything that would place them on the same level as TNCs. They simply wanted increased regulations against Uber and Lyft so that competing wouldn't be so difficult. As Kargbo said about the public-utility nature of taxis, "once that standard is set, I think that all service providers ... should be held to that standard."[5]

Immediately after an hour of comments devoted largely to TNC complaints, the meeting moved into a crash course on how city regulators historically managed taxi services. Carlton Thomas's boss, the director of the Austin Transportation Department (ATD), took pains to stress that taxis were administered as "managed competition," as was common for most cities. The supply of cabs – 756 in Austin – was tightly regulated, he explained.[6]

For some on the Mobility Committee, this was a new and strange concept. On the surface, taxis didn't appear to be a public utility. As one member said skeptically, "That seems to be that we are injecting ourselves into companies' business models."

The director replied that it's always been that way, that in exchange for safety and permitting, the regulators then "make sure that those participants in that market have a fair market wage and so forth." He also emphasized, as Matt Daus often had, that deregulation historically didn't work.

Still, the skeptics wanted to know how other cities were treating the new, dynamic business model of TNCs, and the director was happy to point out that they had access to that information because Carlton Thomas was a member of the International Association of Transportation Regulators (IATR).[7]

As the crash course started to go on indefinitely, Kitchen interrupted to sum up the main point and move on. "The basic question when you're regulating is to what extent do you do that? What are you protecting? You obviously want to protect safety but also want to protect access, you know, from a cost standpoint so that it's not just people of higher incomes that can afford taxicabs."[8]

This was a longstanding complaint of TNC skeptics. If taxis became insolvent because of a competitor, then low-income passengers who couldn't afford a smartphone or credit card would be left in the cold. Implicitly, Kitchen was making the point that to "protect access" to taxis, they needed regulatory cushioning from TNCs like Uber and Lyft. For Thomas, who was feeling out the new council, it was probably music to his ears.

Neither Uber nor Lyft officials were present at this first meeting. Not that they would have done more than promote themselves if they had attended. But ATD staff cherry-picked their arguments, and no one called them out on it. When possible, they emphasized that in mid-2014, TNCs were operating in Austin *illegally*. They didn't mention that deregulation was last attempted in the United States decades before smartphone technology. They didn't mention that the taxi industry kept the supply low to extract the greatest rents out of drivers. They didn't mention their own campaign to push SideCar out of Austin in 2013 or the strong IATR bias in favor of taxis. There was no mention of Yellow Cab's private investigator report or the many sting operations conducted despite police department criticisms. And there was no mention of the most glaring fact of all: that if Uber and Lyft had first asked for permission before entering, they would have been met with a resounding "no."

Instead, ATD staff compartmentalized past conflicts in the softest possible terms. In late 2012, "there was a local company that entered into the market as a TNC, and that was the first round of conversations about how do you regulate this new industry," said an ATD staffer.[9] "Conversations" – they made it sound as though they were lounging on sofa seats and hashing out policy over beers.

The meeting's agenda listed a briefing to finally present the TNC working group's recommendations, which included more rigorous vehicle inspections, greater insurance coverage, and heftier data reporting. Fingerprint background checks were omitted, likely so Carlton Thomas could see where the council members stood.[10] But the Mobility Committee was chomping at the bit for more data about how TNCs were regulated differently from the city's other for-hire vehicles.

A week later, the ATD provided a supercharged response. In a cover letter, they added to the initial TNC working group recommendations to now include "expanded driver background checks." They not only came through with a few spreadsheets, but they also provided a thick, 150-page binder of supporting documentation to showcase their desire to protect the taxi industry. Inside were public taxi reports spanning back several years, including the 2013 overview of ridesharing across the country. The ATD threw in miscellaneous excerpts, such as a 2013 quote from taxi expert Ray

Mundy advocating strongly against SideCar because it "would be detrimental to [the] existing transportation providers;" a page of state law, highlighted in yellow, stating, "A municipality by ordinance: (1) shall license, control, and otherwise regulate each private passenger vehicle ... that provides passenger taxicab transportation;" they even inserted a copy of Craig Leisy's 2001 report of Seattle's experience in deregulating and then re-regulating taxicab services. For anyone reading along, the implicit message was clear: please don't let taxis become deregulated.[11]

Before the ATD could make any headway toward tighter restrictions, Uber and Lyft decided to take their campaign to the state legislature in early 2015. They promoted a bill that would allow them to legalize TNCs statewide without the need to ask for permission city by city. Texas wasn't special in this regard. Uber was on a nationwide quest to duplicate their 2014 victory in Colorado in almost every state legislature in America. Their numbers were difficult to follow, but it seemed clear they had hired hundreds of lobbyists at a cost of several million dollars. In Texas alone, they had reportedly hired an initial twenty-three at a cost of $700,000.[12]

There were several advantages to becoming legal at the state level. For one, the lawmakers were more receptive. Large urban cities tended to favor Democratic constituents, but state legislatures were becoming increasingly Republican controlled. Democrats favored unions and immigrants, which were more prodigious among taxi drivers, and they also didn't care for the fact that TNCs were expanding the workforce of independent contractors. "Good Democrats don't support independent contracting," said one Austin City Council staffer. By contrast, Republican lawmakers had none of those concerns and viewed TNCs as "job creators."

Usually, this meant TNCs could achieve more favorable terms through a state law. In many cities, they had to actively fight against council members who were trying to impose constraints in the name of safety and regulatory equity. Whether it was fingerprint background checks, medical tests for drivers, driver registration, or rigorous insurance coverage, when one city got its way, other cities wanted to negotiate for most-favored-nation constraints. Creating a state law was an effective way to block the domino effect. Not to mention it would allow them to ignore the lion's share of local IATR members.

By March 2015, the insurance issue was still tense but diminishing. Uber was close to signing a long-term agreement with some of the major insurance carriers like USAA, Allstate, and State Farm to work out the kinks in Period One coverage. The road to clear insurance rules was still rocky but less of a concern, and quietly, the Texas legislature was in the middle of passing a separate bill simply to bless the new TNC/insurance marriage.[13] As that issue became less dire, background checks took a more prominent role.

Regulators and Texas lawmakers didn't trust Uber and Lyft's private background checks, which only used information like a name and social security number to research someone. Ordinarily, taxi drivers were fingerprinted and their criminal histories were checked by taxi regulators. The TNCs, conversely, didn't trust taxi regulators to administer their checks quickly. And in all likelihood, there was probably a suspicion that regulators would deliberately stall the process. How could they give one of Matt Daus's disciples the power to control who did or didn't become drivers for their platform?

In public, Uber insisted their private checks were superior, and government regulators said the same about their fingerprint checks. In reality, neither were rock-solid. There was no central database, public or private, that could research every criminal history in the United States. An Uber-sponsored search at best generally reviewed a driver's credit score to determine where they had lived for the past seven years (the legal maximum) and then looked for available criminal records in those cities and counties.

For Uber, this method had a couple of obvious holes that were easy to criticize. For one, because they didn't use a biometric identifier like a fingerprint, they couldn't prove that the driver-applicant was in fact the person who applied. At least with a fingerprint, if a driver matched a criminal history, he couldn't claim to be someone he wasn't. Secondly, some of the government's criminal databases weren't publicly available, not even to private background check companies. For instance, the federal government maintained the National Sex Offender Registry, which was only available to law enforcement agencies. And it was more robust than the US Department of Justice's National Sex Offender Public Website, which intentionally omitted certain lower-level sex offenders. If a driver had been convicted of "sexual exploitation of a child," "felony sexual battery," or a handful of other offenses, a private company might not catch it, but a fingerprint check probably would.[14]

Even before 2015, Uber found it difficult to counter some of these weaknesses and had continued to double down on the thoroughness of its private checks. They claimed they were better suited to find lower-level offenses, like a DUI, that a fingerprint check would miss. But stories would periodically emerge of TNC drivers with criminal backgrounds who had assaulted passengers, creating even more tension with regulators who already didn't trust Uber. In California, the claims of phenomenal background checks pissed off the district attorneys of Los Angeles and San Francisco (who were probably not happy that the CPUC had pre-empted their ability to regulate Uber and Lyft to begin with) so much that they jointly filed suits against Uber and Lyft for false advertisement.[15]

While Uber's lawsuit progressed slowly, the Texas legislature was only a few days from having its first committee hearing in April on the TNC bill when an incident in Houston turned the issue completely on its head. An Uber driver had taken a drunk woman, who was too incoherent to provide an address, back to his own home, where he later admitted to police that he had sex with her. The woman said she was too drunk to consent and accused the driver of rape. Making things worse for Uber, they discovered he was never issued a permit by the City of Houston, as required by the local TNC law passed six months earlier.[16]

As in most cities, Uber had already on-boarded untold hundreds or thousands of drivers to their platform before they were made legal. But after the Houston law passed, Uber and the city were still butting heads during the transition. A huge backlog of drivers had not yet been fingerprinted, and while they waited and continued to drive for Uber, the city issued them several hundred citations. Houston claimed they were moving as fast as possible, even arguing with Uber over who should pay for all of the city's accrued overtime.[17]

The driver accused of rape was among those who had slipped through the cracks, having received neither a permit nor a fine.[18] But quickly, the *Houston Chronicle* also learned he was released from prison three years earlier after serving fourteen years on a felony drug charge. Uber was unable to explain how they had missed it in their own background check and simply issued blanket statements about their commitment to safety. Houston taxi regulators insisted they would have caught the offense had they fingerprinted the driver.[19]

The hearing occurred two days after the *Chronicle* story, putting intense pressure on Uber to defend its practices. When the legislative committee asked about their background checks, Uber's representative was evasive and noncommittal. Getting a straight answer was like trying to pull teeth. The committee chairman asked, if Uber's private checks were indeed more thorough, why not start with a fingerprint check and then simply go above and beyond with a private check?[20]

The Uber rep cheerfully replied, "Well, I think what we see right now is that there's not an additional safety benefit from a fingerprint mandate. And what we see is that when you have to rely on a municipal—"[21]

"I didn't say rely on it," the chairman interrupted. "I mean you can go above and beyond. I think there's a lot of people out there who think this should be a basis, though. And it's going to be difficult to educate 27 million people in Texas that your system is better than the ten-fingerprint background check. So why couldn't you do a ten-fingerprint check and on top of that you as a company have higher standards than the minimum required by a law?"[22]

The Uber rep only relented a little. "I think one thing we see is that if we have to comply with a fingerprint mandate, it typically adds many weeks to the process of getting a driver on board and earning money. So I think if there are ways to reduce that sort of friction, then we can maybe have a conversation about it."[23]

"So, again, your testimony though now is that you wouldn't be opposed if we could get the timeframe less than a couple weeks here and back?" the chairman asked.[24]

"It's quite possible we could have a conversation around that."[25]

The strategy was a common theme of Uber's public testimony. Upsell the brand with positivity, relinquish as little ground as possible, never lose your cool, and commit to little, if anything. It was perhaps modeled as the upbeat, positive version of Travis Kalanick's public testimony style.

But as usual, Uber couldn't rely on the charm of their government relations team alone. In many of their campaigns, it was necessary to obtain an outside expert, and this was no exception. Uber asked Mike Coffey, a Fort Worth owner of an upper-level "white glove" background-check firm, to speak for them (for free). In the world of private checks, there were different degrees of thoroughness, and Coffey's clients typically paid a premium for greater assurance. Having studied the industry up close, he understood the problems with both government and private checks.

Said Coffey, "Everyone watches *CSI* and thinks that all of these databases are out there from the federal government and private companies, and it's all at our fingertips. And it's just not. The courts' records are hard to research. There are a lot of places where the records are difficult to access or the details are really challenging. Every jurisdiction has its own set of computers, and often they don't talk to each other. So getting all of the information from a [single] government entity is almost impossible."

Coffey's own firm had conducted a study in 2008 reviewing Texas's death-row inmates, among other convicts, against a state database of criminal records. He found that over a third were missing the capital murder convictions that put them on death row in the first place.[26] The government was little better than Uber on background checks.

"I used to fear big brother, but now I don't worry about it," Coffey said. "Uber actually asked me to come testify [in the Texas legislature]. I told them, 'You may not like what I'm going to say. I'll definitely be able to explain the problems with the federal database, but I just can't say that what *you're* doing is right.'"

Coffey wasn't content simply to go before lawmakers and promote Uber's brand. Suspicious, he did his own digging and found something disturbing. The Houston driver arrested for rape was previously convicted of a drug charge in *federal* court. Federal cases were a little more difficult to confirm because the database didn't list birthdates to cross-reference against. A private researcher had to put in more effort to make sure the "John Smith" convicted of a federal crime was the same one being researched. But it was also unlikely the feds would accidentally forget to list a conviction in their own database. They were at least thorough enough to include those. To Coffey, it was strange that Uber had missed it.

"I called the guy who owns Uber's background check company and said, 'Help me understand this. What happened?' And he first tried to tell me there was another name and it was confusing, and I said, 'Wait a minute, I pulled the name myself and found the record – it took me thirty seconds.' He said, 'Well, it doesn't have a date of birth on it.' And I said, "Well, *none* of the federal court cases have dates of birth on them.' And he said, 'Well, our policy is that if it doesn't have date of birth in the [criminal] index, we don't report it."

In other words, if a driver-applicant and a matched felon didn't share the same birthdate, Uber's firm didn't report it to them. But because the feds didn't use birthdates at all, Uber was ostensibly going to miss *all* federal convictions. The holes in Uber's checks seemed wider than most people knew.

To Coffey, it appeared as though Uber were using the cheapest form of background check, which made sense to him given the number of drivers they on-boarded. The gaps were bad enough, but with cheap labor came cheap diligence. Criminal records systems were far from pristine. A researcher who was paid a dollar per name might not go the extra mile if criminal files contained slight mismatches, such as typos.

Months later, Coffey's suspicions would be corroborated when the California district attorneys' lawsuit uncovered Uber drivers who were convicted felons released from prison less than seven years earlier. Several could have been detected but, for whatever reason, weren't. At least one was convicted of second-degree murder, used an alternate name to become a driver, and provided over eleven hundred rides. Another was a sex offender who applied to Uber within six months of his release from prison and provided nearly thirty-two hundred rides. Even more were convicted of theft or DUI, and their criminal histories were not detected, either.[27]

Overall, it made Coffey uneasy. He wouldn't speak for or against the TNC bill but instead registered as a neutral expert. For the most safety, he recommended the legislation require both the TNC *and* fingerprint checks. Friction be damned.

When he spoke at the legislature, his comments didn't quite stick with the committee. They were learning the technical details of this process on the fly, and they still had five more hours of speakers ahead of them. Although he was smart and experienced, Coffey's presentation encountered a few hurdles. In the nine minutes allotted, he opened with a dry joke that fell flat, and as he continued, he spoke quickly and somewhat verbosely. The committee thanked him and moved on.[28]

Before and after Coffey, opponents of the bill showed up in full force. Taxi companies complained of the "rule-breaking" and "Wall Street-financed" TNCs; state police showed up to defend the supposedly superior fingerprint checks; and city lawmakers like Kathie Tovo, who was now appointed by the council as mayor pro tem, wanted TNC laws to remain local. She argued that cities should be allowed to "embrace [TNCs] on their own terms."[29]

Making a surprise appearance was Matt Daus himself, who was among the public speakers allowed a maximum of three minutes. Using a loud, intense tone, he took nine minutes, much to the irritation of the committee chair. Daus warned that the bill was unconstitutional and called it a "cookie-cutter law" similar to what other Uber lobbyists around the country were proposing in 2015. Immediately following him was taxi expert Ray Mundy, who made similar points.[30]

The House committee passed the bill, but that's as far as it traveled in the legislature.[31] The Houston incident had cost Uber too much political capital. Other issues dominated their agenda, and no lawmaker wanted to stick their neck out any further at that point. When the session ended, Uber and Lyft had hired a combined thirty-eight lobbyists in Texas, and the result was a stalled bill.[32]

Their lack of success in Texas was somewhat uncharacteristic. That same year, statewide TNC bills passed in twenty-two states across the country, mostly in Republican legislatures. Uber gained legitimacy with stunning ferocity. In Arizona, the new governor met with the state's top taxi regulator, who confided he was going to perform sting operations against Uber and Lyft just weeks before the City of Glendale hosted Super Bowl XLIX. The governor then fired him, dismembered his agency, and pushed forward a TNC law.[33]

Uber was more subtle in some states than in others. Then-Governor Mike Pence signed Indiana's TNC bill in May 2015, and the same day Uber launched in Fort Wayne, catching local officials by surprise. "There's a law that nobody bothered to talk to us about, so we're going to have to research this," the public safety director said just after Uber launched.[34]

Perhaps the greatest upset came in Kansas. Both chambers of the legislature passed similar versions of a TNC bill. But at the last minute, an amendment sponsored by the Kansas Bankers Association passed that would have required TNC drivers with liens on their cars to prove they had purchased comprehensive and collision coverage, which was legally optional in Kansas.[35] It was not only an extra cost to the driver but also an extra on-boarding step for the company, and Uber took great offense.[36] They called it a "poison pill" amendment and threatened to leave if it became law.[37] Republican legislators, in turn, said Uber was bluffing, that if the company ever went public (which was often speculated), leaving state markets would then devastate their IPO valuation.[38] In the conference committee, an additional amendment was inserted requiring regulators to perform fingerprint background checks of their drivers, which Uber equally hated.[39] After the final version passed the Senate, a billboard truck was spotted driving around the capitol with a sign that read, "SB 117 destroys Kansas jobs."[40] Regardless, the final bill passed overwhelmingly, leaving the governor to ponder a veto. Lawmakers noted in the press that there was ample support for a veto override.[41]

Kansas Governor Sam Brownback, who famously used his state as a laboratory to see if deep budget cuts and loosened regulations could promote business growth, ultimately vetoed. In his message, he said he was comfortable with letting Uber regulate itself rather than passing regulations that TNCs felt were too restrictive.[42] A few days after, Uber made another move. While the legislature considered an override, the company launched in four more Kansas cities simultaneously: Manhattan, Topeka, Leavenworth, and Lawrence.[43] They appeared to be expanding both their political and customer bases.

On May 5, the legislature carried through on its promise, passing an override by margins of 4–1 or better in each chamber.[44] The law didn't take effect for nearly two months, but without waiting, Uber immediately carried through on its threat and shut down, just prior to the evening of Cinco de Mayo. Anyone opening the app within Kansas was greeted with a banner reading, "KANSAS JUST SHUT DOWN UBER," and in a byline, "NO PICKUPS EFFECTIVE IMMEDIATELY." The message explained, "KS legislators voted to override Gov. Brownback's veto of SB 117. Effective immediately, Uber can no longer operate in KS. We're saddened by the loss of hundreds of jobs, safe rides, and consumer choice in Kansas."[45] And just in case they didn't see the message in the app, Uber sent mass emails to their Kansas customers stating, "Farewell, Kansas."

Uber's messaging was wildly clever and effective. Their service was not deemed illegal, but thousands of residents nonetheless interpreted it that way. The new law simply inserted more "friction" in their on-boarding than they were willing to accept. Still, the public didn't track such details. Their response was visceral, a fiery white-hot contempt. A few of the 20 percent of lawmakers who voted against the override felt the need to point out their opposition on Twitter, followed by Uber's newest hashtag, #BringBackUberKS.[46]

Within four days, lawmakers were scared back to the negotiating table with Uber representatives.[47] By rule, the deadline had passed to introduce any new bills. Instead, a short while later, the legislature took an unrelated health insurance bill that had passed both chambers but stalled and whitewashed and replaced its language. In a compromise, the background-check requirement was stripped out, but the driver requirement of comprehensive and collision coverage remained.[48] Three weeks after Uber shut down their app, Governor Brownback signed the new TNC bill into law.[49] In Kansas, Uber had accomplished a rare and exceptional feat: within less than a month, they had convinced a legislature to override their own veto override.

Uber's tactic of implying they were being "kicked out" of a city or state whenever fingerprint checks were passed was shockingly effective. They expertly controlled the message. TNC users were attached to the service, and they usually didn't follow the nuance of legislative hearings. In effect, they trusted Uber's interpretation of events and balked when lawmakers tried to explain they were concerned about public safety. That message didn't resonate with them.

Over time, only a few states ever jumped on to Matt Daus's fantasy of outlawing ridesharing services. As part of an agreement with New York State officials, Uber and Lyft agreed to stay out of upstate New York in exchange for operating in NYC. In 2014 Uber launched in Las Vegas, and the Nevada attorney general quickly secured a court injunction in one of the fiercest legal responses Uber faced in the United States. They shut down until the following year when the Nevada legislature made them legal. In Alaska, after a failed attempt to receive their ideal regulations in Anchorage, state regulators came down hard on Uber for using independent contractors instead of employees. Since every other Alaskan city was tiny, Uber declined to fight them and simply left. But these were the few exceptions. Almost everywhere else in the country, Uber found a way to operate.

By the summer of 2015, it became clear even to Matt Daus that transportation network companies were a permanent institution. No longer was he or the IATR as a whole advocating for the prohibition of Uber and Lyft. By then, twenty states and several additional cities had made them legal. Instead, the conversation, and seemingly the tactics, had changed. Of all the places where TNCs were allowed to operate, Uber experienced its only major setback in Houston, where it had agreed to fingerprint background checks thanks to a deal largely negotiated by Houston's taxi regulator, IATR member Tina Paez.

Much like the ATD, two California district attorneys, and several other jurisdictions that openly called for fingerprint checks, Daus followed along.

In May 2015 he released a new report called "One Standard for All," where he listed his credentials not as the IATR president but as a professor at City University of New York. In conjunction with other background check professionals, it was a way of pushing support for the notion that TNC drivers should undergo fingerprint checks – not in addition to but in *replacement of* their own private checks, just as taxis had.[50]

Presumably, Daus was pushing on Uber's greatest pain point, the one they had difficulty defending whenever a felon driver slipped through the cracks. Fingerprint checks were still an effective way of making life difficult for Uber and Lyft. With the exception of Houston, neither company agreed to operate in any city or state where a fingerprint check was required of mom-and-pop drivers. If TNCs couldn't be made illegal, then perhaps their own obstinacy could be used against them.

In June, Daus hosted a symposium at the SUNY Global Center in Manhattan titled "The Future of the Taxi Medallion System and For-hire Services in a Disruptive Technology," which was a complex way of describing taxi markets in a TNC world. Partly, Daus used his speech to vent against rumors that taxi markets were doomed, a rumor often theorized as Uber's valuation soared above $40 billion and taxi medallion values plummeted. He lambasted the media for mischaracterizing the decline of taxis, only examining it through the lens of the "Silicon Valley spin machine."[51]

By all signs, Daus now sounded like someone who was on the outside of the debate looking in. Former Governor David Patterson was invited to the symposium, and Daus took a call in the middle of his speech to receive his regrets. He tried to introduce the hokey phrase "irrational app-suberance" to describe the frenzied demand for Uber, which never caught on. And as usual, he chastised Uber for not working with regulators and "other stakeholders," even leaving an open chair for them in the audience if they dared to attend.[52]

The national press seemingly lost interest in Daus's frustrations. No longer were any *New York Times* reporters showing up to report his TNC criticisms. "I see no one from the media showed up here today that I can identify," Daus said. He then noticed one person in the audience raising his hand in objection, and Daus politely corrected himself. "I'm glad we have one member from the press with us today."[53]

"I'm just a – I'm just a photographer," the media member replied.[54]

Daus's motivations were far less veiled than in years past. He talked at length about the survival of the taxi industry and the threat that TNCs presented. He cited New York City as the ideal, the "most level playing field in the world," as he called it. It was the only city where Uber and Lyft relied solely on the overabundance of professional chauffeur drivers rather than the customary amateur drivers. Because they were licensed, the drivers were already fingerprint checked, and Daus argued it should be the same everywhere else. If taxi markets nationwide were to share New York's supposed stability, he argued, the rest of the country should add similar restrictions to Uber and Lyft's business model.[55]

"There's a real legitimate concern that these rideshares ... are running rampant. They need to get a universal app or do something to get it under control," he told the symposium attendees.[56]

While Daus argued that TNC background checks were unreliable and Uber and Lyft's use of licensed chauffeurs should be standardized everywhere, he conveniently omitted an important fact. New York was special. Most cities didn't have nearly as many licensed chauffeurs to meet TNC demand. Not even close. If other cities solely allowed professionally licensed chauffeurs to become TNC drivers, then TNCs would experience a driver shortage, effectively triggering surge pricing and killing their lower-cost advantage. Most cities and states didn't take the idea seriously. Instead it was the push for fingerprint checks of TNC drivers that gained steam across the country – that's where the battle lines shifted.

Daus arrived late to the new front lines. He had talked about background checks in 2014 but mostly in relation to the PASS Act, the Congressional bill that started to move taxi background checks to the IATR itself (which died in committee). Houston's TNC ordinance had already been in place for six months, and independently of Daus, Houston regulators pushed the fingerprinting provision hard.

During the Texas legislative battle, Houston officials passed around a white paper sternly arguing that Uber's checks were not reliable. Houston claimed that after Uber's drivers underwent the secondary screening of a fingerprint check, several were disqualified for offenses such as indecent exposure, DWI, assault, battery, and robbery. The paper never explained why Uber's checks didn't catch the offenses, but then again, it was a one-sided analysis. There was also no discussion of the offenses Uber or Lyft caught that Houston may have missed. The paper was meant to demonstrate that fingerprint checks were inherently superior.[57]

That was a key point Daus tried to make at the SUNY symposium. Neither Uber nor Lyft attended in person, but the presentation was placed online. And if either TNC was watching, it wouldn't have been difficult to conclude this was the next big campaign to harm their business model. If Daus pushed for it, regulators and taxi companies were likely to join in.

To make sure Daus hammered his point home, a few months later at the 2015 IATR Conference, one of the themes presented was "regulatory resiliency."[58] Houston's regulator, Tina Paez, hosted a conference session titled "One Standard for All," the same title as Daus's most recent white paper. She echoed many of the arguments made during the Texas legislative session about the superiority of fingerprint background checks.[59]

At the conference, Paez received a fair amount of acclaim for her "resilience." During an awards ceremony, Carlton Thomas was invited to the center stage to present "Regulator of the Year." Thomas himself had won the award in 2014, presumably for pushing SideCar out of Austin in 2013. This year, it was given as a glass award comfortably sitting in a plush purple box, thanks in large part to TransDev, the largest owner of taxi franchises in the country. Thomas Drischler, the IATR Board chairman and Los Angeles taxi regulator, explained that in recent years, the award had been given to regulators who were in "the firing line" and stood their ground.[60] So it was little surprise when he announced Paez's name.

"Tina has suffered the slings and arrows of a lot of controversy, and I think we all know who the source of the controversy is," said Drischler. "No need to say that name at this happy time."[61]

The award was for Paez's role in passing fingerprint background checks for Uber in Houston. And it was the perfect symbol for how regulators, at least those outside of the twenty states with their own TNC laws, would attack this issue in 2015.

It was all building toward a dangerous game of brinkmanship. Uber would have no way to know who was pushing for fingerprint checks out of a genuine safety concern and who was pushing for them to protect the taxis. There wasn't a way to clearly parse those motives, nor did it benefit them to try. Instead, just as in Kansas, they would demonstrate a simple mentality that all who supported it had ulterior motives.

CHAPTER TWELVE

Prop 1: A Staring Contest

As Daus was penning his "One Standard for All" report, things were not going well for Uber in Austin. All signs suggested that the bubble of resentment was beginning to pop. In May 2015, their local lobbyist quietly complained to a city council member that the Austin Transportation Department was trying to shut them down.

"The [ATD] has decided to terminate its contract with Uber as of midnight tonight, which would effectively force Uber out of Austin with no return date in sight."[1]

It's unclear what specifically set off the letter or even if the claim was true, but there were several likely culprits. Two months before, Uber had launched its "UberPOOL" service, allowing drivers to pick up multiple passengers on overlapping routes.[2] To the ATD, "pooling" was a traditional livery function, and they were probably not thrilled with Uber incorporating it without permission. Uber was also reluctant to turn over data they had agreed to provide in the pilot program.[3] And, ten days after the lobbyist's letter, Carlton Thomas told a San Antonio colleague they were having trouble using the TNC apps.

> We are having a difficult time accessing their respective platforms due to the TNCs continually "disabling," "suspending," or even "banning" our user accounts. One TNC indicated that because it isn't explicitly stated in the contract, they are not required to allow us on their app. Although we have

not violated the "Terms of Service."[4]

The ATD didn't end Uber's contract, and the "termination" threat more or less vanished, never having been mentioned publicly. Even the Mobility Committee was unaware of it. Instead, Council Member Ann Kitchen was busy reviewing the franchise renewals of the three existing taxi companies, an issue which also had unsettling TNC implications. The committee agreed that they would tackle the taxi companies first and hold off on TNC issues until after.

Essentially a contract renegotiation, franchise renewals usually imposed a new wish list of improvements on the local taxi service. In 2015, the top goal focused on labor conditions. Cab drivers were feeling the pressure of their livelihood slipping away after TNCs had received legal legitimacy. Many complained that Uber had too much of a regulatory advantage.[5]

Adding to the strain, none of the three taxi companies reduced their lease fees in light of Uber and Lyft. Drivers still had to pay upwards of $300 per week for the "privilege" of taking a cab on the street and competing with TNCs for fares.[6] In traditional taxi fashion, the risk and also the burden of sacrifice was placed on the taxi drivers themselves.

In the hearings, drivers made clear they were squeezed between the rock of their taxi-company masters and the hard place of Uber. They felt increasingly exploited and victimized. Their chauffeur's licenses were dependent on "sponsorship" by a taxi company, depriving them of leverage as they unionized more actively. Several complained that, as independent contractors, they were summarily terminated or otherwise harassed by the cab companies.[7] Uber and Lyft's relatively lax regulations were simply the icing on an already rancid cake.

Kitchen, for her part, was sympathetic more to the drivers than her taxi-company donors. She pushed for an additional franchise in the form of a taxi cooperative, giving drivers more control over their profits and losses. She also wanted to end the sponsorship requirement and add "due process" provisions so that drivers couldn't be terminated at will. All were measures that took power away from the existing companies, and all passed.[8]

To no one's surprise, the council renewed all three franchises. However, the ATD had recommended a generous renewal term of ten years.[9] The council settled on five.[10]

As the taxi hearings took place, Uber expanded its local territory. In June and July, they launched further around the greater Austin area outside the city limits.[11] Locally, they also launched new products to make themselves more useful: UberESPAÑOL, a service for requesting a Spanish-speaking driver, and UberACCESS, a service for requesting a wheelchair-accessible vehicle.[12] The latter addressed a longstanding complaint of the disability community, who held great sway in taxi matters. It was as though Uber were anticipating a fight and they were taking steps to make sure the "Uber faithful" appreciated them to the maximum extent possible. Regardless of whether the new services were *intentionally* political, more devoted users certainly created more leverage.

In August the Mobility Committee finally returned to the issue of TNCs, and the ATD arrived to the meeting ready to gripe. The companies didn't hand over the promised data. Inexperienced drivers were blocking sensitive areas at airport entrances. They also brought up a list of cities where Uber had agreed to certain compromises they were unwilling to make in Austin: using only chauffeur drivers in New York, allowing fingerprint background checks in Houston, and sharing proprietary trip data with officials in Boston. An ATD spokesperson said they felt the need to revisit their prior recommendations that the 2014 council had ignored. Once more, Mobility Committee members reaffirmed their desire to "have a level playing field" between taxis and TNCs.[13]

To an extent, the ATD understood the regulatory arbitrage that former Council Member Spelman realized in his epiphany the prior year. Uber was so satisfied with the minimalist regulations passed in Austin's 2014 pilot program that they promoted the model to lawmakers in other cities. As the

ATD advocated for more rigorous regulations, they not only asked on Austin's behalf but so that equally rigorous requirements would be adopted elsewhere. Said the ATD spokesperson, "We understand they are also going to other cities and saying, 'Well, this is what Austin approved, so this is the standard that we should use.' So, I think we need to 'up' that standard."[14]

The Mobility Committee typically met once, sometimes twice, per month, and in the interval between August and September, it was likely clear to Uber that they had another uphill battle ahead of them. They were done sitting on their hands and working only behind the scenes. A social media campaign not used since their 2014 victory party, #KeepAustinUber, was reactivated. The local manager organized a rally on the day of the next Mobility Committee meeting in early September (where public testimony was accepted) in the courtyard staging area outside Austin City Hall. Dozens of drivers showed up and were handed neon-blue T-shirts with the same slogan, "Keep Austin Uber."[15]

The TNC hearings started to shift tonally. Large crowds now filled the city hall meeting room, and audience members for taxis or TNCs frequently applauded when they heard a sentiment they liked, as if they were congressmen at a State of the Union address. Even Council Member Kitchen, at the beginning of the September meeting, spoke in a tone that was more upbeat and cheerful than her customary soft, professional monotone. Looking out into an auditorium of neon-blue T-shirts, she said, "I just want to start by saying that I am very appreciative of and I do consider TNCs to be an important part of our transportation system."[16]

Prior to the meeting, Kitchen posted online an informal list of TNC amendments that heavily mirrored the ATD's recommendations. One proposal under the heading of "dynamic pricing" required "advance notification to city when changing pricing."[17] It's not clear that council members fully grasped how TNCs functioned. Surge pricing occurred automatically as the result of an algorithm, not because an Uber employee pulled a lever. Nor did it usually affect all drivers citywide.

Kitchen's amendments seemed based on a zeal to correct the perceived mistakes of the pilot program. Some members felt that the prior year's council, of which only Kathie Tovo remained, was either duped or corrupt. And the ATD was happy to ride that wave.

By this point, events were moving so fast that no one even noticed the ATD contradicting their own 2014 recommendations. The prior October, they had envisioned giving taxis more regulatory flexibility so they could compete with TNCs. Cab companies would flip between taxi and TNC regulations so they could select the least burdensome structure. Instead the ATD whitewashed over that recommendation, never once mentioning it in the Mobility Committee's hearings. Kathie Tovo had likely forgotten about it, and the new council, too busy to fact-check old business, simply ran with the ATD's newest recommendations. The ATD artfully took advantage of their missing institutional memory.

As a result, one of the strangest effects of the new council was that the ATD's "hybrid" recommendation mutated from a sensible, technocratic solution in 2014 to a right-wing, libertarian fantasy in 2015. Although the ATD abandoned the idea, one of the conservative council members still pushed for reduced regulations for taxis, but he was among a tiny minority of an otherwise Democratic body. As far as most of the council was concerned, "leveling the playing field" meant bringing TNCs closer in line with taxis, not the other way around.

When the public commented on the committee's proposal, the response was mixed. The disability community, which didn't favor one service over another, applauded Uber for introducing accessible vehicles and asked that the council not do anything to remove that option. It was one of the few compliments Uber and Lyft received from an impartial party. But the response was otherwise slanted. Yellow Cab president Ed Kargbo, who obtained permission to speak on behalf of Austin's three cab companies, made a strong speech in favor of drivers obtaining a chauffeur's permit.[18]

As if reading from Matt Daus's script, he said, "All drivers should be required to get chauffeur's permits through the [ATD].... It both helps identify the person operating ... [and] allows for enforcement from the [ATD]. Fingerprint background checks are one critical example of why having regulations in place are important."[19]

Although the 2015 council had little clue about Uber's prior campaigns or even the role that the IATR played, creating regulatory equity, at least for safety measures, was widely appealing. It was difficult to understand why, among all for-hire vehicles, TNCs were allowed their own exemptions. Even the small handful of horse-and-buggy drivers offering nighttime carriage rides had to obtain a fingerprint check. What made Uber and Lyft so special?

Uber representatives, for their part, were somewhat cagey in their public responses and didn't give any comforting answers. Asked what their main objection was, they had difficulty focusing on a single issue. They said the company normally paid for all background checks, but requiring driver-applicants to pay for a fingerprint check would create a regressive, "highest-in-the-nation tax" for TNCs. They also made dual arguments that their checks were better and that part-time drivers were less likely to complete the on-boarding process if they had to obtain a fingerprint check. Uber reps were asked how they knew the person who applied to be a driver was actually the person they claimed to be. An applicant had to provide several pieces of documentation to match, they replied: insurance, social security number, and most importantly, they'd have to have a bank account in their own name. But once more, the committee didn't find it persuasive.[20]

To counter, Uber attacked the ATD's fingerprint check for its limited usefulness. They had learned that for local taxi drivers, the government's check pulled information only at the statewide – not national – level. It caught the committee off guard, and a council member asked Carlton Thomas to comment.

"If an applicant has lived outside of Texas for a period of time, our process requires that they secure their own background check," he said. "As a standard, we don't do a nationwide check for all applicants."[21]

By contrast, Uber's checks covered most of the United States, and they now had a credible leg up on the process.

After the September committee meeting, it was apparent to Uber that despite the neon-blue-shirted audience and some of their better arguments, they were not going to make any headway. There was never going to come a moment when Kitchen or the council as a whole would say to them, "You've convinced us." Instead, they turned up the heat on their campaign.

Before the next meeting in October, Uber mobilized at a rapid pace for new leverage. They push-polled twelve hundred locally registered voters, positing (among other things), "Some Austin taxi companies want the City Council to pass an ordinance that would create the highest tax in the nation on ridesharing companies. Do you think that's a good idea or bad idea?" Predictably, 70 percent said, "Bad idea."[22] Uber also released a "Mobility Case Study" that argued it was improving the local economy and transportation infrastructure. Filled with maps and graphs, including a chart showing the low wait times for requested rides, the study made the point that Uber was not a niche service for a limited section of town. It was used broadly by the city as a whole.[23] The study was picked up by several local media outlets, and Uber's lobbyist made sure council members noticed both the poll and, especially, the study.

He wrote to them, "Please see below some of the 23 stories about the announcement (the TV stories alone had over 300,000 viewers)."[24]

Before the month was over, Uber would also partner with the NAACP and other minority groups to recruit five thousand new drivers in the predominantly low-income East Austin.[25] The area was not particularly special for its council member, but Uber representatives would later argue that fingerprint background checks were racially discriminatory against minorities, that they flagged people for arrests without listing a disposition if the arrest never led to a court conviction. Minorities, they claimed, were much more likely to match as false positives under a fingerprint scan.[26]

Some council members sensed treachery in this argument, especially since so many fingerprinted taxi drivers were minorities themselves.[27] One possibility was that Uber was taking a vulnerable population and showcasing them to the council as sacrificial lambs. If the city began fingerprinting TNC drivers, then minority activists might see it as non-white applicants having a harder time qualifying for the job. Inherently, Uber pushed the message that to harm their interests likewise harmed minority drivers, a potential wedge issue against Democrats. And they made sure that African American community leaders were watching.

In case all their tactics to date were too subtle, Uber drove their point home. Two days before the next Mobility Committee meeting, they held a press conference featuring their chief political strategist and former Obama campaign manager, David Plouffe, who had flown into town. He addressed the council in much the same way one does in an open letter. "Don't fix what's not broken," he said at an initial briefing.[28] The next day, Uber sent an email to all their local users. "The Uber you know and love is being threatened by a new plan pushed by Councilmember Ann Kitchen," it read.[29]

The gloves were off.

To her credit, Kitchen took it in stride. At the following day's hearing, she addressed the elephant in the room, stating, "There's been a lot of information in the press and some information that's been sent out by TNCs that I want to correct the misinformation that's been sent out. First off, we *do* recognize and appreciate and really value what TNCs offer to our community, so our discussion today is *not about* getting rid of TNCs – it was never that, and that's not what we're about talking about today."[30]

But there were hints the antics had nonetheless soured Kitchen. At the hearing, the conversation shifted toward the calculation of a TNC permit fee, a difficult issue because Uber and Lyft continued to be cagey. Neither company wanted to openly divulge any data about their fares, which was the basis for the permit fee. The Mobility Committee tossed around multiple methods for determining the fee, but the TNC representatives sitting below the dais had difficulty tracking them. An Uber rep said they needed "appropriate consultations" on the matter before they could offer a response. In a knee-jerk reaction, Kitchen retorted, "We've certainly been meeting. All of us have been meeting with all of you, so please don't imply that we haven't met."[31]

Things got worse as the matter turned to fingerprint background checks. For the sake of fairness, the committee was willing to require national checks on taxi drivers and tighten the list of disqualifying offenses so that they were scrutinized as much as TNCs scrutinized their own. And, to reduce the friction, they would have the ATD enter into a third-party contract to expedite the turnaround time.[32] Effectively, it removed any power from Carlton Thomas to slow down the on-boarding process.

But Uber and Lyft were having none of it. When the representatives were asked what specifically they hated about their low-friction proposal, they talked around it, instead listing all the reasons they hated fingerprint checks in general. Lyft explained that half of their drivers were behind the wheel less than ten hours per week. It was such a small investment of time that they didn't believe enough drivers would go through the on-boarding process. Uber, dropping a rare hint, said, "It does not scale – it does not work with the model."[33] Again, they were cagey arguments.

The council members had difficulty buying that it couldn't work. Uber operated in Houston, where fingerprint checks were required. Fingerprinting was considered a best practice among a number of professions. And above all, they felt a biometric scan was stronger. A driver-applicant couldn't be an impostor if they matched to a criminal record.

Back and forth, tensions increased. They got into arguments about which American cities Uber and Lyft were and were not operating in. Kitchen, normally calm and professionally monotone, became visibly frustrated.

"I don't think that if—okay, let me just say this. Public safety is key. It is our job. And I know that you're operating in other cities that have fingerprinting. And to threaten to leave simply because we're trying to protect public safety cannot be my deciding, determining factor because there are other TNC companies. TNCs are part of our—they're part of our present and future, and they will be here."[34]

Kitchen didn't have any market knowledge of other TNCs. She simply took it on faith that if they left, others would replace them.

For much of the council, Uber was losing credibility. The company developed an almost Jekyll-and-Hyde duplicity. Outside the walls of city hall, they were hyperbolic, mud-throwing campaigners. Inside city hall, they were much more cordial and straightforward. The majority of the council would look to Kitchen for a recommendation, and Uber had clearly destroyed her sense of trust with them. She was willing to mitigate the friction of fingerprint checks but not enough to give them everything they wanted.

For the ATD, it was in all likelihood a mixed outcome. Everything to date suggested they wanted the maximum amount of friction for TNCs so that taxis could prosper. Instead, Kitchen made enough concessions that if push came to shove, maybe Uber and Lyft could make it work. But if the TNCs threatened to leave out of their own obstinacy, then it was still a victory for the taxi industry. The outcome was a coin toss, and it all depended on who in this game of brinkmanship would blink first.

Kitchen took her fingerprint recommendations before the full council for a formal vote, which passed overwhelmingly. In testimony, it was clear that Uber's arguments were not gaining traction. A state police official testified that fingerprint checks were superior to TNC background checks, testimony that even the mayor openly characterized as more credible. Once more, a council member admonished Uber for their political attacks against Ann Kitchen and other political antics. Even the local police union, which opposed the 2014 TNC sting operations, was on Kitchen's side.[35]

Uber pushed back even harder to make sure they didn't lose control of the message. In late October, they released the results of an internal audit stating they had rejected drivers who had passed the city's background checks.[36]

A week later, Uber introduced a new local service on the app. Placed next to the regular services of UberPOOL, UberX, and so on, a feature called "KITCHEN" suddenly appeared with an icon of a horse. The service allowed users to request a horse-drawn carriage within thirty square blocks of downtown after 6:00 p.m. It also included a message reading, "TAKE ACTION. Councilmember Ann Kitchen wants to regulate ridesharing companies like a horse and buggy. If you don't want to take Austin back to the 19th century, call the City Council today!"[37] To make sure no one missed it, Uber copied it in a blog post and advertised a thirty-second TV spot showing a couple ordering a ride, only to wait a long time for their carriage to arrive. "Remember life before Uber?" the screen read. "Please tell Ann Kitchen we don't want to go back."[38]

The KITCHEN service was similar to an app feature used to mock NYC Mayor Bill de Blasio a few months earlier. De Blasio had proposed an ordinance to cap the number of TNC vehicles on the streets, just like taxis. Uber's new feature, simply called "DE BLASIO," intentionally showed either no cars or wait times of twenty-five minutes or more.[39] A week after it was introduced, de Blasio backed down from the proposal.[40]

Kitchen had no intention of backing down. Once more, she took it in stride, only demonstrating minor irritation to reporters. Mayors might have been susceptible to such pressures, but Kitchen's district adamantly supported her. Uber exhausted its political bullying against the Mobility Committee, and with no more leverage to pressure them, they simply turned to the mayor's office.

Mayor Steve Adler, a soft-spoken, nonthreatening former real estate attorney, easily felt the political pressures Uber exacted on the city. New email campaigns asked constituents to tweet Adler and explain "#WHYIRIDE."[41] Adler remained on the fence for as long as humanly possible, looking for a compromise both sides could live with. He'd read a

Forbes article in the middle of the fight that suggested Uber was experimenting with fingerprint scanning on smartphones, an idea that excited him.[42]

Neighboring San Antonio had already gone through this drama and offered a potential solution Adler could copy. Uber and Lyft vacated San Antonio earlier in 2015 after fingerprint background checks were mandated.[43] At the time, Carlton Thomas had learned from his counterpart that Uber would still operate outside the city limits. Thomas asked him if San Antonio was verifying that they didn't sneak back in.

Thomas's colleague answered, "Nope, Uber would not lie to me about operating in San Antonio…. Just kidding, Yes, we have smartphones and are checking daily to ensure that the App does not go active."[44]

A few months after, an election was held to fill the power vacuum left by the heavily popular San Antonio Mayor Julián Castro after he was confirmed as the US HUD secretary. Several candidates battled to replace him, and in the process, the local tech industry made Uber's departure a political issue, blaming excessive regulations.[45] After a victor emerged, a deal was struck to make TNC fingerprint checks optional, provided that passengers could request a driver who had elected the government's background check.[46] After it took effect in October 2015, Thomas checked in with his counterpart to see how he was handling it.

"It is Crazy my friend," the San Antonio regulator replied. "I found out yesterday at 10 am that Uber was launching at 3:30. FUN FUN….."[47]

"LOL," Thomas wrote back.[48]

Behind the scenes in Austin, the mayor's office was working hard to adopt something similar, but Adler couldn't give it legs. It was an option that only the two diehard conservative council members were interested in. Everyone else had more or less settled into their position of requiring fingerprint checks, and almost no one was budging.

Uber and Lyft could have made credible arguments that both regulators and the taxi industry were pushing for increased regulations to harm TNCs, but no one cared anymore. They had burned the important bridges. When Kitchen was later asked if it was suspicious that Ed Kargbo showed strong support of fingerprint background checks, she replied, "That was a figment of Uber's imagination. A tool and a lie to obscure the policy issue."

The council decided to finalize the issue at the last meeting of the year, December 17, giving everyone two months to turn ridesharing into one of Austin's most politically charged issues of 2015. Seemingly everyone was galvanized toward a position. The association TX Rides for Hire, which listed Ed Kargbo as a contact person, put out its own push poll on the value of fingerprint background checks.[49] One of the conservative council members penned an op-ed asking the rest of the council to vote against the ordinance.[50] News stories emerged detailing Ann Kitchen's taxi contributions, implying she was a defender of the taxi industry.[51]

More facts and figures were thrown about by one side or the other. Uber bragged about the decline of DWIs since their entry into Austin, a common tactic in most of their cities.[52] A local sexual-assault shelter reported that seven of their patients had been assaulted by TNC drivers between April and August, a statistic Kitchen often promoted to support her position.[53] It was a barrage of information that the average person would find almost impossible to follow.

Uber continued to send its own mass emails, although they were now changing tone as well. Instead of blaming any council member, they made the taxi industry their scapegoat. "Championed by a group of taxicab companies, the new rules target rideshare drivers, and if passed, would cause Uber and other ridesharing apps to shut down in Austin, perhaps immediately."[54] They also began to move away from broad generalizations. In a lengthy blog post, Uber – for the first time – broke down the Austin ordinance and explained their objections point by point.[55]

Meanwhile, Kitchen found a new ally out of the blue, a TNC that was willing to go along with the fingerprint regulations. In October, a small Dallas-based company called "Get Me" attempted to launch in Austin during the ACL Music Festival.[56] Get Me had only existed for six months and specialized in both ridesharing and on-request delivery services, and for ridesharing, they ran into a wall with the ATD. Carlton Thomas's office rejected any new TNC companies, taking a constrained view of the existing pilot program. The 2014 ordinance specified that operating permits would be granted "within 30 days" of its passage, but the ATD narrowly interpreted it to mean no further TNC permits could be authorized *after* the thirty days lapsed.[57] Only Uber and Lyft had received permits.

Get Me executives closely followed the Uber fight and reached out directly to Kitchen's office in late October. "We watched with interest the initial reaction of other rideshare companies from the October 7th [Mobility Committee] meeting," they wrote to her office. They proposed a collaboration. In exchange for allowing them to operate, Kitchen could sell Get Me to the public as the ideal TNC, a "show of strength of unity – based on trust and safety of Austin," they described it to her.[58]

For Kitchen, the partnership allowed the city to demonstrate that the regulations were not unreasonable. A TNC *could* operate under them. Kitchen's staff made sure Get Me had their ducks in a row, reviewing their insurance and other documentation.[59] A month later, the city attorney's office miraculously reinterpreted the ATD's narrow vision of the pilot program language and authorized them to issue a new permit.[60] Regardless of whether the 2015 ordinance would pass, the ATD was now completely powerless to resist the encroachment of TNCs.

Get Me and Kitchen's staff continued to work closely with one another. Within a week of receiving a permit, they coordinated a press release, which the Mobility Committee's vice chair read, highlighting the company's willingness to lead by example.[61] They even traded updated versions of the new TNC ordinance, presumably to make sure Get Me wouldn't suddenly reverse course over any new amendments.[62] Kitchen never publicly took credit for fostering a new taxi competitor into the market, and she would later earn an unfair reputation as a stern defender of taxis. Conservative activists later attempted an unsuccessful recall campaign against her, citing her support of fingerprint background checks.[63] Even though it failed, the taxi stigma never faded.

Finally, December 17 came. As if the issue wasn't exhausting enough, the TNC ordinance was saved for the last item of the agenda on a full day that began at 10:00 a.m., and the council wouldn't reach it until 8:30 p.m. During a midday lunch break, Mayor Adler announced a compromise with Council Member Kitchen designed similarly to San Antonio's revised ordinance. In a new amendment, fingerprint background checks were still required and would be phased in slowly, so that they didn't replicate Houston's continued sting operations after their 2014 ordinance passed. But the penalties were left unspecified and delegated to a future council ordinance.[64] In essence, the bill's teeth were removed, at least temporarily. At the press conference, Adler said, "I don't expect any of the TNCs to leave town based on what we are proposing today."[65]

Neither Uber nor Lyft's lobbyists saw the ordinance language in advance, nor were they on board. Around 2:00 p.m., Uber's lobbyist texted a mayor's aide.

"Someone from your office is saying we have agreed to this. That is an issue."[66]

The aide denied any such claim was made.

"Ok. Great," the lobbyist replied. "We are shutting [the rumor] down."[67]

When the TNC lobbyists finally read the language, they had "heartburn," as one of them put it.[68] Although toothless, it still required fingerprint checks, which was an absolute deal-breaker. It also required that rigorous data be submitted directly to the ATD, with harsh penalties for noncompliance. On the plus side, the city would pay for the fingerprint checks and only administered a permit fee of 1 percent of revenues. Insurance requirements were dropped, as state law had already addressed them. And surge pricing was left untouched (except during abnormal market conditions, like a hurricane).[69] Still, of all the pain points, fingerprinting would envelop that evening's debate.

Uber's and Lyft's lobbyists met with one another, trying to make sense of the newest draft.[70] The language was too uncertain. Nothing protected them from stiff penalties in the future. Mayor Adler seemed to trust that the council would fill in the blanks with reasonable measures later.

His aide texted the TNC lobbyists, "Mayor thinks intent has been made clear on dais and so no need to change, but if what yall fear is true, we can change it on January 28." No message came in response.[71]

Although the aide appeared to have the last word, Uber's lobbyist had failed to mention – at least by text – that "shutting down" the rumors also meant that at 7:00 p.m., when they already had another rally planned, they'd ask their users to keep the pressure against the council on high. Uber emailed its Austin users. "TO BE CLEAR, WE HAVE NOT AGREED TO ANY PROPOSAL," the byline read. "Please tweet at Mayor Adler and your city council member and ask them to work with Uber on smart ridesharing regulations for Austin."[72]

By 8:30 p.m., Mayor Adler introduced the TNC item on the agenda.[73] His aide texted Uber's lobbyist for a last-minute update. "Any word?" he asked.[74]

"They said there is no way they can give this commitment," Uber's lobbyist replied. "It is above them because of the implications in other cities."[75]

In other words, Uber was trying to cut off the domino effect of other cities following Austin's example. They were holding the line.

As the TNC issue started, the council was clearly fatigued, and many members were getting punchy. Several gave long speeches about their feelings on the issue. Adler spoke softly of how much he hated having to choose between fingerprinting and TNCs. He did his best to be a calming presence, but it was somewhat beyond his control.

Over the course of five hours, several invited speakers were grilled like they were being cross-examined in a bitter courtroom battle. Uber was no exception. One could almost taste how much Kitchen reviled them as they continued to put on a facade of cooperation.

"I want to stress we are here to work with you," the young Uber rep said in an opening statement. "We stand here ready and willing to partner with you."[76]

It was almost comical. After everything that Kitchen, Adler, and everyone else had endured, his comments could only come off as insincere. By some miracle, no one laughed when he said it.

Kitchen, among others, pushed for an answer about why Uber had agreed to the fingerprint regulations in Houston. The representative was asked – and unable to answer – how many of their drivers operated there. He continued to say that their business model doesn't scale, nor had it scaled well in Houston. Kitchen laid into him.[77]

"You've been saying that you can't operate in an environment where fingerprints are required, but you are. And you're also saying that the drivers won't be fingerprinted, but they are in Houston. And I'm asking you how many you have in Houston. And you're telling me that you don't know. That's not very credible."[78]

Lyft's representative was more sympathetic, even divulging that "78 percent of [their] drivers work less than fifteen hours per week," a detail she had previously said was too specific to reveal in public.[79] But her gesture of openness didn't resonate with anyone.

The hearing lasted until the early morning, and council members on both sides of the issue politely lambasted speakers who didn't bolster their own positions. The police chief, who supported fingerprint checks in general, hated the idea of TNCs leaving town. Although Kitchen pushed the case that the seven sexual assaults by TNC drivers were seven too many, the chief took a step back and saw matters from a wider perspective. On Friday and Saturday nights, when several thousand intoxicated people left Austin's downtown bars, TNCs took an inherently vulnerable population and (usually) escorted them to safety. If such a service left, he argued, it would cause considerable more harm overall. The county sheriff had made similar comments. Kitchen verbally ruffled the chief, trying to get him to say that fingerprinting was a greater priority.[80] It was clear the chief wanted no part in the political fight.

Even during the hearing, while Mayor Adler sat on the council dais, Uber's lobbyist communicated with him by text. At 11:41 p.m., the lobbyist told him the police chief had misinterpreted the bill.

"The Chief is saying both [types of background] checks, but as written, this only requires fingerprinting. Nothing in here includes our checks. This is another reason we should consider a delay. The other tncs will be required to do both."[81]

"Your missing the forest for the trees," Adler wrote back.[82]

"Ok."

The two ultraconservative members grilled Carlton Thomas's boss. They wanted to know how Get Me had managed to receive a permit when no other

TNC could. And they wanted to know why, in the Mobility Committee's first meeting back in March (when Thomas was still feeling out the new council), fingerprint checks weren't even mentioned as a recommendation. "We maintained that we should seek the safest and most thorough background checks that we could find within the industry," the ATD director replied.[83]

He also argued that not only were TNCs bluffing and wouldn't leave town, but even SideCar would return, too.[84] However, SideCar had ceased passenger transportation four months earlier and completely closed shop a week after his prediction.[85]

Exhausted, they put it to a vote at 1:30 a.m. Instead of going through the normal six-week process, they put it up for a final vote simply to be done with it.[86] "I'm not gonna be bullied," one of the Mobility Committee members said.[87] It passed 9–2, with only the conservative bloc voting against it and Mayor Adler voting in favor.[88]

A short time later, a local taxi driver association praised the ordinance as an "important first step in addressing an injustice that has affected public safety and the ability of taxi drivers to earn a living." In the same announcement, they proclaimed they were not against "any particular business model" but still objected to "fares that change from hour to hour" or "escape from any regulation on the number of vehicles available."[89]

The next day several thousand Austinites were seething in anger, sending angst-filled emails to city hall. Uber announced that the council had "passed an ordinance that will make it impossible for [Uber] to operate," characterizing it more as a disagreement than a willful attempt to push them out of town.[90] The ordinance didn't take effect until February, and unlike in Kansas, they didn't shut the app down. Lyft's lobbyist texted Adler:

Here's where we are. Lyft is disappointed and concerned. They left last night saying this is mandatory. They saw other council members pushing for even more aggressive adoption timelines. They also think the council completely disregarded testimony from [the police chief and county sheriff]. They do not believe most of the council. They do know the mayor got it dialed down some. But they still see mandatory. And we do not operate in cities that have it. We will stay at the table over the next few weeks with you, but between us, they are not optimistic.[91]

Uber, on the other hand, started taking advantage of the city's discontent. By December 28, an Uber employee and former chief of staff for Lee Leffingwell, the Austin mayor prior to Adler who had voted for the TNC pilot program, formed a political action committee (PAC).[92] Calling itself "Ridesharing Works for Austin," the PAC was instantly funded with $10,000 each from Uber and Lyft to push through a ballot initiative.[93] By law, a referendum could be added to a local election if at least twenty thousand verified signatures were collected. Joined by a coalition of ATX Safer Streets, downtown club owners, and the tech community, the PAC sought to reverse the December 17 ordinance.[94]

The language proposed by Ridesharing Works replaced the ordinance with a new version heavily mirroring the 2014 pilot program. Fingerprint checks were expressly prohibited. Ridership data would be independently audited, and only the final audit reports would be turned over to the ATD. The 1 percent fee was retained. And perhaps as a nod to their relationship with the ATD, a brand-new provision stated that if the director determined a TNC was in violation of the ordinance, then the TNC was given a "reasonable opportunity to cure [it]." In other words, no more threats of terminating their contract.[95]

The referendum tactic was similar to a ballot initiative both companies (and SideCar) attempted in Seattle in 2014. After a long, transparent, thoughtful deliberation, the Seattle City Council ultimately decided to cap the number of TNC vehicles to insulate the taxi industry. But none of the companies were willing to agree to it, and they created a PAC called "Seattle Citizens to Repeal Ordinance 124441." Funded almost entirely by Uber and

Lyft, they raised a budget of $1.2 million and generated enough support that Seattle backed off and removed the cap before the referendum could be held.[96] Like Kansas and San Antonio, they blinked.

To get Austin to blink, Ridesharing Works immediately hit the ground running. The ten grand in cash that each TNC threw in was only a drop in the bucket. In the first month alone, Uber and Lyft would contribute roughly half a million dollars.[97] The lion's share of it at first paid for the high-end services of Block by Block, a nebulous field organization believed to have close ties with the DC consulting firm Field Strategies.[98] The latter had worked for a wide variety of Democratic candidates, labor unions, and progressive organizations, including San Francisco Mayor Ed Lee.[99] Block by Block's mission was to find voters sympathetic to TNCs.

As the PAC moved at a brisk pace, its leadership for the first few months was rather vague. It didn't appear to have its own management separate from the TNCs. By funds alone, it was difficult to tell where Lyft and Uber began and Ridesharing Works ended. Both companies not only threw in great sums of money but also subsidized several hundred thousand dollars of company time and materials. The PAC literally couldn't spend money fast enough, and when funds ran low, Uber and Lyft immediately wired matching donations.

While the PAC ran at warp speed acquiring signatures, Mayor Adler was still pushing for an alternative to incentivize – but not require – fingerprint checks. He brought together a group of local app developers and quickly released "Austin Thumbs Up!" an iPad application integrated into a fingerprint scanner that could complete a submission in under five minutes. Drivers who were cleared received a badge and special benefits, such as free metered parking and priority at geofenced events like the ACL Music Festival.[100]

But before Adler could launch it, the PAC had already obtained enough signatures just three weeks after it had formed. Claiming to have over sixty-five thousand signatures, they submitted twenty-five thousand for verification, more than enough to register a ballot proposal.[101]

For the next month, the council reconsidered their December TNC ordinance. Some of the members who had voted for it signed onto bills adopting Ridesharing Works's new language or watering down the December language.[102] One of the most notable reversals was Ann Kitchen's vice chair on the Mobility Committee, a realtor and moderate conservative who supported calls for "a level playing field." However, after the December vote, several of her conservative peers in the realty community admonished her decision.[103]

Adler tethered these bills to the release of his app, trying to substitute it for the city's fingerprint requirements, but Uber and Lyft were no longer interested. They balked, calling it disingenuous since one way or the other, the council would impose some type of penalty on noncompliant drivers.[104] The PAC had good reason to believe they had the upper hand. The last time a referendum was held in a May election, only fifty thousand Austinites showed up to vote.[105] If the TNCs truly had sixty-five thousand supporters, a victory was highly probable.

A majority of the council also turned down all of Mayor Adler's suggested compromises.[106] Both sides wanted a showdown. By law the council had the option to either accept the citizen ordinance or add it as a ballot initiative to the next election, and they selected the latter.

The council was tasked with developing ballot language to reflect the referendum, and as a practical matter, they couldn't simply copy and paste the PAC's six-page proposed ordinance. Instead, they summarized it as follows:

> Shall the City Code be amended to repeal City Ordinance No. 20151217-075 relating to Transportation Network Companies; and replace with an ordinance that would repeal and prohibit required fingerprinting, repeal the requirement to identify the vehicle with a distinctive emblem, repeal the prohibition against loading and unloading passengers in a travel lane, and require other regulations for Transportation Network Companies?[107]

Thus was born Proposition 1, or "Prop 1," as it was commonly called. The language was generally fair. It listed all the major pain points Uber had with the December 17 ordinance. Even one of the two council members who had voted against it two months earlier said the ballot language was clear.[108]

But psychologically, it had a flaw that panicked Uber. On the referendum, voters would select the options of either "for the ordinance," which was effectively *against* the December 17 bill, or "against the ordinance," which was in *favor* of the December language.[109] It was inherently confusing. Would a low-attention-span voter be able to understand which "ordinance" they were voting for or against? It wasn't clear. An activist supported by Uber attempted to challenge the wording in court but was turned down.[110]

There was also another problem. The election date was set for May 7, 2016, which *was* the next available date prescribed by law. But as former Council Member Riley had learned firsthand in 2014, college students don't vote in the last days of a semester. And without them, the referendum was less certain. Plus, Prop 1 would be a standalone election, meaning there were no other candidates or issues on the ballot to draw out more voters.

By late March, the enormity of the obstacles in front of Ridesharing Works had sunk in. They began bearing for war. On March 31, for the first time, Uber dropped half a million dollars into the PAC's account, overtaking Lyft's matching contributions.[111] The PAC changed its website name from RideSharingWorks.com to VoteProp1.com.[112] Left and right, they started to hire specialists. For "campaign consulting," they hired Reed Galen, a Republican strategist who had worked for John McCain and Arnold Schwarzenegger.[113]

On the opposite side of the issue, the PAC "Our City, Our Safety, Our Choice" formed, painting the referendum with a strong message against corporate self-interest. The new committee was headed by former Council Member Laura Morrison, the lone "no" vote against the 2014 pilot program, and David Butts, a retired, longtime, local Democratic campaigner. Butts was considered something of a pope in Austin Democratic politics. To receive his blessing of money or an endorsement opened a lot of doors for aspiring officeholders. Few could afford to ignore him.

With Butts's involvement, the city was split into two camps, with Austin's core Democratic base on one side versus the rest of the city on the other. The county Democratic Party issued a resolution in favor of Kitchen's ordinance, and several area Democratic state officials endorsed the Our City PAC.[114]

As they started to see the lines developing, Ridesharing Works cultivated a public appearance seemingly designed to pull from different Democratic constituencies. They spent heavily on advertising, sometimes on commercials touting their safety and depicting several female users.[115] For a spokesperson, they hired Huey Rey Fischer, an openly gay, Hispanic, twenty-three-year-old, who just lost a primary for state House two months earlier.[116] To chair the PAC, they hired the elderly prior Austin mayor and Yellow Dog Democrat Lee Leffingwell.[117]

When hiring, there was virtually nothing Ridesharing Works couldn't afford. Fischer and other hired guns like him were paid sums far out of scale for normal campaign work. Leffingwell, who used to criticize the intersection of money and politics, was paid $50,000 for his services.[118]

As stories of the campaign disclosures surfaced, it began to create a sense of unease. Over $2 million was spent in the first few months.[119] By contrast, the 2014 free-for-all election with over eighty candidates had expended just over $5 million total.[120] Austin was unprepared for the attention or tactics of high-price campaigns, and the effect was unnerving. The more money Uber and Lyft spent, the more it fed into the message that they were after preferential treatment. Still, Uber continued to throw in dramatic sums of money. In a three-week period, their PAC spent nearly $5 million, more than double their expenditures in the first 3.5 months. Our City never raised nor spent more than five figures.

Toward late April, the endless buffet of campaign advertising turned nauseating. It was everywhere. Lyft's app often redirected to the Ridesharing Works page.[121] In the TNC vehicles themselves, fliers were attached to seat backs or taped to complimentary granola bars.[122] Ridesharing Works hired

Friday Night Lights star Taylor Kitsch to film a new ad and appear on campus to encourage students to vote.[123] There were radio ads, television ads, repeated telephone polls, campaign calls, typed letters, and *on and on*.

There were several negative reactions to the media intensity. Reddit users posted pictures of half a dozen fliers they had received over just a few weeks.[124] Uber sent unsolicited text messages to its users, leading to a lawsuit and FCC complaint.[125] And there were complaints that some of their commercials were misleading.[126] It was overbearing, as though Uber were screaming at people to show up to the polls.

More and more, it seemed Ridesharing Works was worried about the ballot language. Much of their advertising emphasized in large, bold font, "Vote **FOR** Prop 1." But in trying to fix one problem, they also created too much alienation. Several publications following the referendum said they were pushing too hard. The two largest Austin newspapers endorsed an "against" vote, citing too much self-interest.[127] Even Mayor Adler finally came out against the ordinance, stating that an "against" vote was the only way to bring the parties back to the negotiating table.[128]

Toward Election Day, Uber and Lyft each made last-minute appeals, announcing clearly that they would leave if the referendum failed, a question often debated throughout the campaign.[129] Other threats had been made along the way. The US Chamber of Commerce president wrote to the US transportation secretary, recommending (without naming Austin) that any city that insisted on fingerprint checks for TNCs not receive a pending $50 million grant utilizing technology for mobility improvements.[130] State lawmakers also threatened that if the referendum passed, they would strongly consider a law to overturn it.[131]

None of it had any effect. On Saturday, May 7, 2016, voters shot down the referendum by nearly a twelve-point margin. Turnout was generally low citywide – only 18 percent – and even lower in some student precincts. Although Ridesharing Works had claimed months before that they had sixty-five thousand signatories, fewer than thirty-five thousand people showed up to vote in their favor.[132]

As the results came in, several former and sitting council members attended an Our City rally (and impromptu victory party) at a downtown beer garden. A photographer snapped a photo of a custom flier protruding from a shirt pocket, with Uber's logo and an "F" replacing the boxed "U," effectively reading, "F Uber, Austin's Corporate Bully." Smiles and cheers abounded as Laura Morrison and David Butts stood front and center announcing the results. Ann Kitchen, Kathie Tovo, and Mayor Adler stood in the audience.[133]

Uber and Lyft had spent a combined $10 million on Proposition 1 (three-quarters of which came from Uber), the most expensive election in Austin's history, and lost. Depending who you asked, Our City won a moral victory, as Austinites "chose wisely" to rein in TNCs. Some claimed that polls had consistently shown Ridesharing Works that their numbers were poor, which, if true, explained their desperate strategy. To others, TNCs had the votes, but their base stayed home due to a gluttonous media frenzy and the ultimatum of leaving town. Another handful claimed that the ballot language was misleading, even though Uber went to great lengths to make sure voters knew which way to vote.

Uber and Lyft both announced they were shutting down at 9:00 a.m. the following Monday, although they would continue to operate outside the city limits. Both apps posted messages blaming the city council, implying it was their actions that had forced them to leave. In the aftermath, few if any who took an opinion on the referendum followed the nuance of the campaign or the players involved. On his personal website, Mayor Adler copied and pasted a volley of angry tweets he had received, as though he were personally responsible for the outcome.[134] Many publications painted it as the city deliberately kicking Uber and Lyft out, and they would continue to do so for over a year.

The week after the vote, the ATD issued an incredibly strange memo declaring that they would examine intentionally deregulating the local taxi market. Taxis would operate in an "open entry" system with no caps on supply, a provision that had for decades allowed cab owners to get rich extracting rents from drivers. The stakeholder group would be made of taxi companies and drivers, neither of whom wanted to open their industry to even more competitors.[135] Months after the announcement, the stakeholder group fizzled out of existence, forgotten.

Still, the deregulation memo showed that Matt Daus's strategy of seeking increased regulations could go wildly off the rails. The council didn't push regulations to fully insulate the taxi market but rather to meld taxis and TNCs as closely as possible. Background checks were standardized between both markets. The TNC's pain points of fingerprinting were mitigated short of being withdrawn altogether. And even though Uber and Lyft left, the TNC market was nonetheless ripe and inviting.

Within weeks of their departure, several smaller TNCs from coast to coast raced into town to set up shop: FARE (Phoenix, AZ), Fasten (Boston, MA), InstaRyde (Toronto, Canada), Wingz (San Francisco, CA), and domestic nonprofit service RideAustin.[136] Like Get Me, the newcomers agreed to the city's fingerprint checks, and they all satisfied the compliance deadlines set by the December 17 ordinance. Many of them experienced the same technical glitches and flaws Uber had experienced in its early days (especially during peak-demand events like SXSW or New Year's Eve). Some folded and others excelled, but they more or less filled the void with prices roughly comparable to Uber and Lyft.

One of the lingering questions was that if so many competitors could get by with fingerprint background checks, why couldn't Uber and Lyft? In hearings, TNC representatives said that it didn't scale, which was a half-truth. Clearly, competitors could scale. Kitchen attributed it to a "lack of imagination," but what Uber and Lyft consistently failed to mention was that it didn't scale to the level that allowed them to dominate their competitors.

By all indications, Uber had for years attempted to corner the for-hire market. Leaked profit-and-loss statements showed that despite receiving record levels of investment, they operated at a loss.[137] In the United States, part of the blame lied with an ongoing price war with Lyft. Most years, Uber cut the per-mile rate of fares each January deeper and deeper. By 2016, Uber's cuts were so deep that they began subsidizing existing drivers so they didn't quit the platform.[138]

The unaudited P&L statements suggested that Uber had used its cash investments to subsidize rides by as much as 60 percent.[139] Also, *The New York Times* reported that even in 2016, they continued to raise several billion dollars as part of a "mad scramble to starve the competition of cash."[140] They were effectively freezing out the competition.

The domination strategy, which lawmakers seldom noticed, implied a strong insecurity that with a relatively modest investment, rideshare imitators were easy to spawn. It wasn't that the app's algorithm was special, but rather the keys to supposed profits were brand awareness and price. Indeed, Uber had to light staggering sums of cash on fire to remain competitive abroad, most prominently against the Chinese company Didi Chuxing (a fight Uber ultimately lost).

From a regulatory perspective, the domination strategy might explain Uber's caginess when answering questions about why fingerprint background checks didn't work. They could never go before the Austin City Council (or any other body) and explain that they wanted to undercut every other service provider, taxis included. First of all, it was self-serving. It undermined the public safety argument of whether fingerprints or private background checks were more effective. Secondly, it was the antithesis of the free-market strategy they had long argued in favor of. Uber frequently claimed the taxi industry was trying to maintain an oligopoly by blocking ridesharing laws, which was true. But it would have made them look like hypocrites if they announced they were trying to undermine all their competitors as well.

Thirdly, it could have been seen as a borderline-illegal antitrust action. While competitors can get away with cutting prices below cost, they usually can't announce they're doing so to knock their rivals out of the market, a practice known as predatory pricing.[141] And lastly, lawmakers like Ann Kitchen were not going to stand aside while Uber deliberately put struggling taxi drivers out of business.

Austin lawmakers went to great lengths to find a middle ground, removing any hints of friction in driver fingerprinting. And for Uber and Lyft, it still wasn't good enough. The domino effect would spread elsewhere, and even if other cities replicated Austin's model (which was a big "if"), the tail end of driver-applicants would walk away from the process. Uber and Lyft considered them critical to keeping prices low, but it would not have been easy to publicly explain why, nor did they try. Instead, they simply said, "It doesn't scale."

Roughly a year after Prop 1, Texas's legislature finally passed a law undoing the regulations of Austin, Houston, and a handful of other cities that had passed seemingly "excessive" burdens against Uber and Lyft.[142] The session was characterized by a new favorite blood sport of the state's Republicans: undoing local ordinances they felt were too restrictive. The TNC issue was simply one of multiple examples, and after Uber and Lyft returned to the legislature with an army of forty lobbyists (at a reported cost of $2.3 million), they found allies who were much more receptive than two years before.[143]

Locally, Uber's management in Austin had turned over in the year since Prop 1, and when they relaunched on Memorial Day 2017, they posted a halfhearted mea culpa:

> We're sorry Austin – for leaving the way we did; for letting an honest disagreement about regulations and consumer choice turn into a public fight; and most of all, for not being able to serve you for the last year. It was never our intention, but we let down drivers, riders, and the broader Austin community. We've spent the last year listening carefully and learning from the mistakes we made. While we can't change how we got here, we can and

will commit to getting it right this time around.[144]

Anecdotally, several residents did not welcome Uber and Lyft back with open arms. There was a sense that they had usurped both local control and a democratic vote. Their apology seemed like the customary damage control they often employed. For many, Uber wasn't so "sorry" that they felt ashamed to go to the legislature to get their way.

After returning, Uber and Lyft also began a price war against the smaller TNCs that many drivers had become accustomed to in their absence, some of which charged much lower commissions than Uber or Lyft. According to *BuzzFeed*, the war had cut severely into drivers' incomes.[145]

CHAPTER THIRTEEN
Predictions of End Times

As Uber began losing more money each year, there were hints it was willing to work with – and bend just a little to – regulators who showed a willingness to move forward with them. In Massachusetts, for instance, in exchange for a statewide TNC law in late 2016, they agreed to a twenty-cent-per-ride tax, five cents of which would prop up taxis, as well as more thorough (non-fingerprint) background screenings.[1] To partially settle lawsuits over their drivers' status as independent contractors, they agreed to provide more warnings to drivers whose ratings started to slip.[2] And elsewhere, some of their cooperation was more subtle.

At the National Institute of Standards and Technology (NIST), there was still an open question as to whether GPS could be used as a means to measure a taximeter's distance, which was first posed by policy wonk Craig Leisy of Seattle in 2012. The question dragged on for years, as the US National Work Group on Taximeters only met two to three times annually. The pro-taxi members who attended, including Matt Daus's law firm, held intractable viewpoints.

Although Uber attended several of the meetings, their presence was considered "passive" until the San Francisco and Los Angeles district attorneys filed a joint class action against them in late 2014.[3] Part of their complaint was that neither TNC's app was "type evaluated" for accuracy, a practice applied to taximeters.[4] Lyft responded quickly, submitting a type-evaluation application in October 2014, and Uber followed suit in May 2015.

Around the same time, California's weights-and-measures (w&m) regulator, Kristin Macey, wanted to break through the logjam. Although most states simply adopted the federal NIST code, California had reserved the right to create its own, and Macey's office was becoming impatient. Aside from Uber and Lyft, other smaller TNCs were beginning to enter California, and Macey wanted a formal standard in place.

Plus, as one governing document noted, it was "not customary or common" to debate business models when revising w&m regulations.[5] It was inappropriate. In truth, w&m issues were usually mind-numbingly technical, but they were also debated by small committees open to public participation. A regulator, engineer, or business owner might devote a few hours per year to offer a handful of insights. But the discussions were usually dedicated to metrology, the study of measurement, not market strategies. Macey saw w&m policy as a means to promote technological progress, not stifle industries. "We're here to help; we're not here to obstruct," she said.

Macey's office wanted the matter settled so everyone could move on with their lives. In addition to her job as a regulator, she also served as chair of the National Conference of Weights and Measures, the body that voted on standards published by NIST. Holding a fair amount of clout, she intervened to accelerate the process.

As Uber's participation became less "passive," Macey all but floored the gas pedal. She proposed a new, wholly separate w&m code for ridesharing.[6] That got the attention of Lyft, who also started showing up to meetings in earnest.

But in meetings, the taxi industry was still stonewalling. One of the difficulties of w&m "type evaluation" was that it usually involved an examination of low-tech analog equipment: grocery store scales, gas pumps, and traditional taximeters, for example. For software, regulators usually did little more than identify a software version number. Taxi members would argue that w&m officials were not usually equipped to evaluate software.

The meetings tended to drag on. Macey wasn't interested in examining the software but merely ensuring that the outcome was accurate. If TNCs charged a dollar per mile, then ten miles should equal ten dollars. It was that simple

At the suggestion of Uber and Lyft, and with the support of NIST staff, the work group abolished their deadlocked GPS study committee and replaced it with a small task force led by Macey, who would decide who else could join. The task force would create their own recommendations and submit them directly to NIST staff for review. Taxi members of the work group could submit their own comments but with the explicit instruction that "negative comments must be technically persuasive."[7] Taxi members had stalled long enough, and the w&m community was done waiting.

Macey and the task force spent much of 2016 pushing forward a series of w&m recommendations to remove the regulatory ambiguity for TNCs. But in getting Uber and Lyft to cooperate, she was also provided rare access to examine how their mapping system software calculated fares.

"For Lyft, we signed a nondisclosure agreement," said Macey. "For Uber, they trusted our procedures, and if we violated them, there was always the veiled threat of a lawsuit."

But she received cooperation wildly uncharacteristic of most other regulators, even the CPUC. "Once they came to the table, their 'lone wolf' mentality just completely reversed," said Macey.

During the process, one taxi company, Flywheel (formerly Cabulous), broke ranks with the rest of the industry by doing the unthinkable: they started asking for changes to the w&m taximeter code so they could incorporate GPS to measure distance. Up to that point, the industry had difficulty parting ways with their customary taximeters, video advertising, and credit card processing. They had apps to summon a taxi, but functionally little else.

Flywheel made a bet, largely in response to TNCs, that a low-overhead model compartmentalizing all the bulky equipment into a smartphone app was the best way to survive.[8] The technological efficiencies created by TNCs became harder to evade. The direction of the taxi industry changed to adapt or die. Craig Leisy's original 2012 prediction of an industry turning toward a lower-cost smartphone was starting to come true.

The NCWM formally adopted Macey's TNC revisions in July 2017.[9]

For the IATR, their TNC obsession simply carried forward with Matt Daus remaining at the helm. In early 2016, Daus attended a panel session on the sharing economy at his alma mater, NYU Law. Of the five panelists, four predicted a long-term future for TNCs. Daus, on the other hand, went off on a rant, as he was often prone to do until someone cut him off. He argued that regulatory lapses would cost TNCs so much public support there would be a cataclysmic "rethinking of the public safety element."[10] It wasn't the first time Daus predicted a reversal of fortunes against TNCs.

"Taxis and limos are going to make a comeback," he said to the panel. "Autonomous vehicles – it ain't gonna happen in our lifetime."[11]

It's never been clear if Daus genuinely believed in his own predictions or if he was simply speaking as a cheerleader for the taxi industry. One could almost sense a correlation between the widening dominance of TNCs and Daus's need to align himself with taxis. As Uber and Lyft expanded, his close connection with taxis became more obvious, especially in New York. During the 2015 IATR Conference, a vendor tweeted a photo of Daus and wrote, "Can this man save taxis?! We think so!"[12] In early 2016, Daus distributed a Windels Marx promotional email offering to challenge NYC's real-property tax assessment of taxicabs. It read, "No legal fees unless successful!"[13]

At the NYU Law panel, he pointed to Lyft's representative and accused them of pushing TNC laws to hurt the taxi industry. "So why are you killing these guys now? They really are on the ropes – the taxi and limo – just let them become TNCs, too!"[14]

Daus was right about the state of the industry. By 2016, multiple cities where TNCs were present reported declining taxi business. By the following year, small-fleet cab companies in Santa Fe, Albuquerque, and Cleveland, among a handful of others, closed down and cited Uber as a main reason.[15] Credit unions in New York City that specialized in loans for taxi medallions were placed into conservatorship.[16] The stock price for Medallion Financial Corp, a company that invested in medallion securities, peaked to $17 per share since Uber first launched and then fell to less than $3 per share at the end of 2016.[17]

At the 2016 IATR Conference, taxis were hurting so badly that one of the central themes was finding ways to remove regulatory restrictions. Regulators, especially from San Francisco and Toronto, went back to the drawing board and reexamined why they had imposed most of their requirements in the first place. Which were critical and which now seemed burdensome? Whereas the monopoly power of taxis had once allowed cities to practically micromanage the industry, in the wake of Uber and Lyft, those same restrictions made it harder to keep taxis afloat. To most in the room, traditional rules now obviously looked like "over-regulation." And the fact that they were willing to weaken industry standards that had been in place for decades – fare limits, vehicle age limits, universal neighborhood availability, expensive taximeter hardware – spoke to their desperation.

"Babysitting the taxi industry is coming to an end," the Toronto regulator told the audience. "We need do that for their sake. We need to get out of their way."[18]

Even the TLPA was on board with the new program. Their 2016 president spoke of the ways the industry could reduce wait times and improve reliability. He told the regulators, "I urge you that when approached by your local cab company that you'll support these changes we're asking for. Regulators should provide for public safety in an even-handed way that doesn't serve to pick the winners and losers in this battle."[19]

The TLPA apparently didn't recognize the irony of asking regulators not to "pick the winners and losers." Doing so was fine in the past when it served their interests. Now that TNCs had won, regulators should abstain from such overbearing practices. Still, the regulators showed glimmers of hope that taxis could improve. In a Q&A, the Toronto regulator let it slip that she hoped more cabs would enter the market "and give Uber a run for their money," as she put it.[20]

If you looked closely, you could see taxis beginning to adjust and make the best of a bad situation. Large cities began requiring that taxi companies sign onto a citywide "universal dispatch app," an idea the industry had fought since Christiane Hayashi first proposed it in 2013. But there was no choice anymore. Although many lawmakers cheered the idea of letting the market pick the winners, no one really wanted the cab industry to die off. In 2016, New York, Chicago, Houston, and DC each launched their own citywide taxi apps.[21] For most, the taxi industry's participation was mandatory.

Although they took a severe hit in business, taxi drivers themselves adjusted their tactics. At least one in San Francisco became a successful specialist in picking up hospital patients and senior citizens. An economist who reviewed complaints of taxi drivers in New York and Chicago found that as TNC vehicles increased, taxi complaints decreased.[22]

In years past, one of the great fears was that taxi drivers would abandon their cabs to drive for Uber and Lyft, but that worry died out. Over time, a fair number of taxi drivers reported trying Uber but then switching back to taxis because the money was better. In 2014, Uber claimed the median full-time driver in New York earned over $90,000 per year, and in San Francisco, nearly $75,000.[23] In less than year, that promise of a stellar income fizzled away.

In a 2015 academic paper released by Uber, they reported that despite the supposedly high income, close to half of their drivers quit inside of a year.[24] It's likely that in the early days of expansion, the first drivers benefited from a crazed demand and nascent supply, like the $1,600-a-week driver Senator Ted Harvey met in Colorado. But then fares simply fell off as more drivers applied. In later years, a data-aggregating website calculated that after costs, drivers (outside of NYC) earned roughly ten dollars per hour.[25] The Federal Trade Commission, once an ally to Uber, sued them for their 2014 statements about wages and argued that less than 10 percent of drivers earned close to the promised amount.[26] Uber settled out of court for $20 million.[27]

Once or twice, states attempted to reshuffle responsibilities to give taxis a leg up. In 2016, the California legislature passed a bill to transfer all taxi oversight from cities (except San Francisco) to the CPUC. Governor Jerry Brown vetoed it.[28]

That same year, Governor Brown and a handful of other lawmakers pushed a bipartisan bill to scale down the CPUC's regulatory authority, including transferring TNC oversight to another agency. Even the CPUC chairman publicly admitted that his staff had more responsibilities than they could handle. But it was difficult at first to find any other agency to absorb TNC regulations.[29] Uber had become a hot potato; the state might as well have been transferring a headache. But lawmakers also suspected that giving the responsibility back to cities like San Francisco and Los Angeles meant the business model would be constrained in favor of taxis. The bill ultimately died due to last-minute problems unrelated to TNCs.[30] Uber and the CPUC were stuck with one another.

Uber never seemed to have a problem biting the hand that fed them. They consistently quarreled with the CPUC, the agency that had gone out on a limb and first legalized ridesharing in the United States. Uber continued to fight a $7.6 million fine issued for failing to hand over data they had agreed to provide in 2013, and they were fined another $1 million for not handling complaints of drunk drivers as quickly as they had agreed.[31]

Even in their home town of San Francisco, they started to wear out their welcome. The city originally turned a blind eye on regulating Uber like taxis, but by 2017, several agencies and airports were challenging them on issues related to background checks, business filings, and the intense congestion further worsened by the plethora of TNC drivers. In the space of seven years, they had gone from working with San Francisco officials to playing regulatory whack-a-mole.

As the taxi industry deteriorated, the regulators couldn't seem to identify their own role in the animosity with TNCs. Uber had been unquestionably disingenuous, aggressive, and disrespectful, but the regulators still exhibited a moral superiority that blinded them to their own shortcomings. At the 2016 IATR Conference, one of the more outspoken complaints was that Uber and Lyft seldom shared their trip data with regulators, a source of aggravation. Uber (as well as taxis) often worried that the data would leak to competitors and undermine their business. The regulators didn't explore why Uber was so hesitant and distrusting – even as they discussed with one another how to revive the taxi industry. Even as they continued to affiliate themselves with the IATR, an organization that made every effort to prohibit TNCs, and whose leader had taken money from the TLPA to shield the taxi industry.

None of them seemed to understand how their own character flaws had contributed to this outcome. They simply saw themselves as the blameless regulators. And now that the TNCs had won, they wanted them to start cooperating. It was like they wore blinders.

At the conference, it was also obvious that the IATR itself was in dire straits. Matt Daus began a new strategy of partnering with other transportation-related entities to tackle taxi issues.

"A lot of our members have been stripped of their authority," he told the audience. "But we will get it back, and the way we get it back as government regulators is by working with [others] who can make the transportation system better."[32]

To help taxis move beyond Uber, he embraced data analysis and even sponsored a college-level hack-a-thon to explore ways municipal data sets could be used to find taxis more fares.

Where once the association had been cash-rich with sponsorships, Daus sounded as though they were teetering toward bankruptcy. He pleaded with the attendees to make sure they paid their membership dues by the end of the year, especially if the dues were reimbursed by their city governments.[33]

"I will write any letter that you need me to write," he said. "I will beg to anyone that we need to beg to."[34]

He also asked that when regulators went home, they pull their staff together to phone bank other regulators from nearby cities and encourage them to join the IATR. And he emphatically thanked their most generous sponsor that year, a cab-comparison app called "Karhoo."[35]

"You helped us stay solvent," he told them.[36]

In all of the animus, it's worth noting that Lyft was less aggressive than Uber. They worked well with lawmakers, demonstrating grace under pressure. And they were more patient, often (though not always) letting Uber do the heavy lifting. For instance, after receiving a court-ordered injunction in Nevada, Uber successfully requested that the legislature change the law in their favor, but Lyft never once set foot in Vegas until the state law took effect. Nor did they chase SideCar across the country when they rushed to expand in 2013. Lyft initially focused on cities with populations of at least three-hundred thousand, and they waited longer to invest in an international presence. More often than Uber, Lyft eased into communities.

Lyft took pains to bill themselves as the friendly, community-focused alternative. In early 2017, it finally paid off. A month after Donald Trump was elected president, Travis Kalanick agreed to join his newly created Strategy and Policy Forum, an advisory board consisting of CEOs mostly from Fortune 500 companies such as Walmart, Boeing, The Walt Disney Company, and JP Morgan Chase.[37] On Friday, January 27, that participation became toxic when President Trump signed Executive Order 13769, severely restricting the flow of immigration from predominantly Muslim countries into the United States. It was the beginning of a moment in which the culmination of Kalanick's years of antagonistic behavior had become too much to bear.

The following day Kalanick emailed his employees, saying Uber would compensate drivers who were locked out of the country for ninety days. He went on to explain that although he disagreed with the policy, he would make his objections known at the next advisory board meeting. In order to give cities a voice, he said, it was also necessary to have "a seat at the table." In contrast, Logan Green of Lyft sent an email hours after Kalanick simply stating they were firmly against the executive order.[38]

That same day, several protests formed at airports across the nation, including at JFK International. The New York Taxi Workers Alliance, whose Twitter page was already an ongoing gripe-fest about Uber, agreed to go on a one-hour work stoppage at JFK between 6:00 and 7:00 p.m.[39] Many of the drivers were themselves immigrants from Muslim countries and strongly empathized with the cause. At 7:30 p.m., Uber tweeted that it would cease surge pricing at JFK, a common agreement in most of their regulatory contracts during abnormal market conditions.[40] In the event of, for example, a hurricane, Uber's algorithm wouldn't exploit passengers desperately needing a ride. In all probability, a massive political strike qualified as "abnormal."

Before they could explain their intentions, a freelance writer posted a series of replies to Uber's tweet, including:

> Don't like @Uber's exploitative anti-labor policies & Trump collaboration, now profiting off xenophobia? #deleteUber[41]

It wasn't the first time the hashtag was used, especially after Kalanick joined President Trump's advisory board, but it quickly went viral. The writer posted a screenshot of how to delete the Uber app, and many others followed suit. To the world, it looked as though Uber was trying to profit from the disarray caused by the executive order – lowering prices to increase demand. Uber tweeted a clarification for the misunderstanding.[42] But the damage was done.

At an instinctive level, Kalanick's willingness to work with Trump was suspiciously inconsistent with his known behavior. Across the United States, Uber had never been afraid to push back against politicians when it suited their purposes. Now, they were taking a bizarre position best described as "tactful," "moderate," and "mature," words seldom associated with Uber or Kalanick. It was too strange, too uncharacteristic.

On Sunday morning, Logan Green and John Zimmer of Lyft sent a joint letter to users telling them they would donate $1 million to the American Civil Liberties Union (ACLU) over the next four years.[43] Meanwhile, the #DeleteUber frenzy trended on Twitter. By noon, an array of celebrities had joined in, including John Leguizamo, Taraji P. Henson, Rob Corddry, and Jesse Tyler Ferguson, among several others.[44]

Uber went into rapid damage control. They quickly announced that their assistance to overseas stranded drivers would include a $3 million legal defense fund.[45] *The Verge* reported that to make amends, Uber was tying Facebook advertisements to users who "liked" the ACLU.[46] And when customers submitted inquiries on how to delete their account, they were provided with both instructions *and* a link to Uber's statement on the executive order.[47] Little of it, though, could reverse years of ill will.

Within seventy-two hours of the executive order, followed by Uber's disastrous tweet, Lyft's ranking among the top-downloaded free iPhone apps shot up from around number forty to number four, surpassing Snapchat, Instagram, YouTube, and Facebook.[48] Uber remained at number thirteen.

By Tuesday, Kalanick was facing his employees at a regular all-hands meeting where he received a barrage of questions probing his willingness to leave Trump's advisory board. According to *The New York Times*, many expressed concern that Kalanick's cooperation with the Trump administration would not only damage Uber's brand but would also publicly stigmatize them as employees. *The Times* reported that Kalanick nonetheless defended his position. The next day, employees pleaded further by circulating a twenty-five-page Google document titled "Letters to Travis."[49]

On Thursday, Kalanick finally sent an internal memo announcing he'd resign from the advisory board. He chalked up the #DeleteUber campaign to a "perception-reality gap" and said that his participation interfered with his ability to advocate against the executive order.[50] It was reported that the issue had cost the company five hundred thousand users.[51] By August 2017, a credit card-analysis firm reported Uber's US market share had declined to 74.3 percent, with the greatest loss occurring during the #DeleteUber campaign.[52] The same month the data was released, President Trump dissolved the Strategy and Policy Forum after multiple CEOs resigned in the wake of the president's comments on the Charlottesville, Virginia, rallies.[53]

Less than three weeks after Kalanick resigned from the advisory board, another bombshell dropped. Susan J. Fowler, a former Uber software engineer, published a blog post titled "Reflecting on One Very, Very Strange Year at Uber." In it, she detailed an account of a supervisor making sexual advances toward her, an HR department turning a blind eye to her complaints, a "game-of-thrones political war" of Machiavellian maneuvers, a misogynistic corporate culture hemorrhaging female employees, and a shadowy system of performance reviews. Once more, they were qualities the public had come to believe embodied Kalanick's personality. The reports of sexism were practically echoes of Sarah Lacy, the *PandoDaily* author an Uber executive had discussed investigating in front of other journalists. And once more, Uber was in damage control.

The company seemed to spiral, and the press eagerly rode the momentum. In the following months, investigative reporters (especially from *The New York Times)* uncovered a treasure trove of embarrassing secrets, many of which stemmed from when Uber launched ridesharing in 2013–2014. Every week seemed to unfold into a new drama. Kalanick was recorded arguing with an Uber driver about how their price slashing caused his personal bankruptcy.[54] Executives semi-mysteriously resigned. An article detailed how Uber had continued to track iPhones after the app was deleted, a violation of Apple's terms and conditions, and then had tried to cover it up.[55] After a reported rape in India, an executive had obtained and presented to Kalanick medical files of the alleged victim.[56] In Seoul, South Korea, Kalanick had attended an escort bar where Uber managers selected escorts for themselves.[57]

For regulators, one of the most damning reports was a program internally referred to as "Greyball," wherein Uber showed a fake version of their app to trolling taxi regulators. Instead of showing actual cars on their system, it showed "ghost cars" that didn't actually exist. *The Times* reported Greyball was used mostly outside the United States, although one Portland, Oregon, regulator recorded the fake data he had received.[58] The program was also a subset of the "Violation of Terms of Service" program, which Carlton Thomas told a colleague was used against his office to boot regulators off of the app.[59] Within a few months of the report, the US Justice Department began an official inquiry. Austin, Texas, was added as one of the cities they were reviewing.[60]

In Portland, Greyball had irked regulators so much that they instituted a highly aggressive field audit program. Greyball was used in December 2014, the first month Uber barged into Portland after years of fruitless negotiations with the city. Regulators conducting sting operations immediately noticed the pattern – within a half-hour period on the day of Uber's launch, they requested four rides, all of which were canceled. The city soon initiated a lawsuit, and Uber agreed to a temporary cessation of their app while the mayor worked out a pilot program. Part of its language included a provision that Uber could not prevent city officials from using their app. Over the next two years, city regulators conducted two thousand field audits for Uber and Lyft combined, far outpacing most of their peers. Portland officials contacted seventeen other state and local regulators across the US, none of whom reported anything close to that pace. Seven stated they suspected Greyball's use, and another four said they had evidence of it.[61]

By June 2017, the flood of negative press hurt Uber so much that board members successfully pressured Kalanick to resign from his own company.[62] Early reports indicated that after his departure, the company remained popular with millennials.[63] It suggested that Uber was still appreciated over the alternative, but that's as far as it went.

Five days after Kalanick was shown the door, Chicago taxi regulators emailed several peers across the country with a brief, nine-question survey, which regulators often distributed to gauge changes in the industry. In it, they asked whether their colleagues' cities placed caps upon TNC vehicles or drivers, or even whether they were thinking about it. As it spoke to the sorry state of the industry, they also wanted to know what changes they had made to "alleviate or ease burdens on the taxi industry." And they asked, somewhat redundantly, "Has your jurisdiction started dialogue to deregulate the taxicab industry in your jurisdiction?"[64]

When looking at Uber's political tactics, one can parse them in two ways. There were incidents in which they unfairly tarnished lawmakers for the sake of market domination. The very first time they politicized their existence in 2012 was in Washington, DC, so they could charge less than fifteen dollars for a black-car ride at roughly the same time Lyft and SideCar were coming on to the scene. Or in Austin, when they tarnished Ann Kitchen by name, they painted her as a backward-looking curmudgeon even though she removed much of the friction of fingerprint background checks. Uber fought painstakingly for the small, tail-end distribution of drivers because more drivers meant flatter, more competitive pricing. And they wanted to keep a regulatory domino effect from spreading.

But then there were the political events to push back against regulations that would have indeed forced them out of the market. There was Chicago and Massachusetts in 2012. The Colorado PUC's 2013 hearings would have given them the boot, despite an earlier truce. There was also New Orleans, where the regulator sent Uber a cease-and-desist letter before they even launched.

Uber officials wouldn't comment for this book, but for Travis Kalanick, it's likely he didn't see a need to parse such scenarios. Why spend time quibbling over each fight's origin story? If the remedy was effective and the outcome was the same, then what difference did the cause of the fight make? Kalanick – and by extension, Uber's corporate culture – placed an intense premium on efficiency. For the regulatory fights, the solution was usually the same. Simply paint each fight with a broad brush, scare the large base of TNC customers into confronting their elected officials, and spend more time working on new products. Context was thrown to the wind.

It also might explain why Uber, despite attending IATR conferences and hiring lawyers who discretely investigated Matt Daus's ties to the taxi industry, rarely mentioned him or the IATR publicly. Doing so would have gained nothing. The taxi industry's opposition was so self-evident that no one needed convincing it existed. Why bother stamping it with Daus's face and a persona? It was more effective to let everyone's imagination about taxi influence run wild.

But by being cagey, defending themselves with walls of registered voters, and periodically attacking elected officials, they created a profound sense of resentment. Current and former elected leaders who spoke of Uber often had negative things to say about the company, even among TNC supporters. Uber took an approach that the ends justified the means, and for anyone who had to deal with them, it left a bitter taste in their mouths.

In the fight between taxi regulators and transportation network companies, it's difficult to find any honest angels. Karen Cameron, the terminated IATR executive director, shoots near the top. Among everyone who knew of or suspected of Daus's connection to the taxi industry, she was the only one willing to call him out, and for her troubles, she was excommunicated. She was also among the few pushing for a legitimate policy debate between taxis and TNCs. When the rest of the world took a partisan position on one side or the other, she wanted an honest evaluation.

A similar argument could be made for Seattle's Craig Leisy, who had every reason to panic when Uber's high-end black cars entered the market but still remained calm. He looked at it as a watershed moment in the evolution of weights-and-measures regulations. Adapt or die.

Straddling a middle ground between a thoughtful regulator and a taxi partisan was Christiane Hayashi. Among the honest parties, Hayashi at least deserves an honorable mention. Most regulators, like Carlton Thomas or Ron Linton, camouflaged their intentions to defend taxi markets. They maneuvered from the shadows and sometimes used their clout as transportation experts to nudge lawmakers. Although Hayashi protected a broken business model and glossed over Daus's relationship with the TLPA, she at least vocalized her thoughts loudly and often. With no other cards to play, she made her objections publicly known. She defended taxis as a public utility and made it clear she didn't want to see drivers or the paratransit community harmed because of disruptive influences. She publicly stood by her convictions and tried to at least improve taxis' competitiveness. In exchange for her tireless dedication, she earned a lot of grief and no material rewards. Hayashi stated that if she had never become a taxi regulator and instead remained in the city attorney's office, she might still be working in San Francisco.

"It was exhausting having to deal with all of that," she said. "I was just getting beaten up on a daily basis."

After retiring in June 2014, she was ceremoniously sent off with an elaborate tribute by the local taxi industry. The community of immigrant cab drivers treated her to an exotic potluck buffet and provided a cover band called The Temporary Hails, where she donned a funny hat and sang along. She was presented with a wooden plaque with a bulky, vintage taximeter reading "Taxi Goddess."[65]

Hayashi moved to Nevada, where she owned a home. As the state legislature was passing their TNC bill in 2015, she applied for the position of Las Vegas taxi administrator and earned consideration as a finalist.[66] In her spare time, she's continued on a long-term project translating the works of a scholar in the Afro-Cuban Santeria religion.

She also concedes that she once took a Lyft ride to the airport.

As she looked back on it a few years later, Hayashi had difficulty consistently explaining whether she wanted to kick Uber, Lyft, and SideCar out of San Francisco. She denied that was her motivation and instead claimed that her primary concern was always to ensure public safety and consumer protections. Yet, in 2013, she often warned others that San Francisco's taxi system was on the verge of collapse, thanks in large part to ridesharing. She tried to sound the alarm and warn others it could happen to them, too.

She said she disagreed with Matt Daus's model regulations because they were unrealistic. "The horse was already out of the barn," as Hayashi put it. Still, she forwarded copies to the CPUC and endorsed Daus's ridesharing definition that ultimately booted SideCar out of Austin, a city fight she jumped into without permission.

It's not that Hayashi was lying; she often spoke bluntly of the hell that Uber and taxi drivers sometimes put her through. But living these fights was different than trying to remember them with the benefit of 20/20 hindsight, especially as Uber and Lyft gradually improved their safety problems. And she recognized that ridesharing was a more efficient service.

"I agree that it's not necessarily a bad business model," Hayashi said. "The people who implemented it did it in a really difficult way. But look at the barriers they broke. I give them credit. At a time of underemployment, that's not necessarily a bad thing. But the economics of it have to balance out."

The experience of the taxi regulators spawned a question that no one wanted to discuss: If taxi regulators stood firm in their position that new companies had to conform to old business models, then how was the industry supposed to evolve and improve? The financial incentives rewarded a limited supply of taxis that would never come close to reaching demand. Truly, one of the most puzzling questions of taxi regulators was when a more efficient business model appeared at their doorstep, why did the gatekeepers refuse to open the gates? Why did they insist on defending a service that charged higher rates, often refused credit cards, had worse customer service, and served fewer areas of a city? Aside from a couple of exceptions, there's no indication the regulators themselves took money from the taxi industry. And in all of their conferences and hundreds of emails, they never seemed to panic that TNCs jeopardized their own government jobs. So what was it?

The answer appears to be little more than an instinctive, knee-jerk reaction. Like Ron Linton, the regulators saw the taxi industry as their core constituent, and they acted accordingly. As former Federal Trade Commission Director Andy Gavil put it, "Somehow, they got the message they are there to protect the industry instead of consumers." In a way, the relationship between regulator and taxi was similar to parent and child. A parent will discipline their child and set boundaries, but when possible, they'll shield them from any outside harm. Regulators were the lions protecting their young.

No side in this fight was completely innocent. Regulators would probably look at their own actions and say, "Uber lied and embellished. They evaded basic safety requirements. And they acted above the law. How could we ever try to work with them?"

And they'd be right. Trust could not come easily. Uber was shameless and irritating. They made it difficult for policymakers to step back and evaluate the business model impartially. And only a small few, like the California PUC or Austin Council Members Riley and Spelman, looked past the negative qualities to support them.

In turn, Uber would probably evaluate their own actions and say, "What choice did we have? If we had asked for permission first, we would have been stonewalled. The model doesn't work without competitive pricing and a large customer base. And almost no one objected to regulators collaborating with our incumbent competitor, taxis."

And they'd be right. Many critics of Uber have argued they should have obtained permission before launching in a city, that it was dishonorable and unseemly to just jump in and politically bully local council members. But even Hayashi acknowledged that if Uber had asked for permission, they would have been shown the door. Uber's tactics were inevitable because nothing else would have worked.

Uber not only had to battle taxi protectionism but the safety aspects that were blended within it. Usually, neither regulators nor TNCs could split them apart and evaluate the safety aspects independently. They went hand in hand.

To protect taxis *was* to protect safety, they claimed. In an alternative universe, regulators could have been honest brokers, putting aside their feelings to solely evaluate how TNCs impacted public safety and then letting the market sort out the winners and losers. At any time, they could have insisted on a handful of safety regulations – appropriate insurance, frictionless background checks, and a trade dress – and left it at that. But they seldom did. They usually squandered that opportunity to protect the incumbents.

At the time of this writing, many have suspected that the ridesharing business model will eventually be replaced by self-driving cars, a burgeoning industry that several companies have tripped over themselves to master as quickly as possible. The benefits are cold but straightforward: fewer labor costs, fewer liability issues, greater productivity, and coming within arm's reach of eliminating personal car ownership. It's led many to wonder if ridesharing was little more than a stepping stone.

But the regulatory implications are longstanding. At the corporate extremes of transportation (Uber/Lyft) or hotels (Airbnb/HomeAway), the sharing economy is an extremely tempting investment regardless of its disruptions. Other industries may follow suit and even look to Uber's experiences as a model practice. For the regulators empowered to grant operating permits, new fights and roadblocks seem likely. In part, it will depend on the mindset of the players involved and the regulatory culture in each industry.

The rapidly changing landscape is a thought that already flickers in a few minds. During the middle of Austin's Prop 1 campaign, Carlton Thomas traded emails with his Houston counterpart to make a simple inquiry about documentation requirements for taxi drivers. Thomas wished her well, and she replied:

From: Cooper, Nikki (Houston)
Sent: Wednesday, February 17, 2016 12:01 PM
To: Thomas, Carlton (Austin)

We are holding okay. You keep your chin up. We are watching what's going on in Austin. Regardless of the outcome, I truly believe the next 3 years will have so much change that we won't recognize the industry.

Notes on Sources, Quoted Materials, and Interviews

The vast majority of materials from this book came from several broadly-scoped public records requests, dozens of interviews, videos posted online that were publicly accessible when I viewed them, government documents, lawsuits, and various news outlets. Some of the written material has been edited for clarity (substituting similar terms in brackets) or brevity (cutting off paragraphs or sentences with ellipses). Also, some of the quoted verbal comments have been similarly edited for clarity of brevity. Most of the written quotes include their original typos, where applicable.

In the summer of 2016, I flew to the Bay Area to conduct a dozen in-person interviews for this book. When I arrived, I was told that I was late. Brad Stone, a prolific writer for the *New York Times*, *Newsweek*, and *Bloomberg*, had already spoken to some of them for his upcoming book, *The Upstarts*. As had a couple of curious students from the Harvard Graduate School of Design, who were writing a case study on ridesourcing in San Francisco. When I started talking to interviewees, some of them had their answers down pat because they had already provided them to Stone and/or the grad students, both of whom would publish before I could.

In cases where the three of us were given similar anecdotes, I've credited those comments as a firsthand source. However, in cases where Stone or Harvard were given unique information that I did not receive, I've made every effort to credit them appropriately.

Several interview requests were made to current and former Uber employees, most of whom would not respond, and the few who did declined to comment. Similar attempts were made with Lyft representatives. Also, several years ago during the 2005-06 school year, Lyft co-founder John Zimmer and I attended Cornell University at the same time. I don't recall ever meeting Mr. Zimmer – he was an undergraduate senior, and I was a first-year grad student. Although, it's possible we took the same class or drank from the same keg.

In July of 2017, I made contact with Matthew Daus, but he would only reply with a polite introduction. Upon his staff's request, I provided a summary of my personal background to Windels Marx, who noted they could not find me associated with any major publishing house, which was true. After that, I never heard back before this book went to print.

Acknowledgments

First and foremost, I'd like to thank Nick Lealos, my friend and attorney. Nick and I have known each other since middle school, and he's not only a sharp jurist who can accurately predict Supreme Court rulings, but he's also far savvier with political and regulatory landscapes than I am. I like to believe that I'm an accomplished researcher, but Nick can contextualize information with stunning speed. For several months, I treated him to coffee at Starbucks each Saturday morning to relay what I'd learned, but thoughts and ideas kept popping up in the middle of the week. At the aggravation of his wife, I relentlessly called him for insights I might have missed. In 2016, he also helped me navigate several difficult public information requests, which was the crux of this book.

Thanks all to those who not only accepted my interview requests but took the time to answer my questions and help me fill in the blanks.

I'd also like to thank Nell McPherson, a skilled freelance editor based out of Jacksonville, Florida. In the summer of 2017, she and I both worked on the final version of this book as we were evading our respective hurricanes. Nell has a sharp eye and is well versed in the Chicago Manual of Style. She helped me smooth out a lot of the rough edges.

Also thanks to Annie Smith of SmithWordsmith.com, another freelance editor who graciously offered me a few pointers when I needed them most.

Special thanks to the University of Texas Libraries, the reference staff at the University of Texas Tarlton Law Library, the TexShare program, and the incredible digital resources of the Austin Public Library. All were instrumental in the research of this material.

ENDNOTE CITATIONS

Chapter 1

1. New York Racing Association, *Belmont Park, 1905-1968* (Jamaica, New York: The New York Racing Association, 1968), 40-41; "Kenny Fights for Life; Assailant Eludes Net," *New York Times*, Jan. 31, 1925.
2. "Dennis Kenny Shot by Taxicab Driver," *New York Times*, Jan. 30, 1925.
3. "Dennis J. Kenny Dies of Taxi Man's Shot," *New York Times*, Feb. 13, 1925.
4. "Kenny Fights for Life..."
5. "Taxi Driver Admits That He Shot Kenny," *New York Times*, Feb. 6, 1925.
6. Ibid.
7. Ibid.
8. "Food Groceries and Toiletries in the 1920's prices 50 examples from The People History Site," Thepeoplehistory.com, accessed August 7, 2017, http://www.thepeoplehistory.com/20sfood.html.
9. "Taxi Driver Admits That..."
10. Ibid.
11. "Dennis Kenny Shot by..."; "Smith and Kenny Friends in Boyhood," *New York Times*, May 11, 1928; Mark Kingwell, *Nearest Thing to Heaven: The Empire State Building and American Dreams* (New Haven, Connecticut: Yale University Press, 2006), 4.
12. Richard F. Welch, *King of the Bowery: Big Tim Sullivan, Tammany Hall, and New York City from the Gilded Age to the Progressive Era* (Madison: Fairleigh Dickinson University Press, 2008), 23-33.
13. "Smith and Kenny Friends..."
14. "Kenny Fights for Life..."; "John H. McCooey Joins Tammany Society," *New York Times*, June 2, 1925.
15. "Dennis Kenny Shot by..."; "Kenny Fights for Life..."
16. "Taxi Driver Admits That..."
17. "Taxi Driver Admits Shooting Yale Man," *Hartford Courant*, Feb. 6, 1925.
18. "Taxi Driver Admits That..."
19. Ibid.
20. "Taxi Driver Admits Shooting..."
21. "Taxi Driver Admits That..."
22. "Police Continue Taxicab Clean-Up," *New York Times*, Feb. 14, 1925.
23. "Felons Drive Taxis, Many Have Records," *New York Times*, Oct. 12, 1921.
24. Ibid.
25. "New York's 15,000 Cruising Taxis Make City Unsafe – Tie Up Traffic," *New York Times*, Feb. 4, 1923; "'Yellow Peril' Spreads Daily as Taxicab Fleet Increases," *New York Times*, Feb. 25, 1923; Gorman Gilbert and Robert E. Samuels, *The Taxicab: An Urban Transportation Survivor*, 2nd printing (Chapel Hill: The University of North Carolina Press, 1982), 38-39.
26. Gilbert and Samuels, 38-39.
27. Gilbert and Samuels, 66.
28. "New York's 15,000 Cruising..."
29. Graham Russell Gao Hodges, *Taxi! A Social History of the New York City Cabdriver* (Baltimore: The Johns Hopkins University Press, 2007), 21.
30. "Reduce Taxi Fares, Fosdick Suggests," *New York Times*, Jan. 24, 1912; "'Yellow Peril' Spreads Daily..."
31. "'Yellow Peril' Spreads Daily..."
32. "Whole Police Force Hunts Taxi Slayer," *New York Times*, Jul 29, 1923.
33. "Taxi Driver Admits That..."
34. Ibid.
35. Ibid.
36. "Taxi Man Indicted for Killing Kenny," *New York Times*, Feb. 14, 1925; "Dennis J. Kenny Dies..."
37. "Police Continue Taxicab Clean-Up..."
38. "All Taxis Halted as 5,000 Policemen Question Drivers," *New York Times*, Feb. 13: 1925.
39. Ibid.
40. Ibid.
41. Ibid.
42. "Police Continue Taxicab Clean-Up..."; "All Taxis Halted as..."
43. "All Taxis Halted as..."

44   "48 Taxi Drivers Held; Slain Youth is Buried," *Washington Post*, Feb. 15, 1925.

45   "Hylan Tells Police of His Plan to End Taxicab Outrages," *New York Times*, Feb. 24, 1925; Hodges, 35.

46   "Slayer of Kenny Gets 20-Year Term," *New York Times*, Mar. 10, 1925.

47   "Police Hold 3 for Pool Selling Following Raid," *Hartford Courant*, Nov. 16, 1921; "Bookie Gets $300 Fine, Suspended Sentence," *Hartford Courant*, May 16, 1962.

48   Gilbert and Samuels, 42.

49   Ibid, 71-72.

50   Hodges, 44-45.

51   Gilbert and Samuels, 68.

52   Raymond S. Tompkins, "The Taxicab Runs Amuck," *American Mercury*, August 1932, 385-394.

53   Hawley S. Simpson, "The Taxicab Industry Faces a Crisis," *American Electric Railway Association* 23, no. 4 (Mar. 1932); Hawley S. Simpson, "Regulation of the Taxicab as a Public Utility," *American Electric Railway Association* 23, no. 4 (Apr. 1932); Hawley S. Simpson, "Essential Features of Taxicab Laws and Ordinances," *American Electric Railway Association* 23, no. 5 (May 1932),

54   Gilbert and Samuels, 62-64.

55   Hawley S. Simpson, "The Carpet-Bagger Appears in the Transportation Industry," *American Electric Railway Association* 22 (Dec. 1931).

56   Simpson, "The Taxicab Industry Faces..."

57   City of New York, *Report of the Mayor's Commission on Taxicabs*, Chairman Frank P. Walsh, New York City: Sep. 23, 1930.

58   Ibid.

59   Simpson, "The Taxicab Industry Faces..."

60   Simpson, "Essential Features of..."; Gilbert and Samuels, 70-71.

61   Bruce Schaller, "Entry Controls in Taxi Regulation: Implications of US and Canadian experience for taxi regulation and deregulation," *Transport Policy* 14 (2007): 490-506, accessed Feb. 3, 2016, http://schallerconsult.com/taxi/entrycontrol.pdf.

62   Ibid.

63   Craig Leisy, "Taxicab Deregulation and Reregulation in Seattle: Lessons Learned," Paper presented at the *International Association of Transportation Regulators (IATR) Conference, Quebec, Canada, September 11, 2001*; *Capitol Taxicab Co. v. Cermak*, 60 F.2d 608 (ND Illinois 1932).

64   Hodges, 49-50.

65   Herbert Mitgang, *Once Upon a Time in New York: Jimmy Walker, Franklin Roosevelt, and the Last Great Battle of the Jazz Age* (New York: The Free Press, 2000), 200-203.

66   Ibid, 57-59.

67   Stanley Lebergott, "Labor Force, Employment, and Unemployment, 1929-39: Estimating Methods," Monthly Labor Review 67 (July 1948): 50-53, accessed Aug. 9, 2017, https://www.bls.gov/opub/mlr/1948/article/pdf/labor-force-employment-and-unemployment-1929-39-estimating-methods.pdf; "The New York City Taxicab Fact Book," Schaller Consulting, Mar. 2006, p. 30, accessed Apr. 10, 2016, http://schallerconsult.com/taxi/taxifb.pdf.

68   *Rudack v. Valentine*, 295 NYS 976 (Sup. Ct. NY Co. 1937).

69   "Taxi Limit Law Signed," *New York Times*, Mar. 10, 1937; Gilbert and Samuels, 184 (SEE endnote no. 15 of Chapter 5).

70   Hodges, 66-67.

71   Gilbert and Samuels, 83-85, 92.

72   Schaller, "The New York City...," 30.

73   Ibid, 41.

74   Ibid, 27.

75   Gilbert and Samuels, 91-94.

76   Hodges, 147-150; Gilbert and Samuels, 103-106.

77   Ibid.

78   Anna Quindlen, "City Studies Leasing of Cabs to Drivers," *New York Times*Error! **Bookmark not defined.**, Dec. 1, 1978.

79   Robin Herman, "Taxi Panel Votes 5-2 to Allow Cab Leasing by Owners to Drivers," *New York Times*, Feb. 15, 1979.

80   Joseph Longmeyer, "See Bloodshed in Cab Lease Fight," *Chicago Defender*, Jul. 8, 1975; "Plans to Lease Taxis is Debated," *New York Times*, Dec. 2, 1978.

81   Hodges, 149-150.

82   Ibid, 158-160.

83   Gilbert and Samuels, 161-164; Hodges, 172.

84   Hodges, 172.

85   Gilbert and Samuels, 185 (see endnote no. 1).

86   Sam Peltzman, "The Economic Theory of Regulation After a Decade of Deregulation," *Brookings Papers on*

Economic Activity: Microeconomics (1989), accessed Aug. 10, 2017, https://www.brookings.edu/wp-content/uploads/1989/01/1989_bpeamicro_peltzman.pdf.

87 "Airlines Move to Meet Regulatory Shifts," *Aviation Week & Space Technology*, Nov. 6, 1978, accessed Aug. 10, 2017, http://aviationweek.com/site-files/aviationweek.com/files/uploads/2015/06/1978-U.S.%20Airline%20Deregulation.pdf.

88 Clifford Winston, "The Success of the Staggers Rail Act of 1980," AEI-Brookings Joint Center for Regulatory Studies, October 2005, accessed Aug. 10, 2017, https://www.brookings.edu/wp-content/uploads/2016/06/10_railact_winston.pdf.

89 Federal Trade Commission, Bureau of Economics Staff Report, *An Economic Analysis of Taxicab Regulation*, by Mark W. Frankena and Paul A. Pautler, May 1984, pp. 155-156, accessed Feb. 6, 2016, https://www.ftc.gov/sites/default/files/documents/reports/economic-analysis-taxicab-regulation/233832.pdf; Richard B. Coffman, 1977, "The Economic Reasons for Price and Entry Regulation of Taxicabs: A Comment," *Journal of Transportation Economics and Policy* 11(3): 288-304; David J. Williams, 1980, "The Economic Reasons for Price and Entry Regulation of Taxicabs: A Comment," *Journal of Transportation Economics and Policy* 14(1): 105-112.

90 Price Waterhouse, "Analysis of Taxicab Deregulation and Re-Regulation," study funded by the International Taxicab Foundation, Nov. 8, 1993, p. 6, accessed Aug. 10, 2017, https://www.colorado.gov/pacific/sites/default/files/0708TransAttachI.pdf.

91 Ibid, 7.

92 Ibid, 11-16.

93 Ibid, 8-9.

94 Paul Stephen Dempsey, "Taxi Industry Regulation, Deregulation & Reregulation: the Paradox of Market Failure," *Transportation Law Journal* 24 (Summer 1996): 869-871.

95 Ibid.

96 Price Waterhouse, 17-19.

97 For example, see: Robert M. Hardaway, "Taxi and Limousines: The Last Bastion of Economic Regulation," *Hamline Journal of Public Law and Policy* 21 (No. 2), Spring 2000, pp. 382-383.

Chapter 2

1   Hodges, 154.

2   Ibid, 134.

3   City of Los Angeles, Department of Transportation (DOT), *Annual Review of the Bandit Taxicab Enforcement Program for 2011*, memorandum from DOT General Manager Jaime de la Vega to the Board of Taxicab Commissioners, Jun. 21, 2012

4   Ibid.

5   "Final Chapter Written in Saga of Westgate," New York Times, May 6, 1982, accessed Aug. 10, 2017, http://www.nytimes.com/1982/05/06/business/final-chapter-written-in-saga-of-westgate.html; Heidi Machen and Jordanna Thigpen, "Overview of the San Francisco Taxi Industry and Proposition K," accessed Feb. 21, 2016, http://www.taxi-library.org/overview-of-prop-k.pdf.

6   "Overview of the San Francisco…"; "2010 Conference – Session 5 – Christiane Hayashi – Taxi Medallion Sales Pilot Program – Part 1," Youtube video, 14:46, posted by "taxicabregulators," May 20, 2011, https://youtu.be/D7T1QM-7GO8.

7   Ibid.

8   Ibid.

9   Ibid.

10 JL Pimsleur, "SF Commission Extends Freeze on Taxi Permits," *San Francisco Chronicle*, Dec. 6, 1985; JL Pimsleur, "Cab Permit Debate Overheats," *San Francisco Chronicle*, Dec. 12, 1986; JL Pimsleur, "Panel Delays Decision on Taxi Permits," *San Francisco Chronicle*, May 15, 1987; LA Chung, "Cabbies Protest at City Hall," *San Francisco Chronicle*, Mar 7, 1991; Clarence Johnson, "SF's Taxi Measure Prompts Bitter Fight," *San Francisco Chronicle*, Oct. 25, 1993; Emerald Yeh and Christine McMurry, "Are San Francisco Cabs a Bit Too Rare?" *San Francisco Chronicle*, Sep. 15, 1996; Stephen Schwartz, "SF Panel Votes to Allow Additional Taxis in City," *San Francisco Chronicle*, Jul. 39, 1998; Edward Epstein, "SF Taxi Deal Rejected by Supervisors," *San Francisco Chronicle*, Apr. 13, 1999.

11 "Overview of the San Francisco…"

12 "2010 Conference – Session 5 – Christiane Hayashi – Taxi Medallion Sales Pilot Program – Part 1."

13 Ibid.

14 Bernie Langer, "Counties with the Highest Population Density in 2009," *PolicyMap.com*, Apr. 20, 2010, accessed Aug. 11, 2017, https://www.policymap.com/2010/04/top-10-counties-with-the-highest-population-density-in-2009/;

Robbie Gonzalez, "Half of the US lives in these 146 counties – is yours one of them?" *Gizmodo*, Sep. 5, 2013, http://io9.gizmodo.com/half-of-the-u-s-lives-in-these-146-counties-is-yours-1258718775.

15   Daytime residents based on: US Census Bureau, "Commuter-Adjusted Population Estimates: ACS 2006-10," by Brian McKenzie, William, Koerber, Alison Fields, Megan Benetsky, and Melanie Rapino, p.12, accessed Aug. 11, 2017, https://www.census.gov/content/dam/Census/library/working-papers/2010/demo/commuter-adjusted-population-paper.pdf.

16   City and County of San Francisco, Office of the Controller, City Services Auditor, *2005 Taxi Commission Survey Report*, Feb. 7, 2006., accessed Jan. 1, 2016, http://sfcontroller.org/ftp/uploadedfiles/controller/reports/Taxi_020806.pdf.

17   City and County of San Francisco, Taxi Commission, *Public Convenience and Necessity Report*, February 13, 2007, accessed Feb. 27, 2016, http://web.archive.org/web/20100416034036/http://www.sfgov.org/site/uploadedfiles/February13_2007PublicConvenienceNecessityReport.pdf.

18   Kyle Russell, "This One Intersection Explains Why Housing is So Expensive in San Francisco," *Business Insider*, Apr. 8, 2014, accessed Aug. 11, 2017, http://www.businessinsider.com/why-housing-is-so-expensive-in-san-francisco-2014-4.

19   Chris McCann, "1979 to 2015 – Average Rent in San Francisco," *Medium*, Aug 17, 2015, accessed Aug. 11, 2017, https://medium.com/@mccannatron/1979-to-2015-average-rent-in-san-francisco-33aaea22de0e; Jonathan Miller, "Tracking New York Rents and Asking Prices Over a Century," *Curbed*, Jun 2, 2015, accessed Aug. 11, 2017, https://ny.curbed.com/2015/6/2/9954250/tracking-new-york-rents-and-asking-prices-over-a-century.

20   FailCon, "Home," accessed Aug. 11, 2017, http://thefailcon.com.

21   "FailCon 2011 – Uber Case Study," Youtube video, 26:18, posted by "BAMM.tv," Nov. 3, 2011, https://youtu.be/2QrX5jsiico.

22   Ibid.

23   "Travis Kalanick of Uber – TwiST #180," Youtube video, 1:21:38, posted by "This Week in Startups," Aug. 16, 2011, https://youtu.be/550X5OZVk7Y.

24   Karl Taro Greenfeld, "Meet the Napster," *CNN*, Sep. 25, 2000, accessed Aug. 11, 2017, http://edition.cnn.com/ALLPOLITICS/time/2000/10/02/napster.html.

25   Jefferson Graham, "Scour Seeks Post-Napster Path Despite Access to Bootlegs," *USA Today*, May 30, 2000.

26   Benny Evangelista, "Scour Expands Napster's Concept Beyond Swapping Music," *San Francisco Chronicle*, May 18, 2000.

27   "FailCon 2011..."

28   Ibid.

29   Jefferson Graham, "Scour Seeks Post-Napster..."

30   "Travis Kalanick of Uber..."

31   "FailCon 2011..."

32   "Travis Kalanick of Uber..."

33   "FailCon 2011..."

34   For example, see Ibid.

35   Ibid; "Travis Kalanick of Uber..."

36   Alyson Shontell, "All Hail the Uber Man! How Sharp-Elbowed Salesman Travis Kalanick Became Silicon Valley's Newest Star," *Business Insider*, Jan. 11, 2014, accessed Oct. 27, 2016, http://read.bi/1cOCY5i; Maya Kosoff, "This is the First YouTube Video Ever Uploaded – It Was Posted 10 Years Ago Today," *Business Insider*, Apr. 23, 2015, accessed Aug. 11, 2017, http://www.businessinsider.com/first-youtube-video-2015-4.

37   "Travis Kalanick of Uber..."

38   Shontell, "All Hail the Uber..."

39   "FailCon 2011..."

40   Shontell, "All Hail the Uber..."

41   "Failcon 2011..."

42   Ibid; "Travis Kalanick of Uber..."

43   Ibid.

44   Ibid.

45   US Securities and Exchange Commission, *Akamai Technologies, Inc., Form 10-Q, For the Quarterly Period Ended June 30, 2007*, Commission file no. 0-27275 (Washington, DC, 2007), Note no. 2 to Unaudited Condensed Consolidated Financial Statements, accessed Aug. 11, 2017, https://www.sec.gov/Archives/edgar/data/1086222/000119312507177435/d10q.htm.

46   "Travis Kalanick of Uber..."

47   "Travis Kalanick, Founder and CEO of Uber – Tech Cocktail Startup Mixology," Youtube video, 34:35, posted by "TechCo Media," Jun. 14, 2012, https://youtu.be/Lrp0me9iJ_U.

48   Ibid – see presentation slide at 11:23.

49 "Travis Kalanick Startup Lessons From the Jam Pad – Tech Cocktail Startup Mixology," Youtube video, 38:34, posted by "TechCo Media," May 5, 2011, https://youtu.be/VMvdvP02f-Y.

50 "Travis Kalanick, Founder and CEO..."

51 "Travis Kalanick of Uber..."

52 Nick Gonzalez, "eBay's StumbleUpon Acquisition…," *TechCrunch*, May 30, 2007, accessed Sep. 21, 2017, http://tcrn.ch/2hhQjzn.

53 Stone, Brad, *The Upstarts: How Uber, Airbnb, and the Killer Companies of the New Silicon Valley are Changing the World* (New York, NY: Little, Brown and Company, 2017), 48-52.

54 "Travis Kalanick, Founder and CEO..."; "How Travis Kalanick Decided Uber Should Take On the Taxi Industry | Inc. Magazine," Youtube video, 2:55, posted by "Inc.," Apr. 9, 2012, https://youtu.be/Ets-mAfdHQ0.

55 "Travis Kalanick of Uber..."; Travis [Kalanick], "Uber's Founding," *Newsroom* (blog), Uber, Dec. 22, 2010, accessed Jan. 6, 2016, https://newsroom.uber.com/ubers-founding.

56 Ibid.

57 Kalanick, "Uber's Founding."

58 "How Travis Kalanick Decided..."

59 Jennifer Steinhauer, "California Joblessness Reaches 70-Year High," *New York Times*, Sep. 18, 2009, accessed Aug. 11, 2017, http://nyti.ms/2eLd8qq.

60 Kalanick, "Uber's Founding."

61 "Ryan Graves | LinkedIn," LinkedIn.com, accessed Mar. 26, 2016, https://www.linkedin.com/in/ragraves; "Thinc Iowa 2012 – Ryan Graves," Youtube video, 39:20, posted by "Big Omaha," Nov. 1, 2012, https://youtu.be/JdNmG1CtPMw.

62 "Thinc Iowa 2012..."

63 Kalanick, "Uber's Founding."

64 Andy Kessler, "Travis Kalanick: The Transportation Trustbuster," *Wall Street Journal*, Jan. 25, 2013, accessed Mar. 12, 2016, http://www.wsj.com/articles/SB10001424127887324235104578244231122376480.

65 Ryan (the guy at the wheel) [Graves], "Why Taxi's Suck.," *The Uber Blog*, Mar. 25, 2010, accessed May 7, 2016, https://web.archive.org/web/20150626015125/http://ubercab.tumblr.com/post/472859174/why-taxis-suck.

66 Ibid.

67 For example, see: [Untitled Twitter re-post], *The Uber Blog*, Mar 27, 2010, accessed May 7, 2016, https://web.archive.org/web/20150626015119/http://ubercab.tumblr.com/post/477502007/can-you-believe-this-crap-send-your.

68 [Untitled], *The Uber Blog*, Apr. 16, 2010, accessed May 7, 2016, https://web.archive.org/web/20150626015024/http://ubercab.tumblr.com/post/525843121/so-not-uber-via-gawker-is-this-what-happens.

69 [Untitled], *The Uber Blog*, Apr. 17, 2010, accessed May 7, 2016, https://web.archive.org/web/20150626015028/http://ubercab.tumblr.com/post/528092438/according-to-the-taxi-limousine-commission.

70 Ryan [Graves], "Entrepreneurial, Rockstar Engineer Needed. Ground Floor Opportunity With Amazing Advisors & Team," *The Uber Blog*, Mar. 30, 2010, accessed May 7, 2016, https://web.archive.org/web/20151030070803/http://ubercab.tumblr.com/post/485301492/entrepreneurial-rockstar-engineer-needed-ground.

71 Ibid.

72 "UberCab Mashups, a Match Made in Heaven.," *The Uber Blog*, Apr. 14, 2010, accessed May 7, 2016, https://web.archive.org/web/20150626015055/http://ubercab.tumblr.com/post/522545356/ubercab-mashups-a-match-made-in-heaven.

73 Ryan [Graves], [Untitled], *The Uber Blog*, May 27, 2010, accessed May 7, 2016, https://web.archive.org/web/20150626015029/http://ubercab.tumblr.com/post/638639298/this-weekend-were-really-hoping-to-get-things.

74 "We're Running Our Own Groupon, 50% Off Rides!!!" *The Uber Blog*, Aug. 8, 2010, accessed May 7, 2016, https://web.archive.org/web/20150626015008/http://ubercab.tumblr.com/post/909175057/were-running-our-own-groupon-50-off-rides.

75 Michael Arrington, "What if UberCab Pulss an Airbnb? Taxi Business Could (Finally) Get Some Disruption," *TechCrunch*, Aug. 31, 2010, accessed Aug, 12, 2017, http://tcrn.ch/2eKCrcc; Jon, "Physical Web: how Apps Can Move Atoms & Bend Time," *TrueVentures*, Sep. 3, 2010, accessed Aug 12, 2017, https://web.archive.org/web/20110703210813/http://www.trueventures.com/2010/09/03/physical-web-how-apps-can-move-atoms-bend-time/.

76 "An Integrated Enterpise is Within Reach – Curtis Chambers, Uber," Youtube video, 13:59, posted by "TIBCO Mashery," Oct. 18, 2013, https://youtu.be/fO83dyxa0Vo.

77 Ryan Graves, "Uber Service Disruption: Friday 12/10/2010," *The Uber Blog*, Dec. 11, 2010, accessed Jan. 16, 2016, https://web.archive.org/web/20110112074509/http://blog.uber.com/2010/12/11/uber-service-disruption-friday-

12102010/.

78   "2013 State of the Net Luncheon Keynote: Rep Goodlatte w/ Travis Kalanick, CEO of UBER," Yooube video, 36:35, posted by "Congressional Internet Caucus Advisory Committee," Jan. 24, 2013, https://youtu.be/gFgjEGgS5-o.

79   Henry [Lin], "When Google ETAs Fail," *Newsroom* (blog), Jun. 14, 2011, accessed Jan. 16, 2016, https://newsroom.uber.com/when-google-fails.

80   Graves, "Uber Service Disruption..."

81   Ryan Graves, "Huge Hurts: Demand Prediction in Uberland," *The Uber Blog*, Nov. 17, 2010, accessed May 7, 2016, https://web.archive.org/web/20101126031555/http://blog.uberapp.com/2010/11/17/huge-hurts-demand-prediction-in-uberland/.

82   "2010 Conference – Session 5 – Christiane Hayashi – Taxi Medallion Sales Pilot Program – Part 1."

83   City and County of San Francisco, Department of Elections, Ballot Simplification Committee, *Voter Information Pamphlet*, Sep. 17, 2007, p. 116, accessed Oct. 30, 2016, https://sfpl4.sfpl.org/pdf/main/gic/elections/November6_2007.pdf.

84   "2010 Conference – Session 5 – Christiane Hayashi – Taxi Medallion Sales Pilot Program – Part 1."

85   *Voter Information Pamphlet*, 46.

86   Rachel Gordon, "Propositions A and H Inflame Passions Over Parking," *San Francisco Chronicle*, Oct. 20, 2007.

87   Rachel Gordon, "SF Supervisors Move to Hold Hearings Into Elections Mismanagement Charges," *San Francisco Chronicle*, May 22, 2001.

88   Edward Epstein and Jonathan Curiel, "Runoff for Most Supervisor Spots," *San Francisco Chronicle*, Nov. 8, 2000.

89   Matthew Yi, "California's Budget Crisis – Fiscal Emergency: Gap Will Leap By Millions Each Day," *San Francisco Chronicle*, Jul. 2, 2009.

90   Rachel Gordon, "San Francisco's Budget Deficit," *San Francisco Chronicle*, Nov. 20, 2009; Rachel Gordon, "Muni Facing Financial Crisis," *San Francisco Chronicle*, Apr. 1, 2009.

91   Erin Allday, "Newsom Sees Budget Relief in Coveted Taxi Medallions," *San Francisco Chronicle*, Jan. 13, 2009.

92   "2010 Conference – Session 5 – Christiane Hayashi – Taxi Medallion Sales Pilot Program – Part 2," Youtube video, 14:15, posted by "taxicabregulators," May 20, 2011, https://youtu.be/nqvbeQAAZ64.

93   "2010 Conference – Session 5 – Christiane Hayashi – Taxi Medallion Sales Pilot Program – Part 1."

94   "2010 Conference – Session 5 – Christiane Hayashi – Taxi Medallion Sales Pilot Program – Part 2."

95   "How Demoting Christiane Hayashi Backfired," *The Phantom Cab Driver Phites Back* (blog), May 19, 2014, accessed Jul 27, 2016, http://phantomcabdriverphites.blogspot.com/2014/05/how-demoting-hayashi-backfired.html.

96   "2010 Conference – Session 5 – Christiane Hayashi – Taxi Medallion Sales Pilot Program – Part 2," see presentation slide at 4:56.

97   Ibid.

98   Ibid.

99   San Francisco Municipal Transportation Agency, Taxi Services, Taxi Advisory Council, *Sept. 13, 2010 minutes*, Item 5 – Public Comment, accessed Jan. 1, 2016, http://archives.sfmta.com/cms/ctac/TACSept.132010minutes.htm.

100 SFMTA Division of Taxis & Accessible Services, "Uber Cab advertising," email to Christiane Hayashi, et al, Sep. 24, 2010.

101 Onesimo Flores Dewey and Lisa Rayle, "How Ridesourcing Went From 'Rogue' to Mainstream in San Francisco," p. 13, working paper, Harvard University Graduate School of Design, accessed Nov. 4, 2016, www.transformingurbantransport.com/s/San-Francisco-Case-2016.pdf.

102 Michael Arrington, "UberCab Closes Uber Angel Round," *TechCrunch*, Oct. 15, 2010, accessed Aug. 12, 2017, http://tcrn.ch/2wMEwyZ.

103 SFMTA Enforcement and Legal Affairs Manager Jarvis Murray to Ryan Graves, Oct. 20, 2010, San Francisco Municipal Transportation Agency.

104 Ibid.

105 Ibid.

106 Ibid.

107 Ibid.

108 CPUC Investigator Brian Kahrs to Ryan Graves, Oct. 19, 2010, California Public Utilities Commission, Consumer Protection and Safety Division, Transportation Enforcement Section.

109 "We've Always been Uber, Now It's Official.," *The Uber Blog*, Oct. 25, 2010, accessed May 7, 2016, https://web.archive.org/web/20150926093621/http://ubercab.tumblr.com:80/post/1400235579/weve-always-been-uber-now-its-official.

110 "Travis Kalanick of Uber..."

1   Daniel T. Rockey, "FTC Investigates Ann Taylor…," Boulivant Houser Bailey, PC (blog), May 2010,
    http://web.archive.org/web/20100620175804/http://www.bullivant.com/Blogger-Endorsement-Guidelines.

2   Daniel Rockey to CPUC Senior Investigator Edward A. Rouquette, Nov. 8, 2010, California Public Utilities
    Commission, Consumer Protection and Safety Division.

3   Ibid; "Uber Has Been Served," *The Uber Blog*, Oct. 24, 2010,
    https://web.archive.org/web/20150626014923/http://ubercab.tumblr.com/post/1391350687/uber-has-been-served.

4   Kahrs to Graves.

5   Rockey to Rouquette.

6   Ibid.

7   Ibid.

8   Ibid.

9   Christiane Hayashi, "RE: Uber," email to Jarvis Murray, Dec. 6, 2010.

10 San Francisco Municipal Transportation Agency, Taxi Services, Taxi Advisory Council, *Minutes – Monday, April
    25, 2011*, Item 5 – Public Comment, accessed Jan. 1, 2016,
    http://archives.sfmta.com/cms/ctac/TACApril252011minutes.htm.

11 Paul Rogers, "San Bruno Blast: PG&E Settles Nearly All Remaining Lawsuits for a $565 Million Total," *Mercury
    News* (San Jose, California), Sep. 9. 2013, accessed Aug. 12, 2017, http://www.mercurynews.com/2013/09/09/san-
    bruno-blast-pge-settles-nearly-all-remaining-lawsuits-for-a-565-million-total/.

12 US National Transportation Safety Board (NTSB), *Pipeline Accident Report – Pacific Gas and Electric Company,
    Natural Gas Transmission Pipeline Rupture and Fire, San Bruno, California, September 9, 2010*, NTSB/PAR-11/01
    PB2011-916501, p. x, https://www.ntsb.gov/investigations/AccidentReports/Reports/PAR1101.pdf.

13 NTSB, p. x.

14 Lee Ferran, Leezel Tanglao, and Bradley Blackburn, "San Bruno Gas Explosion: Fire Contained, But Homes Still
    Too Hot to Search," *ABC News*, Sep. 10, 2010, accessed Aug 12, 2017, http://abcn.ws/2gM3tRe.

15 NTSB, p. x.

16 Dan Weikel, "San Bruno Pipeline Explosion: 'A Failure of the Entire System,'" *Los Angeles Times*, Aug. 30, 2011,
    accessed Nov. 5, 2016, http://lat.ms/2wNV47g.

17 NTSB, 87.

18 Ibid, 75.

19 Ibid, 135.

20 Business Advantage Consulting, "California Public Utilities Commission Safety Culture Change Project – Initial
    Discovery Report," Jan. 25, 2013.

21 "Disrupting Offline Businesses: Brian Chesky, Airbnb and Travis Kalanick, Uber," Ustream.tv video, May 25, 2011,
    http://www.ustream.tv/recorded/14949255.

22 Ryan Graves and Travis Kalanick, "1 + 1 =3," *The Uber Blog*, Dec. 20, 2010, accessed Jan. 16, 2016,
    https://web.archive.org/web/20110112070219/http://blog.uber.com/2010/12/22/1-1-3/.

23 Ibid.

24 Angie Chang, "Expensify Raises $1M for Online Expense Reporting," *VentureBeat*, Aug. 12, 2009, accessed Nov.
    16, 2016, http://venturebeat.com/2009/08/12/expensify-raises-1m-for-online-expense-reporting/.

25 "An Integrated Enterprise is Within…"

26 Ibid.

27 "Kevin Love Shows his Love for Uber…," *Newsroom* (blog), Oct. 1, 2012, accessed Sep. 21, 2017,
    https://newsroom.uber.com/us-minnesota/kevin-love-shows-his-love-for-uber-secret-ubers-take-over-the-twin-
    cities/.

28 [Bradley] Voytek, "Comparing Uber to Cabs' Hidden Costs," *Newsroom* (blog), Apr. 11, 2011, accessed Jan. 16,
    2016, https://newsroom.uber.com/uberdata-the-hidden-cost-of-cabs.

29 [Bradley] Voytek, "Mapping the San Franciscome," *Newsroom* (blog), Jan. 9, 2012, accessed Jan. 16, 2016,
    https://newsroom.uber.com/sf/uberdata-san-franciscomics.

30 "How Crime Location Knowledge is a Proxy for Uber Demand," *Newsroom* (blog), Sep. 13, 2011, accessed Jan. 16,
    2016, https://newsroom.uber.com/crime-knowledge-demand-proxy.

31 [Bradley] Voytek, "Uberdata: The Ride of Glory," *Uber Blog*, Mar. 26, 2012, accessed Nov. 6, 2016,
    http://web.archive.org/web/20120330113815/http://blog.uber.com/2012/03/26/uberdata-the-ride-of-glory.

32 "Disrupting Offline Businesses…"; [Bradley] Voytek, "Mapping San Francisco, New York, and the World with
    Uber," *Newsroom* (blog), May 16, 2011, accessed Jan. 1, 2016, https://newsroom.uber.com/uberdata-mapping-san-
    francisco-new-york-and-the-world.

33 [Bradley] Voytek, "Mapping San Francisco, New York, and the World with Uber," *Newsroom* (blog), May 16, 2011,

accessed Jan. 16, 2016, https://newsroom.uber.com/uberdata-mapping-san-francisco-new-york-and-the-world.

34   Travis [Kalanick], "Halloween Surge Pricing: Get an Uber at the Witching Hour, *The Uber Blog*, Oct. 26, 2011, accessed Nov. 6, 2016, http://web.archive.org/web/20111031081700/http://blog.uber.com/2011/10/26/halloween-surge-pricing-get-an-uber-at-the-witching-hour.

35   Austin [Geidt], "NYE Madness: Fare Increase & VIP Auction," *The Uber Blog*, Dec. 28, 2010, accessed Nov. 6, 2016, http://web.archive.org/web/20110112074530/http://blog.uber.com/2010/12/28/nye-madness-fare-increase-vip-auction.

36   Kalanick, "Halloween Surge Pricing..."

37   "A Data Science Chat with Kevin Novak from Uber," Youtube video, 38:00, posted by "Rackspace," Jul. 8, 2014, https://youtu.be/HIbzibEAcr8.

38   Travis [Kalanick], "Surge Pricing Followup," *Newsroom* (blog), Jan. 3, 2012, accessed Apr. 15, 2016, https://newsroom.uber.com/surge-pricing-followup.

39   Ibid.

40   Ibid.

41   Jenna Wortham, "With a Start-Up Company, a Ride is Just a Tap of an App Away," *New York Times*, May 4, 2011; Travis [Kalanick], "You are Now Free to Move About Seattle," *Newsroom* (blog), Aug. 12, 2011, accessed Mar. 27, 2016, https://newsroom.uber.com/uswashington/you-are-now-free-to-move-about-seattle; Alex Wilhelm, "Uber Comes to Chicago, Makes You Feel Important: Guest," *NBCchicago.com*, Sep. 27, 2011, accessed Aug. 13, 2017, http://www.nbcchicago.com/blogs/inc-well/Uber-Comes-to-Chicago-Makes-you-Feel-Important-Guest-130629798.html; Travis [Kalanick], "Uber Bahsstuhn is Live!" *Newsroom* (blog), Oct. 24, 2011, accessed Apr. 4, 2016, https://newsroom.uber.com/usmassachusetts/uber-bahsstuhn-is-live; Travis [Kalanick]," Uber and DC: Opposites Attract," *The Uber Blog*, Dec. 15, 2011, accessed Jan 16, 2016, https://web.archive.org/web/20120108144712/http://blog.uber.com/2011/12/15/uber-and-dc-opposites-attract.

42   James [Aviaz], "Celebrating Uber's NYC Launch!" *The Uber Blog*, May 4, 2011, accessed Jan. 16, 2016, https://web.archive.org/web/20110516224547/http://blog.uber.com:80/2011/05/04/celebrating-ubers-nyc-launch; "The Top Angel Investors: Behind the Rankings," *Bloomberg.com*, Feb. 25, 2010, accessed Aug. 13, 2017, https://bloom.bg/2xaG4CX.

43   Stone, 156, 163-164.

44   Stephanie Mehta, "Meet Uber's Political Genius," *Vanity Fair*, Jun. 17, 2016, accessed, Nov. 7, 2016, http://www.vanityfair.com/news/2016/06/bradley-tusk-fanduel-uber.

45   New York City Taxi & Limousine Commission, "ATTENTION: FHV Bases Using Smartphone Apps for Dispatch and Developers of Smartphone Apps for Dispatch," Jul. 18, 2011, Industry Notice #11-16, http://www.nyc.gov/html/tlc/downloads/pdf/industry_notice_11_16.pdf.

46   New York TLC Assistant General Counsel Christopher C. Wilson to Uber, Dec. 12, 2011, New York Taxi & Limousine Commission.

47   Schaller, "Entry Controls...," p.6.

48   In 1930, the US Senate proposed S. 3615, allowing DC to regulate taxis by issuing certificates of convenience and public necessity, but the certificate language was eventually removed. See: US Congress, Senate, Subcommittee of the Committee on the District of Columbia, *Hearing on S. 3615, a Bill to Amend Section 8 of the Act...*, 71st Cong., 2nd sess., Apr. 28, 1930, 6; US Congress, House of Representatives, Committee on the District of Columbia, *Report (to Accompany S. 3615)*, 71st Cong., 2nd sess., 1930, H. Rep. no. 2046.

49   Kriston Capps, "Which is More Evil...," *Citylab*, Jan. 6, 2015, accessed Sep. 21, 2017, https://www.citylab.com/transportation/2015/01/which-is-more-evil-uber-or-dcs-old-taxi-zone-system/384232/.

50   Sue Anne Pressley Montes, "Is Meters vs. Zones Debate Over?" *Washington Post*, Jun 23, 2006.

51   Joshua Zumbrun, "Fenty to Start Taxi Meter at $3 for All," *Washington Post*, Jan. 17, 2008; Sam Staley, "A Cab Medallion System in DC? The Neighborhoods Will Pay the Price," *Washington Post*, Apr. 2, 2011; Mike DeBonis, "Cheh to Propose Bill to Overhaul Taxi Service," *Washington Post*, Dec. 19, 2011.

52   Del Quentin Wilber, "DC Taxi Official Turned FBI Informant Recalls Role in Corruption Probe," *Washington Post*, Apr. 2, 2012.

53   Benjamin Freed, "Former DC Taxi Commissioner Ron Linton Dies at 86," *Washingtonian*, Jun 29, 2015, accessed Apr. 26, 2016, http://www.washingtonian.com/2015/06/29/former-dc-taxi-commissioner-ron-linton-dies-at-86.

54   DeBonis, "Cheh to Propose Bill..."

55   Freed, "Former DC Taxi Commissioner..."

56   Thomas Heath, "Technology Firms Heat Up in Taxi Wars in Washington Region," *Washington Post*, Dec. 15, 2011.

57   District of Columbia, Taxicab Commission, *Full Commission Meeting – [transcript]*, Wednesday, January 11, 2012, DC Taxicab Commission, pp. 27-29.

58   Rachel [Holt], "Life, Liberty, and the Pursuit of Uberness: @Uber_DC Needs YOU!" *The Uber Blog*, Jan. 11, 2012, accessed Jan. 16, 2016, https://web.archive.org/web/20120113020339/http://blog.uber.com/2012/01/11/uberdc-needs-you; Eric Eldon, "Here We Go Again: DC Taxi Head Says Uber is 'Operating Illegally,' to be 'Dealt With,'" *TechCrunch*, Jan. 11, 2012, accessed Nov. 9, 2016, https://techcrunch.com/2012/01/11/uberalles; Benjamin Freed,

"Uber is Hacking Into Washington's Taxi Industry, Linton Says," *DCist,* Jan. 11, 2012, accessed Apr. 15, 2016, http://dcist.com/2012/01/uber_is_hacking_into_washingtons_ta.php.

59   Mike DeBonis, "Taxi Panel Probes Uber Car Service," *Washington Post*, Jan. 12, 2012.

60   Holt, "Life, Liberty, and..."

61   Ibid.

62   Ryan Graves, Twitter post, Jan. 11, 2012, 1:36 PM, https://twitter.com/ryangraves/status/157184242944708608; Allen Penn, Twitter post, Jan 11, 2012, 1:38 PM, https://twitter.com/allenpenn/status/157184584264589312; Curtis Chambers, Twitter post, Jan. 11, 2012, 1:40 PM, https://twitter.com/curtischambers/status/157185250034855937; DC Taxi Watch, Twitter post, Jan. 11, 2012, 3:03 PM, https://twitter.com/DCTaxiWatch/status/157205908307451907.

63   Freed, "Former DC Taxi Commissioner..."

64   Mike DeBonis, "Uber Car Impounded, Driver Ticketed in City Sting," *Washington Post*, Jan. 13, 2012, http://wapo.st/2xqAT1i.

65   Travis Kalanick, Instagram picture, Jan. 13, 2012, https://www.instagram.com/p/gy4g8.

66   John Hendel, "DC Superfans Hope to Save Pricey Car Service, Crucify Ron Linton," *TBD*, Jan. 13, 2012, accessed Nov. 12, 2016, http://web.archive.org/web/20120204124747/http://www.tbd.com/blogs/tbd-on-foot/2012/01/d-c-uber-fans-hope-to-save-pricey-car-service-crucify-ron-linton-14238.html.

67   Ibid.

68   Carol Ross Joynt, "A Q&A With Travis Kalanick, CEO of Uber," *Washingtonian*, accessed Nov. 12, 2016, http://web.archive.org/web/20120219185117/http://www.washingtonian.com/blogarticles/people/capitalcomment/22263.html.

69   Freed, "Former DC Taxi Commissioner..."

70   Sam Ford, "Is Uber Illegal or Just Competition?" *WJLA.com* (ABC affiliate), press video, last edited Jul. 11, 2015, accessed Aug. 14, 2017, http://wjla.com/news/local/is-uber-illegal-or-just-competition--71415.

71   David Greene, "Upstart Car Service Butts Heads with DC's Taxis," *NPR.org* (audio transcript), Jan. 31, 2012, http://n.pr/2wNwhjS; Council of the District of Columbia, Committee on the Environment, Public Works, and Transportation, *Public Oversight Hearing on Innovations in the Public Vehicle-For-Hire Industry*, Sep. 24, 2012, Ron Linton (Government Witness), http://dc.granicus.com/MediaPlayer.php?view_id=23&clip_id=1395.

72   Carl Pierre, "Council Member Cheh Gives Uber (and DC Innovation) Some Love," *American Inno*, Jan. 17, 2012, accessed Jan. 16, 2016, https://www.americaninno.com/dc/council-member-cheh-gives-uber-and-dc-innovation-some-love/.

73   Uber DC, "Uber DC Cocktails, Innovation, and Transportation," Eventbrite.com RSVP, event of Jan. 26, 2012, accessed Jan. 16, 2016, http://www.eventbrite.com/e/uberdccocktailsinnovationandtransportationtickets2828041749.

74   "Uber CEO Travis Speaks to DC," Vimeo video, 3:03, posted by "InTheCapital," Jan. 27, 2012, https://vimeo.com/35755484.

75   Ibid.

76   Ibid.

77   Ibid.

78   Jennifer Beermann, "Life, Liberty, and the Pursuit of Uberness," *The Georgetown Dish*, Jan. 26, 2012, accessed Jan. 17, 2016, http://www.thegeorgetowndish.com/thedish/lifelibertyandpursuit%C3%Bcberness.

79   Ibid.

80   Greene, "Upstart Car Service..."

81   "Chris Sacca – Travis Kalanick Competitiveness," Youtube video, 0:50, posted by "Clemens van der Linden," Oct. 11, 2016, https://youtu.be/l-FW6oNAFhc.

Chapter 4

1   Matthew Daus, "Conference Expense Comparison," email to Craig Leisy, et al [IATR Board of Directors], Aug. 9, 2013, attachment: "ConferenceBudgetComparison.xls."

2   "Bylaws of the International Association of Transportation Regulators, Inc.," *IATR.org*, captured August 2000, http://web.archive.org/web/20000816163802/http://www.iatr.org/Bylaws/bylaws.html.

3   IATR, "News Snippets," email to Malachi Hill, Aug. 19, 2012.

4   Matthew Daus, "Professor Matthew W. Daus, Esq. Visits Washington, DC," *Black Car News*, June 2012, p. 25, accessed Aug. 14, 2017, http://www.evergreeneditions.com/publication/?i=114492&p=25.

5   US Library of Congress,

6   Matthew Daus, "PASS Act Update," email to Craig Leisy, et al [IATR Board of Directors], Jun. 28, 2013, attachment: "Fact Sheet (10852468-7).DOC.X."

7   Ibid (email only).

8   Karen Cameron, "FW: Google Alert – taxi regulation," email to Craig Leisy, Jan. 31, 2012.

9   New York City, Taxi and Limousine Commission, *Thursday, March 1, 2012, Commencing at 10:30 AM* [meeting transcript], NYC TLC, p. 12; San Francisco Municipal Transportation Agency (SFMTA), Division of Finance and Information Technology, *[staff report related to calendar item no. 13 for meeting of Jun. 5, 2012]*, SFMTA, p. 4, https://www.sfmta.com/sites/default/files/agendaitems/6-5-12item13pim.pdf.

10   NYC TLC, *March 1, 2012.*

11   New York City (NYC), Taxi and Limousine Commission (TLC), *Notice of Solicitation – Request for Proposals, Development of a Smart Phone Application for Medallion Taxicabs...*, NYC TLC, PIN: 156 12P00120.

12   Christiane Hayashi, "FW: square, uber etc," email to Matthew Daus, Feb. 15, 2012.

13   Christiane Hayashi, "RE: Uber," email to Richard Mucha, Feb. 14, 2012.

14   Gary Titlow, "UBER Service," email to Nikki Cooper, et al, Jul. 10, 2012.

15   Corey R. Pilz to Executive Director Elizabeth Lint, memorandum, RE: "Initial Review of Uber Car Service," Mar. 20, 2012, City of Cambridge, Massachusetts, Consumer's Council.

16   Ibid.

17   Malachi Hull, "Re: Uber discussion on Quora," email to Jeremy Cooker, Jul. 19, 2012.

18   Pilz to Lint, memorandum.

19   Benjamin Freed, "Cheh Shelves Uber Amendment After Backlash from CEO and Customers," *DCist*, Jul. 10, 2012, accessed Jan. 17, 2016, http://dcist.com/2012/07/cheh_shelves_uber_amendment_after_b.php.

20   Juanda Mixon, "FW: TLPA Media Watch," email to Ron Linton, May 3, 2012.

21   Ron Linton, "FW: TLPA Media Watch," email to Sharon McInnis, May 4, 2012.

22   Sharon McInnish to Chairman [Ron] Linton, memorandum, Subject: "After Action Report – Uber Ride," May 22, 2012, Government of the District of Columbia, Taxicab Commission.

23   Benajmin R. Freed, "Linton Stings Uber After Calling Livery Service 'Illegal,'" *DCist*, Jan. 13, 2012, accessed Aug. 14, 2017, http://dcist.com/2012/01/linton_stings_uber_leaves_driver_ho.php.

24   Sharon McInnis, "Uber – After Action Report," email to Ron Linton, Jun. 25, 2012, attachment: "SCAN0660_000."

25   Pedro Ribeiro, "Uber," email to Ron Linton, May 22, 2012.

26   Ron Linton, "RE: Uber," email to Pedro Ribeiro, May 23, 2012.

27   Andrew Newman, "RE: Draft Uber Amendment," email to Ron Linton, Jun. 29, 2012, 1:52 AM.

28   Andrew Newman, "Draft Uber Amendment," email to Ron Linton, Jun. 28, 2012, 4:57 PM.

29   Ron Linton, "RE: Draft Uber Amendment," email to Andrew Newman, Jun 28, 2012: 5:06 PM.

30   Ron Linton, "FW: Draft Uber Amendment," email to Dena Reed, Jun. 29, 2012, 8:58 AM.

31   Dena Reed, "RE: Draft Uber Amendment," email to Ron Linton, Jun 29, 2012, 10:23 AM.

32   Ibid.

33   Andrew Newman, "Draft Taxi Amendments," email to Ron Linton, Jul. 7, 2012, 10:42 AM, attachment: "2012 07 10 Taxi Amendments.pdf."

34   DCMR 801.3(a) [effective Apr. 20, 2012], 801 Passenger Rates and Charges, *DC Municipal Regulations and DC Register*, 59 DCR 3154, http://dcregs.dc.gov/Notice/DownLoad.aspx?NoticeID=2274667.

35   Newman email to Linton, Jul 7, 2012, attachment.

36   Dena Reed, "RE: Draft Taxi Amendments," email to Ron Linton, Jul. 9, 2012, 11:51 AM.

37   Ron Linton, "FW: Draft Taxi Amendments," email to Andrew Newman, Jul 9, 2012, 11:58 AM.

38   Andrew Newman, "RE: Draft Taxi Amendments," email to Ron Linton, Jul 9, 2012, 12:24 PM.

39   Freed, "Cheh Shelves Uber Amendment..."

40   Joshua Brustein, "A New Ride-Sharing Service Turns Private Cars Into Taxis," *New York Times*, Jun. 26, 2012, accessed May 1, 2016, http://nyti.ms/2vJNKs6.

41   Mickey Meece, "Car-Pooling, a Tough Sell, Makes a Surge on Apps and Social Media," *New York Times*, Jul. 5, 2012.

42   Brian [McMullen], "SF, You Now Have the Freedom to Choose," *Newsroom* (blog), Jul. 3, 2012, accessed Jan. 16, 2016, https://newsroom.uber.com/sf/sf-vehicle-choice.

43   Freed, "Cheh Shelves Uber Amendment..."

44   Benjamin R. Freed, "DC Council Moves Closer to Making Uber Street Legal, But Uber's Not Happy About It," *DCist*, Jul. 9, 2012, accessed Aug. 14, 2017, http://dcist.com/2012/07/dc_council_moves_closer_to_making_u.php.

45   Christopher Murphy, "Uber," email to Janene Jackson, et al., Jul. 9, 2012, 11:29 PM.

46   Ron Linton, "Re: Uber," email to Christopher Murphy, Jul. 10, 2012, 3:27 AM.

47   Alex [Priest], "Never Underestimate the Power of #UberDCLove," *The Uber Blog*, Jul. 10, 2012, accessed Jan. 17, 2016, https://web.archive.org/web/20120718230709/http://blog.uber.com/2012/07/10/never-underestimate-the-power-of-uberdclove.

48   Ron Linton, "Re: Uber," email to Christopher Murphy, Jul. 10, 2012, 7:51 AM.

49   Freed, "Cheh Shelves Uber Amendment," Eric Eldon, "DC City Council Shelves 'Uber Amendment' Against Discounted Private Cars, Road Clears for UberX (For Now)," *TechCrunch*, accessed Jan. 16, 2016, http://tcrn.ch/2xSXCBj.

50 Dena Reed, "Re: Uber Ride…," email to Ron Linton, Jul. 10, 2012, 9:05 AM.
51 Brian Chen, "Uber, an App That Summons a Car, Plans a Cheaper Service Using Hybrids," *New York Times*, Jul 1, 2012, accessed Aug. 15, 2017, https://nyti.ms/LqNgdk.
52 Council of the District of Columbia, Legislative Hearing, *Forty-First Legislative Meeting, John A. Wilson Building, Council Chamber, Tuesday, July 10, 2012*, Item VIII(B)(5), "Taxicab Commission Service Improvement Act of 2012, (Bill 19-630), http://dc.granicus.com/MediaPlayer.php?view_id=3&clip_id=1352&meta_id=42516.
53 Ibid.
54 Ibid.
55 Ibid.
56 Ibid.
57 Ibid.
58 "Uber Wars: How DC Tried to Kill a Great New Ride Technology," Youtube video, 11:01, posted by "ReasonTV," Oct. 22, 2013, https://youtu.be/4U9tMTni9dU?t=3m30s.
59 Stone, 194.
60 James Ney, "Fwd: Uber: DC," email to Christiane Hayashi, et al., Jul. 10, 2012.
61 TLD@PhilaPark.org, "Illegal Limousine Operators," email to "Taxi & Limo" [list serv], Jun. 22, 2012.
62 James Ney, "RE: Uber: DC," to Matthew Daus, Jul. 13, 2012.
63 David Yassky," The Taxi of Tomorrow and a Quick Note on Outer-Borough Hail Service," *Black Car News*, June 2011, p. 20.
64 "News and Noteworthy" [press release], WindelsMarx.com, Jun. 29, 2012, accessed Nov. 25, 2016, http://www.windelsmarx.com/news_detail.cfm?id=127.
65 Ibid; "Taxi & Livery Issues of Today & Tomorrow" [event flyer], event of Jun. 26, 2012.
66 "Legislative Forum – Taxi & Livery Issues of Today & Tomorrow," [University Transportation Research Center via] TotalWebCasting.com, Jun. 26, 2012, accessed 2016, http://www.totalwebcasting.com/view/?id=utrc.
67 Matthew W. Daus, esq, "'Rogue' Smartphone Applications for Taxicabs and Limousines: Innovation or Unfair Competition?" WindelsMarx.com, June 29, 2012, accessed Aug. 15, 2017, http://www.windelsmarx.com/resources/documents/Rogue%20Applications%20Memo%20(updated%208.6.12)%20(10777883).pdf.
68 Ibid, p. 2.
69 Ibid.
70 Ibid, p. 3; Matthew Daus, "White Paper on Smartphone Apps," email to Jim Ney, et al. [IATR Board of Directors], Jun 30, 2012.
71 Craig Leisy, "'Uber' Limousine Dispatching," email to Conan Freud and Brian Switzer, Aug. 16, 2011.
72 Justin William Moyer, "Whole Foods to Pay $500,000 for Overcharging NYC Customers," *Washington Post*, Dec. 29, 2015, accessed Aug. 15, 2017, http://wapo.st/2eQTwVL.
73 "Many Advocates for Taxicab Law," *New York Times*, Apr. 15, 1909.
74 Lesiy, "'Uber' Limousine Dispatching" (email).
75 Craig Leisy, "WMMA – S&T Committee – Developing Item – Amend NIST…," email to Don Onwiler, Oct. 7, 2011.
76 Craig Leisy, "RE: GPS Use-Vehicle Charges," email to Juana Williams, Oct. 4, 2011.
77 Craig Leisy, "RE: Your Inquiry Re: Uber Trip Booking…," email to Michelle Broderick, Dec. 27, 2011.
78 Craig Leisy, "RE: Uber Car Impounded, Driver Ticketed in DC Sting," email to Eli Darland, Jan. 19, 2012.
79 "Lawmakers Approve Tougher Regulations on Town Car Chauffeurs," *Seattle Post-Intelligencer*, Apr. 20, 2011.
80 Washington State, Department of Licensing, *2012 Supplemental Budget*, Washington DOL, pp. 29-31, accessed Aug. 15, 2017, http://www.dol.wa.gov/about/docs/2012supBudget.pdf.
81 US Department of Commerce, National Institute for Standards and Technology, *NIST Handbook 44 Taximeter Code, Initial Meeting August 17-18, 2011, CADMS – Sacramento, CA, Meeting Summary*, NIST, accessed May 24, 2016, http://www.taxilibrary.org/nistmeetingsummary2011.pdf.
82 John Barton, "RE: Virtual Taximeter – NCWM Developing Item," email to Craig Leisy, et al., Mar. 8, 2012.
83 Craig Leisy, "FW: White Paper on Smartphone Apps," email to Matthew Daus, Jul. 2, 2012.
84 US Department of Commerce, National Institute for Standards and Technology, *USNWG TXMTRS 23 May 2012* [handwritten notes], NIST.
85 Commonwealth of Massachusetts, Division of Standards, *RE: Hearing Decision Civil Citation No. 4576 Issued by City of Cambridge*, Aug. 1, 2012, Mass. Division of Standards.
86 Travis Kalanick, Twitter Post, Jun. 22, 2012, 9:28 PM, https://twitter.com/travisk/status/216357100698349568.
87 *Hearing Decision Civil Citation No. 4576…*
88 Ibid.
89 Ron Linton, "Uber," email to Mary Cheh, Aug. 6, 2012; Ron Linton, "Re: Uber," email to Roy Spooner, Sr., Aug. 6, 2012.

90   Mike DeBonis, "Uber Runs Afoul of Massachusetts Regulators," *Washington Post*, Aug. 10, 2012.

91   Travis [Kalanick], "Uber Boston Has Been Served," *Newsroom* (blog), Aug. 14, 2012, accessed Mar 23, 2016, https://newsroom.uber.com/usmassachusetts/uber-boston-has-been-served.

92   Debonis, "Uber Runs Afoul..."

93   Jason Henrichs, "Petition – Allow Uber to continue to operate," Change.org, accessed Mar. 23, 2016, https://www.change.org/p/division-of-standards-of-the-commonwealth-of-massachusetts-allow-uber-to-continue-to-operate.

94   Brendan Ryan, Twitter Post, Aug. 15, 2012, 12:35 PM, accessed Mar. 23, 2016, https://twitter.com/brendanbrendan/status/235791964929392641.

95   Brendan Ryan, Twitter Post, Aug. 15, 2012, 12:54 PM, accessed Mar. 23, 2016, https://twitter.com/brendanbrendan/status/235796729017024512.

96   Commonwealth of Massachusetts, Division of Standards, *RE: Modified Hearing Decision Civil Citation N. 4576 Issued by City of Cambridge*, Mass. DOS, http://www.mass.gov/ocabr/docs/dos/massachusetts-gives-green-light-for-uber-technologies.pdf.

97   Craig Leisy, "GPS-Based Systems for Computing Fares," email to Jim Cassidy, Jul. 11, 2012.

98   Mass. DOS, *Modified Hearing Decision...*

99   Ibid.

100   Colman Herman, "Drive On: Cambridge Loses Lawsuit to Keep Uber Off the Roads," *Boston.com*, Jun. 25, 2013, accessed Jul. 30, 2017, https://www.boston.com/news/innovation/2013/06/25/drive-on-cambridge-loses-lawsuit-to-keep-uber-off-the-roads.

Chapter 5

1   San Francisco Municipal Transportation Agency, Finance and Information Technology, *Monthly Report – January 2012*, by Sonali Bose, p. 4, https://www.sfmta.com/sites/default/files/2012-01%20Monthly%20Report-%20Taxis.pdf.

2   Hayashi to Mucha (email).

3   SFMTA, *[report related to calendar item no. 13...]*

4   Michael Cabanatuan, "All SF Cabs to Get Rear-Seat Credit Card Readers," *SFGATE*, Jun. 6, 2012, accessed Jul. 30, 2017, http://www.sfgate.com/bayarea/article/All-S-F-cabs-to-get-rear-seat-credit-card-readers-3612140.php.

5   Jim Motovalli, "California Takes a Giant Step Toward Personal Car Sharing," *New York Times*, Jun. 9, 2010.

6   Matthew Gryczan, "Shepherd Leads Riders to Buses on time," *Crain's Detroit Business*, Sep. 11, 2011, accessed Nov. 26, 2016, http://www.crainsdetroit.com/article/20110911/FREE/309119974/shepherd-leads-riders-to-buses-on-time.

7   "Logan Green (Lyft & Zimride) at Startup Grind San Francisco," Youtube video, 59:19, posted by "Startup Grind," Oct. 3, 2013, https://youtu.be/ul1-zFwB21A.

8   Ibid.

9   "PandoMonthly Presents: A Fireside Chat with Lyft's John Zimmer," Youtube video, 1:49:37, posted by "PandoDaily," Feb. 20, 2015, https://youtu.be/YoED63gy7iI.

10   Ibid.

11   Ibid.

12   Sam Gustin, "LyftL Ride Sharing Startup Zimride hits the Gas Pedal in San Francisco," *Time*, Sep. 4, 2012, http://ti.me/2wN0sKi.

13   Taylor Soper, "SideCar Expands Community-Based Ride-Sharing Platform to Seattle, Offers $10 Credit," *GeekWire*, Nov. 2, 2012, accessed Aug. 16, 2017, https://www.geekwire.com/2012/sidecar-expands-instant-ridesharing-platform-seattle.

14   Dewey and Rayle, p. 25.

15   Ibid, p. 18.

16   San Francisco Municipal Transportation Agency, Division of Taxis and Accessible Services, *[staff report related to calendar item no. 11 for meeting of Sep. 4, 2012]*, SFMTA, https://www.sfmta.com/sites/default/files/agendaitems/9-4-12item11temporarytaxipermits.pdf.

17   "Travis Kalanick Onstage at Disrupt," Youtube video, 20:48, posted by "TechCrunch," Sep. 21, 2012, https://youtu.be/O7iokgEsWcM.

18   Ibid.

19   Ibid.

20   Ibid.

21   Ibid.

22   Rebecca Grant, "Car Service Uber to Foes: If You Don't Evolve, I'm Going to Kick Your Ass," *VentureBeat*, Sep.

12, 2012, accessed May 2, 2016, http://venturebeat.com/2012/09/12/uber-founder-proclaims-comfortable-convenient-rides-for-all.

23   Matthew Daus, "Uber Is Going to Kick the Ass of Crony Regulators?" email to Christiane Hayashi, et al. [IATR Smartphone App Committee], Sep. 14, 2012.

24   Ibid.

25   "2012 IATR Membership Information" [brochure], IATR.org, accessed Aug. 16, 2017, http://web.archive.org/web/20160717200340/http://www.iatr.memberlodge.org/Resources/Documents/2012%20MembershipConference/Membership-Recruitment-Ebro-2012.pdf.

26   International Association of Transportation Regulators, "2012 IATR Conference Attendees" [conference document], created by Karen Cameron, Nov. 13, 2012.

27   San Francisco Municipal Transportation Agency, Taxis, *Monthly Report – September 2012*, by Christiane Hayashi, p. 1, https://www.sfmta.com/sites/default/files/2012-09%20Monthly%20Report-%20Taxis.pdf.

28   Matt, "TAXI is Arriving in San Francisco," *Newsroom* (blog), Oct. 17, 2012, accessed Jan. 16, 2016, https://newsroom.uber.com/sf/taxi-is-arriving-in-san-francisco.

29   Hansu Kim, "Fwd: UBER," email to Christiane Hayashi, et. al., Oct. 14, 2012.

30   Christiane Hayashi, "FW: UBER," email to Matthew Daus, Oct. 15, 2012.

31   Matthew Daus, "Re: UBER," email to Christiane Hayashi, Oct. 15, 2012.

32   Christiane Hayashi, "RE: Uber Taxi and Licensed Color Schemes," email to Charles Rathbone, et al., Oct. 26, 2012.

33   Ibid.

34   Leena Rao, "Uber Sued by Taxi and Livery Companies in Chicago for Consumer Fraud and More," *TechCrunch*, Oct. 5, 2012, accessed Mar. 6, 2016, http://tcrn.ch/2gMmeE1.

35   Rosemary Krimbel, "RE: IATR App Committee Conference Call..." email to James Ney, et al. [IATR Smartphone App committee], Aug. 15, 2012; City of Chicago, Department of Business Affairs and Consumer Protection, Public Vehicle Operations Division, *Draft for Public Comment – Public Passenger Vehicle, Other Than Taxicabs...*, October 22, 2012, City of Chicago BACP Department, p. 6.

36   *Draft for Public Comment...*, pp. 6-7.

37   City of Chicago, Office the City Clerk, *Journal of the Proceedings of the City Council of the City of Chicago, Illinois*, January 18, 2012 (Vol. I), Chicago City Clerk, p. 19160, https://chicityclerk.com/file/6648/download?token=32T95oNK.

38   Maxim Lott, "Tech Freedom: Tech Start-Ups Strain Against Regulatory Headaches," *FoxNews.com*, accessed Mar. 9, 2016, http://fxn.ws/2gQPFZe.

39   US Department of Commerce, National Institute for Standards and Technology (NIST), *USNWG on Taximeters, September 24-26, 2012, Gaithersburg, MD, Meeting Summary*, NIST, accessed Mar. 12, 2016, https://www.nist.gov/sites/default/files/documents/pml/wmd/Sept-2012-Summary-Final.pdf.

40   Ibid.

41   Ibid.

42   Ibid, p. 31.

43   Ibid, p. 31.

44   Ibid, p. 32.

45   Ibid, pp. 33-34.

46   District of Columbia, Taxicab Commission (DCTC), Notice of Proposed Rulemaking, *Chapter 14, Sedan Vehicles and Operators of Title 31...*, Sep. 2012, DCTC.

47   Ron Linton, "RE: New Limousine License," email to Roy Spooner, Sr., Aug. 2, 2012, 2:50 PM.

48   Ibid.

49   Travis [Kalanick], "Here We Go Again: DC Taxi Commission Proposes New Rules to Shut Down Uber," *Newsroom* (blog), Sep. 20, 2012, accessed Feb. 8, 2016, https://newsroom.uber.com/usdc/here-we-go-again-dc-taxi-commission-proposes-new-rules-to-shut-down-uber.

50   Council of the District of Columbia, Committee on the Environment, Public Works, and Transportation, *Public Oversight Hearing on Innovations in the Public Vehicle-For-Hire Industry...*, Sep. 24, 2012, DC Council, http://dccarchive.oct.dc.gov/services/on_demand_video/channel13/September2012/09_24_12_PUBWKS.asx.

51   Ibid.

52   Ibid.

53   Ibid.

54   Ibid.

55   Freed, "Cheh Shelves Uber Amendment..."

56   *Public Oversight Hearing...*, Sep. 24. 2012.

57   Nitasha Tiku, "Uber Wants Its Yellow Cab App to Cost Riders the Meter Plus a 20 Percent Tip," *Observer.com*, Sep. 9, 2012, accessed May 27, 2016, http://observer.com/2012/09/uber-yellow-cab-taxi-app-20-percent-tip-hailo-verifone.

58   Ibid.

59   Andrew J. Hawkins, "Taxi-App Shutdown is Called 'A Matter of Justice,'" *Crain's New York Business*, Oct. 17, 2012, accessed Jul. 8, 2016, http://www.crainsnewyork.com/article/20121017/BLOGS04/310179986#more237.

60   Travis [Kalanick], "UberTAXI in NYC Shutting Down for Now – NO CHANGES to UberNYC Black Car Service," *Uber Blog*, Oct. 16, 2012, https://web.archive.org/web/20121017234947/http://blog.uber.com/2012/10/16/ubertaxi-in-nyc-shutting-down-for-now-no-changes-to-ubernyc-black-car-service.

61   Brian Ries, "Hurricane Sandy: Grocery Stores' Empty Shelves," *The Daily Beast*, Oct. 29, 2012, accessed Aug. 16, 2017, http://www.thedailybeast.com/hurricane-sandy-grocery-stores-empty-shelves; Ted Mann, "New York City Subways to Shut Down as Sandy Nears," *Wall Street Journal*, Oct. 28, 2012, http://on.wsj.com/2wLZQE4.

62   Paul Carr, "As NY Floods, 'Robin Hood' Uber Robs from the Rich and… Nope, That's About It," *Pando*, accessed Mar. 12, 2016, https://pando.com/2012/10/31/assholes-shrug.

63   Marcus Wohlsen, "For Uber, Doubling Fares Post-Storm Could Exact a Price," *Wired*, Nov. 1, 2012, accessed Mar. 12, 2016, http://www.wired.com/2012/11/uber-rides-pricey-post-sandy.

64   Edward Casabian, "Hurricane Sandy/Pricing Update," *Newsroom* (blog), Nov. 1, 2012, accessed Mar. 12, 2016, https://newsroom.uber.com/usnewyork/hurricane-sandy-pricing-update.

65   Brad Whittle, "FW: UBER," email to Doug Dean and Ron Jack, Aug. 8, 2012.

66   "Introducing MTData," *The Metro Traveler: A Newsletter by Metro Taxi, Denver's Largest Taxi Company*, August 2012, accessed Aug. 17, 2017, http://static1.1.sqspcdn.com/static/f/722021/21663063/1358373409137/August+2012+Metro+Taxi+Newsletter_08-07-12_page+2.pdf?token=6uOkqaniIlRibuRN3sHiceJEACg%3D; Greg Avery, "Uber Plans Denver Operation by Mid-August," *Denver Business Journal*, Aug. 3, 2012, accessed Mar. 13, 2016, http://www.bizjournals.com/denver/print-edition/2012/08/03/uber-plans-denver-operation-by.html.

67   Whittle to Dean and Jack, email.

68   Ibid.

69   Ibid; "Robert McBride | LinkedIn," *LinkedIn.com*, accessed Aug. 17, 2017, https://www.linkedin.com/in/robertmcbride1/.

70   Colorado General Assembly, 2012 Interim Committees, Transportation Legislation Review Committee, *Public Utilities Commission Report*, Meeting of Aug. 10, 2012, http://coloradoga.granicus.com/MediaPlayer.php?view_id=54&clip_id=1908&meta_id=34437.

71   Joel Warner, "Are Denver Cab Companies Ready for an Uber-Bumpy Ride?" *WestWord*, Mar. 20, 2014, accessed Jul. 30, 2016, http://www.westword.com/news/are-denver-cab-companies-ready-for-an-uber-bumpy-ride-5123724.

72   Ibid.

73   Shane Stickel, "Fwd: Avis," email to Cliff Hinson and Dorothy Harris, Jul. 27, 2012.

74   Ibid, email attachment: "Event in NJ Violating Limo Law.doc"; Port Authority of NY and NJ Retail Concessions Manager Carol Caldas to Avis Budget Group Senior Vice-President Robert Bouta, May 12, 2009.

75   Windels Marx, "Windels Marx Announces Formation of, and Leadership role in, Coalition of Transportation Associations ('COTA')," *PR Newswire*, Nov. 7, 2011, accessed Aug. 17, 2017, http://prn.to/2f7LZ1F.

76   Stickel to Hinson and Harris, email.

77   Salle Yoo, "Follow-Up," email to Larry Herold, Sep. 11, 2012; "Salle Yoo | LinkedIn," *LinkedIn.com*, accessed Apr. 14, 2016, https://www.linkedin.com/in/salle-yoo-67aa29b.

78   Olga V. Mack and Katia Bloom, "Embracing Risk: How Uber GC Salle Yoo Defines Her Career," *Above The Law*, Sep. 19, 2016, accessed Aug. 17, 2017, http://abovethelaw.com/2016/09/embracing-risk-how-uber-gc-salle-yoo-defines-her-career/.

79   Larry Herold, "RE: Colorado PUC – Uber," email to Salle Yoo, Sep. 19, 2012.

80   Brian [McMullen], "Uber 2.0 - #TheRideAhead," *Newsroom* (blog), Dec. 5, 2012, accessed Mar. 25, 2016, https://newsroom.uber.com/uber-2-0-therideahead.

81   Herold to Yoo, email.

82   Mike Percy, "FW: Emailing: $37 Flat To & From DIA or Metro Local," email to Cliff Hinson and Gary Gramlick, Sep. 20, 2012.

83   Cliff Hinson, "RE: Emailing: $37 Flat To & From DIA or Metro Local," email to Mike Percy and Gary Gramlick, Sep. 20, 2012.

84   Larry Herold, "09-26-12 Denver Taxi Advisory Council – notes," email to Ron Jack and Cliff Hinson, Oct. 1, 2012

Chapter 6

1   Carolyn Rinaldi, "Minutes of the IATR Smartphone Application ('App(s)') Committee," email to Ashwini Chabra, et al., Nov. 8, 2012, attachment: "IATR App Committee Minutes – 11.7.12 Meeting (10799443-3).doc."

2   Windels Marx Lane & Mittendorf, LLP, "Proposed Model Regulations for Smartphone Applications in the For-Hire Industry," WindelsMarx.com, Nov. 16, 2012, accessed Aug. 17, 2017,

http://www.windelsmarx.com/resources/documents/Windels%20Marx%20-%20IATR%20Proposed%20Model%20Regulations%20for%20Smartphone%20Applications%20(10801287).pdf.

3   Ibid.

4   Ibid, p. 3.

5   "IATR App Committee Minutes – 11.7.12…"

6   Ibid.

7   Ibid.

8   Ibid.

9   Ibid.

10   Ibid.

11   Matthew Daus, "Daus Embarks on International Smartphone App Tour," *TLC-Mag.com*, Nov. 2012, accessed Dec. 4, 2016, http://tlc-mag.com/archive_issues/in_focus_nov12.html.

12   Matthew W. Daus, Esq. "The Law and the Taxi: The Right Regulatory Mix – The Challenge of Emerging Technologies and Smart Phone Applications," Presentation made before the *5th International Road Transport Union Taxi Forum, Cologne, Germany, November 10, 2012*, accessed Dec. 4, 2016, https://www.iru.org/sites/default/files/2016-05/en-daus-the-law-and-the-taxi.pptx.

13   Ibid.

14   "IATR Conference 2012," International Association of Transportation Regulators, accessed Mar. 9, 2016, http://iatr.global/index.php/2012; "Day 2 Session1 h264 2mbps," Youtube video, 35:34, posted by "taxicabregulators," Dec. 5, 2012, https://youtu.be/fHma9XIibqg.

15   "2012 IATR Conference Attendees"

16   "Day 2 Session 1…"

17   Ibid.

18   Ibid.

19   Ibid.

20   Ibid.

21   Ibid.

22   Matthew Daus, "Conference Expense Comparison," email to Craig Leisy, et al. [IATR Board of Directors], Aug. 9, 2013, attachment: "ConferenceBudgetComparison.xls."

23   Philadelphia Parking Authority Director James Ney to Matthew W. Daus, esq, November 5, 2012.

24   "Windels Marx Announces Formation…"; "Timothy Rose | LinkedIn," LinkedIn.com, accessed Aug. 17, 2017, https://www.linkedin.com/in/timothy-rose-2289869/.

25   James Ney, "American Limo," email to Matthew Daus, Jun. 25, 2012.

26   "2010 Conference – Session 5 – Christiane Hayashi – Taxi Medallion Sales Pilot Program – Part 1."

27   Matthew Daus, "RE: News Snippets," email to Rosemary Krimbel, Oct. 11, 2012, 5:22 PM.

28   "IATR Conference 2012."

29   Matthew Daus, "RE: News Snippets," email to Rosemary Krimbel, Oct. 11, 2012, 5:28 PM.

30   Rosemary Krimbel, "RE: News Snippets," email to Matthew Daus, Oct. 11, 2012, 6:21 PM.

31   Matthew Daus, "RE: News Snippets," email to Rosemary Krimbel, Oct. 11, 2012, 6:22 PM.

32   Karen Cameron, "Confirmed Panel Members – There's an App for That," email to Matthew Daus, Sep. 14, 2012.

33   "2012 IATR Conference Attendees," Nitasha Tiku, "TLC Testimony Foreshadows October Ruling on Smartphone Apps for Yellow Taxis" *BetaBeat*, Sep. 27, 2012, http://web.archive.org/web/20121116111223/http://betabeat.com/2012/09/new-york-city-tlc-taxi-limousine-commission-ehailing-smartphone-apps-ruling-rfp.

34   International Association of Transportation Regulators, "2012 IATR Conference, Sponsorship and Membership Information" [conference document].

35   "IATR Conference 2012."

36   Ibid; For an example of follow-up correspondence from the Day on the Hill session, see: James Ney, "Fwd: Access to Federal Criminal Background Check Information," email to Ben Barasky, Nov. 21, 2012.

37   "IATR Conference 2012."

38   "2012 IATR Conference – A LA CARTE SPONSORSHIP," IATR.org, http://web.archive.org/web/20121109051548/http://www.iatr.org/2012ConfWeb/sponsors.html#pkg.

39   "Conference Expense Comparison."

40   Ibid.

41   Christopher N. Osher, "Denver Supervisor Pleads Guilty to Conflict-of-Interest Charges," *Denver Post*, Aug. 31, 2015, accessed Jul. 30, 2016, http://www.denverpost.com/2015/08/31/hancock-friend-and-former-denver-supervisor-pleads-guilty-to-conflict-of-interest-charges.

42   Matthew Daus, "RE: IATR Conference," email to Tom Downey, Sep. 28, 2012.

43   "2012 IATR Conference Attendees."

44   "Day2 Session2A TLPA," Youtube video, 11:50, posted by "taxicabregulators," Dec. 5, 2012,

https://youtu.be/J3_DUMVXkfc.
45   Ibid.
46   City of Los Angeles, Department of Transportation (LADOT), *Los Angeles Taxicab Review and Performance Report (2010 Annual Review)*, http://web.archive.org/web/20120423134935/http://www.ladot.lacity.org/pdf/PDF200.pdf.
47   "Day2_Session2C," Youtube video, 59:53, posted by "taxicabregulators," Jan. 3, 2013, https://youtu.be/oBOEj4LHs-s.
48   Ibid.
49   International Association of Transportation Regulators, "2012 IATR Program Booklet" [conference document].
50   Ibid; Ray Rivera and Matt Flegenheimer, "Comptroller is Expected to Try to Upset Deal for New Taxis," *New York Times*, Dec. 13, 2012, http://nyti.ms/2wNBzfb; Christian Seabaugh, "Updated: NYC Taxi Operators Sue TLC, Mayor Bloomberg Over Nissan NV200 Taxi of Tomorrow," *MotorTrend.com*, Dec. 11, 2012, accessed Aug. 17, 2017, http://www.motortrend.com/news/nyc-taxi-operators-sue-tlc-mayor-bloomberg-over-nissan-nv200-taxi-of-tomorrow-302961.
51   "Day2_Session2C."
52   Ibid.
53   Ibid.
54   Ibid.
55   Uber, "Uber 101 – Please Join us at 5 PM Today," email to "supportdc@uber.com" [list serv], Nov. 16, 2012, 2:57 PM.
56   Ted Mann, "Cities Move to Rein in Smartphone Taxi Services," *Wall Street Journal*, Nov. 16, 2012; Brian X. Chen, "Popular Ride-Calling App Under Pressure from Regulators," *International New York Times*, Dec. 3, 2012.
57   Charlie Anderson, "Smartphone Taxi Service," email to Matthew Daus, Nov. 16, 2012; Andrea James, "GPS is Good Enough for the US Military," email to Matthew Daus, Nov. 16, 2012.
58   Matthew Daus, "FW: GPS is Good Enough for the US Military," email to Craig Leisy, et al. [IATR Board of Directors], Nov. 17, 2012.
59   Matthew Daus, "FW: Smartphone Taxi Service," email to Craig Leisy, et al. [IATR Board of Directors], Nov. 17, 2012.
60   "2012 IATR Conference Attendees"; Karen Cameron, "Re: Smartphone Taxi Service,", email to Craig Leisy, et al. [IATR Board of Directors], Nov. 17, 2012.
61   Cameron, "Re: Smartphone Taxi Service."
62   Dan Solomon, "Going Places," *Austin Chronicle*, Nov. 23, 2012, accessed Apr. 18, 2016, http://www.austinchronicle.com/screens/2012-11-23/going-places.
63   Edward Kargbo, "Rogue Smartphone Apps," email to Carlton Thomas and Steve Grassfield, Jul. 26, 2012.
64   Cindy George, "Houston Advocate Fix: Yellow Cab Sets Things right for Mentally Challenged Couple," *Houston Chronicle*, Jul. 24, 2012, accessed Aug. 18, 2017, http://blog.chron.com/advocate/2012/07/houston-advocate-fix-yellow-cab-sets-things-right-for-mentally-challenged-couple.
65   "Texas Taxi Launches MTData Developed Hail A Cab App," MTData.com, Oct. 23, 2012, accessed Dec. 11, 2016, http://mtdata.us/texas-taxi-launches-mtdata-developed-hail-cab-app.
66   Dan Solomon, "Heyride Has a Hitch in Its Get-Along," *Austin Chronicle*, "Nov. 21, 2012, accessed Apr. 18, 2016, http://www.austinchronicle.com/daily/screens/2012-11-21/heyride-has-a-hitch-in-its-get-along.
67   Edward Kargbo, "Illegal Operator," email to Carlton Thomas, Nov. 12, 2012, attachment: "Heyride.pdf."
68   "2012 IATR Program Booklet"; "2012 IATR Conference Attendees."
69   "2012 IATR Conference Attendees."
70   "Day2_Session2C."
71   Edward Kargbo, "Heyride Driver (Self Promoting)," email to Carlton Thomas, Nov. 7, 2012; Edward Kargbo, "Heyride on the Radio," email to Carlton Thomas, Nov. 29, 2012; Edward Kargbo, "Heyride Stories (to date)," email to Carlton Thomas, Nov. 30, 2012.
72   Robert Spillar, memorandum to Marc A. Ott, "'Heyride' Cease and Desist Order," Nov. 21, 2012.
73   Kahrs to Graves, 2010; California Public Utilities Commission (CPUC), Consumer Protection and Safety Division, *Citation for Violation of Public Utilities Code*, citation no. F-5195, Nov. 13, 2012, CPUC.
74   Jaxon Van Derbeken, "Hagan Retires from PUC; Resisted Fining PG&E," *SFGATE*, Jan. 22, 2014, accessed Aug. 18, 2017, http://www.sfgate.com/news/article/Hagan-retires-from-PUC-resisted-fining-PG-amp-E-5166240.php.
75   "Jack Hagan | LinkedIn," Linkedin.com, accessed Aug. 18, 2017, https://www.linkedin.com/in/jack-hagan-87891320.
76   Phyllis White, "Non-Licensed Public Transportation Service in SF," email to Paul King, et al., Sep. 7, 2012.
77   Benny Evangelista, "Ride-Share Services Run Into Roadblocks," *San Francisco Chronicle*, Nov. 19, 2012.
78   Christina Farr, "Fight the Power! Ride-Sharing Startup Lyft Rallies to Fight Legal Charges," *VentureBeat*, Nov. 14, 2012, accessed Aug, 18, 2017, https://venturebeat.com/2012/11/14/ride-sharing-startup-lyft-rallies-the-tech-community-to-fight-illegal-operations-charges.

79   Benny Evangelista, "PUC Fines 3 SF App-Using Taxi Firms," *San Francisco Chronicle*, Nov. 15, 2012
80   "Day 2 Session 1..."
81   Terrie Prosper, "Chron Editorial Call," email to Jack Hagan, et al., Nov. 14, 2012.
82   Christiane Hayashi, "FW: Model Regulations for the IATR App Committee," email to Brian Kahrs, Dec. 4, 2012.
83   Brian Kahrs, "RE: Model Regulations for the IATR App Committee," email to Christiane Hayashi, Dec. 4, 2012.
84   California Public Utilities Commission, "CPUC to Evaluate Ridesharing Services," press release, Dec. 20, 2012,
      http://docs.cpuc.ca.gov/PublishedDocs/Published/G000/M039/K594/39594708.PDF.
85   California Public Utilities Commission (CPUC), Safety and Enforcement Division (SED), *Term Sheet for Settlement
      Between the [SED] of the [CPUC] and Uber Technologies...*, January 24, 2013, CPUC SED,
      http://www.cpuc.ca.gov/uploadedFiles/CPUC_Public_Website/Content/Safety/Transportation_Enforcement_and_Li
      censing/Enforcement_Actions_Transportation_Network_Companies/UberTermSheetforSettlement.pdf.
86   Ibid.

Chapter 7

1   Mina [Radhakrishnan], "The Uber Resolution – Always a Reliable Ride!" *Newsroom* (blog), Dec. 28, 2012,
      accessed Mar. 25, 2016, https://newsroom.uber.com/surge2012.
2   Colorado Department of Regulatory Agencies, Public Utilities Commission, *Attachment A, Decision No. C13-0054,
      Proposed Revisions in Legislative Format to Current Rules Adopted in Docket No. 11R-792TR*, Docket no. 13R-
      0009TR, Jan. 11, 2013,
      https://www.dora.state.co.us/pls/efi/efi_p2_v2_demo.show_document?p_dms_document_id=188800.
3   Ibid, pp. 8, 21, 55.
4   Ibid, p. 18.
5   Will [McCollum], "Colorado PUC Trying to Shut Down UberDenver!" *Newsroom* (blog), Jan. 29, 2013, accessed
      Mar. 12, 2016, https://newsroom.uber.com/us-colorado/uberdenverlove.
6   Ibid.
7   John W. Hickenlooper's Facebook page, post dated Jan. 30, 2013, accessed Mar. 16, 2016,
      https://www.facebook.com/JohnHickenlooper/posts/10151215192111437; John Hickenlooper, Twitter Post, Jan. 30,
      2013, 7:11 PM, accessed Mar. 13, 2016, https://twitter.com/hickforco/status/296772772804296704.
8   Hickenlooper, Facebook post.
9   Andy Vuong, "Transport Efforts Could 'Harm Consumers,'" *Denver Post*, Mar. 8, 2013; Andy Vuong, "Proposed
      Rule Changes Could Halt Uber in Denver," *Denver Post*, Jan. 30, 2013.
10   Uber_Colorado, Twitter Post, Jan. 30, 2013, 5:56 PM, accessed Mar. 13, 2016,
      https://twitter.com/Uber_CO/status/296753699064262656.
11   Will McCollum, "CORA Request," email to Doug Dean, Feb. 21, 2013.
12   Andy Vuong, "Denver Cabbies vs. Uber," *Denver Post*, Mar. 10, 2013; Whittle to Dean and Jack, email.
13   Jasmine Le Veaux, "DRAFT Testimony to Colorado PUC," email to Christiane Hayashi, et al. [IATR Smartphone
      App Committee], Mar. 6, 2013.
14   Matthew Days, "RE: Minutes of the IATR Smartphone Application ('App(s)') Committee," email to Christiane
      Hayashi, et al., Mar. 6, 2013.
15   Uber_Colorado, Twitter Post, Mar. 11, 2013, 10:35 AM, accessed Aug. 18, 2017,
      https://twitter.com/Uber_CO/status/311138347584192514.
16   Colorado Department of Regulatory Agencies, Public Utilities Commission (PUC), *In the Matter of the Proposed
      Rules Regulating Transportation by Motor Vehicle, 4 Code of Colorado Regulations 723-6* [transcript], Docket no.
      13-R0009TR, Mar. 11, 2013, pp. 35-36 & 43-44,
      https://www.dora.state.co.us/pls/efi/efi_p2_v2_demo.show_document?p_dms_document_id=228316&p_session_id
      =.
17   Ibid, pp. 109-110.
18   Ibid, p. 111.
19   Ibid, p. 115.
20   Ibid.
21   Ibid, pp. 51-52.
22   Andy Vuong, "App Maker Uber Scores a Regulatory Victory, But Review Continues," *Denver Post*, Mar. 11, 2013.
23   Denver Post Editorial Board, "Uber's Survival is No Sure Thing," *Denver Post*, Mar. 15, 2013.
24   Ilya Abyzov, "Uber," email to SFParatransit [SFMTA email address], Nov. 30, 2012.
25   "2012 IATR Conference Attendees."
26   Christiane Hayashi, "RE: Uber," email to Ilya Abyzov, Nov. 30, 2012.
27   Ibid.
28   Kessler, "Travis Kalanick: Transportation Trustbuster."

381

29   Christiane Hayashi, "RE: WSJ Article Uber," email to Matthew Daus, Jan. 27, 2013.
30   San Francisco Municipal Transportation Agency (SFMTA), Division of Taxis and Accessible Services, *[staff report related to calendar item no. 11 for meeting of Nov. 20, 2012]*, SFMTA, https://www.sfmta.com/sites/default/files/agendaitems/11-20-12item11tcamendmentmedallionwaitlist.pdf.
31   San Francisco Municipal Transportation Agency (SFMTA), *RFI SFMTA-2013-11 Request for Information/Qualifications*, Oct. 30, 2012, SFMTA, accessed Aug. 18, 2017, http://www.taxi-library.org/sfmta-taxi-data-rfi-rfq.pdf; SFMTA, Division of Taxis and Accessible Services, *[staff report related to calendar item no. 11 for meeting of Mar. 19, 2013]*, SFMTA, https://www.sfmta.com/sites/default/files/agendaitems/3-19-13%20Item%2011%20Electronic%20Taxi%20Access.pdf.
32   Christiane Hayashi, "11x17 Chart," email to Cheryl Leger, Jan. 10, 2013, attachment: "RFI chart.docx."
33   Ibid.
34   Ibid.
35   Leslie Caplan, "Response to RFI," email to Ashish Patel, Dec. 27, 2012, attachment: "Hailo_LettertoSFMTA_RFI_December2012.pdf"
36   Kessler, "Travis Kalanick..."
37   Ibid.
38   Ibid.
39   Matthew Daus, "Wall Street Journal article," email to Christiane Hayashi, et al., Jan. 29, 2013.
40   Devon Glenn, "Facebook's Public Policy Manager to Join Uber," *AdWeek.com*, Jan. 25, 2013, accessed Aug. 18, 2017, http://www.adweek.com/digital/facebooks-public-policy-manager-to-join-uber.
41   Matthew Daus, "Uber," email to Julianne Befeler, et al., Jan. 29, 2013. Note: That same day, Daus forwarded this email to the IATR Smartphone App Committee.
42   Brian X. Chen, "Uber to Roll Out Ride Sharing in California," *New York Times*, Jan. 31, 2013, https://nyti.ms/2xfCR5Q; Ryan Lawler, "It's On. Uber Will Soon Go Up Against Lyft and SideCar with a Ride-Sharing Service of its Own," *TechCrunch*, Jan. 31, 2013, accessed Aug. 18, 2017, https://techcrunch.com/2013/01/31/uber-ride-share.
43   Carl Macmurdo, "Uber to Challenge Lyft, SideCar With its...," email to Christiane Hayashi, Feb. 2, 2013.
44   Christiane Hayashi, "FW: Uber to Challenge Lyft, SideCar With its...," email to Matthew Daus, Feb. 3, 2013.
45   Ryan Lawler, "See, Uber – This is What Happens When you Cannibalize Yourself," *TechCrunch*, Mar. 15, 2013, accessed Oct. 1, 2016, https://techcrunch.com/2013/03/15/see-uber-this-is-what-happens-when-you-cannibalize-yourself.
46   *Alatraqchi v. Uber*, 2013 WL 4517756 (ND Cal. 2013).
47   Lawler, "See, Uber..."
48   Anthony Ha, "Uber Drivers Gather Outside SF Office to Protest...," *TechCrunch*, Mar. 15, 2013, accessed Oct. 1, 2016, https://techcrunch.com/2013/03/15/uber-protest.
49   Matthew Daus, "Happy St. Patrick's Day to All...," email to Christiane Hayashi, et al. [IATR Smartphone App Committee], Mar. 17, 2013.
50   California Public Utilities Commission (CPUC), *Order Instituting Rulemaking on Regulations Relating to Passenger Carriers, Ridesharing, and New Online-Enabled Transportation Services*, docket no. R.12-12-011, Dec. 27, 2012, CPUC, http://docs.cpuc.ca.gov/PublishedDocs/Published/G000/M040/K862/40862944.PDF.
51   Christiane Hayashi, "FW: R.12-12-011—Notice of Ruling Setting Workshop," email to Mark Cohen, et al. [IATR Smartphone App Committee], Mar. 8, 2013; California Public Utilities Commission (CPUC), *Initial Comments... Filed on Behalf of the San Francisco Municipal Transportation Agency*, docket no. R.12-12-011, Jan. 28, 2013, pp. 4-5, http://docs.cpuc.ca.gov/PublishedDocs/Efile/G000/M042/K159/42159581.PDF.
52   California Public Utilities Commission (CPUC), *Reply Comments... Filed on Behalf of the San Francisco Municipal Transportation Agency*, docket no. R.12-12-011, Feb. 11, 2013, p. 2, http://docs.cpuc.ca.gov/PublishedDocs/Efile/G000/M042/K156/42156522.PDF.
53   California Public Utilities Commission (CPUC), *Comments of Uber Technologies, Inc. on Order Instituting Rulemaking*, docket no. R.12-12-011, Jan. 28, 2013, p. 1, http://docs.cpuc.ca.gov/PublishedDocs/Efile/G000/M042/K157/42157058.PDF.
54   Ibid, pp. 10-13.
55   Tomio Geron, "SideCar Raises $10 Million from Google Ventures, Lightspeed," *Forbes*, Oct. 10, 2012, accessed Aug. 18, 2017, https://www.forbes.com/sites/tomiogeron/2012/10/10/sidecar-raises-10-million-from-google-ventures-lightspeed/#544e82c14473.
56   "Sidecar Acquires Austin Rideshare Community Heyride; Takes Rideshare Nationwide," *SideCar Blog*, Feb. 14, 2013, accessed May 2, 2016, http://blog.side.cr/sidecar-acquires-austin-rideshare-community-heyride-takes-rideshare-nationwide.
57   Ibid.
58   "It's Time to Reclaim Rideshare," *SideCar Blog*, Apr. 17, 2013, accessed May 2, 2016, http://blog.side.cr/its-time-to-reclaim-rideshare.

59   Ryan Lawler, "SideCar Acquires Austin-Based Ride-Sharing…," *TechCrunch*, Feb. 14, 2013, accessed Apr. 18, 2016, http://techcrunch.com/2013/02/14/sidecar-heyride-7-new-markets.
60   Robert Spillar to Sunil Paul, Feb. 15, 2013, City of Austin (Texas) Transportation Department.
61   Ordinance no. 20130228-030, City of Austin (Texas) (2013).
62   Ibid; Austin City Council, *Minutes of Regular Meeting*, "Consent Agenda," Feb. 28, 2013, http://www.austintexas.gov/edims/document.cfm?id=185324.
63   James Ney, "RE: Minutes of the IATR Smartphone Application…," email to Christiane Hayashi, et al., Mar. 6, 2013.
64   Paul Nausbaum, "Parking Authority Halts 'Gypsy' Cab Service," *Philadelphia Inquirer*, Feb. 26, 2013.
65   Ney, "Re: Minutes of the…"
66   Sunil Paul, "Do You Believe in Sharing?" *SideCar Blog*, Feb. 27, 2013, accessed May 2, 2016, http://blog.side.cr/do-you-believe-in-sharing; Sunil Paul, "Our Case to #defendsharing," *SideCar Blog*, Mar. 8, 2013, http://web.archive.org/web/20130324052022/http://blog.side.cr/2013/03/08/our-case-to-defendsharing.
67   Justin Schmidt and Steve Harrell, "Hey Austin and Philly, Ride Free Tonight!" *SideCar Blog*, Mar. 2, 2013, http://web.archive.org/web/20130305091018/http://blog.side.cr:80/2013/03/02/hey-austin-and-philly-ride-free-tonight; "SXSW – Your Rides are FREE!" *SideCar Blog*, Mar. 7, 2013, http://web.archive.org/web/20130314034929/http://blog.side.cr/2013/03/07/sxsw-your-rides-are-free.
68   Resolution no. 20130307-067, City of Austin (Texas) (2013).
69   Austin City Council, *Regular Meeting, Mar. 7, 2013*, Agenda Item 67 (hearing), http://austintx.swagit.com/play/03072013-513/26/.
70   Ibid.
71   Ibid.
72   "A Tale of Two Processes," *HB 2286*, Hearing before the House Committee on Insurance, Kansas Legislature, 2015-2016 Legislative Session, Mar. 20, 2015, exhibit by Larrie Ann Brown of the Property and Casualty Insurers Association of America, http://www.kslegislature.org/li_2016/b2015_16/committees/ctte_h_ins_1/documents/testimony/20150320_08.pdf.
73   Austin City Council, Mar. 7, 2013, Agenda Item 67.
74   Ibid.
75   "Hey Austin and Philly…," *SideCar Blog*.
76   James Ney, "RE: Minutes of the IATR Smartphone Application…," email to Christiane Hayashi, et al., Mar. 6, 2013.
77   Matthew Daus, "RE: More Fuel in Your Tank!" email to Christiane Hayashi, et al. [IATR Smartphone App Committee], Mar. 8, 2013.
78   Travis [Kalanick], "Uber Policy White Paper 1.0," *Uber Blog*, Apr. 12, 2013, https://web.archive.org/web/20130424071807/http://blog.uber.com/2013/04/12/uber-policy-white-paper-1-0.
79   Ibid.
80   Ibid.
81   Ibid.
82   Ibid
83   Matthew Daus, "FW: Uber's White Paper – Ridesharing," email to Craig Leisy, at al. [IATR Board of Directors], Apr. 12, 2013; Joseph Chernow, "Joseph M. Chernow, PC, Curriculum Vitate," accessed Aug. 19, 2017, http://media2.expertpages.com/ep/media/4503_cv_11_25_chernow.pdf.
84   Colorado Department of Regulatory Agencies, Public Utilities Commission (PUC), *Hearing Exhibit 10: Proposed Revisions to Attach B to Decision No. C13-0054 in Legislative Format*, Docket no. 13R-0009TR, p.88, Colorado PUC.
85   Ibid, p. 18.
86   Ibid, p. 54.
87   Colorado Department of Regulatory Agencies, Public Utilities Commission (PUC), *In the Matter of the Proposed Rules Regulating Transportation by Motor Vehicle, 4 Code of Colorado Regulations 723-6* [transcript], Docket no. 13-R0009TR, Apr. 16, 2013, p. 47.
88   G. Harris Adams, "Re: (Service of R.12-12-011) – Cmmr…," email to Jason Zeller, Aug. 2, 2013.
89   Colorado PUC, Apr. 16, 2013 [trascript], p. 52.
90   Federal Trade Commission to the Colorado Public Utilities Commission, Mar. 6, 2013 (letter signed by Andrew Gavil, et al.).
91   Organization for Economic Co-Operation and Development (OECD), Policy Roundtables, *Taxi Services: Competition and Regulation*, 2007, OECD, accessed Aug. 19, 2017, http://www.oecd.org/regreform/sectors/41472612.pdf.
92   Colorado PUC, Apr. 16, 2013 [transcript], pp. 136-140.
93   Ibid, p. 183.
94   Ibid, pp. 204-207.

95   Matthew Daus, "Looks Like Victory for IATR in Colorado!!" email to Craig Leisy, et al. [IATR Board of Directors], Mar. 27, 2013.

96   "Google DC Talks Presents: Uber Co-Founder and CEO Travis Kalanick..." Youtube video, 52:36, posted by "googlepublicpolicy," May 2, 2013, https://youtu.be/HedsdfCGbqs.

97   Ibid.

98   Colorado Secretary of State, Colorado Cumulative Report, *Official Results – General Election*, Nov. 24, 2010, http://web.archive.org/web/20101230222620/http://www.sos.state.co.us/pubs/electionresults2010/general/Colorado Report.html.

99   Norma Engelberg, "Innovation Makes SENSE at Sturman," *Pikes Peak Courier View* (Woodland Park, Colorado), Apr. 14, 2010; Alicia Wallace, "Hickenlooper Highlights Innovation, Business at Boulder Speech," *Daily Camera* (Boulder, Colorado), Mar. 21, 2011.

100   "Gov. Backs 'Angels' Bill – Investment in Startup Companies Rewarded," *Daily-Reporter Herald* (Loveland, Colorado), May 24, 2011; Aldo Svaldi, "State Alliance Will Promote Innovation," *Denver Post*, Nov. 29, 2011; Bill Radford, "Colorado Launches Statewide Innovation Challenge," *Gazette* (Colorado Springs, Colorado), May 23, 2013.

101   Svaldi, "State Alliance..."

102   "Google DC Talks..."

103   Andy Vuong, "Uber CEO: Hickenlooper is All Talk When it Comes to...," *Denver Post*, May 7, 2013.

104   Farzad Mashhood, "Ride Service Suing Austin," *Austin American-Statesman*, Mar. 12, 2013.

105   State of Texas 200th District Court, *Re: Cause No. D-1-GN-13-000838; In the 250th... [ruling]*, Apr. 19, 2013, letter to Peter D. Kennedy, et al.

106   Ordinance No. 20130620-051, City of Austin (Texas) (2013).

107   Matthew W. Daus, Esq, "Ridesharing Applications: Illegal 'Hitchhiking-for-Hire' or Sustainable Group Riding?" WindelsMarx.com, May 2013, accessed Aug. 20, 2017, http://www.windelsmarx.com/resources/documents/Ridesharing%20%20Report.pdf.

108   Austin City Council, Regular Meeting, *Agenda Item 54, Recommendation for Council Action*, April 25, 2013, http://www.austintexas.gov/edims/document.cfm?id=188124.

109   Jasmine Le Veaux, "Proposed Model Regulations Relevant...," email to Christiane Hayashi, et al. [IATR Smartphone App Committee], May 10, 2013.

110   Austin City Council, Urban Transportation Commission, *Austin Mobility: Ground Transportation Code Amendments – Rideshare*, May 14, 2013, Austin (Texas) City Council; http://www.austintexas.gov/edims/document.cfm?id=191045;

111   Thomas Drischler, "Re: Newly Revised Proposed Definition...," email to Christiane Hayashi, et al. [IATR Smartphone App Committee], May 16, 2013; Christiane Hayashi, "Re: Newly Revised Proposed Definition...," email to Craig Leisy, et al. [IATR Smartphone App Committee], May 16, 2013

112   Christiane Hayashi, "FW: Monthly App Report & Conf Call," email to James Ney, May 29, 2013.

113   Christiane Hayashi to Austin Mayor Lee Leffingwell, May 22, 2013.

114   Ibid.

115   Ibid.

116   Austin City Council, Urban Transportation Committee, *Item 3A: Presentation of "Going My Way" the Proliferation of Rogue Ridesharing Services*, May 14, 2013, http://austintx.swagit.com/play/05152013-538/5.

117   Ibid.

118   City of Austin, Transportation Department, *Ridesharing, A Report to the Austin City Council from the Austin Transportation Department*, May 31, 2013, http://www.austintexas.gov/edims/document.cfm?id=191048.

119   Ibid.

120   Ibid.

121   Ibid.

122   City of Austin, Police Department, *Public Information Request no. 26979*, May 31, 2016, attachment: "Response Citations.pdf"; City of Austin, Municipal Court, *Public Information Request no. 31557*, Dec. 27, 2016, attachment: "Request.pdf."

123   Ibid.

124   Matthew W. Daus, Esq., "Rocky Road Ahead for Rogue Apps in Colorado...," *TLC-Mag.com*, May 2013, accessed Mar. 30, http://www.tlc-mag.com/archive_issues/in_focus_may13.html.

125   Sunil Paul, "Hey @MikeBloomberg, NYC Wants You to #DefendSharing!" *SideCar Blog*, May 1, 2013, accessed May 4, 2016, http://blog.side.cr/its-time-to-stand-up-for-sharing-in-new-york-city.

126   Matthew Daus and Jasmine Le Veaux,

127   Yuliya Chernova, "NY Shutdowns for SideCar, RelayRides Highlights Hurdles...," *Wall Street Journal*, May 15, 2013, accessed Apr. 23, 2016, http://blogs.wsj.com/venturecapital/2013/05/15/ny-shutdowns-for-sidecar-relayrides-highlight-hurdles-for-car-and-ride-sharing-startups.

128   Jasmine Le Veaux, memorandum to Alfred LaGasse, "TLPA Monthly Report – Update on App Activity in...," May

24, 2013.
Note: For the above memo, see source: Christiane Hayashi, "FW: Monthly App Report & Conf Call," email to Michael Jones, Jul. 1, 2013, attachment: "TLPA Monthly App Report – May 2013.pdf."

129 Ibid.
130 Matthew Daus and Jasmine Le Veaux, "The Ride Stops Here – Regulatory Pushback Against Rogue Apps," IATR.org, June 2013, http://web.archive.org/web/20140716035134/http://www.iatr.org/PresidentUpdate-June2013.html.
131 Jim Gillespie, "Fw: Monthly App Report & Conf Call," email to Christiane Hayashi, May 28, 2013.
132 Colorado PUC, *In the Matter of...*, Mar. 11, 2013, p. 109.
133 State of Rhode Island, Public Utilities Commission, *In Re: Rules and Regulations Governing the Transportation of Passengers Via Public Motor Vehicles* [transcript], Docket no. 13 MC 121, Apr. 30, 2014, pp. 39-40.
134 Hillsborough County (Florida), Public Transportation Commission, *Regular Meeting, July 29, 2014* [transcript], p.28, accessed Aug. 20, 2017, https://webapps.hillsboroughcounty.org/htv/caption/scripts/pt140729.doc.
135 John Barton, "USNWG on Taximeters," email to Pat Russo, Jul. 10, 2012.

Chapter 8

1   Frias Transportation Infrastructure, "SFMTA Moves Forward With Comprehensive Taxi App Data," *PR Newswire*, Mar. 22, 2013, accessed Aug. 21, 2017, http://www.prnewswire.com/news-releases/sfmta-moves-forward-with-comprehensive-taxi-app-data-199568111.html.
2   San Francisco Municipal Transportation Agency, Division of Taxis and Accessible Services, *[staff report related to calendar item no. 11 for meeting of Mar. 13, 2013]*, SFMTA, https://www.sfmta.com/sites/default/files/agendaitems/3-19-13%20Item%2011%20Electronic%20Taxi%20Access.pdf.
3   Jane Ann Morrison, "Case Closed on Claims of Ex-Legislator's Sex, Drug Addictions," *Las Vegas Review-Journal*, Oct. 1, 2012, http://www.reviewjournal.com/jane-ann-morrison/case-closed-claims-ex-legislators-sex-drug-addictions.
4   San Francisco Municipal Transportation Agency, "Best Practices Studies of Taxi Regulation: Managing Taxi Supply," report provided by Hara Associates, March 2013, p. "2-4," https://www.sfmta.com/sites/default/files/Draft%20ManagingTaxi%20Supply%2045%20WEBversion04042043.pdf
5   Ibid.
6   Ibid, p. iii.
7   Hayashi, "FW: R.12-12.011 -- Notice of..." (email).
8   Jessica Gelt, "Night Life; the Enabler; Getting a Lyft at Night," *Los Angeles Times*, May 17, 2013; "SideCar Acquires Austin..."; Travis [Kalanick], "Uber LA Officially Launched, *Newsroom* (blog), Mar. 8, 2012, accessed Apr. 17, 2016, https://newsroom.uber.com/us-california/uber-la-officially-launched.
9   Samantha, "San Diego – UBER Expands into North County!" *Newsroom* (blog), Apr. 8, 2013, accessed Aug. 21, 2017, https://newsroom.uber.com/us-california/north-county-expansion; Tess, "Urijah Faber Enters the Octagon as Sac's 'Rider Zero,'" *Newsroom* (blog), Jan. 23, 2013, accessed Aug. 17, 2017, https://newsroom.uber.com/us-california/ubersacramento.
10   California Public Utilities Commission, Workshop, *Rulemaking on Regulations Relating to Passenger Carriers, Ridesharing...*, April 10-11, 2013, http://web.archive.org/web/20140426005849/http://www.cpuc.ca.gov/NR/rdonlyres/A8EE9CD5-5764-481F-BE2D-3604ABCCD708/0/Rideshare_agenda_v1.pdf.
11   "California – California Public Utilities Commission – Workshop," AdminMonitor.com, Apr. 10, 2013, accessed Aug. 21, 2017, http://www.adminmonitor.com/ca/cpuc/workshop/20130410.
12   Ibid.
13   Ibid.
14   Ibid.
15   "California – California Public Utilities Commission – Workshop," AdminMonitor.com, Apr. 11, 2013, accessed Aug. 21, 2017, http://www.adminmonitor.com/ca/cpuc/workshop/20130411.
16   Ibid.
17   Ibid.
18   California Public Utilities Commission (CPUC), *Additional Comments of Uber Technologies, Inc...*, docket no. R.12-12-011, Jun. 3, 2013, http://docs.cpuc.ca.gov/PublishedDocs/Efile/G000/M075/K768/75768659.PDF.
19   California Public Utilities Commission (CPUC), *Workshop Statement of SideCar Technologies, Inc...*, docket no. R.12-12-011, Apr. 3, 2013, http://docs.cpuc.ca.gov/PublishedDocs/Efile/G000/M064/K140/64140247.PDF.
20   California Public Utilities Commission (CPUC), *Motion of [TPAC] to Compel Responses to Discovery...*, docket no. R.12-12-011, Jun. 14, 2013, http://docs.cpuc.ca.gov/PublishedDocs/Efile/G000/M075/K391/75391676.PDF.

21   Salvador Rodriguez, "Lyft and UberX to Keep Operating in LA Despite City Orders," *Los Angeles Times*, Jun. 25, 2013, accessed May 7, 2016, http://www.latimes.com/business/technology/la-fi-tn-lyft-uberx-continue-operating-la-cease-and-desist-letters-20130625-story.html.

22   Los Angeles City Council, Transportation Committee, *New Online-Enabled Transportation Services (NOETS) / Ridesharing Services*, Council File no. 13-0794, Jun. 20, 2013, http://clkrep.lacity.org/onlinedocs/2013/13-0794_MOT_06-19-13.pdf.

23   Los Angeles City Council, Transportation Committee, *Meeting, Wednesday, June 26, 2013*, accessed Aug. 21, 2017, http://lacity.granicus.com/MediaPlayer.php?view_id=46&clip_id=11969.

24   Tom Dotan, "Why Does LA Tech Love Eric Garcetti?" *Los Angeles Business Journal*, May 21, 2013, accessed Aug. 21, 2017, http://labusinessjournal.com/news/2013/may/21/why-does-l-tech-love-eric-garcetti.

25   Gene Maddaus, "Eric garcetti Muzzles Taxi Czar Who Criticized Uber," *LA Weekly*, Sep. 16, 2013, accessed Mar. 29, 2016, http://www.laweekly.com/news/eric-garcetti-muzzles-taxi-czar-who-criticized-uber-4171837.

26   California Public Utilities Commission (CPUC), *Decision Adopting Rules and Regulations to Protect...*, docket no. R.12-12-011, Jul. 30, 2013, http://docs.cpuc.ca.gov/PublishedDocs/Efile/G000/M073/K768/73768000.PDF.

27   Ibid, section 2.

28   Ibid, pp. 17-18.

29   Ibid, p. 18.

30   California Public Utilities Commission (CPUC), *Opening Comments of SideCar Technologies... on Proposed Decision...*, docket no. R.12-12-011, Aug. 19, 2013, pp. 4-5, http://docs.cpuc.ca.gov/PublishedDocs/Efile/G000/M075/K768/75768539.PDF.

31   California Public Utilities Commission (CPUC), *Comments of Lyft... Regarding Proposed Decision...*, docket no. R.12-12-011, Aug. 19, 2013, pp. 5-6, http://docs.cpuc.ca.gov/PublishedDocs/Efile/G000/M076/K386/76386741.PDF.

32   CPUC, *Decision Adopting Rules..."*

33   California Public Utilities Commission (CPUC), *City of Los Angeles [DOT] Comments on Proposed Decision*, docket no. R.12-12-011, Aug. 19, 2013, http://docs.cpuc.ca.gov/PublishedDocs/Efile/G000/M075/K768/75768264.PDF.

34   Christiane Hayashi, "RE: Uber," email to Craig Leisy, et al. [IATR Smartphone App Committee], Jul. 31, 2013.

35   Nairi, "CPUC Proposed Decision Paves Path Forward," *Newsroom* (blog), Jul. 30, 2013, accessed Mar. 12, 2016, https://newsroom.uber.com/cpuc-proposed-decision-paves-path-forward.

36   California Public Utilities Commission (CPUC), *Opening Comments of Uber Technologies, Inc on Proposed Decision*, docket no. R.12-12-011, Aug. 19, 2013, http://docs.cpuc.ca.gov/PublishedDocs/Efile/G000/M075/K768/75768751.PDF.

37   Ibid.

38   Ibid.

39   California Public Utilities Commission (CPUC), *Decision Adopting Rules and Regulations to Protect...*, docket no. R.12-12-011, Sep. 19, 2013, p. 75, http://docs.cpuc.ca.gov/PublishedDocs/Published/G000/M077/K192/77192335.PDF.

40   Ibid, p. 16.

41   Ibid, p. 75.

42   "SideCar and Lyft Switch from Donations to Minimum Fares in California," *PCWorld*, Nov. 15, 2013, accessed Aug. 21, 2017, http://www.pcworld.com/article/2064280/sidecar-and-lyft-switch-from-donations-to-minimum-fares-in-california.html.

43   Laura Nelson, "No Appeal of Ride-Share Rules," *Los Angeles Times*, Oct. 23, 2013.

44   City of Austin (Texas), Transportation Department, *Rideshare Report – Addendum*, Aug. 13, 2013, http://www.austintexas.gov/edims/pio/document.cfm?id=195399.

45   Ibid.

46   Ibid; Ordinance No. 20130822-081, City of Austin (Texas) (2013).

47   Jasmine Le Veaux, "Austin Adopts Model Rule on Rideshare," email to Christiane Hayashi, et al. [IATR Smartphone App Committee], Aug. 22, 2013.

48   Sunil Paul and Jahan Khanna, "So Long SideCar and Thanks," *Medium*, Dec. 29, 2015, accessed Aug. 21, 2017, https://medium.com/@SunilPaul/so-long-sidecar-and-thanks-74c8a0955064; Sunil Paul, "Why We Sold to GM," *SideCar Blog*, Jan. 20, 2016, accessed May 2, 2016, http://blog.side.cr/why-we-sold-to-gm.

49   Paul, "Why We Sold..."

50   "2013 Program," 2013 *Fortune* Brainstorm Tech [agenda], accessed Aug. 22, 2017, https://www.fortuneconferences.com/brainstorm-tech-2013/2013-program/.

51   "Travis Kalanick CEO of Uber Technologies Speaks at Brainstorm Tech 2013 | Fortune," Youtube video, 31:05, posted by "Fortune Magazine," Jul. 23, 2013, https://youtu.be/vGbuitwkZiM.

52   Colorado Department of Regulatory Affairs, Public Utilities Commission, *Recommended Decision of [ALJ] G. Harris Adams*, Decision no. R13-0943, Docket no. 13R-0009TR, Aug. 2, 2013,

https://www.dora.state.co.us/pls/efi/efi_p2_v2_demo.show_document?p_dms_document_id=226382&p_session_id =.

53   Ibid, p. 16.
54   Will McCollum, email to Doug Dean, Aug. 5, 2013.
55   Andy Vuong, "Hickenlooper: Proposed Uber Rules 'Overreach,' Not in Public Interest," *Denver Post*, Aug. 9, 2013, accessed Mar. 13, 2016, http://www.denverpost.com/breakingnews/ci_23831263/hickenlooper-proposed-uber-rules-overreach-not-public-interest.
56   Ibid.
57   Colorado Department of Regulatory Affairs, Public Utilities Commission, *Exhibit B to Uber's Exceptions*, Aug. 22, 2013, docket no. 13R-0009TR, https://www.dora.state.co.us/pls/efi/efi_p2_v2_demo.show_document?p_dms_document_id=232095&p_session_id =.
58   Colorado Department of Regulatory Affairs, Public Utilities Commission, *Uber Technologies, Inc.'s Exceptions to Recommended Decision...*, docket no. 13R-0009TR, Aug. 22, 2013, https://www.dora.state.co.us/pls/efi/efi_p2_v2_demo.show_document?p_dms_document_id=232092&p_session_id =.
59   Colorado Department of Regulatory Affairs, Public Utilities Commission, *Response of the [IATR] to the Exceptions of Uber...*, Sep. 5, 2013, docket no. 13R-0009TR, https://www.dora.state.co.us/pls/efi/efi_p2_v2_demo.show_document?p_dms_document_id=238811&p_session_id =.
60   Jack Finlaw to Colorado Public Utilities Commission, Aug. 22, 2013; Erik Mitisek to Joshua Epel, Aug. 22, 2013.
61   Colorado Department of Regulatory Affairs, Public Utilities Commission, *Recommended Decision of [ALJ] G. Harris Adams*, Decision no. R13-0943, Docket no. 13R-0009TR, Aug. 2, 2013,
62   Ibid, p. 8.
63   Ibid, p. 3.
64   Andy Vuong, "Denver Startup Week: Second Galvanize...," *Denver Post*, Sep. 17, 2013.
65   William Schlitter, "Re: PUC Case #103619," email to Casey George, May 30, 2012; Andy Vuong, "Details on Lyft's Ridesharing Service...," *Denver Post*, Sep. 18, 2013.
66   Vuong, "Details on Lyft's Ridesharing..."
67   Andy Vuong, "UberX Denver, a Low-Cost E-Hailing...," *Denver Post*, Oct. 4, 2013.
68   Karen Cameron, "See You in St. Louis," email to Christiane Hayashi, et al., Sep. 21, 2013, attachment: "FINAL 2013-09-19 2013-ConferenceAttendeeListforSponsors.xlsx."
69   "Karen Cameron | LinkedIn," LinkedIn.com, accessed May 24, 2016, https://ca.linkedin.com/in/karen-cameron-37b53516.
70   Matthew Daus, "FW: Uber Blog – IATR," email to Craig Leisy, et al. [IATR Board of Directors], Sep. 26, 2013.
71   Karen Cameron, "Re: Introduction," email to Corey Owens, May 3, 2013.
72   Karen Cameron, "RE: Draft Testimony to Colorado PUC," email to Tom Drischler, et al. [IATR Board of Directors], Mar. 11, 2013.
73   Karen Cameron, "FW: President's Update - 'The Ride Stops...,'" email to Corey Owens, Jun 17, 2013, 7:45 AM.
74   Corey Owens, "Re: President's Update - 'The Ride Stops...,'" email to Karen Cameron, Jun. 17, 2013.
75   Karen Cameron, "Re: President's Update - 'The Ride Stops...,'" email to Corey Owens, 8:25 AM.
76   Ibid.
77   Karen Cameron, "RE: uber," email to Craig Leisy, et al. [IATR Board of Directors], Jul. 31, 2013.
78   Matthew Daus, "RE: uber," email to Craig Leisy, et al, [IATR Board of Directors], Jul. 31, 2013.
79   Corey Owens, "Fwd: Press Release: Regulators Join Rising...," email to Karen Cameron, Jul. 19, 2013.
80   "IATR Conference 2013," IATR.global, accessed Mar. 26, 2013, http://iatr.global/index.php/2013; Cameron, "See You in St. Louis" (email attachment).
81   Matthew Daus, "Uber," email to Karen Cameron, Sep. 19, 2013.
82   Corey Owens, "Re: FW: Uber," email to Karen Cameron, Sep. 19, 2013.
83   Karen Cameron, "Re: Uber," email to Matthew Daus, Sep. 19, 2013.
84   Matthew Daus, "FW: Uber," email to Malachi Hull, Sep. 19, 2013.
85   Matthew Daus, "RE: IATR Workshops," email to Craig Leisy, et al. [IATR Board of Directors], Sep. 19, 2013.
86   Karen Cameron, "RE: Report on Deregulation and Re-Regulation," email to Matthew Daus, et al., Sep. 22, 2013.
87   Ron Linton, ""RE: Report on Deregulation and Re-Regulation," email to Matthew Daus, et al., Sep. 22, 2013.
88   "State of the IATR Speech," Youtube video, 26:32, posted by "taxicabregulators," Oct. 11, 2013, https://youtu.be/VJfZbmVfc7Q.
89   Ibid.
90   Ibid.
91   Ibid.
92   Daus, "Rocky Road Ahead..."

93   Cameron, "See You in St. Louis" (email attachment).

94   "Day 2 Lunch Keynote," Youtube video, 47:51, posted by "taxicabregulators," Oct. 15, 2013, https://youtu.be/AubraHDHltc.

95   Ibid.

96   "Day 2 Session 6," Youtube video, 2:01:54, posted by "taxicabregulators," Oct. 12, 2013, https://youtu.be/R9spOyTKI9k.

97   "Day 2 Session 7," Youtube video, 1:13:02, posted by "taxicabregulators," Oct. 12, 2013, https://youtu.be/ZdvctFb_8-U.

98   Karen Cameron, email to Corey Owens, Sep. 20, 2013.

99   Corey Owens, "On Consumers, Competition & Collusion," *Newsroom* (blog), Sep. 24, 2013, accessed Apr. 4, 2016, https://newsroom.uber.com/on-consumers-competition-and-collusion.

100   Ibid.

101   Ibid.

102   Ibid.

103   Matthew Daus, "RE: Uber Blog – IATR," email to Craig Leisy, et al., [IATR Board of Directors], Sep. 26, 2013, 3:27 PM.

104   Patrick Hoge, "Regulators' Rep Slams Uber's Confrontational Style," *San Francisco Business Journal*, Sep. 25, 2013, accessed Aug. 22, 2017, https://www.bizjournals.com/sanfrancisco/blog/2013/09/regulators-rep-slams-ubers.html?page=all.

105   Matthew Daus, "FW: Uber Blog – IATR," email to Craig Leisy, et al. [IATR Board of Directors], Sep. 26, 2013, 1:46 PM.

106   Karen Cameron, "Re: Uber Blog – IATR," email to Craig Leisy, et al. [IATR Board of Directors], Sep. 26, 2013, 3:13 PM.

107   Ibid.

108   Ibid.

109   Matthew Daus, "RE: Uber Blog – IATR," email to Craig Leisy, et al. [IATR Board of Directors], Sep. 26, 2013, 3:27 PM.

110   Louis Hamilton, "Re: Uber Blog – IATR," email to Craig Leisy, et al. [IATR Board of Directors], Sep. 26, 2013.

111   Karen Cameron, "FW: Uber – Final Word for Now!" email to Craig Leisy, Christiane Hayashi, and Thomas Drischler, Oct. 4, 2013.

112   Matthew Daus, "Uber – Final Word for Now!" email to Karen Cameron, Sep. 26, 2013.

113   Karen Cameron, "Re: Uber – Final Word for Now!" email to Matthew Daus and Tom Drischler, Sep. 26, 2013.

114   Ibid.

115   Thomas Drischler, "IATR," email to Karen Cameron, Oct. 8, 2013.

116   James Bisson, "RE: Cessation of Business Relationship…," email to Tom Drischler, et al. [IATR Board of Directors], Oct. 8, 2013.

117   Tom Drischler, "RE: Cessation of Business Relationship…," email to James Ney, et al., Oct. 9, 2013.

118   "Regulators' Forum" [home page], http://web.archive.org/web/20141114134204/http://www.regulators-forum.com.

119   Matthew Daus, "RE: Regulators Forum – News Nuggets…," email to Malachi Hull, Dec. 20, 2013.

120   Tom Drischler, "FW: IATR Board Meeting Docs," email to James Ney, et al. [IATR Board of Directors], Mar. 23, 2014, attachment: "K Cameron Separation Agreement – General Release (10941134).PDF."

121   Ibid, p. 2.

122   *Wallen v. St. Louis Metro. Taxicab Commission*, Case No. 4:15-cv-01432 (E.D. Mo. Sept. 18, 2015).

123   City of San Antonio (Texas), Police Department, Open Records Request no. W023544-012014, Jan. 20, 2014.

124   Michael Barfield, "Records Request," email to Stephen Todd, Feb. 16, 2017.

Chapter 9

1   Christiane Hayashi, "Re: Feedback Request," email to Michael Jones, et al., Dec. 2, 2013.

2   Thomas Drischler, "Re: Feedback Request," Email to Christiane Hayashi, Dec. 2, 2013.

3   Ibid.

4   Ibid.

5   Jim Epstein, "Uber and Its Enemies," *The Daily Beast*, Feb. 10, 2014, accessed Sep. 21, 2017, http://www.thedailybeast.com/uber-and-its-enemies.

6   Henry K. Lee, "Arrests in 2 SF Crashes That Killed Pedestrians," *SFGATE*, Jan. 2, 2014, accessed Aug. 22, 2017, http://www.sfgate.com/crime/article/Arrests-in-2-S-F-crashes-that-killed-pedestrians-5108718.php.

7   Christiane Hayashi, "RE: Uber Claims It's Not…," email to Rupal Bapat, Jan. 2, 2014.

8   Rosemary Krimbel, "RE: Uber X Driver Killed a Girl…," email to Christiane Hayashi, Jan. 3, 2014.

9   Elyce Kirchner, David Paredes, and Scott Pham, "UberX Driver Involved in New Year's…," *NBCBayArea.com*, Jan. 15, 2014, accessed Aug. 22, 2017, http://www.nbcbayarea.com/news/local/UberX-Driver-Involved-in-New-Years-Eve-Manslaughter-Had-A-Record-of-Reckless-Driving-240344931.html.

10 CPUC, Decision no. 13-09-045, p. 27.

11 Christiane Hayashi, "Another Uber Article," email to Ron Linton, et al. [IATR Smartphone App Committee], Jan. 6, 2014.

12 Barry Lefkowitz, "RE: Uber," email to Christiane Hayashi, Jan. 16, 2014.

13 Sean Patrick Farrell, "Questions of Responsibility at Uber," *New York Times* video, Jan. 27, 2014, http://nyti.ms/1e62K6K.

14 California Department of Insurance, Investigatory Hearing, Background White Paper, *Insurance and [TNCs]: Solving the Insurance Challenge…*, Mar. 21, 2014, http://www.insurance.ca.gov/01-consumers/105-type/82-TNC-Ridesharing/upload/TNCBackground.pdf; Christiane Hayashi, "RE: Uber's Policy," email to Matthew Daus, Mar. 24, 2014.

15 San Francisco Board of Supervisors, Neighborhood Services and Safety Committee, *140020 Hearing – Regulatory Status of Private Transportation Networks*, Regular Meeting – Mar. 6, 2014, http://sanfrancisco.granicus.com/MediaPlayer.php?view_id=164&clip_id=19516&meta_id=378395.

16 Ibid.

17 "Baltimore, Your UberX is Arriving Now!" *Uber Blog*, Oct. 22, 2013, accessed Aug. 23, 2017, https://www.uber.com/blog/baltimore/baltimore-your-uberx-is-arriving-now/; "Bringing #LyftLove to Baltimore," *Lyft Blog*, Oct. 17, 2013, accessed Aug. 23, 2017, http://web.archive.org/web/20131022181348/http://blog.lyft.com:80/.

18 "Nashville UberX: Better, Cheaper, Faster Than a Taxi," *Uber Blog*, Dec. 11, 2013, accessed Aug. 23, 2017, https://www.uber.com/blog/nashville/nashville-uberx-better-cheaper-faster-than-a-taxi; "Lyft Rolls into Nashville," *Lyft Blog*, Dec. 6, 2013, accessed Aug. 23, 2017, https://blog.lyft.com/posts/lyft-rolls-into-nashville.

19 Freed, "Former DC Taxi Commissioner…"

20 Andrew J. Hawkins, "Taxi Mogul Suspects City Official Moonlighted for Uber," *Crain's New York*, May 20, 2014, accessed Aug. 23, 2017, http://www.crainsnewyork.com/article/20140520/BLOGS04/140529985/taxi-mogul-suspects-city-official-moonlighted-for-uber.

21 "For Boston Cabbies, a Losing Battle Against the Numbers," *Boston Globe*, Mar. 31, 2013, accessed Jul. 22, 2016, https://www.bostonglobe.com/metro/2013/03/30/spotlight/9eVWW7Y6RaOIqII62n2XlI/story.html.

22 Mark Cohen, "Resignation Board IATR," email to Matthew Daus and Thomas Drischler, Jan. 13, 2014.

23 Malachi Hull to Travis Kalanick, Oct. 10, 2013.

24 Travers Mackel, "I-Team: City Leader Threatens Transportation Company…," *WDSU.com*, Nov. 21, 2013, accessed Mar. 30, 2016, http://www.wdsu.com/investigations/iteam-city-leader-threatens-transportation-company-with-arrest-fines-if-it-brings-business-to-nola/23094732.

25 Richard A. Webster, "Ousted New Orleans Taxicab Bureau Director Slammed…" *Times-Picayune* (New Orleans, LA), Jul. 7, 2014, accessed Aug. 23, 2017, http://www.nola.com/politics/index.ssf/2014/07/ousted_new_orleans_taxicab_bur.html.

26 Richard A. Webster, "Former New Orleans Taxicab Bureau Chief Sues…," *Times-Picayune* (New Orleans, LA), Mar. 12, 2015, accessed Aug. 23, 2017, http://www.nola.com/politics/index.ssf/2015/03/former_new_orleans_taxicab_bur.html.

27 Joel Connelly, "Seattle Suspends Ride Sharing Regulations a Month After Passage," *Seattle Post-Intelligencer*, Apr. 17, 2014.

28 Cameron, "See You in St. Louis" (email attachment); City of Cambridge, License Commission, *Regulations for Smartphone Technology for Taxicabs and Limousines*, accessed Aug. 23, 2017, http://www.cambridgema.gov/license/Calendar/~/media/55B6A848D40C434B8299A95F80E91FD6.ashx.

29 Nick, "The Cambridge License Commission vs. The People of Cambridge," *Newsroom* (blog), June 16, 2014, accessed Mar. 23, 2016, https://newsroom.uber.com/us-massachusetts/74056.

30 Art, Twitter post, Jun. 17, 2014, 3:22 PM, https://twitter.com/sorstz/status/479026230109290496.

31 "Cambridge License Commission to Hold Public Hearings…," *WickedLocal.com*, Jun 30, 2014, accessed Aug. 23, 2017, http://cambridge.wickedlocal.com/article/20140630/News/140639913.

32 Andy Vuong, "Ride-Share Outfits Draw PUC Letters," *Denver Post*, Dec. 11, 2013.

33 "Lyft and UberX are Latest Threat to Taxi Oligopoly," *Denver Post*, Jan. 8, 2014.

34 Colorado Senate, Sixty-Ninth General Assembly, Second Regular Session, *[SB14-125], Concerning the Regulation of [TNCs]*, Introduced version, Colorado: General Assembly, http://www.leg.state.co.us/clics/clics2014a/csl.nsf/fsbillcont3/70364091166B28FC87257C4300636F6B?open&file=125_01.pdf.

35 Andy Vuong, "Ticket to Ride (Share)," *Denver Post*, Jan. 29, 2014.

36 Colorado General Assembly, Senate Business, Labor & Technology (BLT) Committee, *SB14-125 [TNCs] Regulation* Hearing, Feb. 5, 2014, http://coloradoga.granicus.com/MediaPlayer.php?view_id=41&clip_id=4907.

37 Ibid.
38 Ibid.
39 Ibid.
40 Ibid.
41 Ibid.
42 Ibid.
43 Ibid.
44 Ibid.
45 Colorado General Assembly, Senate Business, Labor & Technology (BLT) Committee, *SB14-125 [TNCs] Regulation* Hearing (For Action Only), Feb. 11, 2014, http://coloradoga.granicus.com/MediaPlayer.php?view_id=41&clip_id=4983 and http://coloradoga.granicus.com/MediaPlayer.php?view_id=41&clip_id=4989.
46 Ibid.
47 Ibid.
48 Ibid.
49 Doug Dean to Senators Jahn and Harvey, et al., Feb. 24, 2014.
50 Andy Vuong, "A Debate Hops In," *Denver Post*, Feb. 19, 2014.
51 Colorado General Assembly, Senate Journal, *59th Day – March 7, 2014*, Sixty-Ninth General Assembly, Second Regular Session, pp. 438-441.
52 Colorado General Assembly, Senate Journal, *62nd Day – March 10, 2014*, Sixty-Ninth General Assembly, Second Regular Session, p. 446.
53 Andrew, "UberX Eliminates Ridesharing Insurance Ambiguity," *Uber Blog*, Mar. 14, 2014, http://web.archive.org/web/20140331163138/http://blog.uber.com/uberxridesharinginsurance.
54 Vincent Carroll, "Doug Dean's Dogged Crusade to Quash Competition," *Denver Post*, Feb. 19, 2014.
55 Senate BLT Committee, *SB14-125 Hearing*, Feb. 5, 2014.
56 Colorado General Assembly, House Transportation and Energy Committee, *SB14-125 [TNCs] Regulation* Hearing, Apr. 2, 2014, http://coloradoga.granicus.com/MediaPlayer.php?view_id=24&clip_id=5559&meta_id=100159.
57 Robert McBride, "Taxi Safety Should be Paramount," *Denver Post*, Feb. 16, 2014.
58 Will {McCollum], "Keep UberX Rolling in Colorado!" *Newsroom* (blog), Mar. 10, 2014, accessed May 14, 2016, https://newsroom.uber.com/us-colorado/keep-uberx-rolling-in-colorado.
59 House Transportation Committee, *SB14-125 Hearing*, Apr. 2, 2014.
60 Ibid.
61 Ibid.
62 Ibid.
63 Ibid.
64 Ibid.
65 Ibid.
66 Christopher N. Osher, "Hancock Friend and Former Denver Supervisor Pleads…," *Denver Post*, Apr. 22, 2016, accessed Jul. 30, 2016, http://dpo.st/2xfZbfx.
67 House Transportation Committee, *SB14-125 Hearing*, Apr. 2, 2014.
68 Colorado General Assembly, House Transportation and Energy Committee, *SB14-125 [TNCs] Regulation (For Action Only)* Hearing, Apr. 9, 2014, http://coloradoga.granicus.com/MediaPlayer.php?view_id=24&clip_id=5647&meta_id=101833.
69 Colorado General Assembly, House Transportation and Energy Committee, *SB125_L.031* (amendment), Sixty-Ninth General Assembly, Second Regular Session (2014), http://www.leg.state.co.us/CLICS/CLICS2014A/commsumm.nsf/58e6d054c29cbe1287256e5f00670a70/a1824b316ae5996287257cb5007401f5/$FILE/140409%20AttachC.pdf.
70 Colorado General Assembly, House Transportation and Energy Committee, *SB125_L.062* (amendment), Sixty-Ninth General Assembly, Second Regular Session (2014), http://www.leg.state.co.us/CLICS/CLICS2014A/commsumm.nsf/58e6d054c29cbe1287256e5f00670a70/a1824b316ae5996287257cb5007401f5/$FILE/140409%20AttachH.pdf.
71 Colorado General Assembly, House Transportation and Energy Committee, *Final Bill Summary for SB14-125, Amendment L.068*, Sixty-Ninth General Assembly, Second Regular Session (2014), http://www.leg.state.co.us/CLICS/CLICS2014A/commsumm.nsf/CommByBillSumm/A1824B316AE5996287257CB5007401F5.
72 House Transportation Committee, *SB14-125 Hearing*, Apr. 9, 2014.
73 Ibid.
74 House Transportation Committee, *Final Bill Summary*, Amendment L.057.
75 House Transportation Committee, *SB14-125 Hearing*, Apr. 9, 2014.
76 Ibid.

77   House Transportation Committee, *Final Bill Summary*, Amendment L.033, Section 3.
78   House Transportation Committee, *SB14-125* Hearing, Apr. 9, 2014.
79   Ibid.
80   Ibid.
81   House Transportation Committee, *Final Bill Summary*, Amendment L.044.
82   House Transportation Committee, *SB14-125* Hearing, Apr. 9, 2014.
83   Ibid.
84   House Transportation Committee, *Final Bill Summary*, Amendment L.034.
85   House Transportation Committee, *Final Bill Summary*, Amendment L.056.
86   House Transportation Committee, *Final Bill Summary*, SB14-125 (as amended).
87   House Transportation Committee, *SB14-125* Hearing, Apr. 9, 2014.
88   Colorado General Assembly, House Finance Committee, *SB14-125 [TNCs] Regulation* Hearing, Apr. 16, 2014, http://coloradoga.granicus.com/MediaPlayer.php?view_id=19&clip_id=5740&meta_id=104169.
89   Colorado General Assembly, House Appropriations Committee, *SB14-125 [TNCs] Regulation* Hearing, Apr. 23, 2014, http://coloradoga.granicus.com/MediaPlayer.php?view_id=14&clip_id=5809&meta_id=106513.
90   Colorado Senate, Sixty-Ninth General Assembly, Second Regular Session, *[SB14-125], Concerning the Regulation of [TNCs]*, Rerevised version, Colorado: General Assembly, http://www.leg.state.co.us/clics/clics2014a/csl.nsf/fsbillcont3/70364091166B28FC87257C4300636F6B?open&file=125_rer.pdf.
91   Ibid.
92   Colorado General Assembly, House Journal, *111ᵗʰ Day – April 28, 2014*, Sixty-Ninth General Assembly, Second Regular Session, pp. 1250-1252.
93   Colorado General Assembly, Senate Journal, *112ᵗʰ Day – April 29, 2014*, Sixty-Ninth General Assembly, Second Regular Session, p. 997.
94   Colorado General Assembly, *Summarized Bill History for Bill No. SB14-125*, Colorado: General Assembly (2014).
95   "Did PUC Director Take Legislators for a Ride?" *Denver Post*, May 11, 2014.
96   Doug Dean, "PUC Did Not Mislead Legislators," *Denver Post*, May 18, 2014.
97   Vincent Carroll, "How Doug Dean Blindside Lawmakers," *Denver Post*, May 22, 2014.
98   Dave Cook, "My Uber Got Pulled Over by the Denver Police – And Then Things Got Really Weird," *GeekWire*, Jul. 19, 2014, accessed May 14, 2016, http://www.geekwire.com/2014/hey-denver-police-harrass-riding-uber; Taylor Soper, "Denver Police Chief Opens Investigation Into Uber Incident…," *GeekWire*, Jul. 21, 2014, accessed May 14, 2016, http://www.geekwire.com/2014/denver-police-chief-opens-investigation-uber-incident-issues-public-apology.
99   Colorado Secretary of State (SOS), Friends of Max Tyler (candidate committee), *July 1, 2014 – Report of Contributions and Expenditures*, SOS ID no. 20095608268; Colorado Secretary of State (SOS), Friends of Max Tyler (candidate committee), *August 1, 2014 – Report of Contributions and Expenditures*, SOS ID no. 20095608268.
100   Colorado Secretary of State (SOS), Friends of Max Tyler (candidate committee), *January 15, 2014 – Report of Contributions and Expenditures*, SOS ID no. 20095608268.
101   "Contribution Limits," Colorado Secretary of State, http://web.archive.org/web/20150130042224/http://www.sos.state.co.us/pubs/elections/CampaignFinance/limits/contributions.html.
102   Friends of Max Tyler, *July 1, 2014 – Report…*
103   "Uber Plays Hardball But Fails to Win the Game," *San Francisco Business Journal*, Sep. 3, 2014, accessed Jun. 10, 2016, https://www.bizjournals.com/sanfrancisco/blog/techflash/2014/09/uber-plays-hardball-but-fails-to-win-the-game.html.
104   Tamara Chuang, "Rideshare Coverage for Insurance Gap," *Denver Post*, Jan. 16, 2015.
105   Justin Kintz, "Insurance Aligned," *Newsroom* (blog), Mar. 24, 2015, accessed May 7, 2016, https://newsroom.uber.com/introducing-the-tnc-insurance-compromise-model-bill.

Chapter 10

1   Mike Isaac, "Uber Picks David Plouffe to Wage Regulatory Fight," *New York Times*, Aug. 19, 2014, https://nyti.ms/2mGaAQh.
2   Matthew Panzarino, "Uber Offering Lyft Drivers Free $50…," *TechCrunch*, Dec. 11, 2013, accessed Apr. 2, 2016, http://tcrn.ch/2wdmeTn.
3   Rip Empson, "Black Car Competitor Accuses Uber of DDOS-Style…," *TechCrunch*, Jan. 24, 2014, accessed Feb. 4, 2017, http://tcrn.ch/2xs8S7w.
4   Erica Fink, "Uber's Dirty Tricks Quantified," *CNNMoney*, Aug. 12, 2014, accessed Apr. 23, 2016,

http://cnnmon.ie/XdRf8E.

5   Casey Newton, "This is Uber's Playbook for Sabotaging Lyft," *The Verge*, Aug. 26, 2014, accessed Aug. 28, 2017, https://www.theverge.com/2014/8/26/6067663/this-is-ubers-playbook-for-sabotaging-lyft.
6   Ibid.
7   Kim Lyons, "PUC Comes Down Hard on Ride-Share Drivers and Companies," *Pittsburgh Post-Gazette*, Jun. 10, 2014.
8   Kim Lyons, "Yellow Cab Readies App for Ride Shares," *Pittsburgh Post-Gazette*, Jul. 23, 2014.
9   Brian Bowling, "PUC Slams Brakes on Ride-Sharing," *Pittsburgh Tribune-Review*, Jul. 1, 2014.
10 Kim Lyons, "Lyft and Uber are Allowed to Operate for Now," *Pittsburgh Post-Gazette*, Jul. 24, 2014; Kim Lyons, "PUC Vote Gives Uber a License to Roll," *Pittsburgh Post-Gazette*, Nov. 14, 2014.
11 "Michael Arrington in Conversation with Uber's Travis Kalanick | Disrupt SF 2014," Youtube video, 31:00, posted by "TechCrunch," Sep. 8, 2014, https://youtu.be/s5zXIjGlzDU.
12 Ibid.
13 Ibid.
14 Johana Bhuiyan, "Uber's Travis Kalanick Takes 'Charm Offensive to New York City," *Buzzfeed*, Nov. 14, 2014, accessed Apr. 25, 2016 http://bzfd.it/2wk4RSk.
15 Ben Smith, "Uber Executive Suggests Digging Up Dirt on Journalists," *Buzzfeed*, Nov. 17, 2014, accessed Apr. 25, 2016, http://bzfd.it/2iCh3e9.
16 Sarah Lacy, "The Horrific Trickle Down of Asshole Culture," *Pando*, Oct. 22, 2014, accessed Jun. 28, 2017, https://pando.com/2014/10/22/the-horrific-trickle-down-of-asshole-culture-at-a-company-like-uber.
17 Smith, "Uber Executive Suggests Digging..."
18 Johana Bhuiyan and Charlie Warzel, "'God View': Uber Investigates its Top New York Executive...," *Buzzfeed*, Nov. 18, 2014, accessed Feb. 11, 2017, http://bzfd.it/2wktyOG.
19 Nairi, "Uber's Data Privacy Policy," *Newsroom* (blog), Nov. 18, 2014, accessed Feb. 13, 2017, https://newsroom.uber.com/ubers-data-privacy-policy; "Uber CEO Offers Lengthy 13 Tweet Apology...," *6ABC.com*, Nov. 18, 2014, accessed Apr. 25, 2016, http://6abc.com/technology/uber-ceo-offers-lengthy-13-tweet-apology-for-an-executives-controversial-remarks/400914.
20 Rosalind S. Helderman, "Uber Pressures Regulators by Mobilizing Riders and Hiring...," *Washington Post*, Dec. 13, 2014, accessed Aug. 29, 2017, http://wapo.st/2vCbJtf.
21 Senator Al Franken to Travis Kalanick, Nov. 19, 2014; Senator Al Franken to Logan Green, Dec. 2, 2014.
22 Senator Al Franken, "Sen. Franken to Uber: I Still Have Concerns...," Jan. 27, 2015, https://www.franken.senate.gov/?p=press_release&id=3027.
23 Alison Griswold, "While You Were Complaining About Uber's Ethics...," *Slate*, Dec. 4, 2014, accessed Aug. 29, 2017, http://slate.me/2iIC07o.
24 Ordinance No. 2013-03-21-0188, City of San Antonio (Texas) (2013).
25 Ibid; Ordinance No. 20130620-051, City of Austin (Texas) (2013).
26 Robert Wilonsky and Rudolph Bush, "Dallas Officials, Yellow Cab Worked Together...," *Dallas Morning News*, Sep. 14, 2013, accessed Jan. 17, 2016, http://www.dallasnews.com/news/transportation/20130914-dallas-officials-yellow-cab-worked-together-to-thwart-uber-transportation-app.
27 Rayson Media, Twitter post, Mar. 7, 2014, 12:15 AM, https://twitter.com/RaysonMedia/status/441849705606021120.
28 Ryan, "Shining a Light on Uber Austin," *Newsroom* (blog), Mar. 5, 2014, accessed Apr. 23, 2016, https://newsroom.uber.com/us-texas/shining-a-light-on-uber-austin.
29 Jazmine Ulloa and Philip Jankowski, "Owens Found Guilty of Capital Murder," *Austin American-Statesman*, Nov. 7, 2015.
30 Gary Dinges and Christian McDonald, "Austin's Drinking Problem?" *Austin American-Statesman*, Mar. 26, 2014.
31 Ibid.
32 Kevin Schwaller, "Austin Organization Focusing on Safer Streets Celebrates Launch," *KXAN.com*, May 11, 2014, accessed Aug. 29, 2017, http://kxan.com/2014/05/11/austin-organization-focusing-on-safer-streets-celebrates-launch.
33 Resolution No. 201405215-024, City of Austin (Texas) (2014).
34 Resolution No. 201405215-025, City of Austin (Texas) (2014).
35 Ibid.
36 Lily Rockwell, "Rideshare Firm Plans Free-Ride Launch," *Austin American-Statesman*, May 29, 2014.
37 Ben Wear and Lily Rockwell, "Austin Issues Warning as Lyft Launches Ride-Sharing," *Austin American-Statesman*, May 30, 2014.
38 Lily Rockwell, "Ridesharing Firm Uber Launches Austin Service," *Austin American-Statesman*, Jun. 4, 2014.
39 Jennifer Curington, "Ridesharing Service May Become Legal in Austin," *Community Impact Newspaper*, Sep. 15, 2014, accessed Aug. 29, 2017, https://communityimpact.com/austin/city-county/2014/09/15/ridesharing-services-may-become-legal-in-austin-2.

40   Gary Dinges and Claudia Grisales, "'Surge Pricing' Catches Ride-Sharers Off-Guard...," *Austin American-Statesman*, Sep. 6, 2014; Philip Jankowski, "Ride-Sharing Advocates Throw Jabs at Taxi Firms," *Austin American-Statesman*, Jul. 31, 2014.

41   Joshua Fetcher, "City Props 1 and 2 Pass...," *Daily Texan* (Austin, Texas), Nov. 7, 2012, accessed Aug. 29, 2017, http://www.dailytexanonline.com/news/2012/11/07/city-prop-1-and-2-pass-austin-to-have-november-city-elections.

42   "Austin Leaders Announce Plan to Make Uber and Lyft Legal," *KXAN.com*, Sep. 12, 2014, accessed Apr. 24, 2017, http://kxan.com/2014/09/12/austin-leaders-announce-plan-to-make-uber-and-lyft-legal.

43   Austin City Council, *Minutes, Regular Meeting, Thursday, March 7, 2013*, Item 67, http://www.austintexas.gov/edims/document.cfm?id=185972.

44   Mike Morris and Dug Begley, "Uber, Lyft Given Green Light," *Houston Chronicle*, Aug. 7, 2014.

45   Austin City Council, *Item 58 – Approve Second and Third Reading of...* (hearing), Regular Meeting, Oct. 2, 2014, http://austintx.swagit.com/play/10022014-507/18/.

46   Ibid.

47   Austin City Council, *Item 38 – Approve Third Reading of an Ordinance...* (hearing), Regular Meeting, Oct. 16, 2014, http://austintx.swagit.com/play/10162014-582/15/.

48   Nikki Cooper, "RE: Quick Question," email to Carlton Thomas and Steve Grassfield, Oct. 15, 2014, 11:42 AM.

49   Gary Dinges, "Uber Reports Big Hike in Users," *Austin American-Statesman*, Oct. 15, 2014.

50   Nikki Cooper, "Quick Question," email to Carlton Thomas, Oct. 15, 2014, 10:29 AM.

51   Carlton Thomas, "RE: Peer 2 Peer transit resolution," email to Gary Gilbert, Sep. 15, 2014.

52   Lily Rockwell, "Council OKs Ride-Sharing Services," *Austin American-Statesman*, Oct. 17, 2014.

53   Sarah, "Austin: Now We're Yours, Know We're Here," *Newsroom* (blog), Oct. 31, 2014, accessed Apr. 23, 2016, https://newsroom.uber.com/us-texas/austin-now-were-yours-know-were-here.

54   Mark Richardson, "Statesman Rescinds Pressley Endorsement," *Austin Monitor*, Nov. 4, 2014,

55   Travis County Clerk, *November 4, 2014 Joint General and Special Elections, City of Austin Cumulative Results*, http://www.traviscountyclerk.org/eclerk/content/images/election_results/2014.11.04/20141104coacume.pdf.

56   Amy Kamp, "Breaking: Chris Riley Withdraws From Run-Off," *Austin Chronicle*, Nov. 7, 2014, https://www.austinchronicle.com/daily/news/2014-11-07/breaking-chris-riley-withdraws-from-run-off.

Chapter 11

1   "Council Member Ann Kitchen – Biography," accessed Sep. 1, 2017, http://www.austintexas.gov/department/council-member-ann-kitchen-biography.

2   Michael Kanin, "With Finance Numbers In, Shade and Tovo...," *Austin Monitor*, Jun. 13, 2011.

3   City of Austin, Office of the City Clerk, *Reports Filed by Council Members and Candidates, 8th Day Before Election*, Ann Kitchen, Oct. 27, 2014, http://www.austintexas.gov/edims/document.cfm?id=220211.

4   Austin City Council, Mobility Committee, *Items 1 & 2 – Call to Order...* (hearing), Mar. 25, 2015, http://austintx.swagit.com/play/03252015-565/2/.

5   Ibid.

6   Austin City Council, Mobility Committee, *Item 3 - Transportation Network Company...* (hearing), Mar. 25, 2015, http://austintx.swagit.com/play/03252015-565/3/.

7   Ibid.

8   Ibid.

9   Ibid.

10   Robert Spillar to [Austin] Mayor and Council, "Transportation Network Companies...," Mar. 24, 2015, http://www.austintexas.gov/edims/document.cfm?id=228702.

11   Robert Spillar to [Austin] City Council, "Ground Transportation; an Operational..." Mar. 31, 2015, http://www.austintexas.gov/edims/document.cfm?id=228550.

12   Bill Lambrecht, "Uber Seeking to Get a Lift From Lobbyists," *Houston Chronicle*, Mar. 2, 2015.

13   Texas Legislature, HB 1733, 84th Session – Regular (2015).

14   *California v. Uber Technologies Inc.*, CGC-14-543120, California Superior Court, San Francisco County.

15   Ibid.

16   Dug Begley and Dylan Baddour, "Uber Driver Lacked Permit," *Houston Chronicle*, Apr. 7, 2015.

17   Ibid.

18   Ibid.

19   Dug Begley, "Ex-Con Cleared by Uber to Drive," *Houston Chronicle*, Apr. 8, 2015; Dug Begley, "Cleared by Uber But Not the City," *Houston Chronicle*, Apr. 9, 2015.

20   Texas Legislature, House Committee on Transportation, *Hearing, HB 2440*, Apr. 9, 2015, http://tlchouse.granicus.com/MediaPlayer.php?view_id=37&clip_id=10601 (Part 1).

21 Ibid.
22 Ibid.
23 Ibid.
24 Ibid.
25 Ibid.
26 Imperative Information Group, "2008 Study of Criminal Records," accessed Sep. 1, 2017, http://imperativeinfo.com/wp-content/uploads/2011/09/DPS_Criminal.pdf.
27 *California v. Uber Technologies Inc.*, "First Amended Complaint for...," filed Aug. 18, 2015.
28 Texas Legislature, House Committee on Transportation, *Hearing, HB 2440*, Apr. 9, 2015, http://tlchouse.granicus.com/MediaPlayer.php?view_id=37&clip_id=10616 (Part 2).
29 Ibid; Texas Legislature, *Hearing, HB 2440* (Part 1).
30 Texas Legislature, *Hearing, HB 2440* (Part 2).
31 Texas Legislature, *History, HB 2440*, 84th Session – Regular, http://www.capitol.state.tx.us/BillLookup/History.aspx?LegSess=84R&Bill=HB2440.
32 Ben Wear, "Legislation on Uber, Lyft Runs Out of Gas in House," *Austin American-Statesman*, May 16, 2015.
33 Howard Fischer, "Ducey: Dropping Ride-Share Taxi...," *Arizona Daily Star*, Jan. 29, 2015; Howard Fischer, "Ducey: Firing Forestalled Sting on Uber, Lyft," *Arizona Daily Star*, May 16, 2015; Jesse A. Millard, "Arizona Weights and Measures Department Folding...," *Arizona PBS*, https://cronkitenews.azpbs.org/2015/09/02/arizona-weights-and-measures-department-folding-duties-moving.
34 Jeff Wiehe and Chris Meyers, "Uber Quietly Enters Under New State Law," *Journal Gazette* (Fort Wayne, IN), May 8, 2015.
35 Kansas Bankers Association, "Proposed Comprehensive and Collision...," provided to the Kansas House Committee on Insurance, Mar. 20, 2015, http://www.kslegislature.org/li_2016/b2015_16/committees/ctte_h_ins_1/documents/testimony/20150320_14.pdf; Kansas House of Representatives, Committee of the Whole, SB 117, *Amendment by Representative Proehl*, Mar. 25, 2015, http://www.kslegislature.org/li_2016/b2015_16/measures/documents/fa_2015_sb117_h_1907.pdf; Kansas Insurance Department, "Introduction to Auto Insurance," http://web.archive.org/web/20150428163435/http://www.ksinsurance.org/autohome/auto/auto-info.php.
36 Emily Behlmann, "Uber's Problem With this Bill in Kansas?...," *Wichita Business Journal*, Apr. 2, 2015, accessed Jun. 27, 2016, http://www.bizjournals.com/wichita/morning_call/2015/04/uber-s-problem-with-this-bill-in-kansas-it-s-more.html.
37 Zack Slezak, "Save UberX in Kansas," *Newsroom* (blog), Mar. 30, 2015, accessed Jun. 27, 2016, https://newsroom.uber.com/us-missouri/saving-kansas.
38 Austin Alonzo, "Kansas Nears Passing a Bill That May Force Uber Out," *Kansas City Business Journal*, Apr. 1, 2015, accessed Jun. 27, 2016, http://www.bizjournals.com/kansascity/news/2015/04/01/kansas-nears-passing-a-bill-that-may-force-uber.html.
39 Kansas Legislature, SB 117, *Conference Committee Report*, Apr. 2, 2015, http://www.kslegislature.org/li_2016/b2015_16/measures/documents/ccr_2015_sb117_h_2015.pdf.
40 "Truck Displaying 'SB 117 Destroys...,'" *Topeka Capital-Journal*, Apr. 3, 2015.
41 Bryan Lowry, "Brownback May Veto Rules for Uber...," *Wichita Eagle*, Apr. 17, 2015.
42 Kansas Governor's Office, "Governor Sam Brownback Cites Importance of Innovation..." Apr. 20, 2015, https://governor.kansas.gov/governor-sam-brownback-cites-importance-of-innovation-in-economic-growth-as-he-vetoes-sb-117/.
43 Dave, "Uber is Expanding Across Kansas," *Newsroom* (blog), Apr. 23, 2015, accessed Jun. 27, 2016, https://newsroom.uber.com/us-kansas/uber-is-expanding-across-kansas.
44 Jonathan Shorman, "Legislature Forces Bill Opposed by...," *Topeka Capital-Journal*, May 5, 2015.
45 KC Startup Village, Twitter post, May 5, 2015, 9:07 PM, https://twitter.com/KCSV/status/596526804388614145.
46 Brett Hildabrand, Twitter post, May 5, 2015, 1:27 PM, https://twitter.com/Brett4ks/status/595686163219935232; Stephanie Clayton, Twitter post, May 5, 2015, 1:45 PM, https://twitter.com/SSCJoCoKs/status/595690749523587074.
47 Bryan Lowry, "Lawmakers Negotiate to Bring Uber Back to Kansas," *Wichita Eagle*, May 9, 2015.
48 Bryan Lowry, "Kansas House, Senate Approve Measure to Bring Back Uber," *Wichita Eagle*, May 19, 2015.
49 Tim Carpenter, "Brownback Takes Political Trip Before...," *Topeka Capital-Journal*, May 22, 2015.
50 Matthew Daus and Pasqualino Russo, "One Standard for All," accessed Sep. 3, 2017, http://docs.cpuc.ca.gov/PublishedDocs/Efile/G000/M166/K503/166503004.PDF.
51 University Transportation Research Center, "The Future of the Taxi Medallion System...," Presentation at the SUNY Global Center, Jun. 23, 2015, video available at "Part 1...," Vimeo video, 59:41, posted by "Univ. Transp. Research Center," Jun. 25, 2015, https://vimeo.com/131789222.
52 Ibid.
53 Ibid.

54 Ibid.
55 Ibid.
56 Ibid.
57 Ed Kargbo, "Houston White Paper Exposes TNC Background Checks," email to Carlton Thomas, Apr. 17, 2015, attachment: "4.7.2015 Updated City of Houston Complete...pdf."
58 Tom Drischler, "IATR 2015 Conference," email to Matthew Daus, et. al. [IATR Board of Directors], Jun. 1, 2015, attachment: "IATR Conference 2015 Narrative.docx."
59 Nikki Cooper, "RE: Background Check," email to Carlton Thomas, Nov. 23, 2015, attachment: "IATR .pdf."
60 "2015 IATR Conference: Gala Awards Dinner," Youtube video, 30:05, posted by "The IATR," Oct. 11, 2015, https://youtu.be/ahUTOIjQexk.
61 Ibid.

Chapter 12

1 Sarah Clemons, "URGENT: Meeting with Adam Goldman TODAY," email to John Lawler, May 1, 2015.
2 Lauren Rigney, "uberPOOL Arrives in Austin," *Newsroom* (blog), Mar. 5, 2015, accessed Apr. 29, 2017, https://newsroom.uber.com/us-texas/5-uber-pool-rides-2.
3 Carlton Thomas, "RE: Checking In," email to Gary Gilbert, et. al., May 11, 2015.
4 Ibid.
5 Chase Hoffberger, "Crash Course," *Austin Chronicle*, Aug. 7, 2015.
6 Ibid.
7 Austin City Council, Mobility Committee, *Items 9-11 (Part 1 of 2) – 0 Consider and...* (hearing), Apr. 29, 2015, http://austintx.swagit.com/play/04292015-763/7.
8 Ordinance no. 20150604-055, City of Austin (Texas) (2015).
9 Austin Transportation Department, "Taxicab Franchise Renewal Process," presentation before the Austin Mobility Committee, Mar. 25, 2015, http://www.austintexas.gov/edims/document.cfm?id=228527.
10 Ben Wear, "City Backs Fourth Cab Franchise," *Austin American-Statesman*, Jun. 5, 2015.
11 Rachel, "Lake Travis Love," *Newsroom* (blog), Jul. 1, 2015, accessed Apr. 8, 2017, https://newsroom.uber.com/us-texas/lake-travis-love; Rachel, "Cedar Park Love," *Newsroom* (blog), Jul. 16, 2015, accessed Apr. 8, 2017, https://newsroom.uber.com/us-texas/cedar-park-love; Rachel, "Georgetown Love," *Newsroom* (blog), Jun. 3, 2015, accessed Apr. 8, 2017, https://newsroom.uber.com/us-texas/georgetown-love; Rachel, "Round Rock Love," *Newsroom* (blog), May 20, 2015, accessed Apr. 8, 2017, https://newsroom.uber.com/us-texas/round-rock-love.
12 Salmaa, "UberESPANOL Has Arrived," *Newsroom* (blog), Jul. 6, 2015, accessed Apr. 8, 2017, https://newsroom.uber.com/us-texas/uber-espanol-has-arrived-2; Shelley Adams, "uberACCESS: Wheelchair Accessible Vehicles...," *Newsroom* (blog), Jul. 29, 2015, Apr. 8, 2017, accessed Apr. 8, 2017, https://newsroom.uber.com/us-texas/uberaccess-wheelchair-accessible-vehicles-available-at-the-tap-of-a-button.
13 Austin City Council, Mobility Committee, *Item 7 – Staff Briefing on Ground Transportation...* (hearing), Aug. 5, 2015, http://austintx.swagit.com/play/08052015-659/8.
14 Ibid.
15 Jordan M. Gentry, Instagram photo, uploaded Sep. 2, 2015, https://www.instagram.com/p/7JAOReohCs/.
16 Austin City Council, Mobility Committee, *Item 5 (Part 1 of 2) – Discussion and Possible...* (hearing), Sep. 2, 2015, http://austintx.swagit.com/play/09022015-680/4.
17 City of Austin Council Message Board, "Mobility Committee – TNC Ordinance Proposed Amendments," by Ann Kitchen, Sep. 2, 2015, http://austincouncilforum.org/viewtopic.php?f=2&t=361&hilit=motion+sheet+safety&view=print.
18 Ibid.
19 Ibid.
20 Ibid.
21 Ibid.
22 Brent Wistrom, "Uber's New Poll Shows 68% of Austin Opposes...," *Austin Inno*, Sep. 23, 2015, accessed Sep. 3, 2017, https://www.americaninno.com/austin/uber-regs-tax-survey-shows-austin-opposition.
23 Russ Garcia, "Case Study Shows Our Impact in Austin," *Newsroom* (blog), Oct. 5, 2015, accessed Apr. 8, 2017, https://newsroom.uber.com/us-texas/case-study-shows-our-impact-in-austin.
24 Adam Goldman, "ICYMI," email to Gregorio Casar, Oct. 7, 2015.
25 Claudia Grisales, "Wanted: 5,000 East Austin Drivers," *Austin American-Statesman*, Sep. 17, 2015.
26 Austin City Council, Mobility Committee, *Item 4 – Staff Briefing and Discussion...* (hearing), Oct. 7, 2015, http://austintx.swagit.com/play/10072015-704/7.
27 Austin City Council, *Regular Meeting, Oct. 15, 2015*, Agenda Items 50 and 51 (hearing), http://austintx.swagit.com/play/10152015-556/26.

28   Aman Batheja, "Uber, Lyft Shun Driver Fingerprint Requirements," *Texas Tribune*, Oct. 7, 2015, accessed Sep. 3, 2017, https://www.texastribune.org/2015/10/07/background-checks-center-city-fights-uber.

29   Uber Austin, "Sign Petition to Keep Austin Uber," email to Austin Uber users, Oct. 6, 2015.

30   Mobility Committee, *Item 4*, Oct. 7, 2015.

31   Ibid.

32   Ibid.

33   Ibid.

34   Ibid.

35   Austin City Council, *Regular Meeting, Oct. 15, 2015*, Agenda Items 50 and 51.

36   "Uber Audit Finds City Granted Licenses to Failed Applicants," *KVUE.com*, Oct. 27, 2015, accessed Sep. 3, 2017, http://www.kvue.com/news/local/uber-audit-finds-city-granted-licenses-to-failed-applicants/309924580.

37   Audrey McGlinchy and Andrew Webber, "Uber Launches In-App...," *KUT.org*, Nov. 5, 2015, accessed Sep. 3, 2017, http://kut.org/post/uber-launches-app-online-campaign-against-austin-city-council-member.

38   Russ Garcia, "Kitchen's Uber: Horse & Carriage," *Newsroom* (blog), Nov. 4, 2015, accessed Apr. 8, 2017, https://newsroom.uber.com/us-texas/kitchens-uber-horse-carriage; "Giddy Up | Uber," Youtube video, 0:30, posted by "Uber," Nov. 5, 2015, https://youtu.be/row9kXygETU.

39   Fitz Tepper, "Uber Launches 'De Blasio's Uber' Feature...," *TechCrunch*, Jul. 16, 2015, accessed Jul. 14, 2017, http://tcrn.ch/2gM2nVr.

40   Matt Flegenheimer, "De Blasio Administration Dropping Plan for Uber Cap, for Now," *New York Times*, Jul. 22, 2015, https://nyti.ms/2kuk2Sl.

41   Uber Austin, "Tell Mayor Adler: #WhyIRide," email to Uber Austin users, Oct. 16, 2015.

42   Ellen Huet, "Uber Publicly Resisting Fingerprinting But is...," *Forbes*, Oct. 14, 2015, accessed Apr. 8, 2017, https://www.forbes.com/sites/ellenhuet/2015/10/14/uber-publicly-resists-fingerprinting-its-drivers-but-is-quietly-testing-it-live-scan; Austin City Council, *Regular Meeting, Oct. 15, 2015*, Agenda Items 50 and 51.

43   Drew Joseph, "City Takes Tougher Stand on Ride-Share," *San Antonio Express-News*, Mar. 19, 2015.

44   Gary Gilbert, "RE: Checking In," email to Nikki Cooper, et al., May 8, 2015.

45   Iris Dimmick, "Mayor Taylor Calls for the Return of Rideshare to San Antonio," *Rivard Report*, Jun. 26, 2015, accessed May 14, 2016, http://therivardreport.com/mayor-calls-for-return-of-rideshare-to-san-antonio.

46   Josh Baugh, "Residents Again Can Get a Lyft," *San Antonio Express-News*, Aug. 14, 2015.

47   Gary Gilbert, "RE: Survey...," email to Carlton Thomas, Oct. 14, 2015.

48   Carlton Thomas, "RE: Survey...," email to Gary Gilbert, Oct. 14, 2015.

49   Ed Kargbo, "PRESS RELEASE," email to Carlton Thomas, Dec. 2, 2015, attachment: "12-2-2015 Voter Survey Press Release.pdf."

50   Ellen Troxclair, "Troxclair: Don't Drive Ridesharing Out of Austin," *Austin American-Statesman*, Dec. 16, 2015, accessed May 14, 2016, http://www.mystatesman.com/news/news/opinion/troxclair-dont-drive-ridesharing-out-of-austin/npk4R.

51   Brent Wistrom, "Street Fight: Taxi Companies...," *Austin Inno*, Nov. 5, 2015, accessed Jul 6, 2017, http://austininno.streetwise.co/2015/11/05/taxi-industry-campaign-contributions-austin-cabs-vs-uber.

52   W. Gardner Selby, "Uber Says Drunk-Driving Crashes...," *PolitiFact*, Dec. 16, 2015, accessed Sep. 5, 2017, http://www.politifact.com/texas/statements/2015/dec/16/uber/uber-says-drunk-driving-crashes-down-austin-advent.

53   Kate McGee, "After Sexual Assault Reports...," *KUT.org*, Dec. 14, 2015, accessed Sep. 5, 2017, http://kut.org/post/after-sexual-assault-reports-uber-lyft-may-face-expanded-background-checks.

54   Uber Austin, "[ALERT] Austin City Council to Vote...," email to Austin's Uber users, Dec. 11, 2015.

55   Debbee, "Uber Statement on Mobility Committee Recommendations," *Newsroom* (blog), Dec. 8, 2015, accessed Apr. 8, 2017, https://newsroom.uber.com/us-texas/uber-statement-on-mobility-committee-recommendations.

56   Get Me USA's Facebook page, post dated Oct. 1, 2015, accessed Apr. 22, 2016, https://www.facebook.com/GetMe.Texas/.

57   Mobility Committee, *Item 5*, Sep. 2, 2015.

58   Derek Dunlop, "FAO Ann Kitchen," email to Austin City Council District 5, Oct. 28, 2015.

59   Jonathan Laramy, "Fwd: City of Austin Documentation," email to Ken Craig, Nov. 1, 2015.

60   Austin City Council, *Regular Meeting, Dec. 17, 2015*, Agenda Item 75 (Hearing, Part 4 of 4), http://austintx.swagit.com/play/12172015-590/43; Ben Wear, "A Third Ride-Hailing Company Joins Fray," *Austin American-Statesman*, Dec. 15, 2015,

61   Jonathan Laramy, "Fwd: Press Release for GetMe," email to Ken Craig, Dec. 11, 2015.

62   Ann Kitchen, "Ordinance Language," email to Jonathan Laramy, Dec. 11, 2015.

63   Mac McCann, "Ann Kitchen Not Going Anywhere for Now," *Austin Chronicle*, Mar. 11, 2016, accessed Sep. 5, 2017, https://www.austinchronicle.com/news/2016-03-11/ann-kitchen-not-going-anywhere-for-now/.

64   Austin City Council, *Regular Meeting, Dec. 17, 2015*, Agenda Item 75, "Motion Sheet – Mayor Adler and CM Kitchen," http://www.austintexas.gov/edims/document.cfm?id=245513.

65   Michael Theis, "Austin Mayor Announces 11th-Hour...," *Austin Business Journal*, Dec. 17, 2017, accessed May 6,

2017, http://www.bizjournals.com/austin/blog/techflash/2015/12/austin-mayor-announces-11th-hour-compromise-for.html.

66 City of Austin (Texas), Law Department, Public Information Request (PIR) no. 826772, Jan. 11, 2016, document: "PIR 826772 Mayor."

67 Ibid.

68 Ibid.

69 "Motion Sheet – Mayor Adler and CM Kitchen."

70 "PIR 826772 Mayor."

71 Ibid.

72 Nicole Forbes, Twitter post, Dec. 17, 2015, 8:53 PM, https://twitter.com/livehappy8/status/677656834514243584.

73 Austin City Council, *Regular Meeting, Dec. 17, 2015*, Agenda Item 75 (Hearing, Part 2 of 4), http://austintx.swagit.com/play/12172015-590/41.

74 "PIR 826772 Mayor."

75 Ibid.

76 Austin City council, *Dec. 17, 2015*, (Hearing, Part 2 of 4).

77 Ibid.

78 Ibid.

79 Ibid.

80 Austin City Council, *Regular Meeting, Dec. 17, 2015*, Agenda Item 75 (Hearing, Part 3 of 4), http://austintx.swagit.com/play/12172015-590/42.

81 "PIR 826772 Mayor."

82 Ibid.

83 Austin City Council, *Dec. 17, 2015*, (Hearing, Part 3 of 4); Austin City Council, *Regular Meeting, Dec. 17, 2015*, Agenda Item 75 (Hearing, Part 4 of 4), http://austintx.swagit.com/play/12172015-590/43.

84 Austin City Council, *Dec. 17, 2015*, (Hearing, Part 4 of 4).

85 Ellen Huet, "Sidecar Puts Passengers Aside…," *Forbes*, Aug. 5, 2015, https://www.forbes.com/sites/ellenhuet/2015/08/05/sidecar-pivots-to-mostly-deliveries-company/#2c68ef14119e.

86 Austin City Council, *Dec. 17, 2015*, (Hearing, Part 4 of 4).

87 Austin City Council, *Dec. 17, 2015*, (Hearing, Part 3 of 4).

88 Austin City Council, *Dec. 17, 2015*, (Hearing, Part 4 of 4).

89 Dave Passmore, "Re: Stand Strong on TNCs!" email to Steve Adler, et al., Dec. 21, 2015.

90 Uber Austin, "Austin City Council Adopts Anti-Ridesharing Rules," email Uber's Austin users, Dec. 18, 2015.

91 "PIR 826772 Mayor."

92 Andy, "Petition Drives Aims to Give Uber/Lyft…," *Travis Tracker* (blog), Dec. 28, 2015, accessed May 14, 2017, http://thetravistracker.blogspot.com/2015/12/petition-drive-aims-to-give-uber-lyft.html.

93 Ridesharing Works for Austin, *Reports Filed by Committees, January 15, Campaign Finance Report*, Jan. 15, 2016, http://www.austintexas.gov/edims/document.cfm?id=246592.

94 Michael Theis, "Austin Groups Aim to Undo New Rules for Uber, Lyft," *Austin Business Journal*, Dec. 28, 2015, accessed Apr. 13, 2016, https://www.bizjournals.com/austin/blog/techflash/2015/12/austin-groups-aim-to-undo-new-rules-for-uber-lyft.html.

95 Ordinance no. 20160217-001, City of Austin (Texas) (2016).

96 City of Seattle, Ethics and Elections Commission, *Contributions to Seattle Citizens to Repeal Ordinance 124441, 2014 Election Cycle*, accessed May 7, 2017, http://web6.seattle.gov/ethics/elections/poplist.aspx?cid=374&listtype=contributors; Joel Connelly, "Seattle Suspends Ride Sharing Regulations…," *Seattle Post-Intelligencer*, Apr. 17, 2014.

97 Ridesharing Works for Austin, *January 15, Campaign Finance Report*; Ridesharing Works for Austin, *Reports Filed by Committees, 30th Day Before Election, Campaign Finance Report*, Apr. 7, 2016, http://www.austintexas.gov/edims/document.cfm?id=251679.

98 Ibid; Jeffrey Anderson, "The Brandon Todd Team Struggles…," *Washington City Paper*, Apr. 30, 2917, accessed Sep. 5, 2017, http://www.washingtoncitypaper.com/news/loose-lips/article/20859858/the-brandon-todd-team-struggles-to-explain-its-largest-campaign-expenditure.

99 Home page, accessed Sep. 5, 2017, http://fieldstrategies.com.

100 Brent Wistrom, "Did Mayor Adler Just Launch His First…," *Austin Inno*, Jan. 29, 2016, accessed Sep. 30, 2016, https://www.americaninno.com/austin/thumbs-up-app-gets-backing-in-uber-lyft-debate-in-austin.

101 Ben Wear, "Group: 65,000 Have Signed Petition…," *Austin American-Statesman*, Jan. 19, 2016; Ben Wear, "Petition for Uber, Lyft Rules Validated," *Austin American-Statesman*, Feb. 3, 2016.

102 Austin City Council, *Regular Meeting, Feb. 11, 2016*, Agenda Items 2, 16, and 59, http://www.austintexas.gov/department/city-council/2016/20160211-reg.htm.

103 Blake Houston, "Re: Uber, Lyft, & TNC Issue…," email to Austin City Council District 10, Dec. 18, 2015; JB Goodwin, "Re: Uber, Lyft, & TNC Issue…," email to Austin City Council District 10, Dec. 21, 2015.

104   Mac McCann, "Uber Says 'Thumbs Down,'" *Austin Chronicle*, Jan. 29, 2016, accessed May 7, 2017, http://www.austinchronicle.com/news/2016-01-29/uber-says-thumbs-down.

105   Wear, "Group: 65,000..."

106   Michael Theis, "Uber, Lyft Compromise Fails...," *Austin Business Journal*, Feb. 12, 2016, accessed Sep. 5, 2017, https://www.bizjournals.com/austin/blog/techflash/2016/02/uber-lyft-compromise-fails-sending-ride-hailing.html.

107   Ordinance no. 20160217-001.

108   Austin City Council, *Special Called Meeting, Feb. 17, 2016*, Agenda Item 1 (hearing), http://austintx.swagit.com/play/02172016-629/4/.

109   City of Austin, Office of the City Clerk, *May 7, 2016 Special Election: Ballot Language*, http://www.austintexas.gov/edims/document.cfm?id=248576.

110   Michael Theis, "Uber Ballot Rewrite Denied by Texas Supreme Court," *Austin Business Journal*, Mar. 15, 2016, accessed Sep. 5, 2017, https://www.bizjournals.com/austin/news/2016/03/15/uber-ballot-rewrite-denied-by-texas-supreme-court.html.

111   Ridesharing Works for Austin, *Campaign Finance Report*, Apr. 7, 2016.

112   Casey Claiborne, "'Vote for Prop 1' Supporting...," *Fox7Austin.com*, Mar. 23, 2016, accessed Sep. 5, 2017, http://www.fox7austin.com/news/local-news/112689308-story.

113   Ridesharing Works for Austin, *Campaign Finance Report*, Apr. 7, 2016; Home page, accessed Sep. 5, 2017, http://www.jedburghs.com/.

114   Audrey McGlinchy, "The Uber and Lyft Proposition...," *KUT.org*, Mar. 31, 2016, accessed Sep. 5, 2016, http://kut.org/post/uber-and-lyft-proposition-doesn-t-fall-neatly-along-party-lines; Our City, Our Safety, Our Choice PAC, "Public Supporters," accessed Apr. 11, 2017, https://www.ourcityoursafetyourchoice.org/public-supporters/.

115   "Safety We Can Count On," Youtube video, 1:00, posted by "Vote for Prop 1," Apr. 7, 2016, https://youtu.be/NlsXwysXj-w.

116   Nicholas Richard Rees, "Is Grindr the Next Campaigning Platform?" *Out Magazine*, Feb. 25, 2016, accessed Sep. 5, 2017, https://www.out.com/news-opinion/2016/2/25/grindr-next-campaigning-platform; "HD 49," Elected Officials Directory, *Texas Tribune*, accessed Sep. 5, 2017, https://www.texastribune.org/directory/districts/tx-house/49; Michael King, "Where the Money Goes," *Austin Chronicle*, Apr. 15, 2016, accessed Apr. 8, 2017, http://www.austinchronicle.com/daily/news/2016-04-15/where-the-money-goes.

117   King, "Where the Money Goes."

118   Ibid.

119   Ibid.

120   Brent Wistrom, "When Unicorns Campaign...," *Austin Inno*, Apr. 8, 2016, accessed Apr. 28, 2016, http://austininno.streetwise.co/2016/04/08/uber-and-lyft-campaign-finance-and-spending-in-austin-election.

121   Kristen V. Brown, "Are Uber and Lyft Going Too Far...," *Fusion*, May 4, 2016, accessed Sep. 6, 2016, http://fusion.net/story/298317/uber-lyft-austin-proposition-one/.

122   Brent Wistrom, "Prop 1. Ad Blitz in Austin...," *Austin Inno*, Apr. 25, 2016, accessed Apr. 28, 2016, http://austininno.streetwise.co/2016/04/25/austins-prop-1-campaigns-ads-big-spending-questionable-content.

123   Brent Wistrom, "Friday Night Lights Star...," *Austin Inno*, Apr. 28, 2016 (accessed same day), http://austininno.streetwise.co/2016/04/28/uber-and-lyft-austin-prop-1-vote-rally-taylor-kitsch-joins-ridesharing-works; "Join Taylor Kitsch in Voting for Prop 1," Youtube video, 1:01, posted by "Lyft," May 2, 2016, https://youtu.be/5tmFK1x4PSQ.

124   "Why Prop. One Failed (At Least for Me)," Imgur post, May 7, 2016, http://imgur.com/pTEiiII.

125   Nolan Hicks, "Uber Facing Suit Over Text Barrage," *Austin American-Statesman*, May 5, 2016.

126   Ben Wear, "Prop. TV Ad Deceives, Say Opponents," *Austin American-Statesman*, Apr. 13, 2016.

127   Editorial Board, "Vote No On Prop. 1," *Austin Chronicle*, Apr. 22, 2016, accessed same day, http://www.austinchronicle.com/news/2016-04-22/chronicle-endorsements; "No on Prop. 1," *Austin American-Statesman*, Apr. 24, 2016.

128   "Austin Mayor Steve Adler Comes Out Against Prop 1," Youtube video, 6:07, posted by "Joe Deshotel," Apr. 25, 2016, https://youtu.be/qHe6LzcvmzY.

129   Michael Theis, "Updated: Both Uber, Lyft Ready...," *Austin Business Journal*, May 6, 2016, accessed Sep. 6, 2017, https://www.bizjournals.com/austin/blog/techflash/2016/05/lyft-says-bags-already-packed-to-leave-town-if.html.

130   Amanda Eversole to US Secretary Anthony Foxx, Apr. 21, 2016.

131   Jeff Stensland, "Texas Lawmaker Warns State Could Set Ridesharing Rules," *Time Warner Cable News*, Apr. 28, 2016, accessed Apr. 30, 2016, http://www.twcnews.com/tx/austin/news/2016/04/28/texas-lawmaker-warns-state-could-set-ridesharing-rules.html.

132   Travis County Clerk, *Results, May 7, 2016, Official Cumulative Results, City of Austin Election, Proposition 1*, accessed May 12, 2017, http://traviselectionresults.com/enr/results/display.do?criteria.electionId=201605&electionId=201605&tabType=C&criteriaId=-1959870787&formSubmitted=1.

133   "Election Day in Central Texas, 05.07.16" (photo gallery), *Austin American-Statesman*, accessed May 12, 2017,

http://www.statesman.com/news/local-govt--politics/election-day-central-texas/Zs0szcyR72QrokzcnuFuqN/#1.
134   Steve Adler, "Twitter Feedback on Ridesharing in Austin," *MayorAdler.com* (blog), May 11, 2016, accessed May 12, 2016, http://www.mayoradler.com/twitter-feedback-on-ridesharing-in-austin.
135   Robert Spillar to [City of Austin] Mayor and Council, May 11, 2016.
136   Michael Theis, "Ride-Hailing App Gears Up…," *Austin Business Journal*, May 20, 2016, https://www.bizjournals.com/austin/news/2016/05/20/ride-hailing-app-gears-up-for-imminent-austin.html; Michael Theis, "Canadians Want Slice of Austin's Ridesharing Pie," *Austin Business Journal*, Jun. 6, 2016, https://www.bizjournals.com/austin/news/2016/06/06/canadians-want-slice-of-austins-rideshare-pie.html; Ben Wear, Tech Leaders Start Ride-Hailing Firm," *Austin American-Statesman*, May 24, 2016; "Wingz Launches WingzAround in Austin..." *Business Wire*, May 20, 2016, http://www.businesswire.com/news/home/20160520005932/en/Wingz-Launches-WingzAround-Austin-Offering-Pre-Booked-Private; "Quickly, Fasten is a Ridesharing Success in Austin…," *Business Wire*, Jun. 21, 2016, http://www.businesswire.com/news/home/20160621005889/en/Quickly-Fasten-Ridesharing-Success-Austin-Weeks.
137   Sam Biddle, "Here Are the Internal Documents that Prove…," *Gawker*, Aug. 5, 2015, accessed May 13, 2017, http://gawker.com/here-are-the-internal-documents-that-prove-uber-is-a-mo-1704234157.
138   Ellen Huet, "Facing a Price War, Uber Bets on Volume," *Bloomberg*, Jan. 21, 2016, https://bloom.bg/2vRoX9H.
139   Samantha Cole, "The True Cost of Your Uber Ride is Much..." *Vice.com*, Dec. 2, 2016, https://motherboard.vice.com/en_us/article/uber-true-cost-uh-oh.
140   Andrew Ross Sorkin, "Why Uber Keeps Raising Billions," *New York Times*, Jun. 20, 2016, http://nyti.ms/28J6nlF.
141   Federal Trade Commission, "Predatory or Below-Cost Pricing," accessed Sep. 6, 2017, https://www.ftc.gov/tips-advice/competition-guidance/guide-antitrust-laws/single-firm-conduct/predatory-or-below-cost.
142   Texas Legislature, 85th Legislative Session – Regular, *HB 100*, 2017.
143   Patrick Sisson, "Uber and Lyft are Coming Back to Austin," *Curbed*, May 18, 2017, accessed Sep. 6, 2017, https://www.curbed.com/2017/5/18/15657684/uber-lyft-austin-texas-ridehailing-state-law.
144   "The Road Ahead," *Newsroom* (blog), May 26, 2017, accessed same day, https://newsroom.uber.com/us-texas/the-road-ahead.
145   Caroline O'Donovan, "Uber and Lyft Are Back in Austin…," *Buzzfeed*, Jul 5, 2017, accessed Jul 14, 2017, http://bzfd.it/2uL7V85.

Chapter 13

1
      "Why Massachusetts' New Tax on Ride-Hailing Companies…," *Slate*, Aug. 22, 2016, accessed Aug. 25, 2016, http://slate.me/2bgJNSQ; Adam Vaccaro, "Uber, Lyft Drivers to Face Background Checks…," *Boston Globe*, Nov. 28, 2016, accessed Sep. 6, 2017, https://www.bostonglobe.com/business/2016/11/28/uber-lyft-drivers-face-state-background-checks-sooner-than-expected/nZcwLaRqlImyYSpTLWdKRK/story.html.
2   Travis [Kalanick], "Growing and Growing Up," *Newsroom* (blog), Apr. 21, 2016, accessed same day, https://newsroom.uber.com/growing-and-growing-up.
3   National Institute of Standards and Technology (NIST), Weights and Measures, Taximeters: US National Working Group, *General Information About the GPS Subcommittee*, accessed May 14, 2017, https://www.nist.gov/pml/weights-and-measures/legal-metrology-devices/taximeters-us-national-work-group.
4   *California v. Uber.*
5   National Institute of Standards and Technology (NIST), Weights and Measures, *NIST OWM Strategy for GPS Subcommittee Task Group – White Paper*, accessed Sep. 6, 2017, https://www.nist.gov/file/357211.
6   NIST, *General Information...*
7   NIST, *NIST Own Strategy...*
8   Megan Rose Dickey, "Flywheel Launches Uber-Like Operating…," *TechCrunch*, Dec. 22, 2015, accessed Sep. 9, 017, http://tcrn.ch/2eHHr1y.
9   National Conference of Weights and Measures, *Voting Record of the 102nd Annual Meeting*, July 16-20, 2017, see item no. 3504-2, accessed Sep. 6, 2017, https://www.ncwm.net/_resources/e30d:otyk24-nm/files/75857199z35033f4d/_fn/2017-Voting-Record.pdf.
10   "2016 Annual Survey Symposium: The Sharing Economy…," Youtube video, 1:19:34, posted by "NYU School of Law," Feb. 23, 2016, https://youtu.be/gGM1A0Or7K8.
11   Ibid.
12   Daniel Fedor, Twitter post, Sep. 29, 2015, 7:21 PM, https://twitter.com/Dan_Fedor/status/649046479772889088.
13   Matthew W. Daus, "Challenge Your NYC Real Property…," email to Dafna Gauthier, Jan. 19, 2016.
14   "2016 Annual Survey Symposium..."
15   Shelby Perea, "Santa Fe Cab Service Closes..," *Albuquerque Business First*, Apr. 14, 2017, accessed Sep. 7, 2016, https://www.bizjournals.com/albuquerque/news/2017/04/14/santa-fe-cab-service-closes-after-31-years-in.html;

Peter Krouse, "Uber and Lyft Hurt Traditional…," *Cleveland.com*, May 25, 2017, accessed Sep. 7, 2017, http://www.cleveland.com/metro/index.ssf/2017/05/uber_and_lyft_hurt_traditional.html.

16   "Uber, Lyft Take Down Not Just Cab Drivers…," *CNBC*, Jul. 15, 2017, accessed Sep. 7, 2017, http://cnb.cx/2wKYMjC.

17   Google Finance, "Medallion Financial Corp," accessed Sep. 7, 2017, https://finance.google.com/finance?q=mfin.

18   † "2016 IATR Annual Conference – Saturday September 24 – Session 6 (Part 2)…," Vimeo video posted by "IATR," Jun. 2017, https://vimeo.com/219862913.

19   † "2016 IATR Annual Conference – Saturday September 24 – Breakfast Keynote…" Vimeo video posted by "IATR," Jun. 2017, https://vimeo.com/219860213.

20   † "2016 IATR Annual Conference – Saturday September 24 – Session 6 (Part 2)…"

21   Dug Begley, "City Cabs to Unite Under One App…," *Houston Chronicle*, Sep. 13, 2016; Kate Shepherd, "Chicago Taxi App to Compete With Uber…," *Chicagoist*, Jan. 6, 2016, accessed Sep. 7, 2017, http://chicagoist.com/2016/01/06/the_city_of_chicago_is.php; Christina Sturdivant, "DC Taxicab Commission's E-Hailing…," *DCist*, Feb. 11, 2016, accessed Sep. 7, 2017, http://dcist.com/2016/02/taxi_app.php.

22   Emily Badger, "Why Taxi Drivers are Suddenly Getting Nicer," *Washington Post*, Jan. 5, 2016, accessed Apr. 13, 2016, http://wapo.st/1S2eZ9f.

23   *Federal Trade Commission (FTC) v. Uber Technologies, Inc.*, Case no. 3:17-cv-00261 (N.D. Ca. Jan. 19, 2017).

24   Jonathan V. Hall and Alan B. Krueger, 2015, "An Analysis of the Labor Market for Uber's Driver-Partners…," Princeton University, Industrial Relations Section Working Papers (January), http://arks.princeton.edu/ark:/88435/dsp010z708z67d.

25   "How Much do Uber Drivers Make in 2017?" *Ridester*, Aug. 30, 2017, accessed Sep. 7, 2017, https://www.ridester.com/how-much-do-uber-drivers-make.

26   *FTC v. Uber.*

27   Federal Trade Commission, "Uber Agrees to Pay $20 Million…" (press release), Jan. 19, 2017, https://www.ftc.gov/news-events/press-releases/2017/01/uber-agrees-pay-20-million-settle-ftc-charges-it-recruited.

28   California General Assembly, AB 650 – Taxicab Transportation Services, 2015-2016 Session.

29   Liam Dillon, "No One Wants to Regulate Uber…," *Los Angeles Times*, Mar. 1, 2016, accessed May 20, 2017, http://lat.ms/1XYn5Dw.

30   Liam Dillon, "How a Bid to Overhaul California's Energy…," *Los Angeles Times*, Sep. 2, 2016, accessed May 20, 2017, http://lat.ms/2bVFGug.

31   David Pierson, "Uber Fined $7.6 Million by California Utilities Commission," *Los Angeles Times*, Jan. 14, 2016, accessed Sep. 7, 2017, http://lat.ms/1USCdwr; Marisa Kendall, "Uber Slow to Boot Alleged Drunk Drivers…," *Mercury News* (San Jose, CA), Apr. 13, 2017, accessed Sep. 7, 2017, http://bayareane.ws/2odClw9.

32   † "2016 IATR Annual Conference – Saturday September 24 – State of the IATR Speech," Vimeo video posted by "IATR," Jun. 2017, https://vimeo.com/219859251.

33   Ibid.

34   Ibid.

35   Ibid.

36   Ibid.

37   Trump-Pence Transition Team, "President-Elect Donald J. Trump Announces Travis Kalanick…" (press release) GreatAgain.gov, Dec. 14, 2016, accessed Sep. 7, 2017, https://greatagain.gov/president-elect-trump-announces-additional-members-of-presidents-strategic-and-policy-forum-8aa8822eced9.

38   Priya Anand, "The Battle Between Uber and Lyft Has Become Political," *Buzzfeed*, Jan. 29, 2017, accessed Jan. 30, 2017, http://bzfd.it/2xSIbZP.

39   NY Taxi Workers Alliance, Twitter post, Jan. 28, 2017, 4:55 PM, https://twitter.com/NYTWA/status/825462249468919808.

40   Uber NYC, Twitter post, Jan. 28, 2017, 7:36 PM, https://twitter.com/Uber_NYC/status/825502908926066688.

41   Dan O'Sullivan, Twitter post, Jan. 28, 2017, 9:54 PM, https://twitter.com/Bro_Pair/status/825537545211637761.

42   Uber NYC, Twitter post, Jan. 29, 2017 12:33 AM, https://twitter.com/Uber_NYC/status/825577611816468481.

43   Anand, "The Battle Between…"

44   Jackie Strause, "Celebrities Spread #DeleteUber After Lyft's…," *Hollywood Reporter*, Jan. 29, 2017, accessed Jan. 30, 2017, http://www.hollywoodreporter.com/news/celebrities-spread-deleteuber-lyfts-donates-1m-aclu-969670.

45   Travis [Kalanick], "Standing Up for the Driver Community," *Newsroom* (blog), Jan. 29, 2017, accessed Sep. 7, 2017, https://newsroom.uber.com/standing-up-for-the-driver-community/.

† In June 2017, the IATR publicly posted a list of these videos on its website, http://IATR.global. Google's CacheView saved a copy of this page as it appeared on June 16, which can be found at http://archive.is/BLtjx. On June 26, the page also provided the password to view these videos. The following month, the page was moved to the Member's Only section of the IATR website.

46   Kaitlyn Tiffany, "Uber Appears to be Interest-Targeting…," *The Verge*, Jan. 30, 2017, accessed May 22, 2017, https://www.theverge.com/2017/1/30/14441770/uber-aclu-facebook-twitter-ad-targeting.
47   Biz Carson, "Some People Had to Wait Before Uber…," *Business Insider*, Jan. 31, 2017, accessed same day, http://read.bi/2wOmzxQ.
48   Andrew J. Hawkins, "Lyft Surpasses Uber in App Downloads…," *The Verge*, Jan. 30, 2017, accessed Sep. 7, 2017, https://www.theverge.com/2017/1/30/14443560/lyft-surpass-uber-app-downloads-deleteuber.
49   Mike Isaac, "Uber CEO to Leave Trump Advisory…," *New York Times*, Feb. 2, 2017, https://nyti.ms/2k5WBBb.
50   Ibid.
51   Mike Isaac, "Uber Board Stands by Travis Kalanick…," *New York Times*, Mar. 21, 2017, https://nyti.ms/2nyYUzi.
52   Rani Molla, "Uber's Market Share Has Taken a Big Hit," *Recode*, Aug. 31, 2017, accessed same day, https://www.recode.net/2017/8/31/16227670/uber-lyft-market-share-deleteuber-decline-users.
53   Adam Edelman and Stephanie Ruhle, "Trump Dissolves Business Advisory Councils…," *NBC News*, Aug. 17, 2017, accessed Sep. 7, 2017, http://nbcnews.to/2gMM4HU.
54   "Uber CEO Kalanick Argues with Driver Over Falling Fares," Youtube video, 6:10, posted by "Bloomberg," Feb. 28, 2017, https://youtu.be/gTEDYCkNqns.
55   Mike Isaac, "Uber's CEO Plays with Fire," *New York Times*, Apr. 23, 2017, https://nyti.ms/2p9ON43.
56   Kara Swisher and Johana Bhuiyan, "A Top Uber Executive, Who Obtained…," *Recode*, Jun. 7, 2017, accessed Sep. 7, 2017, https://www.recode.net/2017/6/7/15754316/uber-executive-india-assault-rape-medical-records.
57   Amir Efrati, "Uber Group's Visit to Seoul Escort Bar…," *The Information*, Mar. 24, 2017, accessed Sep. 7, 2017, https://www.theinformation.com/uber-groups-visit-to-seoul-escort-bar-sparked-hr-complaint.
58   Mike Isaac, "How Uber Deceives the Authorities Worldwide," *New York Times*, Mar. 3, 2017, https://nyti.ms/2lngDck.
59   Ibid; Carlton Thomas, "RE: Checking In."
60   Philip Jankowski, "Austin: Uber Operations in City Part of Federal Probe," *Austin American-Statesman*, May 9, 2017.
61   Portland Bureau of Transportation, *Greyball Audit Report*, April 2017, https://www.portlandoregon.gov/saltzman/article/638525.
62   Mike Isaac, "Uber Founder Travis Kalanick Resigns as CEO," *New York Times*, Jun. 21, 2017, https://nyti.ms/2sOtmaJ.
63   Polina Marinova, "Millennials Vote Uber 'Most Improved' Brand in 2017," *Fortune*, Jul. 6, 2017, accessed Sep. 9, 2017, http://fortune.com/2017/07/06/uber-millennials.
64   Rupal Bapat, "TNC/TNP and Taxicab Regulation Questions from Chicago," email to Tina Paez, et al., Jun. 26, 2017.
65   "Chris Hayashi Goes Out in Song," *The Phantom Cab Driver Phites Back* (blog), Apr. 21, 2014, accessed May 6, 2016, http://phantomcabdriverphites.blogspot.com/2014/07/chris-hayashi-goes-out-in-song.html.
66   Richard N. Velotta, "Taxicab Authority Trims Field in…," *Las Vegas Review-Journal*, Jul. 27, 2015, accessed Sep. 7, 2017, https://www.reviewjournal.com/business/taxicab-authority-trims-field-in-hunt-for-new-administrator/.

INDEX

272, 349

www.ingramcontent.com/pod-product-compliance
Lightning Source LLC
Chambersburg PA
CBHW060114200326

41518CB00008B/819

www.ingramcontent.com/pod-product-compliance
Lightning Source LLC
Chambersburg PA
CBHW060423200326
41518CB00009B/1461